THE

# HISTORY OF WISCONSIN.

IN THREE PARTS,

Historical, Documentary, and Descriptive.

COMPILED BY DIRECTION OF THE LEGISLATURE OF THE STATE.

BY

WILLIAM R. SMITH,

PRESIDENT OF THE STATE HISTORICAL SOCIETY OF WISCONSIN.

---

PART I.—HISTORICAL.

VOL. I.

---

MADISON, WIS.:
BERIAH BROWN, PRINTER.
1854.

# This Work,

Commenced under their direction, and fostered by their generosity; designed as a compilation of ancient annals in relation to this portion of the Mississippi Valley; intended to form the foundation of a truthful History of the State, to be collected and preserved from time to time, while passing events are fresh in the memories of contemporaries; professing to exhibit an accurate picture, at the present day, of a region of country whose beauty of scenery, fertility of soil, mineral wealth, facilities of commerce internal and external, and healthy climate, are unsurpassed in the Union, and whose rapid growth in population, and still increasing prosperity, have hitherto been unexampled in the history of our land; the compilation of the same being now published under legislative authority, it is most properly, and very respectfully,

**DEDICATED**

## To the People of the State of Wisconsin,

By their Fellow-Citizen,

WILLIAM RUDOLPH SMITH.

Mineral Point, Iowa County,
*Wisconsin, July 4th,* 1854.

# CONTENTS.

INTRODUCTORY ........................................................ *Page* 11

## CHAPTER I.

### NEW FRANCE AND LOUISIANA.

Early History—Mississippi Valley—Discovery of Florida—Ponce de Leon, Miruelo, Narvaez, De Soto—Discovery of the Mississippi, and fate of De Soto—Charter Grant of New France—Jesuit Missionaries, zeal and success—Reach the Western Lakes—Enterprising views of Discovery—Mesnard, Allouez, Marquette—Views of the Intendant Talon—Great Congress of Indian Nations at the Falls of St. Mary—Enterprise of Marquette and Joliet—Dangers pointed out by the Indians—Fox River, Portage, and Wisconsin—Upper Mississippi discovered—The Illini Indians hospitable—The Missouri passed, the Ouabache reached, and the Mississippi descended to below the Arkansas—Return of Marquette and Joliet to Green Bay—Joliet's papers lost—Death of Marquette—De la Salle, his enterprise, protected and encouraged by Colbert and Seignelay—Builds a vessel on Niagara River, and navigates the Upper Lakes—He reaches the sources of the Illinois River—Descends and builds a Fort—Learns the course of the Mississippi River, loses his vessel on the Lakes, and resolves to build a new one—Despatches Hennepin on a voyage of discovery up the Mississippi—Leaves Tonti in command, and returns on foot to Fort Frontenac—Tonti builds Rock Fort—Is driven away by the Indians—La Salle returns, descends the Mississippi to the sea, and takes possession of the country, by the name of Louisiana—Returns to France, procures a fleet, and endeavours to discover the mouth of the Mississippi by sea—Passes the mouth, and lands in St. Bernard's Bay—His misfortunes, fruitless searches, and assassination—Joutel and Anastasius return by the Mississippi to Fort Crevecœur, and thence to Quebec—Attempts to decry the merits of La Salle's discoveries—Hennepin's alleged discoveries—His two publications, and interpolations—The claims of England to the Mississippi founded on Hennepin's books—The claims of France—Conflicting opinions of French and English Colonists—New France neglected—French possessions in the West include the whole Valley of the Mississippi—Iberville and his brothers—Expedition fitted out to discover the mouth of the Mississippi—Iberville successful—Passes up the River—Finds a letter from Tonti to La Salle—Builds a Fort at Biloxi, and returns to France—Possession taken of the whole basin of the Mississippi, by France, under the name of Louisiana.............. 23

NOTES TO CHAPTER I.......................................................... 301

## CHAPTER II.

### VALLEY OF THE MISSISSIPPI.

Settlement by Iberville—Progress of the French in Settlements from the St. Lawrence to the Mississippi Valley—Kaskaskia, Peoria—Fathers Gravier and Marest, Montigny and Davion—Religious zeal and commercial enterprise—

Views of La Salle with respect to the Illinois country—Communication between Quebec and the Gulf of Mexico—Jealousy, and claim of England—Exploring Expedition on part of England—Explorations by Bienville and Sauvole—Application of French Protestant emigrants—Bienville prevents the English from taking possession of the Mississippi—Belief still entertained of the route by water to the South Sea—Also of the existence of gold and silver mines, &c. in the country—French views not agricultural—Le Sueur on the Upper Mississippi—Fallacious views as to the natural productions of the country—Baron La Hontan, his travels and discoveries—Mixture of the true, and the romantic and fabulous—The Illinois country, its extent—The Five Nations, their relations to France and England—Grand Council called by De Callieres—The post and settlement of Detroit founded—Other posts growing up, in the West—Allies of the English in Wisconsin—Attempt on Detroit—Trade of the West—Armed occupation by France of the Mississippi Valley—Forts Chartres, Cahokia, Prairie du Rocher, Kaskaskia—Treaty of Utrecht, its want of effect—Unsettled questions of boundaries—Localities of the Indian tribes—The Indians of the Northwest—Colony at the mouth of the Mississippi—Its neglect of agriculture and wild speculations—Le Sueur's copper-mine on Blue Earth River—Louisiana made a government independent of New France—Change in the political system of the colony—unsuccessful attempts of France to colonize—Boundaries of Louisiana—Rio del Norte—Crozat's Patent—Mississippi Scheme—Slavery authorized in Crozat's monopoly—Population of Louisiana—Ill success of Crozat—His losses; surrenders his patent—Delusive hopes of wealth, in France—Wretched state of the French Public Treasury—John Law proposes relief—Paper currency as a substitute for precious metals—Law's Bank established—Its operations—Declared a royal bank—Becomes a commercial company—Great powers granted to the "Mississippi Company"—Bank of France associated with it—Company of the Indies—Monopolies granted to it—The Mint, and Taxes of the nation farmed by it—Law, Comptroller General of France—Emigrants to Louisiana, their character—Routes from the St. Lawrence to the Lower Mississippi—The great bubbles burst—Consequences extend to the settlements of the Mississippi Valley—Similarity of Credit System of 1719 and 1834—Delusion as to the mineral wealth continues—Mining on the Upper Mississippi—War between France and Spain—Chain of forts established on the Mississippi—Site of New Orleans selected—Le Sueur's fort on St. Peter's River—He takes possession of the upper country—Fort Chartres built—Population of the Illinois country—Posts of Michillimackinac, Green Bay, Chicago, St. Joseph's, Sault St. Marie, and Detroit—English and French trade with the Indians—Influence of France unbounded, over the Indians, except the Iroquois—The Five Nations—Ottagamies adhere to the English—Attempt to destroy Detroit—Siege of Detroit—Defeat and great loss of the Ottagamies—Their hostilities and depredations—French expedition against them under Louvigny—Stronghold at Butte des Morts—The Foxes capitulate—Hostages delivered—Treaty not complied with by the Foxes—They renew their depredations—Expedition under De Lignerie unsuccessful—Progress of settlements in the West—Villages in the Illinois country—The Natchez nation, their destruction—The "Company of the Indies" surrenders its charter—War against the Chickasaws—Artaguette and Vincennes—Their death—Situation of the Illinois country—Ambitious views of France as to the Great West—Resisted by the English colonies—George Washington—His mission to the French commander—First signal of the war of the Revolution—Death of Jumonville—Washington capitulates—France in possession of the whole Valley of the Mississippi—English and French encroachments, although with the same intent, not so regarded by the Indians—Peace in Europe, but war in America—Boundaries between English and French possessions the cause—War of 1756—Braddock's defeat; Wolf's victory; surrender of all Canada—Disaffection of the Indians—Rogers takes possession of Detroit, and other western posts—Pontiac—He orders Rogers to stop in his march—Protects him on condition—French power in the West for ever overthrown—Feelings against the English—Henry, the English trader—His interview with an Indian chief—

Attachment of the Indians to the French; its causes—State of settlements in Wisconsin—Carver's account—Prairie du Chien—No establishments west of Green Bay—Traders alone in the country—Sacs and Foxes, their depredations and chastisement—Expeditions against them—Lake Superior, settlements there—Ancient mines—Indications of ancient work........ *Page* 52

NOTES TO CHAPTER II........ 320

## CHAPTER III.

### UNDER BRITISH DOMINION.

Treaty of 1763—England possesses all New France and Louisiana—Protection of eminent domain—Carver's Grant—Illinois and Wabash Companies—Classes of grants in the Territory of Michigan, and in Wisconsin—De Vaudreuil's Grant—French inhabitants under English rule--Indians unfriendly to the English—Pontiac's designs—His great confederacy—Calls a grand council, and states his plans to them—Unexpected attacks on the British posts—Black rain at Detroit—Surprise and capture of Michillimackinac—Henry's personal account of it—Fort at Green Bay abandoned—Fort at St. Joseph's captured—Situation of Detroit—Stratagem of Pontiac—Discovered and prevented—Siege of Detroit—Barbarities of the Indians—Reinforcements arrive—Captain Dalyell's sortie, defeat, and death—Siege abandoned by the Indians—Arrival of General Bradstreet—Concludes a peace with the Indian tribes—Pontiac does not consent—His death—His character—Absence of settlements in Wisconsin—Captain Carver's intentions and attempts—His travels and remarks—No Europeans on the Upper Mississippi, as settlers, in 1766—Evidence as to Carver's Grant—The Illinois country—Peaceable settlements of the French—Their mode of life—Their villages and general regulations of property—Tranquility and happiness—Their religion—Changes under British rule—Settlements decline—Emigration to Spanish Louisiana—Population of the Illinois country—British occupy the forts—Colonel Clark's Expedition—His plan adopted by Virginia—British influence over Indians the source of the depredations on the frontier settlements--Claims of Virginia to the Northwest, by her royal charters—Clark assembles his force—Descends the Ohio—Marches overland to Kaskaskia—Captures the town and fort—Fears of the inhabitants—They apply to Clark—His answer—Their rejoicings—Cahokia surrenders—Fort Sackville, or Vincennes, submits—Oath of allegiance taken—Clark establishes forts—County of Illinois established by Virginia—Indians make treaties with Clark—The British governor collects his forces--Resolves to make Clark prisoner--Governor Hamilton's character—He arrives before Vincennes—Captain Helm alone in the fort--Obtains honorable terms—Clark determines on retaking Vincennes—Marches from Kaskaskia—Hardships suffered by his forces—Arrive at the town and capture it—Attack the fort—Hamilton capitulates, and is sent prisoner to Virginia—Clark's views on Detroit—Captures a convoy of supplies—The result of Clark's enterprises—The five States of the Northwestern Territory—The Northwest during the Revolutionary War—Claims of States proposed to be relinquished—Plans devised and debated in Congress—Deeds of cession by States—Geographical boundaries of the new States not defined understandingly—Revision of deeds of cession proposed—New boundaries of States—Resolutions of Congress on this subject—Ordinance of 1787—Assent of Virginia to alteration of her deed of cession—Review of sixth article of ordinance of 1787........ 123

NOTES TO CHAPTER III........ 349

## CHAPTER IV.

### THE NORTHWESTERN TERRITORY.

British retain the Western posts—Effect on the Indians—Land speculations in the West—Washington's opinion—Cession of title by the States—Retrospective view—Steuben sent to take possession of Western posts—He is refused the possession—Causes assigned—Boundary line not to be crossed—British strengthen the posts—Great council of Indian tribes—Treaties of Fort Harmar—Not adhered to—Brant and the Northern confederacy—St. Clair, governor of the Northwestern Territory—Indians deny the validity of his treaties—State of the case—Ordinance of 1787—Unwise proceeding of government—British policy and agency—Encouragement given to Brant—Influence of McKee, Elliott, and Girty—Mission of Gamelin to the Western tribes, and his report—Conduct of British agents—United States adopt war measures against the Indians—St. Clair's levies, and dissensions—Harmar's Expedition, and two defeats—Discord in his army—Indian villages destroyed—Indian account of the battles—Action of the government in relation to the Indian War—Peace messengers and warlike preparations—British agents and Indians dissatisfied—American policy explained—Scott's Expedition—Wilkinson's Expedition—St. Clair organizes his army at Fort Washington—Commences his march—Builds Forts Hamilton and Jefferson—Reaches the waters of the Wabash—Army encamps—Attacked by the Indians and entirely defeated—Great loss of the Americans—Causes of defeat—St. Clair exculpated—New army authorized by Congress to be raised—General Wayne appointed to its command—Peace still offered to the Indians—The chiefs of the nations are invited to the seat of government—Commissioners meet the Indians in council—Indians insist on the Ohio boundary—Attempts at peace fruitless—The causes—British erect a new fort on the Maumee—Spain offers assistance to Indians—Wayne assembles his forces at Fort Washington—Final report of the peace commissioners—Wayne moves his army—Establishes Fort Greenville—Goes into winter quarters—Buries the bones on the field of St. Clair's defeat—Fort Recovery built—Attack by the Indians on an escort—Wayne learns the movements of the Indians and the British agents—Indians attack Fort Recovery, and are repulsed—Wayne marches from Greenville—Builds Fort Defiance—Sends a peace messenger to the Indians—The reply of the Indians—Wayne marches on—Leaves his heavy baggage—Moves down the Maumee—Battle, and complete victory—Wayne destroys Indian and British property—Effect of the victory on the Indians—The army returns—Fort Wayne built—Fort Loramie built—Army in winter quarters at Greenville—Indian spirit subdued—The tribes disposed to peace measures—Opposition made by the British agents—Great council held—Propositions made by the English governor of Detroit—Brant coincides—Indians do not consent—They send peace messengers to the Americans—The preliminaries of peace entered into—Great council held at Greenville, and treaty made—Terms of the treaty—Other events during the Indian War—Genet, French minister; his schemes to involve the United States in war—His attempts in the West; contemplated invasion of Louisiana and Florida—Separation of the Western States, and revolt in the Spanish provinces, projected—Genet issues commissions—Excitement among the Western people—Action of the United States government—Genet recalled by France, who disowns his acts—Free navigation of the Mississippi insisted on by the United States; denied by Spain—Governor Miro relaxes the stringent measures in relation to duties—He grants special privileges of trade on the Mississippi—Attempts of Spain to dismember the Union—Operations in relation to the navigation of the Mississippi—Unsuccessful attempts of government to treat with Spain—Baron Carondelet's policy and attempts to separate the West—Treaty of Madrid—Free navigation of Mississippi secured—New Orleans a free port of deposit—Yazoo speculation—Projected British invasion of the Spanish provinces, by way of the lakes and the Illinois—Spanish posts withheld from the Americans—The causes—Spanish perfidy and duplicity—Powers proceeds to Detroit, the headquarters of Wilkinson—Conduct of Wilkinson—New Orleans ceases to be a port of deposit, unless duties are paid—The act of the Intendant reversed by the King of Spain—Jefferson sends ministers to France and Spain—Spain cedes Louisiana to France—Diplomacy of the American ministers relative to the purchase of Louisiana—All Louisiana purchased from France—Spain objects, but renounces opposition—Effectual agency of Mr. Livingston—

Spanish and French claims to land—British evacuate the Western posts—Northwestern Territory—Ohio set off—Indiana created—Extent of the United States' possessions in the Northwest........................................*Page* 174

NOTES TO CHAPTER IV........................................................................ 389

## CHAPTER V.

### INDIAN DISTURBANCES.

Principle which governs European title in America—Rights of original inhabitants—Rights of discoverers—Ultimate dominion over the Soil—Political condition of the Indians—Review of the character of Indian treaties—General Harrison appointed governor of Northwestern Territory—His first acts in treaties with the Indians—The Black Sparrow-hawk—His rank and place of residence—Treaty of St. Louis of 1804—Vast territory ceded—Afterward confirmed—Fort Madison built—Jealousy among the Sacs, Black Hawk's band—Attempts to surprise Fort Madison—Territory of Michigan erected—Governor Hull—Fire at Detroit—New town laid out—Lieutenant Pike ascends the Mississippi—Obtains cessions of lands from the Indians—Prospect of Indian disturbances—Tecumthe and the Prophet—Black Hawk—Indian talk of Le Marquois—Enterprise and efforts of Tecumthe and his brother—They attempt to deceive Governor Harrison—The governor prepares for emergencies—Indian hostility apparent—Black Hawk urged to join the confederacy—War parties sent out—Result of their acts—General outbreak expected—Tecumthe assembles a hostile force—Harrison convenes a council of Indians—Violent conduct of Tecumthe—Governor Harrison assembles an army—Marches to the Prophet's town—Indians temporize with Harrison—He encamps, and is attacked in the night—Battle of Tippecanoe—All the Western posts and settlements threatened—War of 1812—Conduct of the English traders—Robert Dickson, his great influence—Predatory warfare of the Indians—Dickson collects the Indians at Green Bay—Gives Black Hawk the command, and sends him to Detroit—Black Hawk remains a short time with the army, and returns to the Mississippi—News of the declaration of war does not arrive quickly in the West—Disastrous consequences—Mackinaw surrenders—Surrender of Detroit—Fate of the garrison at Chicago—Massacre of Captain Heald's forces—Alleged cause of Indian vengeance—Events of the war on the Mississippi—Fort at Prairie du Chien repaired—Captured by the British under McKay—The prisoners sent down the Mississippi—Indian rage—Major Campbell ascends the river from St. Louis—Is attacked by Black Hawk; is wounded and retreats with his boats—British send cannon and soldiers to Rock Island—Major Zachary Taylor ascends the river with a force—Great body of Indians at Rock Island—They attack Taylor, and after a severe fight he returns down the river—Forts Madison and Johnson burned—Peace with Great Britain and consequent peace with Indians by treaties—Fort Armstrong built at Rock Island—Settlements commence there—Keokuk and his band remove—Black Hawk remains—Illinois about to be admitted as a State—Boundary question—Increase of white settlements, and outrages committed—Lead trade with the Indians—Wisconsin a part of Michigan Territory—Settlements at Green Bay—Indian Jealousy—Winnebagoes attack a party of Chippewas—Conduct of American commander at Fort Snelling—Red Bird's resentment—Murders near Prairie du Chien—Red Bird's people attack two boats on the river—Great excitement in the mining regions—General Atkinson ascends the river with his force—Red Bird and other Indians surrender themselves prisoners—General outbreak expected—Prompt action of Atkinson and the volunteers defeats it—Indians tried at Prairie du Chien—Convicted, and pardoned—Red Bird dies in prison—Other prisoners discharged—Country begins to settle—New disturbances on Rock River—Black Hawk returns to his village and threatens the whites—Governor Reynolds declares the State invaded—Applies for assistance to General Government—Raises volunteer force—General Gaines with United States troops proceeds up the river—Confers with the Indians—Is joined by the Illinois volunteers—They take possession of the Sac village, and Indians cross the river—The village destroyed—Treaty at Rock Island—Reflections.......*Page* 221

Notes to Chapter V........ 406

## CHAPTER VI.

### BLACK HAWK IN WISCONSIN.

The treaty of St. Louis—Settlers in Black Hawk's village—Obstinacy of Black Hawk—He again crosses the Mississippi—Governor Reynolds demands aid—General Atkinson ascends the river—Black Hawk refuses to go back—The army follows him—Volunteers at Dixon's Ferry—Major Stillman's attack, and flight of his men—First blood shed in the war—Governor Reynolds demands more aid—Sioux and Menomonies offer their services—Talk with the Winnebagoes—Alarm in the mining district—Colonel Dodge writes to Governor Reynolds—Authority of Colonel Dodge—Assembles volunteers—Marches to Rock Biver—Returns home and prepares for defence—Massacre at Indian Creek and capture of Misses Hall—St. Vrain, Hawley, and others killed—Affair at Buffalo Grove—Major Dement's battle—Attack at Apple River—Affair at Sinsinawa Mound—Dodge talks with the Winnebagoes—Forts and block-houses in Iowa county—The Misses Hall delivered up—Winnebagoes suspected—Aubrey killed at Mound Fort—Dodge's volunteers march—He addresses them—They bury St. Vrain, Hawley, and others—Reach the camp at Dixon—Proceed to General Atkinson's camp—Dodge receives his orders and returns—Murders at Spafford's farm—Dodge assembles a force—Proceeds to Fort Hamilton—Apple killed—Battle of the Pecatonica—Chippewas and Sioux come to Fort Hamilton and return—Force and Green killed at Mound Fort—Dodge joins General Posey's command—Disposition of the forces—March of a portion of the army—General Atkinson at Koshkonong—The White Crow offers to pilot the forces to Black Hawk's camp—His supposed treachery—General Atkinson sends to Fort Winnebago for provisions—General Henry and Colonel Dodge march in search of Black Hawk—They reach Rock River Rapids—Discover the Indian trail, which is followed—Overtake Black Hawk—Battle of the Wisconsin Heights—General Atkinson breaks up his camp and marches in pursuit of Black Hawk—They cross the Wisconsin River and follow the Indian trail—Battle of Bad Axe—Winnebago chiefs bring Black Hawk in as a prisoner—General Scott's rapid movements with his forces—They are attacked with cholera—Loss of the Americans in this war—Subsequent notices of Black Hawk, and reflections—The volunteers of Wisconsin—Increase of population in the mining country—Important Indian treaties—Land speculations—Military road opened—Mail route up the Mississippi—Early private enterprise—Hamilton—Farnsworth—Transportation of troops—Early history of Prairie du Chien—Causes operating against the early settlement of the country—Michigan about to become a State—New Territory to be formed in the West—Jealousy as to the seat of government—Legislative proceedings—Final action of Congress establishing the Territory of Wisconsin........ 257

Notes to Chapter VI........ 416

# INTRODUCTORY.

---

THE object of the present work is sufficiently apparent from its title; the cause and manner of its having been undertaken by the compiler may deserve explanation. In January, 1849, the "State Historical Society of Wisconsin" was formed, through the efforts of a few citizens, whose sanguine anticipations of immediate successful results were unfortunately disappointed. Beyond two annual addresses, the first by the compiler, the second by the Honourable MORGAN L. MARTIN, both by appointments of the Society, no practical labours in the region of Wisconsin history were laid before its annual meetings; indeed, the Society appeared to languish, and all attempts to restore energy to it, or to render it of utility to the State, in conformity with its original design, appeared fruitless.

By the constitution of the Society, the governor of the State was *ex-officio* its president. Soon after the inauguration of Governor FARWELL, in 1852, the compiler was much gratified to find, from conversations with his excellency, how deep an interest he felt in all which, in any degree, related to the development of the actual condition and resources of the State of Wisconsin. The governor expressed to the compiler his regrets that the objects of the

State Historical Society were less regarded, or at least less attended to, than they merited to be; and suggested to him the idea that it might not be a difficult matter, with industry properly directed, to obtain from the prominent residents of each county in the State, such annals and statistics as, when digested and compiled in a correct form, would make a valuable local history. He also spoke of the propriety of collecting, at an early day, every matter of historical interest depending on the memory of individuals, or on perishable records, so that a foundation might be laid for a State history on which a reliance might be placed for its authenticity. On these matters he requested the compiler to reflect, and give him the result of his thoughts in such shape as that it might be advantageously used, if considered of sufficient importance. Accordingly, in a few days afterward, the following letter was addressed to the governor.

*Madison, February 2d*, 1852.

To Leonard J. Farwell, Governor of the State of Wisconsin.

Sir—Within a period of time not longer than that which embraces the political existence of Wisconsin, the attention of many of the States of the Union has been directed to the collection and preservation of all matters shedding light upon, or in any manner properly belonging to their own history—colonial, revolutionary, and federate. The importance of their action on such subjects will not be denied, and the example is worthy to be followed in Wisconsin.

It is due to ourselves—to the enlightened age in which

we live,—it is more especially due to posterity, that we should gather and preserve every evidence within our reach, of such events and transactions, public and individual, as may properly be considered as forming our history, social and political. Much of such evidence is now in our power, but time cannot replace or restore that which his own hand is hourly removing and destroying.

To collect and arrange the documentary history of Wisconsin, from its earliest settlement to the present time, will require much labour and research, and, consequently, considerable expense, independent of the value of the time employed in the work;—expenditure in the collection of records, books, and papers, and in travelling for the desired purpose, will form a considerable portion of the account. The undivided time and attention of the collator must be occupied, and a year or more may elapse before his labours could, in any likelihood, be completed.

I have addressed you, sir, as the executive of the State, to whom properly belongs the superintendence of the general welfare of the community. I am desirous of compiling such matters as will serve as a Documentary History of Wisconsin; comprising, not only public records, but also narratives of private enterprise, the history of the settlement of counties, and their past and present statistics. In the prosecution of this design I would require legislative encouragement; and should my proposed action meet with your approval, I would respectfully ask you to communicate my design and wishes to the legislature.

I have the honour to be your obedient servant,

WM. R. SMITH.

The journal of the Senate, of February 5th, 1852, exhibits the following proceedings, which conclusively show the deep interest which Governor Farwell felt in the accomplishment of the projected undertaking.

"The following communication from his excellency the governor, and accompanying communication from General William R. Smith, was read, and, on motion of Mr. Stewart, it was referred to the Committee on State Affairs."

*Executive Department, Madison Feb. 4th,* 1852.

TO THE SENATE AND ASSEMBLY.

I have the honour herewith to present a communication from General William R. Smith, on the subject of "collecting and arranging the documentary history of Wisconsin."

I most fully concur in the views and suggestions of General Smith upon this subject, and take pleasure in most earnestly commending them to your consideration.

Such a documentary history of Wisconsin would most obviously be a work of immense value to the people of our times, and of still greater value to posterity. We cannot, in my opinion, too soon rescue and save the elements of early history, which year by year are constantly perishing from the records and memories of the past.

Many valuable manuscripts and facts, and much important information now in the possession of the living pioneers of our State, can only in this way be saved; which, after a few more years, can never be reclaimed.

The older States are now expending vast sums of money every year, to search out and explore the relics of their early history, which they might have preserved with but little trouble and expense by giving attention to the subject at an earlier day. I therefore recommend that provision be made by the legislature for this object; and that General William R. Smith be authorized and employed, under such liberal and adequate compensation as may be fixed by law, to prepare and furnish the State such a history as is prefigured in his communication.

His long residence in Wisconsin, his historical and personal knowledge of the country, added to great learning and experience, designate him as the proper person to perform this work.

LEONARD J. FARWELL.

The Senate journal further shows, that on the 9th of February, 1852, the committee on the subject of these communications reported as follows:

The Committee on State Affairs, to whom was referred the message of the governor, enclosing the communication of William R. Smith in relation to the compilation of the documentary history of Wisconsin, report—

That, in the estimation of the committee, it is important to the welfare of all political communities that all records and statistics, and every fact relative to their true history, should be carefully gathered, from time to time, and faithfully preserved. When such collections of public documents are correctly made, a duty which we owe to ourselves is well performed; the history of the past and the present is placed before us, for our instruction, whenever a reference thereto becomes necessary; and we thereby discharge a debt which one generation owes to another.

The example of our sister States in collecting and arranging all matters appertaining to their early history, should not be lost in Wisconsin.

Much difficulty is found at this day in gathering up fragments which time has scattered; and Wisconsin may readily avoid such difficulty by writing her own history in the freshness and vigour of her youth, and yearly preserve her annals with the stamp of truth, for the use of posterity.

We therefore approve of the suggestions contained in the communication of the governor, and report the following bill, recommending its passage. All of which is respectfully submitted.

ELIAB B. DEAN, JR.
HARVEY G. TURNER,
JOEL C. SQUIRES,
*Committee on State Affairs.*

The bill which accompanied this report provided in a generous manner for defraying the expenses of compiling the Documentary History of the State; subsequent legislatures, in the same generous spirit, aided the advancement and progress of the work, by similar appropriations; and, finally, in 1854, authorized the publication of so much of the history as is now ready for the press, at the expense of the State of Wisconsin.

Such has been the liberal action of the legislature. The

compiler, in the performance of his task voluntarily assumed, and in discharge of the duties which devolved upon him, has endeavoured to meet a portion, at least, of the public expectations. Claiming for himself the credit of a zeal which he felt, and an industry which he strove to exercise, he seeks not the name of historian, but will rest satisfied if that of faithful compiler may justly be awarded to him. Yet this remark must be deemed more immediately applicable to the history of events antecedent to the formation of a Territorial government in Wisconsin. For such history, and very often for the language in which the events have been transmitted to us, in various valuable publications, the compiler has acknowledged his indebtedness in the notes to his many quotations; and if in any portion of the work such acknowledgment has been omitted, it is here, in all candour, made. But for that portion of the history relating to the period between the organization of the Territory in 1836 and the present time, the compiler is more immediately responsible, as the events have transpired within his own personal recollections.

The compiler is aware that, in the perusal of almost every page of the early history, observations will present themselves to the reader, which very naturally will suggest the question, "Why is so much matter devoted to the history of portions of country in some degree remote from the immediate Territory of Wisconsin?" It is presumed that a sufficient answer may be given in this:—The history of Wisconsin in early times is essentially embodied in the early history of the Valley of the Mississippi: the country was not integral, but a small portion of the great Northwest; and, as such, the events occurring in, and spreading over, and influentially operating upon the whole, became consequently important *data* in its own history. If it be desirable to obtain a history and description of a single chamber in a vast structure, such desire may best be gratified by obtaining a history and description of the building itself.

Without such an allowance of latitude to the compiler of history, he would necessarily become a mere annalist; his events deprived of all but local interest; the remote causes of such events, and their extraneous effects, would alike remain hidden to the reader, whose attention would thus be unprofitably limited and confined. An early history of Wisconsin, restricted to the present boundaries of the State, would possess no other interest than that derived from an account of the advent of the Jesuit fathers, their religious establishments, their sufferings and endurance, their labours and success. Such a narration might soon be written, and in narrow compass; but would the contemplated design of obtaining what might properly be termed "the History of Early Times in Wisconsin" be thereby accomplished? We have thought it would not, and have pursued a course, in our compilation, which we trust will be at least tolerated, if not commended. The history of the Territory, and of the State of Wisconsin, integral and set apart from the surrounding region, will of course be restricted to those objects alone which will come within its legitimate scope and design. But it has been considered that every prominent event in the history of the settlement of the Valley of the Mississippi had some bearing on the proper history of Wisconsin, immediate or remote, and with such view the subject has been treated.

With regard to the documentary history, a very wide field appears open. All that relates to the civil and political history of the Territory and State; all public papers and public action having reference to any matter in which the improvement, progress, and prosperity of the State is concerned; private narratives of great public events, such as Indian disturbances, and their consequences; interesting narratives of early adventure in the settlement of the State; all matters tending in any degree to establish a foundation for a correct statistical history of the whole country; in fine, all matters which may be considered as affecting the general interests, and not in their nature restricted to private interests, may find a proper place in this field of inquiry. Old States are now searching, with indefatigable care and at very great public expense, into the records and traditions of the past, for every matter which has a bearing on their early history; and this is done at this day, with an acknowledgment of deep regret that the preservation of such matters, in the shape of a Documentary History, had not received their attention at an earlier period. If it be not a source of gratulation that Wisconsin, in her infancy, has the advantage in her power of collecting and preserving such matters belonging to her early history, she may at least be commended for endeavouring to prevent future regrets that her materials for such history were suffered to perish, one by one, for want of compilation in time.

In the descriptive portion of the work the plan is apparent, and needs only an outline explanation. The boundaries of each county are defined and described. The soil and productions, trade and manufactures, of the county are generally set forth. The division of the county into towns is noted, and each town is then separately described. In the description of each township in each county, will be embraced the history of its first settlement, its soil and productions, its streams and water-powers, its woods and prairies, its improvements in machinery and manufactures, its plank-roads and rail-roads, its local advantages, and its farming interests—improved and unimproved; its villages, churches, school-houses, and other public buildings, its population and general statistics, and, in fine, the compiler has endeavoured to give a truthful picture of Wisconsin as she now is, and to lead discerning minds to reflect on the means of rendering her more beautiful still.

Personal visits to every county in the State (with the few exceptions of new counties lately taken from the larger counties in the north) has enabled the compiler to present his views and descriptions generally from actual observation. His indebtedness to gentlemen of intelligence and accuracy of information, in every part of the State, for the highly valuable facts imparted to him, and the facilities afforded him of personal examinations into interesting matters, is most gratefully acknowledged. To name the individuals in each county which the compiler visited, who afforded him such facilities, and gave him such valuable information, would certainly swell an immense list, but could not either increase his gratitude, or add to the satisfaction which he is confident they feel in having conferred upon him benefits so essential to the completion of his labours.

Such has been the design of the compiler of this work; and if, in his earnest endeavours to accomplish the task confided to him, and perhaps rashly assumed, he has materially failed, or embodied incorrect views in any, even the least important, of the many subjects of such a compilation, his sincere regrets for such act may (in the charitable spirit of forbearance to censure mistaken judgment) be allowed to be at least equal to those of his readers.

# HISTORY OF WISCONSIN.

## CHAPTER I.

### NEW FRANCE AND LOUISIANA.

Early History—Mississippi Valley—Discovery of Florida—Ponce de Leon, Miruelo, Narvaez, De Soto—Discovery of the Mississippi, and fate of De Soto—Charter Grant of New France—Jesuit Missionaries, zeal and success—Reach the Western Lakes—Enterprising views of Discovery—Mesnard, Allouez, Marquette—Views of the Intendant Talon—Great Congress of Indian Nations at the Falls of St. Mary—Enterprise of Marquette and Joliet—Dangers pointed out by the Indians—Fox River, Portage, and Wisconsin—Upper Mississippi discovered—The Illini Indians hospitable—The Missouri passed, the Ouabache reached, and the Mississippi descended to below the Arkansas—Return of Marquette and Joliet to Green Bay—Joliet's papers lost—Death of Marquette—De la Salle, his enterprise, protected and encouraged by Colbert and Seignelay—Builds a vessel on Niagara River, and navigates the Upper Lakes—He reaches the sources of the Illinois River—Descends and builds a Fort—Learns the course of the Mississippi River, loses his vessel on the Lakes, and resolves to build a new one—Despatches Hennepin on a voyage of discovery up the Mississippi—Leaves Tonti in command, and returns on foot to Fort Frontenac—Tonti builds Rock Fort—Is driven away by the Indians—La Salle returns, descends the Mississippi to the sea, and takes possession of the country, by the name of Louisiana—Returns to France, procures a fleet, and endeavours to discover the mouth of the Mississippi by sea—Passes the mouth, and lands in St. Bernard's Bay—His misfortunes, fruitless searches, and assassination—Joutel and Anastasius return by the Mississippi to Fort Crevecœur, and thence to Quebec—Attempts to decry the merits of La Salle's discoveries—Hennepin's alleged discoveries—His two publications, and interpolations—The claims of England to the Mississippi founded on Hennepin's books—The claims of France—Conflicting opinions of French and English Colonists—New France neglected—

French possessions in the West include the whole Valley of the Mississippi—Iberville and his brothers—Expedition fitted out to discover the mouth of the Mississippi—Iberville successful—Passes up the River—Finds a letter from Tonti to La Salle—Builds a Fort at Biloxi, and returns to France—Possession taken of the whole basin of the Mississippi, by France, under the name of Louisiana.

THE early history of that portion of the great North-west now known as the State of Wisconsin, is necessarily connected with that of the whole valley of the Mississippi; and in taking a condensed retrospective view of the early explorations of the country bordering on its waters, it cannot be considered as altogether foreign to our immediate subject. Although more than a century had elapsed from the advent of the first European to the banks of the great River of the West, previous to any important exploration of its course, yet that event must be considered as the inception of its history. The first adventurers came, seeking conquest and gold; they found poverty, endured sufferings, and met with death. Religious zeal and persevering self-denial on the part of the early Jesuit missionaries accomplished more with the Red man than the sword, and laid the foundation of that astonishing prosperity of settlement and cultivation by civilized man, which at this day pervades the entire valley of the Mississippi. Wisconsin, as a portion of that valley, is so far connected with the early discovery and settlement of any part of it, that the story of the fortunes of adventurers, and the ultimate reduction of the whole of the Great West to the peaceable possession and occupancy of the United States, necessarily becomes a part of her own history, and cannot justly be omitted in the records of her own proper annals.

The southern coast of the North American continent, near St. Augustine in Florida, was discovered on Easter Sunday, in the year 1512, by Juan Ponce de Leon. In honour of the day, as well as on account of the flowers of the ground, and the blossoms of the trees, he named the new-found country Pascua Florida. Ponce de Leon had been one of the adventurous companions of Columbus, and, in the spirit of the time, he was filled with the hope of finding in his new discovery, not only mines of gold, but even waters imbued with the powers of renovating life. The only advantage he derived from his discovery was the appointment of governor of the region; and on his return thither in 1521 to colonize the country, he was killed in combat with the Indians.[1]

In the mean while, a Spanish sea-captain, Diego Miruelo, sailing from Havana in 1516, had landed in Florida, at some point which he has not distinctly described, and having taken home with him a considerable store of gold, the cupidity of the daring and avaricious among the listeners to his story was effectually aroused. However, ten years elapsed before Pamphilo de Narvaez, in 1526, obtained permission from Spain to prosecute discoveries and make further conquest of Florida. The Spaniards of early times designated by this name all of North America extending from the Gulf of Mexico to the Great Lakes; they certainly claimed, under the name of Florida, the whole sea-coast as far as Newfoundland, and even to the remotest north; in Spanish geography, Canada was a part of Florida.[2]

In 1528, Narvaez landed in Florida, probably near Appalachee Bay, with three hundred men. The success of Cortes in Mexico acted as a powerful stimulant on all contemporary adventurers; and the deluding accounts given by the Indians of the gold regions, led them to believe that Florida was equally wealthy in the precious metals with Mexico or Peru. Narvaez and his companions, (of whom eighty were mounted,) in the fruitless but alluring search for the object of their warmest hopes, wandered over the lands lying north of the Gulf, until disappointment and suffering compelled them, after six months' endurance of unrequited hardships, to seek the sea-shore again. Naked and famished, the remnant of the party, having reached the Bay of Pensacola, manufactured rude boats, in which most of the company, with Narvaez, des-

---

[1] Herrera, as cited by Bancroft, vol. i. 33.

[2] Bancroft, and cited authorities, vol. i. 60.

perately embarked, and finally perished in a storm, and by famine after shipwreck, near the mouths of the Mississippi. Four only of the three hundred ultimately reached Mexico by land, after years of hardships, courageous enterprise, and wanderings that extended across Louisiana and the northern part of Mexico, to the shores of the Pacific Ocean in Sonora; yet even this melancholy remnant, notwithstanding all their sufferings and defeated expectations, still persisted in the tale of the golden regions of Florida, and even confirmed it by the solemnity of an oath before a magistrate.[1] They returned in 1536.

Stimulated by such reports, Ferdinand de Soto, one of the conquerors of Peru under Pizarro, obtained leave to conquer Florida without expense to the Spanish king. In May, 1539, accompanied by a well-armed and brilliant band of six hundred men, with between two and three hundred horses, De Soto landed in the Bay of Spiritu Santo, or Tampa Bay, eager, adventurous, and full of hope in the contemplated enterprise. For the first five months the adventurers toiled in vain, until they reached the neighbourhood of Appalachee Bay; during the year 1540 they passed to the north-east, and climbed the mountains of Georgia; again they turned westward, and in October, having arrived on the Alabama river, they fought with the Indians and captured the town of Mavila, or Mobile; resuming their march toward the Mississippi, they passed the winter near the Yazoo; on the 1st of April, 1541, De Soto reached the Great River not far from the thirty-fifth parallel of latitude; and, after spending a month in preparing barges to transport across the stream such of their horses as still were alive, the explorers crossed, pursued their way northward to the neighbourhood of New Madrid, and turning westward again, marched more than two hundred miles from the Mississippi to the highlands of White River; again they toiled on to the south, and spent a third winter of their wanderings on the Washita. In the spring of 1542, De Soto

---

[1] Bancroft, vol. i. 40.

descended this river to its junction with the Mississippi, anxious to learn the distance and direction of the sea. On reaching the Great River, he was informed, that below, it flowed through endless and uninhabitable swamps; in order to learn the truth, he sent forward horsemen, who advanced only thirty miles in eight days. Disappointment struck the intrepid warrior to the heart; his men and horses were daily wasting and falling around him; the Indians challenged him to the combat with impunity; at length a wasting melancholy seized him—his health sank under a conflict of emotions, and a malignant fever brought his life to a close, in May, 1542. "Thus perished Ferdinand de Soto, the governor of Cuba, the successful associate of Pizarro. His miserable end was the more observed from the greatness of his former prosperity. His soldiers pronounced his eulogy by grieving for their loss; the priests chaunted over his body the first requiems that were ever heard on the waters of the Mississippi. To conceal his death, his body was wrapped in a mantle, and, in the stillness of midnight, was silently sunk in the middle of the stream. The discoverer of the Mississippi slept beneath its waters. He had crossed a large part of the continent in search of gold, and found nothing so remarkable as his burial-place."[1]

His remaining followers, hoping to reach Mexico by land, again turned their steps westward, and penetrated to the Red River, the sport of inimical Indians in their forest wanderings. They were unable to cross the Red River, and once more going eastward, they reached the Mississippi in December, 1542. In despair of rescuing themselves by land, they proceeded to prepare such vessels as they could, to carry them to the sea. They laboured from January to July, 1543, and in that month, in the vessels thus constructed, they reached the Gulf of Mexico, and in September entered the river Panuco. One-half of the six hundred who landed with De Soto full of golden hopes, and gay in the display of war-

[1] Bancroft, vol. i. 57; and for dates and authorities, Bancroft passim. Perkins's Western Annals, p. 1, etc.

like habiliments, had left their bones among the mountains and in the morasses of the South, from Georgia to Arkansas![1] Such is the outline of the history of the expedition, and such the fate of Ferdinand de Soto.

It was reserved for religion to accomplish that enterprise in which a desire of conquest and the thirst for gold had failed; the Mississippi valley had yet to be reached from the north-east, by the route of the great lakes; and all the countless benefits which have flowed from its settlement and cultivation, not only to its own inhabitants and to the United States, but to all mankind, in a commercial point of view, have had their foundation in a prominent degree in the religious zeal of the disciples of Loyola. The discovery of the north-west region was made, missionary posts established, friendship cultivated with the numerous savage tribes, churches erected, and converted red men formed into congregations of worshipping Christians; the country was explored, and the Upper Mississippi not only discovered, but traced from the Falls of St. Anthony of Padua to the Gulf of Mexico; and all these through the privations, the sufferings, the untiring labours of the French missionaries. To use the language of our eloquent historian, they were employed "in confirming the influence of France in those vast regions, mingling business with suffering, and winning enduring glory by their fearless perseverance." Alas, how deplorable the contrast in their enterprises and the results of them, between the warlike and mail-begirt Spanish adventurers, and the meek and robe-clad missionaries of the West!

More than a century had passed from the expedition of De Soto, and no result had sprung from it, except a deadly hatred of the white man, among all the tribes of Indians which had been visited and warred upon by the Spaniard. In 1611, the French settled in Eastern Maine, nine years previous to the landing of the Pilgrims. Early as 1616, Le Caron, a Franciscan friar, the companion of Champlain, had reached the rivers of Lake Huron from the land of the Mohawks, on

---

[1] Bancroft. Perk. West. Annals.

foot, and paddling a bark canoe. In 1627, a number of opulent merchants in France obtained from Louis XIII. a charter grant of New France. After the restoration of Quebec, in 1632, by the English, they entered on the government of their province. Within the limits of their grant was included the whole basin of the St. Lawrence, and of such other rivers as flowed directly into the sea, and also Florida, or the country south of Virginia, which was claimed as a French province, although an attempt by Coligni to settle it had failed. The commercial enterprise of colonizing Canada was attended by the powerful stimulant of religious zeal; but the vowed poverty of life and simplicity of the Franciscans, although the chosen friends of Champlain, the governor of Canada, rendered them free from ambition; and the great office of establishing the honours of the Gallican Church, and converting the heathen of Canada, and thus enlarging the borders of French dominion, was entrusted solely to the rival order of the Jesuits. "The history of their labours is connected with the origin of every celebrated town in the annals of French America; not a cape was turned nor a river entered but a Jesuit led the way."[1]

After undergoing great fatigue and suffering, the Jesuits Brebeuf and Daniel, followed soon by Lallemand, made their way to the West in 1634. They had joined a party of Hurons returning from Quebec, and, by lakes, rivers, and forests, had now penetrated to the heart of the Huron wilderness. Near the shore of Lake Iroquois, north-west of Lake Toronto, was raised the first house of the Society of Jesus, and soon two villages, named St. Louis and St. Ignatius, sprang up among the Huron forests. The mission of Brebeuf gave us a knowledge of the watercourse of the St. Lawrence valley, and from the map published in 1660, it appears that the Jesuits had examined the country from the waters of the "Unghiara," or Niagara, as we write it, to the head of Lake Superior, and had even gained a glimpse of Lake Michigan. Missions were also esta-

[1] Bancroft, vol. iii. 118 et seq.

blished and converts made, but the martyrdom of Daniel, of Jogues, of Brebeuf, and of Lallemand, by their savage enemies, was the price at which they obtained a knowledge of the West, and endeavoured to lay the foundation of the Christian church among the heathen.[1]

As early as 1638, an Indian chief, who dwelt on the head-waters of the Ohio, visited the missions; and constant mention is made in the annals of the Jesuits, of the Algonquins from the West, especially from Green Bay. In 1640, the hostility of the Five Nations prevented the access of Raymbault and Picard to the West, the place of their destination; but in 1641, at a great feast of the dead, held by the Algonquins of Lake Nipising, the Jesuits were invited to visit the nation of the Chippewas at Sault St. Marie;[2] and on the 17th of September, 1641, we find fathers Raymbault and Jogues, the first envoys from Christendom, leaving the Bay of Penetangushe, in a birch-bark canoe, for the Falls of St. Mary, where, after a passage of seventeen days, they met two thousand Indians, who had assembled to receive them. From them the worthy fathers learned of many unknown nations; they heard of the Nadouisses, or Sioux, as living eighteen days' journey further west, beyond the great lake, then without a name; and thus the French were looking toward the homes of the Sioux in the valley of the Mississippi, five years before the New England Eliot had addressed the tribes of Indians that dwelt within six miles of Boston harbour.[3]

The hospitable Chippewas invited the Jesuits to dwell with them as brothers, and expressed a willingness to derive profit from their words; but sickness seized upon Raymbault, the first apostle to the tribes of Michigan, and he died in 1642. In the extent of his enterprising views of discovery, he expected even to reach the ocean that divides America from China. In August, 1654, two fur-traders joined a band of Ottawas, and ventured on a western voyage of five hundred leagues; in two years they returned, accompanied with fifty

---

[1] Bancroft, vol. iii. 328. [2] Ibid. p. 131, and Relations. [3] Ibid.

canoes and two hundred and fifty men; they described the vast lakes of the West, spoke of the Knisteneaux, whose homes stretched to the Northern Sea; and of the Sioux, who dwelt beyond Lake Superior, and demanded commerce with the whites for the wants of the red man. The traders pressed forward to Green Bay, and two of them passed the winter of 1659 on the banks of the Lake Superior; the religious zeal of the bishop of Quebec was thereby excited, and Père Rènè Mèsnard was chosen to visit Green Bay and Lake Superior, and to establish a residence, and a place of assembly for all the surrounding nations. In October, 1660, Mèsnard reached Keweena, on the south shore of Lake Superior, and eight months afterward he left that place for the Bay of Chegoiemegon, with only one attendant, for the purpose of visiting the Hurons in the Isle of St. Michael. He took the route by the way of Keweena Lake and Portage; there, while his attendant was transporting the canoe, Mèsnard wandered in the forest, and was never more seen; long after, his breviary and cassock were kept as amulets among the Sioux.[1]

In 1665, Père Claude Allouez embarked on a mission to the far West. He reached the Falls of St. Mary in September; he entered the lake, and, sailing along the southern shore, in vain search of the mass of pure copper of which he had heard, at length arrived at the great village of the Chippewas at Chegoiemegon. A grand council was there held, of ten or twelve of the neighbouring nations. To this council came the Potowatamies from Lake Michigan; the Sacs and Foxes from the West; the Hurons from north of Lake Superior; the Illinois also came, whose tale of sorrow, of ancient glory and diminished numbers, in consequence of warfare with the Sioux on the one side, and the Iroquois on the other, was accompanied with their enticing description of their noble river flowing to the South, on which they dwelt, their vast prairies, and the absence of forests in their land, although replete with buffalo and herds of deer. There also came the

[1] Bancroft, vol. iii. 148, and Relations.

Sioux from the west of Lake Superior, or the land of prairies and of wild rice, who reported the great river on whose banks they dwelt, and which Father Allouez states as named "Messippi." To the assembled nations Allouez offered commerce, and an alliance with France against their enemies, the Iroquois. In 1667, he returned to Quebec, and in 1668, Claude Dablon and James Marquette repaired to the Chippewas at the Sault, to establish the mission of St. Mary's; it is the oldest settlement began by Europeans within the bounds of the State of Michigan; and the commencement of the old town of Michillimackinac, in 1671, is ascribed to the exertions and the influence of Marquette.[1]

The purpose of discovering the Mississippi, of which the natives had told the grandeur, sprang from Marquette himself, in 1669; in the interval of delay which occurred, he devoted his time to the study of the Illinois tongue, with a view to facilitate his intercourse with the nations he expected to meet in his contemplated voyage of discovery.[2] The protection afforded to the Algonquins of the West, by their commerce with France, confirmed their attachment, and created a political interest which extended to Colbert and the ministry of Louis XIV. The Intendant Talon determined to spread the power of France to the utmost borders of Canada, and for this purpose Nicholas Perrot was despatched to the West, as the agent of Talon, to propose a congress of the nations at St. Mary's. The invitation extended to the tribes of Lake Superior; it was carried to the wandering hordes of the remotest north; and escorted from Green Bay by Potowatamies, Perrot, the first of Europeans, repaired on the same mission of friendship to the Miamis at Chicago.

The day appointed arrived in May, 1671. At the Falls of St. Mary was then gathered a great congress of Indian nations from the whole country from the head-springs of the St. Lawrence, the Mississippi, and the Red River; and it was announced that they were placed under the protection of the

[1] Bancroft, vol. iii. 148, seq., and Relations.

[2] Ibid.

French kings. In the same year, Marquette gathered the remains of one branch of the Hurons at Point St. Ignace, which establishment was long considered as the key to the West. The countries south of this were explored by Allouez and Dablon, who bore the cross through Eastern Wisconsin and the north of Illinois, visiting the Mascoutens and Kickapoos on the Milwaukee, and the Miamis at the head of Lake Michigan, and extending their journeys to the Foxes on the river of that name, fearless of danger, and indefatigable in religious zeal.[1]

The great enterprise projected by Marquette had been favored by Talon, the intendant of New France,[2] who wished to signalize the last period of his stay in Canada, by ascertaining if the French, descending the great river of the central West, could bear the banner of France to the Pacific, or plant it side by side with that of Spain on the Gulf of Mexico. The discovery of the Upper Mississippi, the great western river, whose course was to the south, was now at hand, to be accomplished by Joliet, of Quebec, of whom there is no record but of this one excursion, and by Marquette, who after years of attention to the welfare of the Hurons at the cold extremity of Michigan, entered with equal zeal and humanity upon a career of danger, in which life was perilled, and which in its results has affected the destiny of nations.[3]

On the 13th of May, 1673, Marquette, with the Sieur Joliet, who had been chosen to conduct the enterprise, and five other Frenchmen, in two bark canoes, with a little Indian corn and some dried meat for their only provision, embarked from their mission, on the daring adventure of exploring the country and discovering the nations of the unknown West. The Indians called the Fols Avoine (wild oats or wild rice) tribe, when informed of his design, were astonished, and endeavoured to dissuade him, by representing the distant nations

[1] Bancroft vol. iii. 154, and Relations.

[2] Charlevoix, Nouv. France, tom. ii. 248 et seq.

[3] Bancroft, vol. iii. 156.

as always at war with each other, and never sparing strangers; that the great river was not only dangerous of navigation, but was full of frightful monsters, who devoured men and canoes together; and that there was even a demon, who closed the passage of the river, and swallowed up those who dared to approach; and, in fine, that the heats were so excessive as infallibly to cause death.[1]

Nothing daunted by these terrifying descriptions, Marquette told them that he was willing to lay down his life for that cause in which the salvation of souls was concerned, and after having prayed together, they separated, and the adventurers arrived at the Bay des Puants, now Green Bay.

Leaving the bay, the good father entered the Fox River, and found the ascent difficult on account of the current, and also of the rocks, which cut the feet of those who dragged the canoes when the water was low. At the station which terminated the discoveries of the French, he found a village composed of three Indian nations, as he termed them, the Miamis, the Mascoutens, and the Kikabeaux, and had the extreme consolation of seeing a beautiful cross planted in the middle of the town, ornamented with white skins, red girdles, and bows and arrows, which those good people had offered to the great Manitou, or God, to thank him for the pity he had bestowed on them during the winter, in having given them an abundant chase. Here, also, Marquette drank of mineral waters, and was made acquainted with the secret of the root which cures the venomous bite of the rattlesnake; and he describes the beauty of the site of the village, as being a mound surrounded by extensive prairies, interspersed with woods and groves, and fertile in the production of Indian corn, of plums, and of grapes.[2]

The old men of the village were assembled by the explorers; Marquette told them that Joliet had been sent on the part of

---

[1] Marquette, Voyage, &c., reprint from Thevenot, Recueil, &c. 1681, by O. Rich & Sons, Paris and London, 1845, p. 3, 4.

[2] Idem, 7, 8.

the governor of Canada, to discover new countries, and himself on the part of God, to spread the light of the holy evangelists; that the Sovereign Master of their lives would that he should be known unto all nations; and to obey his will, he feared not death itself, to which he was exposed in his perilous journeys; and that they wished two guides to put them on their route. The request was accompanied with a present, and the guides were furnished to them, together with a mat, to serve as a bed during the voyage.

The following morning, June 10th, 1673, in the presence of a great number of Indians, assembled to witness so extraordinary and hazardous an expedition, seven Frenchmen and two Miami guides embarked in their two canoes, with the knowledge only that at three leagues from the Mascoutens was a river which discharged itself into the Mississippi; that its course was west of south-west; that the route to it was replete with marshes and small lakes, and the channel often so obstructed with wild oats as to render its discovery difficult. "For this," says Marquette, "we had occasion for our guides, and they conducted us, happily, to a portage of two thousand seven hundred paces, and aided us to transport our canoes to enter this river, after which they returned, leaving us alone, in this unknown country, in the hands of Providence."[1]

In 1542, De Soto had crossed the great river of the West, with an army of mail-clad warriors, brilliantly equipped in "pomp and circumstance," in search of conquest and of gold; in 1673 the pious and gentle Marquette, clothed with the coarse habit of his order, with only six companions, embarked in frail bark canoes, on unknown waters, to search their outlet into the same great river of the West, to explore new countries in the spirit of peace, and to spread the knowledge of the gospel in the bonds of love! "And now France and Christianity stood in the valley of the Mississippi!"

---

[1] Marquette, Voyage, reprint, &c. p. 8, 9.

In leaving the waters which flowed toward Quebec, to enter those which henceforth conducted them into strange lands, Marquette and his companions addressed themselves in prayer to the Holy Virgin, which devotion, he meekly says, they practised daily, placing under her protection their persons and the success of their voyage. After having encouraged each other, they stepped into their canoes, and boldly embarked on the bosom of the Mescousin, since known as the Ouisconsin; but when or in what manner the name was altered, is not accurately ascertained. The first mention of the river by this latter name is by Hennepin, when he ascended it from the Mississippi, in 1680, on his return from the Falls of St. Anthony to Quebec. This river is described as very wide, with sandy bottoms, causing many banks, and rendering the navigation very difficult; full of vine-covered isles, and bordered with fine lands, comprising woods, prairies, and rising grounds. The adventurers found roebucks and buffalo in abundant numbers, and perceived appearances of iron-mines. After a navigation of forty leagues on this river, on the 17th of June, 1673, "with a joy," says Marquette, "which I cannot express, we happily entered the Mississippi, in the latitude of forty-two degrees and a half."[1]

It is somewhat remarkable that, during the whole course from the portage to the mouth of the Wisconsin, Marquette neither saw an Indian village, nor met with a native Indian; nor did he, in descending the Mississippi, see an inhabitant of the country, until he reached the fortieth degree of latitude, or near that elevation, when on the 25th of June, footsteps and a path were perceived on the western bank. Leaving the men to guard the canoe, Marquette and Joliet fearlessly followed these indications of human beings, and after a walk of six miles, discovered a village on the banks of a river, and two others on the rising grounds, about half a league distant. They boldly penetrated into the village, and were received not only with great astonishment by the inhabitants, as they

[1] Marquette, Voyage, reprint, p. 10.

were unquestionably the first Europeans who had ever trod the soil of what is now Iowa, but the calumet, or sacred peace pipe, and its accompanying hospitality, was tendered to them. They were informed that the nation was called "Illini," or "the men," and that their village and the river on which it was situated, was called Mou-in-gou-ina, now called by us the Des Moines. The adventurers stayed six days with their new friends, obtaining information of their customs, and, having been accompanied to their canoes by the chief, and hundreds of warriors, they again embarked on their voyage, while Marquette was ornamented by the Illini with the sacred calumet, the mysterious arbiter of peace and war, the safeguard among the nations.[1]

The voyagers proceeded; they passed the Peketanoni, now known as the Missouri, and the good Marquette determined at some future period to explore it to its source, hoping to find thence another river, which flowing westwardly would discharge itself into the Vermilion Sea, or, flowing southwardly, would lead to California: of such streams he had been informed by the natives. In a distance of forty leagues, they passed the Ouabache, as the Ohio was then and long afterward called, and finally descended the Mississippi, until they had reached a point below the Arkansas, about five days' journey from the sea. Having ascertained the fact of the discharge of the Mississippi into the Gulf of Mexico, in Florida, and not in Virginia, on the east, Marquette and Joliet determined on their return, being fearful of falling into the hands of the Spaniards, whereby the rich fruits of their discoveries would be lost to France. Retracing their river path, on the 17th of July they left the village of Akamsca, and ascended the Mississippi until they came into the thirty-eighth parallel of latitude, when they entered a river now called the Illinois, by means of which they reached the Lake of the Illinois, now Lake Michigan, by a shorter route, says Marquette, than by the Mescousin. They were guided by an Illinois chief and his

---

[1] Marquette, Voyage, reprint, p. 11.

young men to the lake, whence the adventurous travellers proceeded to the Bay des Puants, about the end of the month of September, from which they had departed near the beginning of the month of June.

M. Joliet separated from Marquette at Green Bay, and returned to Montreal. In passing the rapids, just before he reached that city, his canoe was overset, and his journal and all his other papers were lost. He dictated a few particulars relative to his voyage down the Mississippi, amounting to no more than three or four pages, which were published,[1] and which agree, as far as they extend, with the narrative of Father Marquette. (NOTE A.)

In addition to this narrative, nothing is known of Marquette, except what is said of him by Charlevoix.[2] After returning from his last expedition, he took up his residence, and remained to preach the gospel to the Miamis who dwelled in the north of Illinois, round Chicago. Two years afterward, while sailing from Chicago along the eastern shore of Lake Michigan, toward Michillimackinac, he entered a small river in Michigan, on the 18th of May, 1675. Having landed, he erected an altar, and celebrated mass according to the rites of the Catholic church; then requesting the two men who conducted his canoe to leave him alone for half an hour, he retired a short distance in the silent woods. When the time had elapsed, the men went to seek for him, and found him dead. They were greatly surprised, as they had not discovered any symptoms of illness; but they remembered that when he was entering the river, he expressed a presentiment that his voyage would end there. The good missionary discoverer of a world, had fallen asleep on the margin of a stream that to this day retains the name of "Marquette." Near its mouth the canoe-men dug his grave in the sand, and ever after, the forest rangers, if in danger on Lake Michigan, would invoke his name. The place of his grave is still pointed out to the traveller, but his remains

[1] They are found in Hennepin, ed. 1698.

[2] Hist. de Nouvelle France, tom. ii. 254.

were removed the year after his death to Michillimackinac.[1] (NOTE B.)

Inseparable from the history of the valley of the Mississippi, and well deserving of honour and fame, is the name of Robert Cavelier de la Salle. In his youth he had entered the seminary of the Jesuits, and thus had relinquished his patrimony; having left the society with honour, but in poverty, we find him in the spirit of enterprise, about the year 1667, seeking fame and fortune in New France. As a fur-trader established near the present site of Montreal, he explored Lakes Ontario and Erie; and having repaired to France full of enthusiasm for the discovery and colonization of the West, he obtained the rank of nobility, valuable grants of land at fort Frontenac, and the protection of Colbert, the French minister, together with the friendship of Seignelay, Colbert's son. In 1678, he returned to fort Frontenac, (now Kingston,) and in a wooden canoe of ten tons, the first that ever sailed into Niagara River, he carried a company to the vicinity of the falls. In 1679, La Salle had built a vessel of sixty tons burthen, and on the 7th of August, on the upper Niagara River, amid the astonishment of the Indians, the discharge of artillery, and the chant of a solemn Te Deum, the "Griffin" was launched, and her sails spread to the breezes of Lake Erie. La Salle passed over the Lake, through the "Detroit," built a trading house at Mackinaw, and cast anchor at Green Bay. Having sent back his "Griffin" to Niagara River, well laden with furs, he repaired with a part of his company (among whom we find Hennepin) along the western shore of Lake Michigan, to its head near St. Joseph's. Determined to penetrate through the country to the great river of the West, he ascended the St. Joseph's, and having discovered a portage over swamps and bogs, entered the Kankakee, and thence descending the Illinois River, he first met with the natives on the banks of Lake Peoria. An alliance offensive and defen-

[1] Bancroft, vol. iii. 161. Sparks' Life of Marquette.

sive was formed between the Illinois and the French, and La Salle learned the course of the Mississippi to its mouth, and received the promise of guides to conduct him there. But misfortunes, then irremediable, and sufficient to cause the stoutest heart to despond and almost despair, overwhelmed De la Salle; his beloved "Griffin" was wrecked in her voyage around the Lakes; his fortune was greatly impaired; his expected store of supplies for colonization was effectually cut off; and his men became discontented and fearful for their situation. Yet under these discouraging circumstances, the great mind, the all-powerful will, and indomitable energy of De la Salle was exhibited in his determination and his acts. He commenced building a fort below Peoria Lake, which was named Crèvecœur, or Broken-heart; he set his men to work to prepare timber for building a bark; he sent Hennepin on a voyage of discovery *up* the Mississippi; and as sails and cordage were necessary for his contemplated exploration of the Mississippi to its mouth, he determined on endeavouring to reach the nearest French settlement, fifteen hundred miles distant, on foot, in the depth of winter, without food or drink, except such as the chase and the brook would supply, and with only three companions for solace and protection. What an exhibition of the energy of De la Salle's character! But in all these well-devised plans for future action in his discoveries, he succeeded only where he himself was present.

During his absence to Fort Frontenac, the Chevalier Tonti had been left in command of Fort Crèvecœur, with directions to build a new fort on a cliff about two hundred feet above the river, near a village of the Illinois, now called Rock Fort. In attempting to fortify this post, men deserted from Crèvecœur; and the Iroquois Indians, in September, 1680, descended the river, threatening destruction to the new colony. Tonti, after a parley with the enemy, fled with the few men that remained with him to the Potawatamies on Lake Michigan, and when La Salle returned, in 1681, with large supplies of men and stores, he found the post at Illinois deserted. In the mean while, Hennepin had proceeded according to his directions, up the Mississippi to the country of the Sioux.[1]

After the unavoidable delay of another year in building a barge, in searching for Tonti and his men, and in visiting Green Bay for the purpose of conducting some traffic there, La Salle descended the Mississippi to the sea, and, formally taking possession of the whole new country watered by the Mississippi, from its mouth to its source, for France, he named it "Louisiana;" erected a column and a cross with an inscription, "Louis the Great, king of France and Navarre, reigning, April 9th, 1682;" issued a procès verbal on the event of his journey and discovery, attested by Jacques de la Metairie, notary, and the men who accompanied him, as witnesses; called the great river "Colbert," after the name of the minister of Louis XIV.; ascertained the three channels by which the river entered the sea, to be in the latitude of about twenty-seven degrees; and, no doubt exulting in the success of his great enterprise and discovery, he ascended the river Illinois, and in May, 1683, returned to Quebec for the purpose of sailing to France.[2] (NOTE C.)

The remaining history of De la Salle is a tissue of misfortunes and disasters, which terminated in his death. When he arrived in France, Colbert was dead, but his son, Seignelay, was minister of marine, and on the reports of La Salle in regard to the importance of Louisiana to the French crown, a fleet was prepared, and great preparations made for colonizing the new country; two hundred and eighty persons, of whom one hundred were soldiers, and a proportion were young women and mechanics, were destined for the work of permanent colonization. From the commencement of the voyage disputes arose between Beaujeu, who had command of the fleet, and La Salle, whose correct judgment on the contemplated objects of the expedition were constantly thwarted.

---

[1] Charlevoix, Nouv. France, vol. ii. 275, 276.

[2] Bancroft, vol. iii. Memoir de le Sieur de la Tonty, 1693. Life of La Salle. French's Hist. Collections of Louisiana.

They entered the Gulf of Mexico, and on the 10th of January, 1685, they were probably near the mouth of the Mississippi, but the fleet sailed by;[1] La Salle wished to return, Beaujeu refused, and persisted in sailing to the west, till they reached the Bay of Matagorda, where La Salle resolved to disembark and search for the mouth of his river Colbert. Having landed his men, his storeship was unfortunately wrecked on entering the harbour, and Beaujeu cruelly deserted him, and sailed for France with the remainder of the ships, leaving on the beach of Matagorda the devoted La Salle with two hundred and thirty followers, crowded in a fort hastily constructed of the fragments of their stranded vessel. Not despairing, La Salle selected a beautiful site for a fort and town, which he named St. Louis; and this is the settlement which made Texas a part of Louisiana.[2]

After various and fruitless searches for the Mississippi, La Salle, in 1685, proposed to seek it in canoes, and after four months' absence, he returned, having failed to find the fatal river. In April, 1686, he turned his steps toward New Mexico, with twenty companions, in hopes to discover the rich mines of St. Barbe, the El Dorado of Northern Mexico.[3] Returning once more, he found his little colony reduced to about forty, and he then resolved to travel on foot to Illinois and Canada, and return to renew his colony in Texas. Accordingly, on January 12th, 1687, La Salle departed with sixteen men for Canada, having left his fort and settlement in the command of the Sieur Barbier, with whom remained nineteen others, including seven women, or maids, and three priests, the Sieur Barbier alone being married.[4] The explorers passed the basin of Colorado, and had reached a branch of Trinity river; there, on the 20th of March, 1687, the enterprising, daring, and unfortunate La Salle was assassinated

---

[1] See Joutel, ed. 1719, p. 19.

[2] Bancroft, vol. iii. passim, and Charlevoix, Nouv. France, vol. iii. livre 13. Joutel, ed. 1719, p. 45.

[3] Ibid, p. 68, 74.

[4] Ibid, p. 77.

by three of his own men. These conspirators had previously, on the 17th of March, murdered Moranget, the nephew of La Salle, and two other men. The absence of these persons induced La Salle to go in search of them, and having reached the spot near which lay their dead bodies, he was shot by the concealed assassins. Father Anastasius, who was with him, expected the same fate, but he was spared, and detailed the facts of the murder to Joutel,[1] who afterward became the accurate historian of the expedition. Joutel, together with the brother and surviving nephew of La Salle and others, in all but seven, obtained a guide from the Cenis Indians to the Arkansas, whence they reached the country above Red River, and at length, on the 20th of July, 1687, came to the Mississippi, where, to their great joy, they discovered a large cross erected, and a house built after the French fashion. Here they found two Frenchmen, who informed them "that they had been six, sent by Monsieur Tonti, when he returned from the voyage he had made down the Colbert or Mississippi River, pursuant to the orders sent him by the late Monsieur De la Salle at his departure from France; and that the said Sieur Tonti had commanded them to build the aforesaid house. That, having never since received any news from the said Monsieur De la Salle, four of them were gone back to Monsieur Tonti at the fort of the Illinois."[2] Joutel and his companions returned by Fort Crèvecœur to Quebec.

Thus perished the father of French settlement in the Valley of the Mississippi. His able biographer says truly of him, "Not a hint appears in any writer that has come under our notice, which casts a shade upon his integrity or honour. Cool and intrepid at all times, never yielding for a moment to despair, or even to despondency, he bore the heavy burden of his calamities to the end, and his hopes expired only with his last breath. To him must be mainly ascribed the discovery of the vast regions of the Mississippi Valley, and the subsequent occupation and settlement of them by the French;

---

[1] Joutel, ed. 1719, p. 99.

[2] Ibid. p. 152, 153.

and his name justly holds a prominent place among those which adorn the history of civilization in the New World."[1]

There were not wanting those, in his lifetime, who employed means to destroy his usefulness, to impede his efforts, and to decry his merits. After his death, Hennepin, who was one of his followers, and under his command, basely attempted to rob him of the reputation justly attached to his discoveries; and yet, it cannot be denied, that in his last expedition to discover the mouth of the Mississippi by sea, other motives than that of mere colonization may have acted on the zeal of De la Salle. In his "Memoir on the Necessity of fitting out an Expedition to take possession of Louisiana," and also in his "Report to Monsiegneur De Seignelay, of the discoveries made by Sieur De la Salle, under the order of his Majesty," he urges the richness of the silver mines of St. Barbe, in New Mexico, and the facility of obtaining an armed possession of them, as powerful inducements for encouraging all his projected undertakings.[2] If Hennepin may in this matter be believed, he had spoken to him on the same subject previous to their leaving Canada, and it is certain that he made one attempt to search for them after his landing in Texas. There is no doubt that De la Salle believed himself to be west of the mouth of the Mississippi; yet, from Joutel's account of his various journeyings, they appear to have been more to the north and north-west, than to the east; it also appears that he was approaching nearer to the Spaniards, and certainly he could have obtained some correct information on the subject from the Cenis Indians. Charlevoix is of this opinion, and very harshly says, that "La Salle finding himself shipwrecked in the Bay of St. Bernard, and having quickly discovered that he was west of the river he was seeking, if he had no other design but to find it, he could have obtained guides from the Cenis, as Joutel did afterward; but he desired to approach the Spanish settlements to take observations respecting the mines of St. Barbe, and wishing to

[1] Sparks. [2] See French's Hist. Collections of Louisiana.

do too much, he not only did nothing, but destroyed himself, and was pitied by no one."[1] (NOTE D.)

To Louis Hennepin belongs the credit of having been the first European who ascended the river Mississippi above the mouth of the Wisconsin. In 1679 he had accompanied De la Salle from Fort Frontenac, on his intended journey of western discovery, and had witnessed the building of the ill-fated "Griffin," sailed in her to Michillimackinac, and afterward had coasted Lake Michigan, ascended the St. Joseph's, crossed the Kankakee Swamps, and descended the Illinois River in canoes, with La Salle and his companions. After the erection of Fort Crèvecœur, La Salle, in order to commence his discoveries, immediately detached one of his men named Dacan, with Father Hennepin, with instructions to ascend the Mississippi above the Illinois River, and, if possible, to proceed to its source. These two voyagers left Fort Crèvecœur on the 28th of February, 1680, and having entered the Mississippi, ascended it until near the forty-sixth degree of north latitude, where they were stopped by a high fall of water, which extended the whole width of the river, and to which Father Hennepin gave the name of the Falls of St. Anthony of Padua. Here they fell into the hands of the Sioux, who detained them a considerable time as prisoners, but did not maltreat them, and they were afterward relieved by Frenchmen arrived from Canada.[2]

This outline of Hennepin's discovery is taken from Charlevoix, who placed very little credit in the narrations of the discoverer; and, indeed, when the two accounts of Hennepin's adventures on this voyage, as they have been related by himself, and published, the one in France in 1684, and the other in England in 1698, are compared together, and their contradictions noted, the charge of gross mendacity and base imposture will not be considered as improperly applied to him.

According to Hennepin's account of Louisiana, "printed at Paris, in 1684," the party, consisting of Anthony Auguel,

---

[1] Charlevoix; Nouvelle France, tom. iii. 59, 60.

[2] Idem, tom. ii. 270.

surnamed the Picard du Gay, Michel Ako, and himself, proceeded to fulfil the instructions of La Salle, and ascended the Mississippi, from the mouth of the Illinois River, which they left in the beginning of March, 1680, having left Fort Crèvecœur on the 29th of February. On the 12th of April, when they had got about one hundred and fifty leagues up the river, from that of the Illinois, they were taken prisoners by the Sioux, and carried two hundred and fifty leagues further up the Mississippi, where they remained at Issati, on the St. Francis River, (or at Lake St. Francis,) until September, when they were liberated by a Canadian trader named St. Luth, and that they returned to Quebec by ascending the Wisconsin River, crossing the portage, and descending the Fox River to Green Bay.[1]

Thus far, perhaps, Hennepin's account of his voyage up the river Mississippi may be relied on as correct, deducting therefrom many gross exaggerations; such as his stating that the Falls of St. Anthony are from fifty to sixty feet in height, and his speaking with confidence of rivers, lakes, and even the source of the Mississippi, and of distances between the mouths of rivers flowing into it; but in many important matters, for the first time made known to the world, he may be believed; he is the first writer who calls the Mescousin of Marquette the Wisconsin.

The pretended claims of his voyage of discovery to the mouth of the Mississippi, and his bold attempt to rob De la Salle of his merited honours, have been often successfully refuted and exposed. Fourteen years after the "Account of Louisiana" was published by order of the King of France, Hennepin, having become in 1698 a sycophant of the King of England, gave to the world his "New Discovery," together with a second part, or "Continuation of the New Discovery, giving an account of the attempts of the Sieur De la Salle upon the mines of St. Barbe," &c. These books were both dedicated to King

---

[1] Hennepin's New Discovery, edition 1698, p. 89, 108, 111, 145, 193, et passim.

William III. and as they contained many things of which Hennepin had not previously spoken in his first account, he makes several strange apologies in his prefaces to his latter volumes, to excuse and account for the omissions in the former; the principal of which is, that he would, by mentioning his discovery of the mouth of the Mississippi, incur the enmity of Monsieur De la Salle.[1] His fabrications and interlopations consist, in part, in his stating that when he was at the mouth of the Illinois River, in March, 1680, he *descended* the Mississippi instead of *ascending* it, to explore the country of the Sioux, as he had been directed by La Salle, according to his own account, and also by the testimony of the Chevalier Tonti, as given in his memoir to the King of France, made in 1693. It may be remarked on the falsities of Hennepin, that so far as they bear on his pretended discovery of the lower Mississippi, they may have been intended as the foundation of a claim, on the part of England, to Louisiana and the whole Valley of the Mississippi. His work is dedicated to the English king, and his protection as a warlike sovereign invoked for the newly discovered country. It is an historical fact, that in September, 1699, vessels of war were sent by England to the Gulf of Mexico, to take possession of the country, under pretext and declaration that the whole south belonged to that power. In the same year an attempt was made by William III. to colonize Louisiana by French refugees, and to take possession of the Mississippi; and to the same effect the private enterprise of Coxe, of New Jersey, to colonize "Carolana" was encouraged by the king in council. It is true that the English vessels returned, when they found that the prior claims of France were not only asserted, but would be defended, and the attempts at colonization altogether failed; but it was then understood that it was on the information contained in, and the supposed authenticity of Father Hennepin's books, that such assumption of claim and attempts to colonize, on the part of England were made, although unsuccessfully.[2]

---

[1] New Discovery, edition of 1698.

[2] Charlevoix, Nouv. France, tom. iii. 384–6.

Thus, at the close of the 17th century, France, in right of occupancy and discovery, claimed not only New France and Acadia, Hudson's Bay and Newfoundland, but also a moiety of Maine of Vermont, and more than a moiety of New York, together with the whole Valley of the Mississippi, including Texas as far as the Rio Bravo del Norte. Throughout that wide region it sought to introduce its authority under the severest forms of the colonial system, and that system was enforced with equal eagerness on the sea-coast by England. Previous to the war declared by France against England in 1689, the strife in the colonies, was, on behalf of their respective mother countries, for the fisheries, for territory at the north and west, and for the possession of colonial monopolies. It has been truly said, that the religious faith and roving enterprise of the French Canadians secured to Louis XIV. their active support; on the other hand, the English colonists sided heartily with England; the English revolution of 1688 was to them the pledge for freedom of mind, as marked by Protestantism; for national freedom as illustrated in the exile of a tyrant, and in the election of a constitutional king. At this period the two principal posts west of Fort Frontenac were at Mackinaw and on the Illinois; but the garrisons were so weak, that English traders with an escort of Indians had ventured even to Mackinaw, and had obtained a large share of the commerce of the lakes. French diplomacy had failed in the attempt to effect an alliance with all the Indian tribes, from Lake Ontario to the Mississippi, as projected in 1687. The keys of the great West were still held by the savages, and no intercourse existed but by means of the traders, who were found in every forest where there was an Indian with skins to sell. In 1688, had it not been for the missions at the West, Illinois would have been abandoned, the fort at Mackinaw lost, and a general rising of the natives would have completed the ruin of New France.[1]

[1] Bancroft, vol. iii. 175–8.

Notwithstanding all the reverses of war, France, by the peace of Ryswick, in 1697, retained in America all Hudson's Bay, and all the places of which she was in possession at the beginning of the war; in other words, with the exception of the eastern moiety of Newfoundland, France retained the whole coast and adjacent islands, from Maine to beyond Labrador and Hudson's Bay, besides Canada and the Valley of the Mississippi. But the boundary lines were reserved for wrangling among commissioners.[1] At this period, of all the portions of New France, no one more occupied the minds of the ministry than Louisiana. Since the unfortunate attempt of De la Salle to enter the Mississippi by sea, the project appeared to have been renounced. At length, in 1697, M. D'Iberville aroused the attention of the ministry on this point, and inspired the Count de Pontchartrain with the design of constructing a fort at the entrance of the Great River, which this officer promised himself to discover.

Two vessels were fitted out for this purpose, the command of one of which was given to the Marquis Chateaumorand, the other to Iberville, and they sailed in October, 1698. In January, 1699, they touched at Pensacola, then in the occupancy of three hundred Spaniards. Having passed the mouth of the Mobile, landed on an isle which he called Massacre Island, (since called Dauphin Island,) Iberville went on the main land, and having discovered the river Pascagoulas, where he met with a number of savages, he departed in barges with his brothers, De Bienville, and the Sieur De Sauvole, a Recollect friar, forty-eight men, besides two Biscayens, and provisions for twenty days, with the design of searching for the Mississippi, of which the savages had spoken to him under the name of "Malbouchia," and the Spaniards by that of "the Pallisade."[2] He at length entered it on the second of March, which was Quinquagesima Monday, and found that the name given by the Spaniards well suited it, for its mouth actually

[1] Bancroft, vol. iii. 192.

[2] Row of trees.

bristled with trees which the current incessantly dragged into it.[1]

After having well reconnoitred this long-sought entrance, he made known his discovery to M. Chateaumorand, who returned to St. Domingo; and Iberville, as soon as he was prepared, ascended the river as far as Bayagoulas, where a letter was sent to him by an Indian chief, which proved to be from the Chevalier Tonti, and was directed to M. De la Salle, Governor of Louisiana. The letter commenced thus: "From the village of Quinipissas,[2] this twentieth of April, 1685. Sir: Having found the posts on which you had set up the king's arms thrown down by the drift wood, I caused another one to be fixed on this side, about seven leagues from the sea, where I have left a letter in a tree by the side of it. All the nations have smoked the calumet with me; they are people who fear us exceedingly, since you had captured this village. I conclude in saying, that it is a great grief to me that we shall return with the ill fortune of not having found you, after we had coasted with two canoes thirty leagues on the Mexican side, and twenty-five on that of Florida."

Reassured by this letter that he was on the Great River, Iberville returned to the Bay of Biloxi, situate between the Mississippi and the Mobile—built a fort there, three leagues from Pascagoulas—left M. de Sauvole in command, with Bienville as his lieutenant, and returned to France.[3]

Thus the possession of the newly-discovered river and adjacent country was taken by France, according to the acknowledged legal custom of nations. Charlevoix quaintly remarks that Spain had made no settlement; for although Ferdinand de Soto had crossed the Mississippi more than once, and was even cast into it after his death, yet he had made no *establishment*.[4] In virtue of the discovery of Florida, Spain had claimed the whole country, from the Gulf of Mexico to the great lakes and the remote north; under the dis-

---

[1] Charlevoix, tom. iii. 377–8, 381.

[2] Bayagoulas and Montgoulatches.

[3] Idem, tom. iii. 381–4.

[4] Charlevoix, tom. iii. 277, (in note.)

coveries of Marquette and De la Salle, the religious establishments of the missionaries, Jesuits, and Recollects, and the occupancy of a few military posts, France claimed the entire basin of the Mississippi, by the name of Louisiana, the government of which was declared, by a royal edict, to be subordinate to, and dependent on the government of New France. (NOTE E.)

# CHAPTER II.

## VALLEY OF THE MISSISSIPPI.

**Settlement by Iberville—Progress of the French in Settlements from the** St. Lawrence to the Mississippi Valley—Kaskaskia, Peoria—Fathers Gravier and Marest, Montigny and Davion—Religious zeal and commercial enterprise—Views of La Salle with respect to the Illinois country—Communication between Quebec and the Gulf of Mexico—Jealousy, and claim of England—Exploring Expedition on part of England—Explorations by Bienville and Sauvole—Application of French Protestant emigrants—Bienville prevents the English from taking possession of the Mississippi—Belief still entertained of the route by water to the South Sea—Also of the existence of gold and silver mines, &c., in the country—French views not agricultural—Le Sueur on the Upper Mississippi.—Fallacious views as to the natural productions of the country—Baron La Hontan, his travels and discoveries—Mixture of the true, and the romantic and fabulous—The Illinois country, its extent—The Five Nations, their relations to France and England—Grand Council called by De Callieres—The post and settlement of Detroit founded—Other posts growing up, in the West—Allies of the English in Wisconsin—Attempt on Detroit—Trade of the West—Armed occupation by France of the Mississippi Valley—Forts Chartres, Cahokia, Prairie du Rocher, Kaskaskia—Treaty of Utrecht, its want of effect—Unsettled questions of boundaries—Localities of the Indian tribes—The Indians of the North-West—Colony at the mouth of the Mississippi—Its neglect of agriculture and wild speculations—Le Sueur's copper mine on Blue Earth River—Louisiana made a government independent of New France—Change in the political system of the colony—Unsuccessful attempts of France to colonize—Boundaries of Louisiana—Rio del Norte—Crozat's Patent—Mississippi Scheme—Slavery authorized in Crozat's monopoly—Population of Louisiana—Ill success of Crozat—His losses; surrenders his patent—Delusive hopes of wealth, in France—Wretched state of the French Public Treasury—John Law proposes relief—Paper currency as a substitute for precious metals—Law's Bank established—Its operations—Declared a royal bank—Becomes a commercial company—Great powers granted to the "Mississippi Company"—Bank of France associated with it—Company of the Indies—Monopolies granted to it—The Mint, and Taxes of the nation farmed by it—Law,

Comptroller General of France—Emigrants to Louisiana, their character—Routes from the St. Lawrence to the Lower Mississippi—The great bubbles burst—Consequences extend to the settlements of the Mississippi Valley—Similarity of Credit System of 1719 and 1834—Delusion as to the mineral wealth continues—Mining on the Upper Mississippi—War between France and Spain—Chain of forts established on the Mississippi—Site of New Orleans selected—Le Sueur's fort on St. Peter's River—He takes possession of the upper country—Fort Chartres built—Population of the Illinois country—Posts of Michillimackinac, Green Bay, Chicago, St. Joseph's, Sault St. Marie, and Detroit—English and French trade with the Indians—Influence of France unbounded over the Indians, except the Iroquois—The Five Nations—Ottagamies adhere to the English—Attempt to destroy Detroit—Siege of Detroit—Defeat and great loss of the Ottagamies—Their hostilities and depredations—French expedition against them under Louvigny—Stronghold at Butte des Morts—The Foxes capitulate—Hostages delivered—Treaty not complied with by the Foxes—They renew their depredations—Expedition under De Lignerie unsuccessful—Progress of settlements in the West—Villages in the Illinois country—The Natchez nation, their destruction—The "Company of the Indies" surrenders its charter—War against the Chickasaws—Artaguette and Vincennes—Their death—Situation of the Illinois country—Ambitious views of France as to the Great West—Resisted by the English colonies—George Washington—His mission to the French commander—First signal of the war of the Revolution—Death of Jumonville—Washington capitulates—France in possession of the whole Valley of the Mississippi—English and French encroachments, although with the same intent, not so regarded by the Indians—Peace in Europe, but war in America—Boundaries between English and French possessions the cause—War of 1756—Braddock's defeat; Wolfe's victory; surrender of all Canada—Disaffection of the Indians—Rogers takes possession of Detroit, and other western posts—Pontiac—He orders Rogers to stop in his march—Protects him on condition—French power in the West forever overthrown—Feelings against the English—Henry, the English trader—His interview with an Indian chief—Attachment of the Indians to the French; its causes—State of settlements in Wisconsin—Carver's account—Prairie du Chien—No establishments west of Greenbay—Traders alone in the country—Sacs and Foxes, their depredations and chastisement—Expeditions against them—Lake Superior, settlements there—Ancient mines—Indications of ancient work.

THE establishment of Iberville was the foundation of the Commonwealth of Mississippi. Although immediate prosperity was highly improbable to the infant settlement, having the Spaniards on its flank, and the Indian tribes around, with an untillable sand for soil, and a burning sun that caused the emigrants to sigh for the cool breezes of Hudson's Bay,[1] yet gleams of light shone upon them. The whites from Carolina, allies of the Chickasaws, invaded the neighbouring tribes of Indians, making it easy for the French to establish alliances. Nearly a century had elapsed since Samuel Champlain, a bold and adventurous mariner, following in the footsteps of Jacques Cartier and La Roche de Robertval, had ascended the St. Lawrence, as far as the Isle of Orleans, and established his little colony, having founded Quebec in 1680, and Montreal in 1613. In 1615, Champlain had explored Lake Huron by way of the Ottawa River, and although France had been too much involved in war to make explorations in distant regions, yet we have seen that the zealous labours of the Jesuit fathers and other missionaries had opened to the world new fields of commerce, and were rapidly spreading civilization and religion in the valley of the Mississippi. Before the year 1700, Kaskaskia had been founded; missionary stations had been formed and had grown into parishes; the labours of Fathers Gravier and Marest, in Illinois, had established many flocks of converted Indians, particularly one near Lake Peoria. The Fathers Montigny and Davion had visited the Yazoo and Tansas; and missionaries had penetrated west of the Mississippi, and as far south as Red River; St. Comè had also established a mission among the Natchez Indians, and in fine the spirit of religious zeal, and of commercial enterprise, was effectually aroused in relation to the Mississippi Valley, at the close of the seventeenth century.

Previous to the discovery of the Mississippi, the Illinois were scarcely known in Canada; Marquette and Joilet, in descending that river, had passed by some of their villages, and had been well received there; the former had projected until his death to establish himself among them. La Salle, in preparing to complete the discovery made by that missionary, thought of making settlements among the Miamis and Illinois,

[1] Bancroft, vol. iii. 201.

which would serve as deposits for his commerce. He had taken with him several Recollect fathers, and it was his design that they should form missions among the Illinois; but they were too much occupied with the excursions which La Salle made them undertake, to make proselytes among the savages, and they left the country without having effected any thing in that way, believing that commerce and religion do not flourish together. The death of La Salle, and other disastrous events, had scattered the French who were established among the Illinois, until Father Gravier, judging the time was now favourable to labour for the salvation of this nation, fixed his residence at Rockfort, the same place where fort St. Louis had been. In a short time he assembled there a considerably numerous flock, and soon had the consolation to see among the savages, so justly reprobated, until then, for corruption of manners, a renewal of as great examples of virtue as had been admired in the most flourishing missions of Canada.[1] Juchereau and Mermet had less success among the Mascoutens, and at the mouth of the Wabash.

At this period, then, we find that a line of communication existed between Quebec and the Gulf of Mexico, where the court of France were taking measures to make a considerable establishment. The jealousy of England was particularly aroused by the success of the enterprise of Iberville, and a claim on the part of that nation to the discovery of the Mississippi was attempted to be set up, in consequence of the impudent falsehoods of Hennepin, as interpolated in the new edition of his work, now just published at London, under the auspices of his new patron, William III. To give effect to the pretended claim on the part of the English, an exploring expedition, under the direction of Coxe, a proprietor of New Jersey, was fitted out for the mouths of the Mississippi, and a naval force was also sent by government to take possession of the much-desired country, and to sound the passes of the majestic stream.[2]

---

[1] Charlevoix, tom. iii. 392.

[2] Bancroft, vol. iii. 202.

Bienville, who, together with Sauvole, had been left in command of the fort at Biloxi by Iberville, spent some time in exploring the forks below the present site of New Orleans, and descended the river on the 16th of September, 1699; at the turn of a point[1] twenty-eight leagues from the sea, he found in the river an English frigate of sixteen guns, commanded by Captain Barr, who had left at the entrance of the river a frigate of the same force, commanded by Mr. Clement. His design was to reconnoitre the western passage of the river, and then to return to Carolina, where an armament was being built, of four Pinks, and several other vessels, to convey an establishment of several families on the river. In this vessel was Mr. Secon, a French engineer, a Protestant in religion, who privately gave M. de Bienville a petition addressed to the king, by which he assured his majesty, that if he would grant liberty of conscience in the colony, more than four hundred religious families would emigrate thither from Carolina. This petition was in the end sent to M. De Pontchartrain, who replied, that the king had not driven the heretics from his kingdom to form a republic of them. The English captain doubted if he had entered the Mississippi; De Bienville, willing to profit by his uncertainty, assured him that the river he sought was more to the west, and that the river he was in was a dependence on Canada, the possession of which had been taken by his most Christian majesty; and he summoned him to leave it. On this opposition, the captain, whose orders were to discover the Mississippi, took the resolution of seeking further off for the river. By this *ruse* De Bienville prevented the English from taking possession of the river and establishing themselves there.[2]

Independent of the great advantages which the commercial world would derive from the anticipated wealth of the natural productions of the newly-discovered country, a belief was still entertained, which had been advanced by Marquette, and cherished by La Salle, that some of the western tributaries

---

[1] Since called "English turn."  [2] La Harpe, Jour. Hist. p. 19.

of the great river would afford a direct route to the South Sea, and thence to China. The long and dangerous voyage around the Cape of Good Hope, or Cape Horn, might be avoided; and this was certainly an object of deep concern, and of important interest to the whole commercial world; consequently this subject was still agitated in Europe, and the solution of the question most anxiously looked for.[1]

The existence of mines of gold and silver, and even the presence of diamonds and other precious stones among the rocks and gravel of the land, together with rich pearls in the shell-fish of its waters, was considered as a matter beyond a doubt. All the early explorers had either spoken of such things as being known to them as true, or as extremely probable from unmistakeable indications. As to the minerals, iron, copper, lead, &c., Marquette, Hennepin, La Hontan, Joutel, and others, had already given their actual locations; Joutel says, "There is no reason to question but that there are in this country, mines of all sorts of metals, and of the richest; the climate being the same as that of New Mexico. We saw several spots where it appeared there were iron-mines, and found some pieces of it in the bank of the river, which nature had cleansed. Travellers who have been at the upper part of the Mississippi affirm they have found mines there, of very good lead."[2] Marquette writes, "A little above this river of which I have just spoken, (Wabash, or Ohio,) are cliffs, where our men perceived an iron-mine which they deemed very rich; there are many veins, and a bed a foot thick: large masses are found combined with pebbles."[3]

We have seen that the petition of the French Protestants to be allowed, under French sovereignty, and in the enjoyment of religious liberty, to plant the banks of the Mississippi, been rejected by the French minister; it appears that

[1] Early conjectures were partially right. The head waters of the P[illegible] almost interlock with the head waters of the Colorado, which flows [illegible] the Gulf of California, or Vermilion Sea of Marquette.

[2] Joutel, p. 172.

[3] Marquette, sec.

policy of France was less directed to the settlement of the country for the peaceful pursuits of agriculture, than to its armed occupation by fortresses, and its exploration for productive mines, the searching for pearls, and even the expected lucrative trade in the wool of the buffalo. In December, 1699, Iberville returned from Europe with two armed vessels and several officers for garrisons, accompanied by Mr. Le Sueur and thirty workmen, to explore the copper-mines of the upper Mississippi and other natural riches of the country.[1] The expected development of the wealth of the Mississippi is thus spoken of by Charlevoix: "They had then two principal objects in this commerce, namely: the wool which they could gather from the buffalo, and the pearl fisheries. Both were expressly marked in the instructions of Monsieur D'Iberville. One of the great objects, said they, which they have given to the king when they engaged him to make the discovery of the mouth of the Mississippi, has been the gathering of the wool of the buffalo; and in order to do this, it is necessary to domesticate these animals, to enclose them in parks, and to transport their young ones to France. Although the pearls which have been presented to his majesty are not of a fine water, nor of a beautiful form, still the search for them must be carried on with care; because others may be found, and his majesty desires that Monsieur D'Iberville bring over as many of them as he can: that he assures himself of the places where the fisheries can be made, and that he has them carried on in his presence."[2]

Up to this period little had been known of the country generally termed the "Upper Mississippi," except from the accounts given by Marquette and Hennepin, the information communicated by Le Sueur respecting the copper-mines on the St. Peter's River, and the romantic statements of the Baron La Hontan of his travels through that region, his discovery and exploration of the "Long River,"[3] and his descrip-

---

[1] See Note A.

[2] Charlevoix, tom. iii. 389.

[3] St. Peter's River, or Cannon River, as supposed by Nicollet, who calls the latter "River La Hontan."

tion of the numerous nations spread over the country. Amid the romance of the baron, some truths undoubtedly appear; but they convey information which was even at that time commonly known, and his voyage from Green Bay, up the Fox River to the portage, and down the Wisconsin to the Mississippi, was no more than a retrace of the steps of Father Marquette. It is only on the upper Mississippi and on the Long River, where he says he sailed for eighty days and more, and yet had not reached halfway to its source; where he asserts that he discovered extensive nations of civilized Indians, and describes their cities, their manners, customs, and commerce, that the baron draws deeply on our credulity. It is true that he may have been up the Mississippi as far as St. Peter's River, but it is somewhat remarkable that he does not speak of "Lake Pepin," nor of the "Falls of St. Anthony," two such prominent features in the river. It is more than probable that the romantic accounts which he has given in his work are the result of ill-interpreted and less understood information received from the Indians, respecting the rivers of the north-west, and the country west of the Mississippi. The descriptions of the baron are not wholly untrue; in all his romance we find glimpses of the "Red River," of "M'Kenzie's River," of the "Rocky Mountains," and of the "Great Salt Lake," as now known to us; but his travels and adventures as related by himself, outrage all probability; and perhaps his best apology may be found in his desire to convey some information to his countrymen, and at the same time have his vanity gratified in receiving the merit of an original discoverer of strange countries and of stranger nations. (See NOTE B.)

On his return from his fabled expedition up the Long River, La Hontan says that he descended the Mississippi as far as the Ouabache, (Ohio,) and on his route met with a body of four hundred Akansas, who were hunting buffalo; they received him well. He re-ascended the Mississippi to the Illinois River, and in six days arrived at Fort Crèvecœur; Tonti was in command, of whom he speaks in terms of high commendation. He afterward arrived at Che-ka-kou, (Chicago,) where his Outagamies (Foxes) left him to return home; and he then descended the Oumamis (Miamis) to where La Salle had some years previous built a fort. There he found four hundred Indian warriors, who were about to burn three Iroquois prisoners. He wished to save them, but was unable, and could with difficulty get away from the savages, who wished him to partake of their festivities.[1] He then coasted the lake, and returned to Michillimackinac.

For a long series of years, the term "Illinois country" embraced all the region east of the upper Mississippi as far as Lake Michigan, and from the Wisconsin on the north, to the Ohio on the south. Mutual confidence and friendship continued between the French and all the western tribes, and emigration continued to advance; yet, in the year 1700, owing to the inveterate hostility of the Five Nations, not a French settlement existed south of the great lakes, from the St. Lawrence to the Illinois country on the west; the whole region, from Fort Frontenac to Green Bay, was a savage wilderness. The Five Nations had always been considered as subjects of England; and, although France asserted its right to dominion over the lands of the Five Nations, yet England claimed to be in possession. Religious sympathies inclined the nations to the French, but commercial advantages brought them always into connection with the English.[2] Under the influence of Monsieur de Callieres, governor-general of Canada, and in order to effect a general peace among the Indian tribes, a grand council of the several nations was held at Montreal, in 1701, at which the four upper nations of the Iroquois attended. After rapid negotiations, peace was ratified between the Iroquois on the one side, and France and her Indian allies on the other; but the question of French jurisdiction over the lands of the Iroquois still remained undecided. France kept the mastery of the great lakes, and De Callieres resolved on founding an establishment at Detroit. The Indians complained of this as an unwarranted encroachment on that

[1] La Hontan, vol. i. 243–250.

[2] Bancroft, vol. iii. 193.

independence of which they were proud; and Te-gan-issorens, (the Rat,) an Iroquois chief, said, "the English had already had the same design on Detroit, and the Iroquois had opposed it." De Callieres insisted upon his intentions with success, and in 1701, in the month of June, De la Motte Cadillac, with a Jesuit missionary and one hundred Frenchmen, was sent to take possession of the site of Detroit, and to form a settlement on the river of the lakes. This is the oldest permanent settlement in Michigan. That commonwealth thus began to be colonized before even Georgia; it may be termed the oldest of all the inland states, except, perhaps, Illinois.[1]

In the mean while, trading-posts, missionary stations, and towns were springing up in the West; Kaskaskia had become the capital of the Illinois country. As early as 1712, land-titles were issued for a common field at Kaskaskia, and deeds and titles came in use to designate the acquisitions of private enterprise. Traders opened a commerce with the remote port of Isle Dauphin, in Mobile Bay; intercourse was established between Quebec in the north, and the infant colony of Louisiana in the south—the latter being a dependence of Canada, or New France.

The English emissaries had already penetrated to the west, and as the conquest of Canada was a favourite project of England, in 1711 every effort was made to weaken and destroy the influence of France with the Indian tribes of the north and west. In Wisconsin, the English had (through the Iroquois) obtained allies in the Ottagamies, who, ever restless, were induced, in 1713, to attempt the destruction of Detroit, and they collected their bands around it. Monsieur Dubuisson, with twenty men, defended the place; and being aware of the intention of the Foxes, he summoned from the chase his allies—the Ottawas, Hurons, Pottowatamies, one branch of the Sacs, Illinois, Menomonies, and even Osages and Missouris, who came to his relief—each nation under its own ensign. Such was the influence of the missionaries in the west.[2] The Fox warriors, far from destroying Detroit, were themselves

[1] Bancroft, vol. iii, 194.

[2] Bancroft, vol. iii. 224.

besieged and finally compelled to surrender at discretion: those who bore arms were ruthlessly murdered; the rest were distributed among the confederates as slaves, to be saved or massacred at the will of their masters.[1]

The incipient settlement and prosperity of the West may be judged by the fact that, in 1720, a lucrative trade had sprung up between the Illinois country and the province of lower Louisiana. Not only the furs and peltries of the northern tribes, but the grain, flour, and other agricultural products of the upper Mississippi were transported down the river to Mobile, and thence to the West Indies and to Europe; and in return, the luxuries and refinements of European capitals were carried to the banks of the Illinois and Kaskasia Rivers.[2]

Settlements continued to be formed on the Mississippi below the mouth of the Illinois, and France resolved to circumvent the English provinces on the Atlantic coast, by a cordon of military posts from the lakes of Canada on the north, to the Gulf of Mexico on the south, as first suggested by La Salle himself, on his visit to Paris in the year 1684. His plans were now about to be adopted, for the purpose of occupying the great valley of the Mississippi before any Englishmen had crossed the mountains from their Atlantic colonies. The first important step in the accomplishment of this great object was taken in the year 1720, at which time Monsieur Boisbriant, the commandant on the Illinois, removed his head-quarters to the bank of the Mississippi, twenty-five miles below the village of Kaskaskia.[3] Near the close of this year, arrangements were made for the construction of a strong fortress in the Illinois country, to serve as the head-quarters of Upper Louisiana. The site had been selected, and Fort Chartres was begun, on the east side of the Mississippi, about sixty-five miles below the mouth of the Missouri. It was designed by the ministers to be one of the strongest fortresses

---

[1] Doc. Hist. [2] Martin's Louisiana, vol. i. 164, 188.

[3] Martin's Louisiana, vol. i. 224.

on the continent, and its walls were built of strong and solid masonry. At the end of eighteen months, and after great labour and expense, Fort Chartres was completed. Its massy ruins, one hundred years afterward, were overgrown with vines and forest trees, almost impenetrable to the traveller.

Soon after the construction of Fort Chartres, the villages of Cahokia, Prairie de Rocher, and some others, sprung into note in its vicinity. All the settlements, from the Illinois to the Kaskaskia continued to extend and multiply. In the year 1721, the Jesuits had established a monastery and a college in the village of Kaskaskia. Four years afterward, this village became a chartered town; and a grant of Louis XV. guarantied "the commons" as the pasture grounds for the stock of the town. Emigrants, under the favour and protection of the crown, continued to settle the fertile region of the "American Bottom," and Fort Chartres became not only the head-quarters of the commandant in Upper Louisiana, but the centre of life and fashion in the West. It was for many years the most celebrated fortress in all the valley of the Mississippi.[1] (NOTE C.)

In April, 1713, the treaty of Utrecht was concluded; which, although it closed the series of universal wars for the balance of power, yet it did not settle any great question of mercantile privileges. As the mercantile system was identified with the colonial system, the political interest, which alone could kindle universal war, was to be sought in the colonies. Henceforward, the question of trade on our borders, the question of territory on our frontier, involved an interest which could excite the world to arms. For about two centuries the wars of religion had prevailed; the wars for commercial advantages were now prepared.[2]

England, by the peace of Utrecht, obtained from France large concessions of territory in America. The Assembly of New York had addressed Queen Anne against French settle-

---

[1] Martin's Louisiana, vol. i. 224. Monette, Val. Miss., vol. i. 164.
[2] Bancroft, vol. iii. 228.

ments in the West; William Penn advised to establish the St. Lawrence as the boundary on the north, and to include in our colonies the valley of the Mississippi. It "will make a glorious country," were his prophetic words. The attention of the English ministry was again and again directed to the progress of the French in the West. The colonization of Louisiana had been proposed to Queen Anne, yet, at the peace, that immense region remained to France. But England obtained supremacy in the fisheries, the entire possession of the Bay of Hudson and its borders, of Newfoundland, and of all Nova Scotia, or Acadia, according to its ancient boundaries. It was agreed, also, that France should never molest the Five Nations, subject to the dominion of Great Britain. But how far did Louisiana extend? It included, according to French ideas, the whole basin of the Mississippi. Did the treaty of Utrecht assent to such an extension of French territory? And what were the ancient limits of Acadia? What were the bounds of the territory of the Five Nations, which the treaty appeared to recognise as a part of the English dominions? These were questions which were never to be amicably adjusted.[1]

The locality of the Indian tribes, from the advent of the early discoverers of North America up to this period, is a matter of necessary consideration; the native occupants of the Illinois country, and the western portion of New France, as seen by the first Jesuit missionaries upon Lake Michigan, were similiar, in all respects, to the tribes previously known to them on the St. Lawrence; for the first aspect of the original inhabitants of the United States was uniform.[2] Between the Indians of Florida and Canada the difference was scarcely perceptible. Their manners and institutions, as well as their organization, had a common physiognomy; and before their languages began to be known, there was no safe method of grouping the nations into families. But when the vast variety of dialects came to be compared, there were found, east

[1] Bancroft, vol. iii. 233. [2] Charlevoix, vol. i. 29.

of the Mississippi, not more than eight radically distinct languages, of which five still continue the speech of powerful communities, and three are known only as memorials of tribes that have almost disappeared from the earth.[1]

The communities and tribes thus distinguished by language, are known as: 1. Algonquin; 2. Dahcota; 3. Huron-Iroquois; 4. Catawba; 5. Cherokee; 6. Uchee; 7. Natchez; 8. Mobillian. The Algonquin tongue, which existed not only on the St. Lawrence, but also on the Des Moines, was most widely diffused. It was heard from Cape Fear to the land of the Esquimaux; from the Cumberland river of Kentucky to the southern bank of the Missinnippi, a thousand miles north-west from the sources of the Mississippi. It was spoken, though not exclusively, in a territory that extended through sixty degrees of longitude, and more than twenty degrees of latitude. It was the mother tongue of those who greeted the colonists of Raleigh, at Roanoke; of those who welcomed the Pilgrims to Plymouth.[2]

Our remarks on the localities of these several communities may properly be restricted to the region of country of which we more particularly speak. The nations which spoke dialects of the Huron-Iroquois, or, as it has also been called, of the Wyandot, were, on the discovery of America, found powerful in numbers, and diffused over a wide territory. The peninsula, inclosed between Lakes Huron, Erie, and Ontario, had been the dwelling-place of the five confederated tribes of the Hurons. After their defeat by the Five Nations, a part descended the St. Lawrence, and their progeny may still be seen near Quebec; a part were adopted on equal terms into the tribes of their conquerors; the Wyandots fled beyond Lake Superior, and hid themselves in the dreary wastes that divided the Chippewas from their western foes. In 1671, they retreated before the powerful Sioux, and made their home first at St. Mary's and at Michillimackinac, and afterward

---

[1] Albert Gallatin's Synopsis. Bancroft, vol. iii. 237.

[2] Bancroft, vol. iii.

near the post of Detroit. Thus, the Wyandots within our borders were emigrants from Canada. Having a mysterious influence over the Algonquin tribes, and making treaties with the Five Nations, they spread along Lake Erie; and leaving to the Miamis the country beyond the Miami of the Lakes, they gradually acquired a claim to the whole territory, from that river to the western boundary of New York.[1]

The immediate dominion of the Iroquois—where the Mohawks, Oneidas, Onondagas, Cayugas, and Senecas were first visited by the trader, the missionary, or the war parties of the French—stretched from the borders of Vermont to Western New York, from the Lakes to the head waters of the Ohio, the Susquehannah, and the Delaware. The number of their warriors was declared by the French, in 1660, to have been two thousand two hundred; this was confirmed by an English agent, sent, in 1677, on purpose to ascertain their strength. Their geographical position made them umpires in the contest of the French for dominion in the West. Besides, their political importance was increased by their conquests. They claimed some supremacy in northern New England as far as the Kennebec, and to the south as far as New Haven, and were acknowledged as absolute lords over the conquered Lenni-Lenape; the peninsula of Upper Canada was their hunting-field by right of war; they had exterminated the Eries and the Andastes, both tribes of their own family, the one dwelling on the south-eastern banks of Lake Erie, the other on the head waters of the Ohio; they had triumphantly invaded the tribes of the West as far as Illinois; their warriors had reached the soil of Kentucky and Western Virginia, and England, to whose alliance they steadily inclined, availed itself of their treaties for the cession of territories, to encroach even on the empire of France in America.[2]

The Shawanese connected the south-eastern Algonquins with those of the West; the basin of the Cumberland river is marked by the earliest French geographers as the home of

---

[1] Bancroft, vol. iii.

[2] Idem, p. 244.

this restless nation of wanderers. Subsequently, they have been found with their cabins in Virginia, in South Carolina, on the head waters of the Mobile River, and on the banks of the Susquehannah. In 1732, when the number of Indian fighting men in Pennsylvania was estimated to be seven hundred, one-half of them were Shawnee emigrants.

The Miamis were more stable, and their own traditions preserve the memory of their ancient limits. "My forefather," said the Miami orator, Little Turtle, at the treaty of Greenville, in 1795, "kindled the first fire at Detroit; from thence he extended his lines to the head waters of the Scioto; from thence to its mouth; from thence down the Ohio to the mouth of the Wabash; and from thence to Chicago, on Lake Michigan. These are the boundaries within which the prints of my ancestors' houses are everywhere to be seen." The early French narratives confirm his words.

The forests beyond Detroit were at first found unoccupied, or, it may be, roamed over by bands too feeble to attract a trader, or win a missionary; the Ottowas, Algonquin fugitives from the basin of the magnificent river whose name commemorates them, fled to the Bay of Saginaw, and took possession of the whole north of the peninsula, as of a derelict country; yet the Miamis occupied its southern moiety, and their principal mission was founded by Allouez, on the banks of the St. Joseph, within the present State of Michigan.

The Illinois were kindred to the Miamis, and their country lay between the Wabash, the Ohio, and the Mississippi. Marquette found a village of them on the Des Moines, but its occupants soon withdrew to the east of the Mississippi; and Kaskaskia, Cahokia, Peoria, still preserve the names of the principal bands, of which the original strength, *perhaps*, has been greatly exaggerated. The vague tales of a considerable population vanished before the accurate observation of the missionaries, who found in the wild wilderness of Illinois scarcely three or four villages. On the discovery of America, the number of the scattered tenants of the territory which now forms the States of Ohio, Michigan, Indiana, Illinois,

Wisconsin, and Kentucky, could hardly have exceeded eighteen thousand.[1]

In the early part of the eighteenth century, the Pottawatamies had crowded the Miamis from their dwellings at Chicago; the intruders came from the islands near the entrance of Green Bay, and were a branch of the Chippewas. That nation, or as properly written, the Ojibwas—the Algonquin tribes of whose dialect, mythology, traditions, and customs we have the fullest accounts[2]—held the country from the mouth of Green Bay to the head waters of Lake Superior, and were early visited by the French at Sault St. Marie and Chegoimegon. They adopted into their tribes many of the Ottowas from Upper Canada, and were themselves often included by the early French writers under that name.

Ottawa is but the Algonquin word for "trader," and Mascoutins are but "dwellers in the prairie." The latter hardly implies a band of Indians, distinct from the Chippewas; but history recognises as a separate Algonquin tribe, near Green Bay, the Menominees, who were found there in 1669, who retained their ancient territory long after the period of French and of English supremacy, and who prove their high antiquity as a nation by the singular character of their dialect.

South-west of the Menominees, the restless Sacs and Foxes, ever dreaded by the French, held the passes from Green Bay and Fox River to the Mississippi, and with insatiate avidity roamed in pursuit of contest, over the whole country between the Wisconsin and the upper branches of the Illinois. The Shawnees are said to have an affinity with this nation; that the Kickapoos, who established themselves by conquest in the north of Illinois, are but a branch of it, is demonstrated by their speech.

North-west of the Sacs and Foxes, west of the Chippewas, bands of the Sioux or Dahcotas had encamped on prairies east of the Mississippi, vagrants, between the head waters of

---

[1] Bancroft, vol. iii. 241; compare Marest, Hennepin, Tonti, Joutel.

[2] Schoolcraft, 1825, p. 360.

Lake Superior and the Falls of St. Anthony. They were a branch of the great family, which, dwelling for the most part west of the Mississippi and the Red River, extended from the Saskatchawan to lands south of the Arkansas. French traders discovered their wigwams in 1659; Hennepin was among them on his expedition to the North; Joseph Marest, and another Jesuit, visited them in 1687, and again in 1689. There seemed to exist an hereditary warfare between them and the Chippewas. Their relations to the colonies, whether of France or England, at this early period, were accidental, and related chiefly to individuals. But one little community of the Dahcota family had penetrated the territory of the Algonquins; the Winnebagoes, dwelling between Green Bay and the lake that bears their name, preferred rather to be environed by Algonquins, than to stay in the dangerous vicinity of their own kindred. Like other Western and Southern tribes, their population appears of late to have been greatly increased.[1]

The Menominees are often called by the Jesuit Fathers, in their Relations, Malouminees, Fols Avoine, People of the Wild Rice; *manomin* being the Indian name of the grain so plentifully growing in their region, *wild oats* being the appellation given to it by the missionaries. The Mascoutins were also called "La Nation du Feu," and "Les Petuns;" Mascoutinech signifies a land bare of trees, such as these people inhabit; the same word signifies "fire;" but why especially called the "Tobacco nation," does not appear to be explained by the early writers, the growing of tobacco being common with several tribes. The above names are indiscriminately given to those people whenever they are spoken of by the Fathers, previous to 1672.[2]

From the time that Iberville took possession of the mouths of the Mississippi, up to 1712, a period of near thirteen years, there had been not less than twenty-five hundred set-

---

[1] Charlevoix, iii. 291. Bancroft, vol. iii. 243.

[2] Jesuit Relations, passim.

tlers of all kinds introduced into Louisiana, who had been distributed in distant explorations, and scattered settlements on the west coast of Mobile; many had died, some had remained in the Illinois country. Yet the colony had been at great expense to the crown; already 689,000 livres, or about $170,000, had been expended, when the value of money was not reduced by paper.[1] Yet the colonists merely lived, prosper they could not, since agriculture was neglected, and the improvident immigrants were scattered over a vast country, vainly searching for gold and silver, and precious stones, or seeking wealth in the paltry traffic of furs and skins, purchased of the Indians. Those who remained stationary, were settled on the barren shores of Mobile, Biloxi, and of St. Louis Bay, with an uncertain dependence upon hunting and fishing, or the precarious bounty of the savages. Many of them, with childish confidence, seemed to have expected annual supplies from France, or that the natives would continue to supply their wants. Led away by the most unreasonable hopes, as to the spontaneous products of the country, they deemed labour or provident attention on their part, wholly superfluous. They even entertained the belief that the wool of the buffalo, which abounded in the prairies, would yield a valuable commodity for export. Instead of building comfortable houses for permanent residence, they roamed to the most remote regions in quest of mines of precious metals. Every new specimen of earth, to their distempered imaginations was some valuable mineral; every brilliant ore, or carburet, was pure gold. Nor was the government of France free from the delusion. The ministry had directed that a number of buffaloes should be caught and tamed, to propagate their species in France, for the sake of their wool. Large quantities of earths were shipped to France from the Upper Mississippi, to be assayed by experienced smelters, in hopes of proving it a valuable oxyd of some precious metal. The most extravagant tales of designing men were received with the greediness of entire be-

[1] Stoddart's Sketches, p. 29.

lief: rewards were paid to those who gave intelligence of valuable mines, and extravagant discoveries multiplied in proportion to the rewards offered.[1]

Such was the condition of the first colonists; hence it is not strange that famine, disease, and death should soon find their way among them. In 1701, the entire number was reduced to one hundred and fifty souls; Sauvole was an early victim to disease, and the chief command devolved on Bienville. Le Sueur returned from St. Peter's River in 1702, with his boats laden with the supposed valuable copper ore from the Blue Earth River; but Fort L'Huillier, which he had built, together with other posts on the Upper Mississippi above the Wisconsin, were abandoned on account of the hostility of the Sioux. Iberville arrived with reinforcements, in December, 1702, and found the whole population of Louisiana reduced, by famine and bilious fevers, to not more than thirty families. Attacked himself by the yellow fever, he escaped with his life, but his health was broken, and although he rendered services to France afterward, yet his efforts were followed by a severe illness, which terminated in his death, in July, 1706.[2] The founder of Louisiana, the hero of Hudson's Bay, the conqueror of the English posts from Fort Rupert to Albany River, was well worthy the deep regret of the colonies and of the French nation. The band of brothers, De Sainte Helene, D'Iberville, Sauvole, Bienville, were Canadians, sons of Charles Lemoine, an early emigrant from Normandy. Their names are worthy the page of American history.[3]

The colony of Louisiana had so far failed to meet the expectations of the crown or the people of France, that the French court began to see that a change in the government and general policy of the province was indispensable. Heretofore the settlements of Louisiana had been a dependence on New France or Canada, although separated by a wilderness of two thousand miles in extent. Now it was to be made an

---

[1] Martin's Louisiana, vol. i. 155. Monette, vol. i. 207.
[2] Bancroft, vol. iii. 205, [3] Idem, p. 179.

independent government, responsible only to the crown, and comprising also the "Illinois country" under its jurisdiction. The government of Louisiana was accordingly, in 1711, placed in the hands of a governor-general. The head-quarters, or seat of the colonial government was established at Mobile, and a new fort erected on the site of the present city of Mobile. Dirou d'Artaguette, as commissary *ordonnateur*, arrived early in the year 1711, and entered upon his duties. De Muys, the governor-general, had died on the voyage.

It was determined that the colonists should depend on their own exertions and industry for the principal necessaries of life; that agriculture should be fostered, and that the land which heretofore had been neglected, should be taxed to support those necessaries; that France would supply only such as could not be produced in the province. But the settlements were as yet confined to a few sandy islands, and the sterile coast from Mobile Bay westward to the Bay of St. Louis.[1]

Bienville had been appointed governor-general of the province; he had before seen the necessity of agricultural settlements, and he sought to form them on the deep alluvions of the Mississippi. Although exploring parties had been sent to the remotest portions of the province, although every Indian tribe had been visited, yet not one permanent settlement had been made on the banks of the Mississippi; not one vestige of civilized life had been made upon the most fertile regions of the vast province; not one field or village greeted the traveller's eye, if we except the small fort of Iberville, toward the mouth, which had now been abandoned. The government of France, embarrassed and burdened with debt, was unable to maintain the helpless colony.[2]

It is proper to view the boundaries of the province of Louisiana as claimed by the French. On the side of Spain, at the west and south, it was held to extend to the river Del Norte; and on the map published by the French Academy, the line passing from that river to the ridge that divides it from the

---

[1] Monette, vol. i. 209. [2] Idem.

Red River, followed that ridge to the Rocky Mountains, and then descended to seek its termination in the Gulf of California. On the Gulf of Mexico, it is certain that France claimed to the Del Norte. At the north-west, where its collision would have been with the possessions of the Company of Hudson's Bay, no treaty, no commission, appears to have fixed its limits.

On the east, the line, as between Spain and France, was the halfway between the Spanish garrison at Pensacola, and the fort which, in 1711, the French had established on the site of the present city of Mobile. With regard to England, Louisiana was held to embrace the whole valley of the Mississippi. Not a fountain bubbled on the west of the Alleghanies but was claimed as being within the French empire. Louisiana stretched to the head springs of the Alleghany, and the Monongahela, of the Kenawha and the Tennessee. Half a mile from the head of the southern branch of the Savannah River, is Herbert's spring, which flows to the Mississippi: strangers, who drank of it, would say they had tasted of French waters.[1] France had obtained, under Providence, the guardianship of this immense district of country, "not, as it proved, for its own benefit, but rather as a trustee for the infant nation by which it was one day to be inherited."[2]

In France it was still believed that Louisiana presented a rich field for enterprise and speculation. The court determined to place the resources of the province under the influence of individual enterprise. For this purpose, a grant of exclusive privileges in all the commerce of the province, for a term of fifteen years, was made to Anthony Crozat, a rich and influential merchant of France, "who had prospered in opulence to the astonishment of all the world. This patent of monopoly of trade, one of the most stupendous that ever was conceded by supreme authority to a subject, was dated September 14th, 1712, and La Motte Cadillac, now the royal Governor of Louisiana, became the partner of Crozat in all

[1] Bancroft, vol. iii. 343. Greenhow's Memoir, p. 216. Adair, p. 231.

[2] Bancroft, vol. iii. 203.

its contemplated advantages; thus, the merchant proprietary, and the founder of Detroit, sought fortune by discovering mines, and encroaching on the colonial monopolies of Spain.[1] (NOTE D.)

The seeds of the Mississippi scheme were already sown in the hearts and minds of the whole French nation; the vision of a fertile empire, with its plantations, manors, cities, and busy wharves, a monopoly of commerce throughout all French North America, the certain products of the richest silver mines, and mountains of gold, were blended in the French mind into one boundless promise of untold treasures.[2] The visionary expectations of the nobility; the churchmen, who competed for favours from the privileged institution; the stock-jobbers, including dukes and peers, marshals and bishops, women of rank, statesmen and courtiers, were soon to become a subject of wonder and astonishment for after-ages; exhibited as they were, in the madness which attended the operations of the Great Western or Mississippi Company, connected as it was with the gigantic banking scheme, both of which were instituted and conducted under the auspices of John Law, who at that period of cupidity was reverenced as the greatest man of the age. The bursting of the bubbles entailed ruin on a nation.

The fourteenth article of the charter to Crozat authorized slavery, and the traffic in slaves, throughout all Louisiana, from the mouth of the Mississippi to its sources, and on all the streams discharging themselves into it. The effects which might have been produced by the full exercise of the power thus granted, together with the proviso stipulations of the Virginia cession, in the ordinance of 1787, and the Missouri compromise, which established the latitude of 36° 30′ as the division line between slavery and anti-slavery, might well constitute a subject of curious abstract investigation. Perhaps it is a most happy and fortunate circumstance in regard to the agitations of the present day, that the extraordinary

---

[1] Bancroft, vol. iii. 347.

[2] Ibid. p. 351.

privileges of so extensive a traffic in slaves in the Mississippi valley, were never taken advantage of, to any extent, by Monsieur Crozat.

At the time of the granting of the charter, the French population in all this region, was comprised in a few hundred indolent and ignorant colonists, and a few troops in the forts. The whole number of settlers in Lower Louisiana consisted of twenty-eight families, whose occupation, besides fishing and hunting, was the cultivation of small garden spots in the sterile regions around the Bays of Biloxi, St. Louis, and Mobile. The soldiers, distributed in the several garrisoned forts, consisted of one hundred and seventy-five men, comprising two companies of infantry, of fifty men each, and seventy-five Canadian volunteers. There were also, at this time, twenty negro slaves, a few Jesuits, and Franciscans, and king's officers. The whole number of Europeans in Lower Louisiana was three hundred and eighty souls, and about three hundred head of cattle. There were also a few settlements on the Kaskaskia and Wabash Rivers.[1] In the far North, and in the vicinity of Lakes Michigan, Huron, and Superior, the missionary establishments, and the recently erected military post at Detroit, constituted the entire white population.

Crozat met with no success in his commercial operations; every Spanish harbour in the Gulf of Mexico was closed against his vessels; the occupation of Louisiana itself was deemed an encroachment on Spanish territory; and having failed in his contemplated trade with the Spaniards, Crozat caused settlements, or trading-posts, to be made in the most remote parts of the province, while explorations were extended into the most distant known tribes. But for the advancement of the colony he accomplished nothing. The only prosperity which it possessed, grew out of the enterprise of humble individuals, who had succeeded in instituting a little barter between themselves and the natives, and a petty trade with neighbouring European settlements. These small sources of

[1] Monette, vol. i. 210.

profit were cut off by the profitless but fatal monopoly of the Parisian merchant. The Indians were too numerous to be resisted by his factors. The English gradually appropriated the trade with the natives; and every Frenchman in Louisiana, except his agents, fomented opposition to his privileges.[1] In all his calculations and expectations, Crozat was doomed to be sadly disappointed. After nearly three years spent in fruitless negotiations with the Spanish viceroy of Mexico, relative to commercial intercourse with the Spanish ports on the Gulf of Mexico, and after much delay, vexation, and expense, his vessels were prohibited from trading in any of the Spanish ports. He then attempted to institute commercial relations by land, for supplying the interior provinces of New Mexico; but his goods were seized and his agents imprisoned, after a persevering effort of nearly five years.[2]

The trade with the Indians also failed to meet his expectations. The English emissaries from Carolina were active in their efforts to excite the tribes east of the Mississippi to hostilities against the French. Where this was impracticable, they endeavoured to annoy the French trade by supplying the the same articles at reduced prices. The mines of Louisiana were principally of lead, copper, and iron, all of which were found in great abundance; but they were not profitable. Much money had been spent in searching for gold and silver, without any recompense. Failing to realize any profit from all his contemplated resources, he was unable to meet his engagements with his workmen, agents, and troops, and dissatisfaction ensued. He had expended 425,000 livres in his operations, and had realized from all the sources of trade only 300,000, leaving him the loser of 125,000 livres, or about $30,000.[3] His partner, La Motte Cadillac, the governor, had died recently, and, at length, Crozat, despairing of the ultimate success of his enterprise in a savage country, petitioned the king to revoke his charter, or to permit him to surrender it to the crown. The king complied with his re-

[1] Bancroft, vol. iii. 348. [2] Monette, vol. i. 213. [3] Martin's Louis., vol. i. 191.

quest, and accepted the surrender of his charter, in August, 1717. The government of the colony reverted solely into the hands of the king's officers, and Crozat retired to France.

At this time the entire population of Louisiana, exclusive of the very few who were at Detroit and the Jesuit missions, did not exceed seven hundred, including persons of every age, sex, and colour. Yet the valley of the Mississippi inflamed the imagination of France; anticipating the future, the French nation beheld the certain opulence of coming ages, as within their immediate grasp; from the mines, great quantities of gold and silver were still hoped to be obtained; and the supposed riches, the commerce, and boundless extent of Louisiana, were now to be invoked to relieve the burden and renew the credit of the mother country.[1] The debt of France, on the death of Louis XIV. in 1715, amounted to the enormous sum of 3,111,000,000 livres, or £222,000,000 sterling. The revenues of the kingdom were in a state of frightful confusion, and there seemed to be no way of avoiding a national bankruptcy. The only means of paying the interest of the state debt, which was 86,000,000 livres, (above £6,000,000 sterling,) was out of the excess of the revenue over the expenditure; but as this amounted only to the small sum of 9,000,000 livres, it was insufficient to meet the demands of the state creditors. By means of strenuous exertions, the Duke of Orleans, who was regent during the minority of Louis XV., had contrived to reduce the national debt to 2,000,000,000 livres, (£142,000,000 sterling,) and the interest to 86,000,000 livres; further reduction was considered impossible, and the state was believed to be on the brink of ruin.

At this crisis, a Scottish theorist, named John Law, came forward, and offered to relieve France from her difficulties. Law had been in some measure favourably known at home and in various parts of the continent, for his mathematical abilities, and acquaintance with all matters relating to banking and finance, accompanied with a knowledge by personal

[1] Bancroft, vol. iii. 349.

observations of the trade and manufactures of the various countries through which he had travelled. His reputation for these qualities stood high in France, and it is said that his plan for remedying the disorders of the finances of the kingdom had been proposed to Louis XIV. by Desmarets, his finance minister, but had been refused by the king, as the schemer was a Protestant, and not a Catholic; therefore he would have nothing to do with him. The true character of Law appears to have been that of a reckless gambler, and a dangerous speculator; a visionary theorist, gifted with an extraordinary capacity in the studies of national economy.

In various interviews with, and by writings addressed to the regent, Law pressed his great idea, the establishment of a paper currency. Gold, silver, copper, or any other kind of coinage, he said, which a nation may agree to use, are not real wealth; they are only signs or representatives of real wealth, and derive their value from public confidence. It does not matter, therefore, what the kind of coinage be which a nation agrees to use; a paper coinage or a leather coinage is as good as a metallic one. A metallic coinage does not constitute real riches, but is valuable only because the public choose to consider it valuable; and if the public will only do the same with paper notes, then paper notes will be on an equality with gold or silver coin. What is a louis-d'or but a bank-note, only made of gold; or a crown but a bank-note, only made of silver? It does not signify, therefore, what a nation chooses to consider as money, be it even oyster-shells; for such will serve as a sign or representative of real wealth the same as a piece of metal.[1]

This reasoning is correct only so far: gold certainly does not constitute real wealth—it is not food, clothing, nor the means of shelter; all which are so many items of real wealth; but it possesses a greater intrinsic value than paper, and therefore is not so completely at the mercy of public opinion. Apart altogether from its fictitious value as a coin, gold is

[1] Chambers's Miscellany, vol. x.

a useful and a precious metal, for which there is a demand in the arts; and the cost of obtaining it from the bowels of the earth, and refining it, being great, every little piece of gold is, as it were, a condensation of a quantity of real wealth: paper, on the other hand, is a valuable commodity likewise; but the cost of its production being less, it really has less intrinsic value, and is more dependent upon public opinion. Paper can be procured as abundantly as we choose, but there is a limit to the production of gold. Gold and silver are dear substances in themselves; paper is a very cheap substance. The value of a metallic currency, therefore, is not so liable to fluctuation as one entirely of paper.

Law maintained that "where there exists no circulating medium but gold and silver, its riches may be greatly augmented by the introduction of paper money;" a proposition true only so long as what is issued represents real wealth, and does not go beyond the legitimate demands of the circulation. What Law proposed to the regent was, to establish a national bank, which should issue notes on the basis of landed property, and of the royal revenues; the bank to be in the king's name, but subject to the control of commissioners appointed by the states-general. This was not approved of, by the Council of Finances, but Law obtained leave to set up a private bank under the name of "Law and Company;" the funds to be furnished by himself and such as chose to become shareholders. The stock was to consist of 1200 shares at 1000 crowns (£250) each, and was, therefore, to amount to £300,000. The most peculiar feature of the establishment, and that which gave it favour in the eyes of the public, was, that its notes were to be payable at sight, in specie of the same weight and fineness as the money in circulation at the period of their issue. This was a novelty, for since the year 1689 the currency had been subject to constant alterations: the value of the livre to-day being, perhaps, not much more than half of what it was yesterday. On this account, as well as from the quickness and punctuality of the payments, and the orders given to the officers of the revenue in all parts of the kingdom, to receive the paper of Law's bank without discount in payment of taxes, the notes of the bank in a short time rose to great repute, and were by many preferred to specie, insomuch that they soon came to pass current for one per cent. more than the coin itself. The most beneficial effects were thereby produced on the industry and trade of the nation; the taxes and royal revenues being by means of the notes remitted to the capital at little expense, and without draining the provinces of specie. The bank subsisted in high credit, to the no small profit of the proprietors, till the close of the year 1718, when the Duke of Orleans, observing the uncommon advantages resulting from the establishment, resolved to take it into his majesty's hands, as at first proposed.[1]

On the 4th of December, 1718, the bank was declared to be a Royal Bank, to be administered thenceforward in the king's name. Law was appointed director-general, and various branches were established. If the bank had continued to perform no other functions than those which are usually understood to belong to a bank, there is every probability that its establishment would have been a considerable advantage to the nation. But in the course of three years after its establishment, the bank had incorporated with itself many other schemes of various characters, so that, instead of continuing a mere bank, it became a gigantic commercial company. In 1717, immediately on the surrender of the charter of Crozat, a new institution was established under the direction of John Law, called the "Company of the West," or more commonly, "The Mississippi Company." Its legal existence was limited to twenty-five years, and the charter conferred upon the "Western Company" much more extensive powers and privileges than those granted to Monsieur Crozat. It was vested with the exclusive privilege of the entire commerce of Louisiana and New France, and with authority to enforce its rights. It was authorized to monopolize the trade of all the colonies in the provinces, and of all the Indian tribes within the limits of

[1] Wood's Life of Law of Lauriston.

that extensive region, even to the remotest source of every stream tributary in any wise to the Mississippi and Mobile Rivers; to make treaties with the Indian tribes; to declare and prosecute war against them in defence of the colony; to grant lands, to erect forts, to levy troops, to raise recruits, and to open and work all mines of precious metals or stones which might be discovered in the province. It was permitted and authorized to nominate and present men for the office of governor, and for commanders of the troops, and to commission the latter, subject to the king's approval; to remove inferior judges and civil officers; to build and equip ships of war, and to cast cannon. The king also granted for the use of the company all the forts, magazines, guns, ammunition, and vessels pertaining to the province.[1]

Among the obligations imposed on the company was the stipulation to introduce into the province of Louisiana within the period of their chartered privileges, six thousand white persons, and three thousand negro slaves, and to protect the settlements against Indian hostilities. It was vainly hoped on the part of France that the western company would exert a powerful influence in colonizing the vast regions of the Mississippi valley, while the company looked forward to certain inexhaustible sources of wealth in the exclusive privileges thus granted to them, although the field of their operations was yet a savage wilderness.

With this company Law associated the Bank of France; their operations, their interests were intimately blended; the extravagant issues of paper by the bank were in a great measure founded on the new shares from time to time created in the "Mississippi Company;" and the stupendous project was formed to pay off the public debt in bank bills, to absorb which, new shares in the company, under its new name of the "Company of the Indies," were to be created and offered for sale. The stock originally consisted of 200,000 shares, at 500 livres each. On the 4th of September, 1718, the farm of to-

[1] Martin's Louisiana, vol. i. 200.

bacco was made over to this company; three months afterward it acquired the charter and property of the Senegal Company; in May, 1719, it obtained from the regent a monopoly of trade with the East Indies, China, and the South Seas: thus enlarged, the company abandoned its original name of the "Company of the West," and assumed that of the "Company of the Indies," at the same time creating 50,000 additional shares at an increased price. In July, 1719, the "Mint" was made over to the Company of the Indies; in August following the farming of the whole taxes of the nation was purchased by the company, and the privilege of receiving other branches of the revenue quickly followed; so that before the end of the year 1719, the Company of the Indies had incorporated within itself nearly all the commercial enterprise of the nation. As director and manager of the two great national institutions, the Royal Bank and the colossal trading company called the Company of the Indies, united in February, 1720—Law, the founder of both, became the most powerful man in France; he had now made himself a Catholic, and was appointed comptroller-general of finance.[1]

One among the first of the operations of the Western Company was to send eight hundred emigrants to Louisiana; they arrived in August, 1718, at Dauphine Island. Bienville had, in the midsummer of the same year, selected the site for the capital of the new empire, which, in honour of the Regent of France, he named "New Orleans." Of the recent emigrants from France, eighty convicts were sent among the coppices that overspread New Orleans, to prepare room for a few tents and cottages. At the end of three years the place was still a wilderness spot, where two hundred persons, sent to construct a city, had but encamped among unsubdued canebrakes.[2] The character of the emigration was not that of industry, energy, or of information: some perished for want of enterprise, some from the climate; and in place of ascending the river in ships, they all blindly disembarked on the miserable coast, to make

[1] See Note E. [2] Bancroft, vol. iii. 352.

their way as best they could to the lands that had been ceded to them. An extraordinary instance of energy may be mentioned: Du Tissenet, a Canadian emigrant, having purchased a compass, and procured an escort of fourteen Canadians, went fearlessly from Dauphine Island by way of the Mobile River to Quebec, and returned to the banks of the Mississippi with his family.[1] At this period the three great avenues from the St. Lawrence to the Mississippi were, one by way of the Fox and Wisconsin Rivers: one by way of Chicago, which had been safely pursued since the days of Marquette; and one by the Miami of the Lakes, where, after crossing the portage of three leagues over the summit level, a shallow stream led into the Wabash and the Ohio.

The bubbles of the Bank, and of the Mississippi scheme, were at their full-blown height in January, 1720: at that time shares in the company, which were originally worth 500 livres, were selling at 10,000 livres each. In March, a decree of council fixed the value of the stock at 9,000 livres for 500, and forbade certain corporations to invest money in any thing else; all circulation of gold and silver, except for change, was prohibited; all payments must be made in paper, except for sums under ten livres. He who would attempt to convert a bill into specie, would have exposed his specie to forfeiture and himself to fines. Confidence suddenly disappeared, and in May, bankruptcy was avowed, by a decree which reduced the value of bank-notes by a moiety. The French people had remained faithful to their delusion, till France was impoverished, public and private credit subverted, the income of capitalists annihilated, and labour left without employment; while in the midst of the universal wretchedness of the middling class, a few wary speculators gloried in the unjust acquisition and enjoyment of immense wealth.[2]

The downfall of Law abruptly curtailed expenditures for Louisiana. But a colony was already planted, destined to survive all dangers, even though, in France, Louisiana was in-

---

[1] Bancroft, iii. 352. Du Pratz, vol. i. 40. [2] Bancroft, vol. iii. 357.

volved in disgrace. Instead of the splendid visions of opulence, the disenchanted public would now see only unwholesome marshes, which were the tombs of immigrants; its name was a name of disgust and terror. Although a change had taken place in the fortunes of the Mississippi Company by its connection with the Bank of Law, its first attempts at colonization were conducted with careless prodigality. The richest prairies, the most inviting fields in the southern valley of the Mississippi, were conceded to companies, or to individuals who sought principalities in the new world. Thus it was hoped that at least six thousand white colonists would be established in Louisiana. To Law himself there was conceded on the Arkansas one of those vast prairies of which the wide-spreading waves of verdure are bounded only by the azure of the sky. There he designed to plant a city and villages; his investments rapidly amounted to a million and a half of livres; through the company which he directed, possessing a monopoly of the slave-trade for the French colonies, he had purchased three hundred negroes; mechanics from France and a throng of German emigrants were engaged in his service, or as his tenants; his commissioners lavished gifts on the tribes with whom they smoked the calumet. But when, in 1727, a Jesuit priest arrived there, he found only thirty needy Frenchmen, who had been abandoned by their employer, and had no consolation but in the blandness of the climate and unrivalled fertility of the soil. The decline of Louisiana was a consequence of financial changes in France.[1]

"The issue of Law's celebrated system left the world a lesson which the world was slow to learn: that the enlargement of the circulation quickens industry *so long only* as the enlargement continues, for prices then rise, and every kind of labour is remunerated; that when this increase springs from artificial causes, it must meet with a check, and be followed by a reaction; that when the reaction begins, the high remunerating prices decline, labour fails to find an equivalent, and

[1] Bancroft. Du Poisson in Lett. Ed. iv. 235.

each evil opposite to the previous advantage ensues; that therefore every artificial expansion of the currency, every expansion resting on credit alone, is a source of confusion, and ultimate loss to the community, and brings benefits to none but those who are skilful in foreseeing and profiting by the fluctuations."[1]

Such was the state of things in Louisiana for several years after the downfall of Law, and his system of finance in France and French America. Who then would have believed that in less than one hundred and fifteen years from that time, the valley of the Mississippi would have been the theatre of delusions almost as great, under a new system of credit held out by a hundred banking institutions and chartered monopolies, as rotten and as baseless as Law's Bank of France? Such was the currency of the valley of the Mississippi among five millions of people for four years after the year 1834.[2] The ruinous disasters which fell on the whole community, at that period, in consequence of the sudden inflation, and as sudden contraction of a paper currency, worthless in its basis, has not yet, it appears, proved a lesson sufficiently instructive—for now, in 1853, in the region of the Upper Mississippi, and the adjacent States, the renewed experiment of a paper currency has obtained favour with the people; the foundation of the existing system of paper issues, apparently, is plausible, but time, which is the parent of truth, may perhaps once again teach that severe lesson to the people of the Mississippi Valley, which they have hitherto been so slow to heed, and by the effects of which they have been so unwilling to profit.

During the first operations of the Western company, the trade of the Illinois country (which had been commenced, although fruitlessly by Crozat, in the establishment of his trading posts) began to assume the regular channels of commerce; and notwithstanding the company had embarked largely in agriculture, and had established large plantations on the river, still it refused to abandon the idea of discover-

[1] Bancroft, vol. iii. 357.

[2] Monette, vol. i. 244.

ing boundless wealth in the mines of Missouri and of the Illinois country and Upper Mississippi. In 1719, Philippe Francis Renault, "Director-general of the mines of Louisiana," with two hundred miners and artificers, arrived in the Illinois country. This arrival gave a great accession to the French population, and introduced many useful mechanics into the settlements. Illinois was deemed by the company to be a region of mines immensely valuable, which were to enrich the capitalists of Europe: and although after much labour and extensive research, Mr. Renault, with his company of two hundred miners, had failed to discover the gold and silver mines of which the most extravagant accounts had been given, yet the "Directory" of the Western Company continued to offer munificent rewards for the much-desired fulfilment of their expectations. The attention of the company continued to be diverted to the search of mines in distant regions, as far as the sources of the St. Peter's, the Arkansas, the tributaries of the Missouri, and even to the Rocky Mountains.[1] Fortunately, the hopes of the company concerning the valuable products of the mines were doomed to disappointment, and the public mind was directed more intensely to agriculture. Mines there were of iron, lead, copper, and perhaps of silver and gold; but they were reserved for a race of men who were to live a century after the dissolution of the company, when monopolies should cease. The richest mines of the country, at this early period, were found in the prolific and inexhaustible soil, which was free to the industry of all classes. Thus an overruling Providence shaped the destiny of the country, which was to become the granary for nations.[2]

Le Sueur had, in April, 1700, set out from Bienville's Fort, with twenty men, and Indian guides for the country of the Sioux, high up the Mississippi, in quest of mineral wealth; many of the two hundred miners of Monsieur Renault were engaged in mining operations, in 1719, on the east and west banks of the Mississippi, far above the Wisconsin River; a

---

[1] Martin, vol. i. 252.

[2] Monette, vol. i. 161.

period of near twenty years had elapsed, and the belief in mineral wealth, and consequent hope of its discovery, had increased with each year's advent. In the mean time, the existing war between France and Spain had created a theatre for hostilities in the valley of the Mississippi, and a late expedition from Santa Fé to the Missouri, although overwhelmed with disaster, evinced the possibility of other expeditions by the same route for the destruction of the French settlements in the Illinois country or Upper Louisiana. To protect the French possessions, as well as to extend French claims to territory, a chain of forts was begun, to keep open a communication from the mouth to the sources of the Mississippi. Fort Orleans, high up the Missouri, was already, in 1720, in progress as an outpost; the Lower Mississippi had also been threatened by the Spaniards, and it became apparent to the Western Company and to Bienville, the royal commandant, that the western bank of the river should be secured against hostile incursions. The complete survey of the mouth of the Mississippi, and all the passes, bars, and channels below the present site of New Orleans city, was made by M. Pauger, a royal engineer, and it was ascertained that the site selected by Bienville might be made a commercial port; that the practicability of bringing shipping up the river was beyond a doubt; and the "Directory" of the Western Company yielded a reluctant assent to the removal of the company's principal depot and their officers to New Orleans, now about to become the great commercial port of the province.[1]

We have seen that Le Sueur, with his detachment, had already advanced up the Mississippi, and up the St. Peter's River, to the Blue Earth River, among the Sioux, by his estimate, a distance of seven hundred and sixty leagues from the sea; and there, at the mouth of the Blue Earth River, having erected a fort and a trading-post for the company, he, with all the usual formalities, took possession of the country in the name of his most Christian majesty.[2] Fort Chartres, one of the strongest French

[1] Martin, vol. i. 233.

[2] Idem.

posts in North America, was commenced at this time, 1720; it was situated on the east bank of the Mississippi, about twenty-five miles below Kaskaskia, and was designed as the head-quarters of the commandant of Upper Louisiana.[1]

From 1670, up to 1720, during a period of half a century, the population and settlement of the Upper Illinois country, and the vicinity of the great lakes, was principally restricted to the forts established to protect the missionaries in their operations with the Indians, and also the commerce with them at the several important trading-posts. Michillimackinac, on the peninsula, was one of the oldest forts erected. Its foundations, together with those of a chapel and missionary dwelling, were laid by Father Marquette in 1671. As early as 1688, the Ottawas and Hurons had villages in the vicinity of the chapel and fort, separated only by the palisades. Near the Huron village, the Jesuits had a college, and the Ottawas had commenced building a fortification in their proximity. Other fortified posts, in this period, had been established at Green Bay, at Chicago, at St. Joseph's, at Sault St. Marie, and at Detroit. The population of these posts was composed of a commander, who was called Governor, Jesuits, soldiers, traders, and savages; the fort and chapel were surrounded with small patches of cultivated land, and the wigwams of the Indians. In 1689, Green Bay contained a fort, chapel, and missionary house, which were situated amid the villages of the Sacs, Potawatamies, and Menominees.[2] This place was at that time a rich market for peltries and Indian corn, which the savages sold to the traders as they passed to and from the Mississippi.

The English and French had long embarked as rivals in the trade with the Indians of the Northwest; the influence of the French over these tribes had not altogether prevented the introduction of the English trade. As early as 1686, a trading expedition of the English had arrived at Michillimackinac, through the connivance of the Ottagamies or Fox Indians,

---

[1] See Note F.

[2] Lanman, p. 39. La Hontan, vol. i. 105.

who then occupied the banks of the Detroit River. These tribes had been for a long time unfriendly to the French, and the English had exercised their policy to strengthen the friendship of the Foxes for their own cause, by frequent messages and valuable presents. At that period, no permanent settlement had been made at Detroit, and, regarded as it was, by both nations, as a most valuable point, commanding a broad tract of country across the peninsula even to the Mississippi, and furnishing a direct channel of navigation to the whole country bordering the lower lakes, the establishment of a military post there was eagerly sought by both the English and French. We have seen that, in this matter, the latter, under La Motte Cadillac, anticipated their rival, although the measure was strongly opposed by the Iroquois, in the great council held at Montreal, where the claims to the country, and the wishes of the two rival nations were discussed, as well as their respective relations to the several Indian tribes. At this council, the Iroquois alleged that the country belonged to them, and that they had, before that time, prohibited the English from erecting a fort, or making an establishment at Detroit; nevertheless Cadillac persisted in his design, and succeeded.

At this time, the influence of France was unbounded over all the Indian nations and tribes in the valleys of the Mississippi and of the St. Lawrence, except the Iroquois, or Five Nations in the latter, and the "implacable Foxes" on the borders of Green Bay. The unrelenting hostility of the Iroquois confederacy to the French, had been such, that the greater portion of the country south of the great lakes and along the Ohio River, was imperfectly known for near forty years after the first exploration of the Mississippi. The English had always claimed jurisdiction over the Five Nations; and although the French had ever disputed the validity of the claim, yet the Treaty of Utrecht, even in referring to the "Five Nations subject to England," did not fix boundaries or limits to the country of the Iroquois. At the period of that treaty, the Five Nations, Senecas, Cayugas, Onondagas,

Oneidas, and Mohawks, received into their confederacy an addition of another nation. The Tuscaroras, once a formidable tribe, had been embroiled with the English in North Carolina, and their power having been weakened, and their tribe divided by British intrigue, the hostile party left their country, the western part of North Carolina, and joined their kindred in the western part of New York. They arrived there late in the summer of 1713, and having been welcomed by the confederates, they settled in the vicinity of Oneida Lake, and were adopted into the confederacy as the sixth nation. From this time the confederacy was known as the "Six Nations."[1]

The Ottagamies, or Fox Indians, who resided along the banks of the Detroit River, were of Iroquois descent, and, adhering to the English cause, soon made their power known, and severely felt, against the French settlements. Even the Ottawas, the fast friends of the French, were induced to attempt the destruction of Detroit, during the third year after it was founded. A number of Ottawa chiefs had visited Albany on an invitation from the English, by whom they were persuaded that the French settlements on the Lakes were designed to wrest the dominion of the country from their hands; and on their return home, acting on this conviction, they set fire to the town. Fortunately, the fire was extinguished before any serious injury was done.[2] About the same time another party of Ottawas, returning from a successful war expedition against the Iroquois, paraded themselves in front of the fort, and endeavoured to induce the other Indians to join in its demolition. Tonti was then the French commandant, and the Sieur de Vincennes was despatched for the purpose of dispersing the hostile bands. He succeeded in defeating and putting them to flight. In their hasty retreat the Ottawas abandoned their Iroquois prisoners, whom they had previously captured, and these were sent back, by the French, to the Iroquois tribes.[3]

---

[1] Bancroft, vol. iii. 322. [2] Cass's Discourse.
[3] Lanman, p. 42.

It was in May, 1712, that the Ottagamies, or Foxes, in secret alliance with the Iroquois, planned the destruction of Detroit, and laid siege to the place. They were doubtless induced to do this by the Five Nations, backed by the English, who wished to destroy this post and erect a fort of their own on its ruins.[1] Du Buisson, the French commandant, called in the aid of the friendly Indian tribes, who promptly came to his rescue. After the arrival of the Pottawatamies, the Ottawas, and the Hurons, the Ottagamies retreated to the eastern boundary of Detroit, where they intrenched themselves within their camp. The French erected a block-house which commanded their position. Here they were attacked with great vigour, and cut off from all supply of water by a constant fire from the French and their Indian allies. Driven to despair by thirst and famine, the Ottagamies rushed from their besieged camp, and succeeded in getting possession of a house near the fort, which they fortified; hence they attacked the French, were again dislodged by the cannon, and driven back to their former intrenchment. Finding their efforts to undermine the French post likely to be unsuccessful, the Foxes sent a deputation to the French commandant, with pacific overtures, in which no confidence was placed, and their offer of capitulation was rejected. Enraged and indignant at what they deemed an insult, and under the influence of a determined and desperate revenge, the Ottagamies discharged showers of blazing arrows upon the fort; the lighted matches which had been affixed to the arrows, coming in contact with many of the roofs of the houses, which were thatched with straw, kindled them into flame, until the precaution was taken to cover the rest with wet skins; by that means they were preserved.[2]

Almost discouraged by the desperation of the Foxes, Monsieur Du Buisson had nearly determined to evacuate the post and retire to Michillimackinac, but was dissuaded from that act by his friendly Indians, who promised redoubled efforts to

---

[1] Lanman, p. 43. [2] Idem, p. 45. Charlevoix, tom. iv. 95.

dislodge the Foxes. The war-song and war-dance being finished, the onset upon the Foxes was recommenced with increased fury; it was successful; the intrenchments were soon heaped with the dying and the dead. A capitulation was again offered, but the Foxes had previously retreated into that portion of the peninsula of Michigan which advances into Lake St. Clair, where they intrenched themselves. This abandonment was made at night, during a storm, without discovery, and on the nineteenth day of the siege.

As soon as their escape was known, they were pursued by the French and their allies, and their camp was attacked. In the first action the Foxes gained considerable advantage, and repulsed the French and Indians, who had attacked them without sufficient precaution and judgment. Other methods were adopted to dislodge them; the French occupied four days for that purpose; a field battery was erected, and the intrenchment of the Foxes fell, battered down by the French cannon, on the fifth day of the siege. Entering the works in arms, the Foxes surrendered at discretion, and the allies and French commenced a deadly slaughter upon the Foxes, destroyed all of their warriors who bore arms, while the rest, about one hundred and fifty, besides the women and children, whose lives they spared, were divided as slaves among the French confederates; but they did not keep them as such any length of time, for they were all massacred before they separated. The loss of the allies amounted to sixty men killed and wounded; the Hurons, among whom were twenty-five Iroquois Christians, distinguished themselves more than the others, and lost more men. But this expedition cost the Ottagamies more than two thousand of their tribe.[1]

The Foxes, more enraged than enfeebled by their great loss thus sustained in their ineffectual attempt to destroy Detroit, collected their scattered bands on the Fox River of Green Bay; this was their natural country, and they filled it with

---

[1] Lanman, p. 45. Cass's Discourse. Charlevoix, tom. iv. p. 94–105. Doc. Hist., Dubuisson's Account.

butcheries, and robberies, of all travellers on the routes from the Lakes to the Mississippi, thereby cutting off all safe communication between Canada and Louisiana. With the exception of the Sioux, who were often associated with them, and the Iroquois, with whom they were allied, all the nations who were on friendly and commercial terms with the French, suffered greatly by their devastations; and it was feared that if a speedy remedy was not taken, the greater number of the Indian tribes would become reconciled with the Foxes, to the prejudice of the French.[1]

This consideration induced the Marquis de Vaudreuil, then the Governor of Canada, in 1714, to propose a union of the tribes with the French, in an expedition to exterminate the common enemy. The consent of the Indians having been obtained, a party of French was raised, and the command given to Monsieur de Louvigny. A number of savages joined him on his route, and he soon found himself at the head of eight hundred men, all resolved not to lay down their arms while an Ottagamie remained in Canada. Every one believed that the Fox nation was about to be destroyed, and so they themselves judged, when they saw the storm gathering against them; they therefore determined to sell their lives as dear as possible.[2]

The Foxes had selected a stronghold on the Fox River, now known as the "Butte des Morts," or Hill of the Dead; here, more than five hundred warriors and three thousand women had shut themselves up in a sort of fort, surrounded by three ranges of oak palisades, with a ditch in the rear. Three hundred men were on the route to reinforce them, but they did not arrive in time. De Louvigny, finding them thus strongly intrenched, attacked them in form; he had two field-pieces and a grenade mortar; the trenches were opened thirty-five toises from the fort, and on the third day he was only twelve toises distant, when the besieged made a great attack by firing on the French. De Louvigny was preparing to undermine

---

[1] Charlevoix, tom. iv. 155.

[2] Idem.

the works, when the Foxes proposed terms of capitulation, which were finally acceded to; a treaty of peace was to be made between the Foxes, and the French, and their Indian allies; all their prisoners were to be given up at once; the dead were to be replaced by slaves, which the Foxes were to obtain from the neighbouring nations with whom they were at war. The expenses of the war were to be paid from the products of the chase, by the Foxes, and their country was to be ceded to the French. Six hostages, chiefs or sons of chiefs, were delivered to De Louvigny, to insure the sending of deputies to Montreal, to perfect the treaty with the governor-general, according to these terms; three of these hostages afterward, in 1716, died at Montreal of the small pox; and De Vaudreuil, fearful that the treacherous Ottagamies would not carry the whole terms of the treaty into effect, sent De Louvigny to Michillimackinac, with orders to have the treaty fully executed, and to bring back with him the chiefs of that nation to Montreal.

In May, 1717, De Louvigny arrived at Michillimackinac with one of the hostages, who had been attacked with the small pox, as the others, and had lost an eye by it. As soon as he arrived, De Louvigny sent this chief to the Ottagamies, with presents to cover the dead, and accompanied by two French interpreters. They were well received, the calumet was smoked, and after some days spent in grieving for the dead, the chiefs met to listen to the hostage. He represented all matters in a proper manner, and reproached the chiefs for not having repaired to Michillimackinac.[1]

The chiefs said, they were sensible of the kindness which Ononthio[2] continued to show them; excused themselves for not having already sent deputies in regard to fulfilling the treaty; and promised to comply with their word the following year, giving this promise in writing, and adding that they would never forget that they held their lives as the gift of their great father. The hostage came away with the inter-

[1] Charlevoix, tom. iv. 157, 158.

[2] The governor-general was so called by all the tribes.

preters, to rejoin De Louvigny at Michillimackinac; but after traveling about twenty leagues, he left them, saying it was necessary he should return to oblige his nation to keep their word.

Nothing further was heard of him; the Foxes did not send deputies to the governor-general; and although he flattered himself for a long time that they would do so, he was only taught by the renewal of their old courses by the Ottagamies, that an enemy driven to a certain point is always irreconcilable.[1] It is true that their pride was greatly humbled, and that in a few years afterward they abandoned their old homes, and retired to the western side of the Mississippi; but in the mean while many battles were fought with them, while they, on their own part, had obliged the Illinois to abandon their river for ever; although, after repeated defeats, it could scarcely be conceived that there remained enough of the Foxes to form a trifling village, yet no one ventured to go from Canada to Louisiana, without taking great precaution against their surprises. "The engagements in which they were defeated at Butte des Morts and on the Wisconsin River, and finally driven beyond the Mississippi, in 1746, left the entire country in possession of the French and their allies, the Chippewas, Menomonies, Winnebagoes, and Pottawatamies.[2]

A second expedition was fitted out against these implacable Foxes, in 1728, by the Marquis de Beauharnois, then governor-general, which, although numerous and well equipped, resulted in nothing more than the destruction of the villages and plantations of the tribe, from Green Bay to the head of the Fox River; the Indians having retired in time, before the approach of an overwhelming force, which, strange to say, had serious expectations of taking them by surprise.

The force was placed under the command of Monsieur de Lignerie, and consisted of four hundred Frenchmen, to whom were joined between eight and nine hundred Indians, princi-

---

[1] Charlevoix, tom. iv. 159. [2] Martin's Hist. Disc. 1851.

pally Iroquois, Hurons, Nipissings, and Ottawas. They commenced their march on the 5th of June, 1728, and ascended the Ottawa River, thence descended a river to Lake Nipissing, and passing over the lake, descended by French River to Lake Huron. Hence the army proceeded to Michillimackinac, which place they left on the 10th of August, and crossing Lake Michigan, ascended Green Bay on the western coast, and arrived at the mouth of Fox River, where the French then had a garrisoned fort. The village of the Saukies, on the eastern side of the Fox River, had been abandoned, as might have been expected, notwithstanding (as the relator of the expedition *naively* says) "the precautions that had been taken to conceal our arrival." As the expedition proceeded up the river, they found all the villages deserted, and were obliged to content themselves with burning wigwams, destroying fields of Indian corn, and burning at a slow fire one old Indian captive. Having passed Lake Winnebago, they ascended the river to the last stronghold of the enemy, "situate on the borders of a small river which empties into another called the Ouisconsin, and found no person there." Here, after destroying the fields of corn, the expedition terminated, and the troops returned to Montreal.[1]

Although at this period no agricultural settlements of any extent had been made north of the Illinois River, and west of Lake Michigan, yet the country below the mouth of the Illinois continued steadily to improve. As early as the year 1705, traders and hunters had penetrated the fertile regions of the Wabash, and from this region, at this early date, fifteen thousand hides and skins had been collected and sent to Mobile, for the European market. In the year 1716, the French population on the Wabash had become sufficiently numerous to constitute an important settlement, which kept up a lucrative trade with Mobile, by means of traders and voyageurs.[2] The Ohio River was comparatively unknown, as all that portion of it below the mouth of the Wabash was designated as a continua-

---

[1] Note G.

[2] Martin's Louisiana, vol. i. 168.

tion of the latter river. In 1746, agriculture on the Wabash was still flourishing, and the same year, six hundred barrels of flour were manufactured and shipped to the city of New Orleans, besides large quantities of hides, peltry, tallow, and bees' wax.[1] In the Illinois country, also, the settlements continued to increase, so that, in 1730, they embraced one hundred and forty French families, besides about six hundred converted Indians, many traders, *voyageurs*, and *couriers du bois*. In 1751, the "Illinois country," east of the Upper Mississippi, contained six distinct settlements, with their respective villages. These were: 1. Cahokia, near the mouth of Cahokia Creek, and nearly five miles below the present site of St. Louis; 2. St. Philip, forty-five miles below the last, and four miles above Fort Chartres on the east side of the Mississippi; 3. Fort Chartres, on the east bank of the Mississippi, twelve miles above Kaskaskia; 4. Kaskaskia, situated upon the Kaskaskia River, five miles above its mouth, upon a peninsula, and within two miles of the Mississippi River; 5. Prairie du Rocher, near Fort Chartres; 6. St. Genevieve, on the west side of the Mississippi, and about one mile from its bank, upon Gabarre Creek. These are among the oldest towns in what was long known as the "Illinois country." Kaskaskia, in its best days under the French regimen, was quite a large town, containing two or three thousand inhabitants. But after it passed from the crown of France, its population for many years did not exceed fifteen hundred souls. Under British dominion, the population, in 1773, had decreased to four hundred and sixty souls.[2]

A different picture from this prosperity was presented in the instance of the French settlement among the Natchez, on the banks of the Lower Mississippi. The nation of the Natchez is now extinct; their very language is at this day a matter of vague conjecture. Their villages were planted in the midst of the most fertile climes of the South-west, and each was distinguished by its sacred building, serving as a recep-

---

[1] Martin's Louisiana, vol. i. 316. [2] Monette, vol. i. 167.

tacle for the dead. In this temple were gathered the fetiches of the tribe, surrounded by the bones of the dead; and there an undying fire was kept burning by appointed guardians, as if to warm, and light, and cheer the departed. The nation was divided into nobles and plebeians, and the grand chief of the tribe could trace his descent with certainty from the nobles, and was revered as of the family of the sun. The inheritance of sovereignty was transmitted exclusively by the female line, and the power of the grand chieftain was nearly despotic. The race of nobles was so distinct, that usage had moulded language into forms of reverence. In other respects their manners hardly differed from those of northern tribes, except as they were modified by climate.[1]

The French who were cantoned among the Natchez coveted their soil, and their commander, Chopart, with brutal avarice, demanded, as a plantation, the very site of their principal village. The Natchez took counsel of their friends, the Chickasas, and a portion of the Choctas, and a general massacre of the intruders was concerted. On the morning of the 28th of November, 1729, the work of blood began, and before noon, nearly every Frenchman in the colony was murdered. The Great Sun, taking his seat under the storehouse of the company, smoked the calumet in complacency, while the head of Chopart was laid at his feet. One after another, the heads of the principal officers at the post were ranged in order around it, while their bodies were left abroad to be a prey to dogs and buzzards.[2]

The news spread dismay in New Orleans, each house was supplied with arms, and the city was fortified by a ditch. Danger appeared on every side, and the negroes, of whom the number was about two thousand, half as large as the number of the French, showed symptoms of revolt. The brave and enterprising Le Sueur repaired to the Choctas, won them to his aid, and was followed across the country by seven hundred

---

[1] Bancroft, vol. iii. 359.

[2] Idem.

of their warriors; the French forces were assembled on the river, and placed under the command of Loubois.

Le Sueur was the first to arrive in the vicinity of the Natchez, who, not expecting an attack, were celebrating festivities gladdened by the spoils of the French. Exulting in their success, they gave themselves up to sleep, and on the morning of the 29th of January, 1730, the Choctas attacked their villages, liberated their captives, and losing only two of their own men, brought off sixty scalps, with eighteen prisoners.[1]

On the 8th of February, 1730, Loubois arrived and completed the victory. Some of the Natchez fled to the neighbouring tribes for shelter; the remainder of the nation crossed the Mississippi to the vicinity of the Natchitoches. They were pursued, and, partly by stratagem, partly by force, their place of refuge was taken. Some fled still further to the west, and of the scattered remnants, some remained with the Chickasas, others found a shelter among the Muskhogees. The Great Sun, and more than four hundred prisoners, were shipped to Hispaniola and sold as slaves.

Thus perished the nation of the Natchez. Their peculiar language—which has been still preserved by the descendants of the fugitives, and is, perhaps, now on the point of expiring—their worship, their division into nobles and plebeians, their bloody funeral rites—invite conjecture, and yet, so nearly resemble in character the distinctions of other tribes, that they do but irritate without satisfying curiosity.[2]

The "Company of the Indies" having found that the cost of defending Louisiana greatly exceeded the returns from its commerce, and from the grants of land, sought wealth by conquest or traffic on the coast of Guinea and Hindostan, and solicited leave to surrender the Mississippi wilderness. Accordingly, on the 10th of April, 1732, the jurisdiction and control over its commerce reverted to the crown of France. The company had held possession of Louisiana for fourteen years, which were its only years of comparative prosperity.

---

[1] Bancroft, vol. i. 363. [2] Idem.

The early extravagant hopes had not subsided till emigrants had reached its soil, and the emigrants, being once established, took care of themselves. In 1735, Bienville reappeared to assume the command for the king.[1]

To secure the eastern valley of the Mississippi, and protect the connection between the Illinois country and New Orleans, it became necessary to reduce the Chickasas, who had ever been the dreaded enemies of France. This nation had excited the Natchez to bloodshed and destruction; they maintained their savage independence, and no settlements on the eastern bank of the Mississippi were safe from their depredations. Resolute in their hatred, they had even endeavoured to debauch the affections of the Illinois, and to extirpate French dominion from the West; but were frustrated in their attempts through the exertions of the young and chivalrous D'Artaguette, who held the command in the Illinois country, and had convened the tribes at Fort Chartres in 1736.

Bienville summoned the whole force of the colony at the south, with D'Artaguette and the troops under his command in Illinois, and probably from the Wabash, to meet on the 10th of May, 1736, in the land of the Chickasas. The friendly chiefs, with "Chicago" at their head, had, through the instrumentality of D'Artaguette, descended the Mississippi to New Orleans, and presented the pipe of peace and friendship to the governor. "This" said Chicago to Monsieur Perrier, as he concluded an alliance offensive and defensive, "this is the pipe of peace or war. You have but to speak, and our braves will strike the nations that are your foes."[2] Chicago was the Illinois chief from the shore of Lake Michigan whose monument was reared, a century afterward, upon the site of his village, and whose name is perpetuated in the most flourishing city of Illinois.[3]

In the mean time, the Choctas, lured by the gifts of merchandise and high rewards for every scalp, gathered at fort Tombecbee to aid Bienville. Of these red auxiliaries the number

---

[1] Bancroft, vol. i. 364. [2] Idem. [3] Monette vol. i. 286.

was about twelve hundred, and the whole party—French and Indians—arrived and encamped, on the evening of the 25th of May, at a distance of a league from the great village of the Chickasas. In the morning, before day, they advanced to surprise the enemy. In vain—the brave warriors were on the watch, and their intrenchments were strong. English flags waved over their fort, and English traders had assisted in preparing their defence. The French made two attempts during the day to storm the log citadel, and were each time repulsed, with a loss of thirty killed, of whom four were officers. The next day, skirmishes occurred between the Chickasas and Choctas; on the 29th, the final retreat began; on the 31st of May, Bienville dismissed the Choctas, having satisfied them with presents, and throwing his cannon into the Tombecbee, his party ingloriously floated down the river. In the last days of June he landed on the banks of the Bayou St. John.[1]

But where was D'Artaguette, the brave commander in the Illinois, the pride of the flower of Canada? And where was the gallant Vincennes, whose name, in honour of the founder of a state, is borne by the oldest settlement of Indiana?[2]

The young Artaguette had already gained glory in the war against the Natchez, and had been advanced to the command in Illinois; he obeyed the summons of Bienville, and with an army of about fifty French soldiers and more than a thousand red men, accompanied by Father Senat, and by the Canadian Vincennes as his lieutenant, the careful hero stole cautiously and unobserved into the country of the Chickasas, and on the 9th of May, the evening before the appointed time, arrived at the place of rendezvous among the sources of the Yalabusha. Here he encamped, and waited in vain for ten days afterward for the arrival of the army from below. His impatient allies threatened desertion, and he at length consented to an attack. His measures were wisely taken; one fort was carried, and the Chickasas driven from the cabins which it protected; at the second, the intrepid youth was equally successful; on

[1] Bancroft, vol. i. 366.

[2] Idem. Lett. ed. vol. iv. 291.

attacking the third fort he received one wound, and then another, and in the moment of victory was disabled. The red men from Illinois, dismayed at the check, fled precipitately. Voisin, a lad of but sixteen years old, conducted the retreat, having the enemy at his heels for five-and-twenty leagues, marching forty-five leagues without food, while his men carried with them such of the wounded as could bear the fatigue. The unhappy D'Artaguette lay weltering in his blood, and by his side fell others of his bravest troops. The Jesuit Senat might have fled; he remained to receive the last sigh of the wounded, regardless of danger, mindful only of duty. Vincennes, too, the Canadian, refused to fly, and shared the captivity of his gallant leader. After the Indian custom, their wounds were stanched; they were received into the cabins of the Chickasas and feasted bountifully. At last, when Bienville had retreated, the Chickasas brought the captives into the field; and while one was spared to relate the deed, the adventurous D'Artaguette—the faithful Senat, true to his mission—Vincennes, whose name will be perpetuated as long as the Wabash shall flow by the dwellings of civilized man—these, with the rest of the captives, were bound to the stake; and neither valour nor pity could save them from death by slow torments and fire. Such is the early history of Mississippi.[1]

Although peace was sued for by the Chickasas, and granted in 1740, yet the communication between the lower country and the Illinois was still interrupted, as the Chickasas remained the undoubted lords of their territory, and in all the expanse of country claimed by France, her jurisdiction was little more than a name. For more than half a century after the first attempt at colonization by La Salle, the valley of the Mississippi was still a wilderness. Its whole population may have been five thousand whites, and half that number of blacks. Its fortunes had been fostered by the liberal expenditures of two monarchs—Louis XIV. and XV.; the opulence of Crozat had been employed to bring into effect its mer-

[1] Bancroft, vol. iii. 367, and authorities there cited.

cantile resources; the Company of the Mississippi, aided by an almost boundless but transient credit, had made it the foundation of their hopes; priests and friars, dispersed through nations from Biloxi to the Dahcotas, propitiated the favour of the savages; yet, all its patrons had not accomplished for it, in half a century, a tithe of the prosperity which, within the same period, sprung naturally from the benevolence of William Penn, to the peaceful settlers on the Delaware.[1]

From the earliest advent of the Jesuit fathers, up to the middle of the eighteenth century, the great ambition of the French was, not only to preserve the possession of all important points in the North-west and West, but also to prevent, in every possible manner, the slightest attempt on part of the English, in the extension of their settlements toward the waters of the Mississippi. "France was resolved on possessing the great territory which her missionaries had revealed to the world;" and French commanders had avowed the purpose of seizing every Englishman within the Ohio Valley.[2] The colonies of Virginia, Pennsylvania, and New York were the most affected by the vast encroachments of France, in the extension of her dominions in America, and particularly in the great plan of uniting Canada with Louisiana; for this purpose possession had been taken of a tract of country claimed by Virginia, and a line of posts had been commenced by the French, extending from the lakes to the Ohio. New York offered no resistance to their progress, and even declined assisting to repel the French from a post which lay within the proprietary domain of Pennsylvania.[3] This state, by her legislature, was at strife with her proprietaries, and refused to grant money or raise troops to repel invasion, although the French were preparing to take possession of all that part of her territory which lay west of the Alleghanies. Virginia was not only alive to her own interests, but attentive to the vast importance of an immediate and effectual resistance on

---

[1] Bancroft, vol. iii. 369.
[2] Bancroft, vol. iv. 111.
[3] Smith's New York, vol. ii. 173.

the part of all the English colonists, to the actual and contemplated encroachments of the French.

In 1753, Governor Dinwiddie, of Virginia, resolved to send "a person of distinction to the commander of the French forces on the Ohio River, to know his reasons for invading the British dominions, while a solid peace subsisted." The envoy he selected was George Washington, a young man then just twenty-one, a pupil of the wilderness, and as heroic as La Salle.[1] Surmounting all the difficulties of a winter journey over mountains and through forests, Mr. Washington met the French commander, Gardeur de St. Pierre, on the head-waters of the Alleghany River, and having imparted to him the object of his journey, received for answer, that the French would not discuss a matter of right, but would conform to instructions, part of which was to make prisoner of every Englishman found trading on the Ohio, or the waters of it; that the country belonged to the French, in virtue of the discoveries of La Salle, and that they would not withdraw from it.[2] In January, 1754, Mr. Washington returned to Virginia and made his report, which was followed by immediate activity; forces were raised, and Washington, with the rank of lieutenant-colonel, was despatched, at the head of one hundred and fifty men, to the forks of the Ohio, "to finish the fort already begun there by the Ohio Company, and to make prisoners, kill, or destroy all who interrupted the English settlements."

On his route through the forests of Western Pennsylvania, Washington received information from friendly Indians, that the French forces were within a short distance of his camp; in conjunction with his Mingo friends, the lodgment of the French, concealed among the rocks, was discovered by Washington, and as they ran to seize their arms, the order was given to fire, and with his own musket he gave the example. "That word of command kindled the world into a flame. It was the signal for the first great war of the revolution."

[1] Bancroft, vol. iv. 108. [2] Washington's Report.

There, in the Western forest, began the battle which was to banish from the soil and neighbourhood of our republic the institutions of the middle age, and to inflict on them fatal wounds throughout the continent of Europe. In repelling France from the basin of the Ohio, Washington broke the repose of mankind, and waked a struggle which could admit only of a truce, till the ancient bulwarks of Catholic legitimacy were thrown down.[1]

An action of about a quarter of an hour ensued. Ten of the French were killed—among them Jumonville, the commander of the party—and twenty-one were made prisoners. The dead were scalped by the Indians, and the chieftain Monacawache bore a scalp, and a hatchet, to each of the tribes of the Miamis, inviting their great war-chiefs and braves to go hand in hand with the Six Nations and the English.

But the numbers of the French were constantly increasing; and Washington, after looking in vain for succour and relief from six colonies, to whom appeals had been made, was compelled to fall back upon Fort Necessity, a rude stockade at the Great Meadows. Here he commenced the work of strengthening his fortification; but, before it was completed, he was attacked on the 3d of July, by Monsieur de Villiers, with about six hundred French, and one hundred Indians. After losing thirty of his men, and being in every respect vastly inferior to the French in discipline, numbers, and position, Washington accepted honourable terms of capitulation, and on the *fourth of July* the English garrison withdrew from the basin of the Ohio. Thus, in 1754, in the whole valley of the Mississippi, to its head springs in the Alleghanies, no standard floated but that of France.[2]

It had ever been the policy of the French, in all their intercourse with the Indian nations, to represent the English as invaders of their country, covetous of their lands, and under the colour of trading with them for their furs, grasping at dominion, while they professed and offered friendship and protection.

---

[1] Bancroft. [2] Idem. vol. iv. 118, 121; Marshall's Wash. vol. i. 5.

The establishment of religious missions, and even the erection of posts of defence by the French, in early days, did not so much alarm the Indian tribes as the encroachments of the cultivator, whose "every step was viewed with jealousy and hate." Every inroad on their hunting-grounds was an aggression and an insult; and although the intention of the French, from the earliest times, was undoubtedly that of colonization, yet their approaches to that object were so much retarded by adventitious circumstances, and apparently restricted to the Jesuit missions in the North-west, that the suspicions of the Indian were not awakened, nor his fears aroused, until he found himself surrounded by white people of different nations, at war with each other, each claiming rights of trade, rights of occupancy, and each holding armed possession of territory which the red man knew to be his own, because it had been the land and the home of his ancestors. The almost unbounded influence of the French over the Indian nations of the basins of Mississippi, the Ohio, and the St. Lawrence, had, hitherto, in a great measure, veiled from their eyes the ultimate design which they entertained of occupying their whole country as a colony: and even the erection of a line of military posts, from Canada to Louisiana, by the French, was regarded by the Indians more as a necessary protection against common enemies, and as proper points of trade and commerce beneficial to themselves, than as strongholds of a power that might one day subjugate their country and drive them as exiles from it. The French contented themselves with an armed, and forted occupancy of the whole West, thereby lulling Indian jealousy under specious pretences; while the English, indefatigably, although slowly, were pushing their settlements farther and farther into the Indian country, thereby confirming every suspicion which had been instilled into the minds of the natives, that they were about to be deprived of their hunting-grounds and their homes.

In 1754, France and England were professedly at peace at home, but the seeds of war had been left in America ever since the peace of Utrecht, and they were now ripening. The attack of Washington upon Jumonville had been denounced in France as an *assassination*, and the use of this word in the capitulation at the Great Meadows was regarded as an acknowledgment, on the part of Washington, that his attack on Jumonville was unjustifiable. But this aspersion on his character, by European writers has been fully answered by all correct authority, and the *mistranslation* of the word *assassination*, to him, when signing the terms of capitulation, would be a sufficient refutation of the slander, in the absence of any other.[1] France saw fit to regard this attack as the commencement of the war, although each party still professed peaceful intentions; and negotiations were still carried on, while each power was making the most vigorous preparations for the conflict which was evidently approaching.

Great Britain insisted that the West of North America must be left as it was at the treaty of Utrecht; France answered, that the old English claims in America were untenable, and offered a new ground of compromise, namely, that the English should retire east of the Alleghanies, and the French west of the Ohio. This offer, after long consideration, was agreed to in March, 1755, provided the French would destroy all their forts on the Ohio and its branches. To which, after twenty days had passed, France answered, "No."[2]

In the mean while, the fleets and the armies of both powers were crossing the Atlantic, and the north and the west of the American colonial settlements were designated as the theatres of the coming contests, and war was formally declared in May, 1756. The signal and unfortunate defeat of General Braddock, near Fort Du Quesne, on the banks of the Monongahela, occurred on the 9th of July, 1755, and from that period to the victory of General Wolfe, at Quebec, on the 13th of September, 1759, various engagements had taken place between the English and French, and their Indian allies, with various fortunes. At length, on the 8th of September, 1760, Ticonderoga,

---

[1] Marshall's Wash., vol. i. 6, and Note.

[2] Secret Journals, vol. iv. 74.

Crown Point, Niagara, and Quebec itself, having previously fallen, Montreal, Detroit, and all Canada were given up to the English, by Vaudreuil de Cavagnal, the French governor. The principal posts on the Ohio were in possession of the English at this time, and, notwithstanding the success of their arms, and their occupation of the former strongholds of the French in the North-west, the inimical feelings of the Indian tribes were yet unallayed. Distrust of the British was general, and disaffection spread rapidly in the West, no doubt fostered and increased by the Canadians and the French.

Although this war had been chiefly carried on east and south of the great lakes, detachments of the French had occasionally been levied from Detroit, Green Bay, and Michillimackinac, to oppose the advances of the English toward the Lakes.[1] A few days after the capitulation of Montreal, General Amherst despatched Major Robert Rogers, a brave and energetic officer, with a proper force, to take possession of the posts at Detroit, Michillimackinac, and others in that district. Major Rogers arrived with his detachment at the mouth of the Chogage River, on the 7th of November, 1760; here he was met by a body of Ottawa messengers, who requested him to halt his forces until Pontiac, the king of the country he was in, and who was a little distance off, should come up.[2]

Pontiac was one of the most remarkable savages with whom we are acquainted in Indian history; he was the chief of the Ottawa tribe, claiming to be the oldest of the Indian nations in this quarter, and he was acknowledged to be the principal sachem and warrior of the Algonquin confederacy, exercising the power and influence of an emperor, by which name he was sometimes known.[3] Distinguished for his noble form, commanding address, and proud demeanour, he acquired the respect and confidence of all the Indians in this region. In point of native talent, courage, magnanimity, and integrity,

---

[1] Lanman's Michigan, p. 85. [2] Idem, p. 91.

[3] Thatcher, Ind. Biog., vol. ii. 84.

he will compare, without prejudice, with the most renowned of civilized potentates and conquerors. He was an avowed friend of the French, and an enemy to the English, and he combined all those traits of character which distinguish men among civilized states, whether in the forum or on the field. He was grasping in his projects, while he had sufficient dissimulation to conceal them; his courage was unconquerable; his pride was the pride of the proudest chief of the proudest nation on the earth; and as an orator he was more remarkable for pointedness and vigour than for burning eloquence. He had watched with jealousy the progress of the English arms, and had imbibed a hatred of the English, which had been handed down to his race. He had seen them pushing their conquests through his country, destroying his tribes, driving the game from his hunting-grounds, which had been bequeathed from his forefathers, and crimsoning his land with the blood of his friends and companions, the French. He had fought with with the French, at the head of his Indian allies, against the English, in 1746; he had been a conspicuous commander of the Indian forces in the defence of Fort Du Quesne, and took an active part in the memorable defeat of the British and Provincials, under Braddock, in 1755. His residence, in summer, was on Pechee Island, about eight miles above Detroit; and in winter, at the Ottawa village opposite, on the Canadian bank of Detroit River—the beautiful land of his fathers, held by them and himself under patent from the Great Spirit! but the possession of which was soon to pass from his hands.[1]

When Pontiac was informed that the first English detachment which had ever advanced into this quarter was on its march toward Detroit, "he aroused like a lion attacked in his den." He instantly sent his messengers to Major Rogers, to arrest his onward progress. When Pontiac and Rogers met, the savage chieftain asked, "How have you dared to enter my country without my leave?" "I come," replied the Eng-

---

[1] Lanman, p. 90. Monette, vol. i. 326.

lish agent, "with no design against the Indians, but to remove the French out of your country;" and he gave the wampum of peace. But Pontiac told him he should "stand in his path" until the next morning, and at the same time presented him with a *small string* of wampum, indicating that he must not advance farther without his leave. On departing, Pontiac asked Rogers if he wanted any thing that his country contained; and if so, his warriors should bring it. He was answered, that any thing which was furnished by the Indians, should be purchased. The next day, the chief sent presents of parched corn, and, a council having been held, Pontiac appeared at the English camp, and stated that he had made peace with the English detachment, and, as a pledge, Major Rogers and Pontiac, by turns, smoked the calumet. He informed Rogers that he would protect his party from the assaults of the Indians, who were collected at the mouth of Detroit River to oppose his progress, and gave him an escort of warriors to assist in driving his herd of oxen along the shore; he sent to the Indian villages on the north and west end of Lake Erie, to inform them that the English had his consent to pass through the country; but he at the same time spoke as an independent prince, who would not brook the presence of white men within his dominions but at his pleasure.[1]

After some correspondence between Major Rogers and Monsieur Pign Bellestre, the French commandant of Detroit, in relation to the capitulation signed by De Vaudreuil and General Amherst, and the surrender of all Canada to Great Britain, the post of Detroit was given into the hands of Major Rogers, by Bellestre, on the 25th of November, 1760; and the British commander, having made a treaty with several tribes of Indians in the neighbouring country, advanced toward Lake Huron, for the purpose of taking possession also of Michillimackinac. The ice in the lake, however, obstructed his passage, and having been informed by the Indians that

[1] Rogers's Concise Account of North America, p. 240. Rogers's Journal, p. 214. Bancroft, vol. iv. 362. Lanman, p. 91.

he could not cross the country by land, without the use of snow-shoes, he returned to Detroit without accomplishing his object. Nevertheless, it may be considered that, from this period, the French power in this region was forever overthrown.[1]

In the spring of 1761, the year following the visit of Rogers, the English trader Alexander Henry went to Michillimackinac, for purposes of business, and he found everywhere the strongest feeling against the English, who had done nothing, by word or act, to conciliate the Indians. Even then, there were threats of reprisals and war. Although Henry had been advised and obliged to disguise himself in a Canadian dress, in order to reach Michillimackinac in safety, as a Frenchman, yet he was there discovered to be an Englishman, and was waited on by an Indian chief, who was (as has been with all probability conjectured) Pontiac himself.[2] Henry was told by the chief, that their French father would soon awake and utterly destroy his enemies, and continued: "Englishman! although you have conquered the French, you have not yet conquered us! We are not your slaves! These lakes, these woods, these mountains, were left to us by our ancestors. They are our inheritance, and we will part with them to none. Your nation supposes that we, like the white people, cannot live without bread, and pork, and beef. But you ought to know that He, the Great Spirit and Master of Life, has provided food for us upon these broad lakes, and in these mountains."

He then spoke of the fact that no treaty had been made with them, no presents sent them, and while he announced their intention to allow Henry to trade with them unmolested, and to regard him as a brother, he declared that with his king the red men were still at war.[3]

At the time the British took possession of the French forts in the West and North-west, and by the influx of traders and

---

[1] Rogers's Conc. Ac. of North Am., p. 240. Rogers's Jour., p. 214. Bancroft, vol. iv. 362. Lanman, p. 91. See Note H.

[2] Thatcher, Ind. Biog., vol. ii. 75.

[3] Henry's Travels in Canada.

the arrival of soldiers, had shown the savages that the influences and positions of their ancient friends, the French, were about to be encroached upon, and supplied in the country, by those of their enemies, the English: the language of the Indian chief to Mr. Henry was the expression of the general feeling among the tribes. They could with difficulty realize to themselves the fact of the existence of any power superior to that of the French, and were ever unwilling to submit to the dictation of any authority, or even to listen to the admonition or advice of any one, save that of the Governor-General of Canada, or Onontbio, as the French commandant was always called. The affection of the Indians to the French was deeply rooted, and to the present day, through the changes of time, the total loss of power, and the widely different positions in which the Indians stand in relation to the whites and their government, such affectionate attachment has never been in any great degree eradicated. The causes of this attachment may, perhaps, be found in the peaceful and religious character of the Jesuits, the early explorers; the comparative advantages derived by the Indians from the trade first established with them by the French; the absence of any *bold* attempts to wrest the country from the natives, for the purpose of colonization, during all their intercourse, however insidious the erection of fortresses among the tribes may have been in fact; for these places were also trading-posts and religious stations; and perhaps as a cause superior to all, has been the facility with which the adventurers adapted themselves to the social manners and customs of the Indians, and by the commingling of bloods creating the strong ties of nature between them, which even now continues. Although more than two centuries have passed away since a Frenchman first trod the land through which flows the Outagamie and the Wisconsin Rivers, yet there is not a tribe of the native inhabitants of that country among whom may not be found an individual with white blood in his veins: not only does this friendly feeling between the Indian and the descendant of the early French settlers still continue, but through all the changes in the country that time has wrought, the French language still, partially, holds its place. Although the Canadian dialect predominates among the French descendants, yet there is not wanting at this day, in portions of Wisconsin, instances where the pure Parisian language is spoken, and the courtly manner of a polite people preserved, notwithstanding all the changes that have occurred since the dominion of France over the Northwest was ceded to Great Britain. In the vicinity of Green Bay and Prairie-du-Chien, these instances may readily be found.[1]

Hitherto we have viewed the gradual, although tardy attempts at the settlement of the Lower Mississippi, and of the Illinois country, which, at best, was an armed occupation of fortified posts, religious establishments of zealous missionaries, the partial cultivation of small spots of ground for immediate sustenance, and the casual presence of the adventurous Indian trader. We have observed that in 1746, several hundred barrels of flour went from the Illinois country to New Orleans, and it appears from representations made to the British ministry in 1770, in regard to the former trade of this region, that convoys annually went down in December with the produce.[2] But up to the time when the British took possession of the West, it is believed, that within the boundaries of that district of country which is now properly known as "Wisconsin," there were few white inhabitants besides the roaming Indian trader; and of these few, the locations were separated by a distance of more than two hundred miles in a direct line, and nearly double that distance by the usual water route. There was no settlement of agriculturists, no missionary establishments, no fortified posts at other points than at Green Bay and Des Pères at the mouth of the Fox River, and at Prairie-du-Chien near the junction of the Wisconsin with the Mississippi. On the left bank of the Fox River, at the present site of Fort Howard, the French had built "Fort La Baye;" and five miles up the river, on the right bank, the Jesuit fathers had, nearly

[1] See Note I.

[2] Pownall's Memorial.

a century before, established the mission of St. Francis Xavier, now called, in honour of their labours, "Des Pères." Fort La Baye was a small post built for the protection of trade, and was surrounded by a stockade; in 1728, on the arrival of De Lignerie's forces destined for the destruction of the Outagamies, there was an officer and a garrison in Fort La Baye, and a village of Saukies on the opposite side of the river, where the village of Green Bay is now built. On the surrender of Canada and its dependencies to the English, it was immediately garrisoned by them with an officer and thirty men, but soon after the surprise and capture of Michillimackinac, this fort was also taken possession of by the Indians, and the British left this quarter of the country. On the east side of Fox River, the French settlers had some land in cultivation, and a few families lived in the fort. On the eastern side of Green Bay, near the Red banks, there are many indications of early cultivation, and from the fertility of the soil, (it being superior to that, at the mouth of the river,) and the locality being not more than ten miles from the fort, it is probable that this cultivation was the work of the settlers in this neighbourhood; but the whole matter remains in doubt and obscurity, in the absence of records or tradition.

About five miles from the mouth of the Wisconsin River, the Outagamies formerly had a large town in a pleasant situation on the right bank of the river; they had been induced, from a superstitious belief that the Great Spirit had so ordered them, to remove from their location, and to build a town on the banks of the Mississippi; this place was called by the French, "La Prairie-du-Chien," the Dog Plain; or perhaps more properly in the plural, "Les Prairies des Chiens," the Dogs' Prairies; as it has been stated by one of the French settlers,[1] that on his arrival there in 1781, he was informed that it derived its name from a large family called "Des Chiens," who formerly resided there, and that the descendants of the same family then resided at the same place, and were called "Des Chiens."

---

M. Brisbois. See Public Lands, vol. iv. 866.

The village on the Wisconsin River was in ruins when Carver visited the country in 1766, and he received the following account of the causes of the desertion of it by the Foxes :—"About thirty years ago, (1736,) the Great Spirit had appeared on the top of a pyramid of rocks, which lay at a little distance from the village, toward the West, and warned them to quit their habitations; for the land on which they were built belonged to him, and he had occasion for it. As a proof that he who gave them these orders, was really the Great Spirit, he further told them that the grass should immediately spring up on those very rocks from whence he now addressed them, which they knew to be bare and barren. The Indians obeyed, and soon after discovered that this miraculous alteration had taken place. They showed me the spot, but the growth of the grass appeared to be no ways supernatural. I apprehend this to have been a stratagem of the French or Spaniards to answer some selfish view; but in what manner they effected their purpose, I know not."[1]

When Carver was at the Dog Plains, he says there was a large town containing about three hundred families, the houses being well built after the Indian manner, pleasantly situated on a very rich soil, from which every necessary of life was raised in great abundance; many horses were there of good size and shape; the town was a great mart, where all the adjacent tribes and even those who inhabit the most remote branches of the Mississippi annually assemble about the latter end of May, bringing with them their furs to dispose of to the traders. But it is not always that they conclude their sale here; this is determined by a general council of the chiefs, who consult whether it would be more conducive to their interest, to sell their goods at this place, or carry them on to Louisiana, or Michillimackinac. According to the decision of this council, they either proceed farther or return to their different homes.[2]

It is difficult to ascertain with any certainty the time when

---

[1] Carver's Travels. [2] Idem.

the first settlement of the French took place at Prairie-du-Chien. It is said that in 1755, the government of France established a military post near the mouth of the Wisconsin, many French families settled themselves in the neighbourhood, and established the village.[1] But it is somewhat strange, that when Captain Carver was at this place in 1766, he found no white inhabitants; at least he does not speak of meeting with any, although he describes the large *Indian* town, and its commercial importance, as a point where the traders and the hunters of the tribes annually met to conduct their traffic in peltry. Surely, if the traveller had here met with a village inhabited by civilized men, he would have not only described the settlement, but have dilated with pleasure on the advance of colonization so far in this western region: his silence on this subject is almost conclusive proof that there were no white inhabitants at Prairie-du-Chien in 1766, or, at least, that the only whites then in this part of the country, were the industrious but wandering traders; but the following extract from his travels, in speaking of this town, will set the question at rest. He says, "A little farther to the west, on the contrary side (of the Mississippi,) a small river falls into the Mississippi which the French call La Jaune Riviere, or the Yellow River. Here the traders, who had accompanied me hitherto, took up their residence for the winter." Doubtless, the traders would not have crossed the river, to remain during the winter, if there had been a settlement of whites near the mouth of the Wisconsin.[2]

The hostility of the Ottagamies to the French, and their occupation of the Fox River from Green Bay to the Portage, was an insurmountable obstacle to the establishment of any trading-post between the mission of St. Francis Xavier and the mouth of the Wisconsin River; even the labours of the Jesuit fathers had not extended in this direction, since the time of Marquette; their attention having been wholly devoted to the missions in the country along the Illinois and the Lower

[1] Public Lands, vol. iii. 341.

[2] See Carver's Travels.

Mississippi. We have seen that nearly a century had passed since the discovery of the Great River, and yet the whole country north of the Illinois River, and west of Lake Michigan, had yet been unexplored; the vast extent of the prairies in this region may have caused the neglect of the Jesuit fathers to penetrate the interior country, and all its beauties, all its advantages in soil and production, remained unknown. We have faint glimpses of some little information, in regard to its being a mineral region, having been given to the reverend fathers and early traders; but not in any respect equal to the knowledge which they had of the rich mines around the shores of Lake Superior. But the absence of information touching the appearance, quality, and productions of the interior country, among the early explorers, can be accounted for, when we reflect that the native inhabitants had their dwellings along the banks of the large streams, and that the most practicable mode of travel through the land was by the aid of canoes, the water-courses furnishing both the highway and the means of supporting life.

Nevertheless, unexplored as was the interior, and although no religious establishment or occupied post afforded a welcome to adventurous traders, they had already been found in the Upper Mississippi country, crossing what is now Northern Wisconsin, from Lake Superior to the Falls of St. Anthony, and carrying back their furs to Green Bay, by means of the Wisconsin and Fox Rivers. This had been done for at least eighty years, as we hear of De Luth, the trader, in the journal of Hennepin; but the risk of the adventurers had ever been very great, however profitable may have been a result to justify so dangerous a hazard.

The "ever restless" Ottagamies and Saukies, as they are often termed, occupied the great thoroughfare of the traders, and their exactions and depredations upon them, had several times been visited with signal vengeance by the French, in expeditions sent against them. In 1706, Captain Morand's expedition was successful in surprising, capturing, and killing a great number of this united people: of this affair, Carver gives the following anecdote, as related to him by an Indian, in 1766.

"About sixty years ago, the French missionaries and traders having received many insults from these people, (the Sacs and Foxes) a party of French and Indians, under the command of Captain Morand, marched to revenge their wrongs. The captain set out from the Green Bay in the winter, when they were unsuspicious of a visit of this kind, and pursuing his route over the snow to their villages, which lay about fifty miles up the Fox River, came upon them by surprise. Unprepared as they were, he found them an easy conquest, and consequently killed, or took prisoners, the greatest part of them. On the return of the French to the Green Bay, one of the Indian chiefs in alliance with them, who had a considerable band of the prisoners under his care, stopped to drink at a brook; in the mean time his companions went on; which being observed by one of the women whom they had made captive, she suddenly seized him with both her hands, while he stooped to drink, by an exquisitely susceptible part, and held him fast till he expired on the spot. As the chief, from the extreme torture he suffered, was unable to call out to his friends, or to give any alarm, they passed on, without knowing what had happened; and the woman, having cut the bands of those of her fellow-prisoners who were in the rear, with them made her escape. This heroine was ever after treated by her nation as their deliverer, and made a chiefess in her own right, with liberty to entail the same honour on her descendants; an unusual distinction, and permitted only on extraordinary occasions."[1]

After the severe chastisement which the Foxes had received at the siege of Detroit in 1712, and which we have already noticed, they had retired to their stronghold on the Fox River. Against this post, the expedition of De Louvigny, in 1714, as has been seen, was successful, although no advantage was derived by the French by its capitulation. The fruitless march

[1] Carver's Travels.

of the large force of French and Indians, under de Lignerie, in 1728, is the last expedition of which we have any accurate account; and this account, as we have given it, was procured from the archives at Paris. Much information relative to the early history of this portion of New France and Louisiana, undoubtedly yet remains among those archives, which has never yet been given to the world; its production is certainly much to be desired.

In 1746, the northern tribes, under Mackinac, (the Turtle,) combined against the French at Detroit: these tribes are said to have been the Iroquois; it is not said that the Foxes were a party. Pontiac assisted the French, and, in 1763, he spoke of such aid as having been given by him, seventeen years before. There is no certain record of any expedition against the Foxes in 1746, and yet it is said that an engagement took place in that year, at the Great Butte des Mort, the old stronghold of the Foxes.[1] It is very probable that about this period, or at some time between 1728 and 1746, the Sacs and Foxes removed from their old dwelling-places along the Fox River, and went down the Wisconsin and Rock Rivers, and across the Mississippi, where they have ever since remained.

A traditionary account of the expedition against the Foxes was given by an aged French settler[2] at Prairie du Chien, a few years since, to this effect:

"A detachment of a considerable number of men, under the command of Monsieur Morand, was sent from Mackinac in a boat, in all respects resembling a traders' boat, which ascended the Fox River from Green Bay. The soldiers were concealed in the boat by a covering of skins, and they cautiously proceeded undiscovered, in this manner, up the river as far as the Great Butte des Morts, since so called, at which place was the great village of the Ottagamies. On their arrival here, the Foxes, as usual, appeared in full force on the banks of the river, in order to stop the boat, and exact from the supposed traders the customary payment of tribute.

---

[1] Martin's Hist. Disc.

[2] Michael Brisbois.

Capt. Morand had with him in the boat a swivel gun, well charged with canister and grape; the signal was given; the covering of the boat was immediately thrown off, and a volley from the concealed soldiers, together with a discharge from the swivel, did murderous execution on the thickly crowded Ottagamies. Scarcely had they time to recover from their first surprise, when a repetition of discharges from the musketry and the cannon nearly annihilated the whole tribe. It is believed that more than a thousand of their chiefs and braves, with women and children, fell at this time. Their burial subsequently has given to this spot the name of 'Le Butte des Morts,' the Hill of the Dead.[1]

"The expedition returned to Mackinac without loss, and the remainder of the band of Foxes soon after left this part of the country, and moved west of the Mississippi."

There is certainly a confusion of dates, or blending of incidents, in these accounts. One expedition is said to have been in the winter, by land; the other in the summer, by water, and both under Captain Morand. Carver's account, having been obtained in 1766, refers distinctly to the year 1706; the traditionary account of the water expedition must refer to a much later period, and the commander's name is inaccurately given. As to the great battle on the Fox River in 1746, there is no account of it, to which we can refer with any certainty; and with respect to the period and the cause of the building up of the Great Butte des Morts, we are altogether lost in uncertainty. It is worthy of remark that Carver, who was there in 1766, or in the immediate vicinity, does not mention it; and it is probable that if such mound was then there, it was an ancient mound, and the account that it was raised over the dead who had fallen in Morand's expedition, is incorrect; for Carver received his tradition of that expedition from an old Indian, and surely the remarkable circumstances respecting the great burial mound would not have been forgotten, if such facts existed, and the mound was then to be seen.

---

[1] See Note K.

Around Lake Superior there had hitherto been no attempts at settlement and cultivation, except at the immediate missionary establishments at the Sault de St. Marie, and at Chagouemegon; the few trading-posts, which were frequented at stated seasons, could not be looked upon as settlements. Although it is known that the early missionaries were well acquainted with the richness of that region in the production of copper, and that their letters speak not only of the vast mass of native copper found in the Ontonagon, but of numerous other places where the mineral was found in abundance; yet there is no evidence of any attempts having been made, to any extent, to turn these mineral discoveries to advantage. After the conquest of Canada by the English, a company of adventurers from England had undertaken to work these mines, but the distracted situation of American affairs obliged them to relinquish their scheme.[1] There is abundant evidence, at this day found in the copper region, of a working of these mines, at some far distant period, and by some unknown people, that excites our curiosity, without in any degree satisfying it. In some of the old mines have been found various matters indicating a knowledge of mining as pursued at the present day, and the possession of tools, the manufacture of which could not with much propriety be attributed to our present races of Indians. Stone hammers have been found in large quantities, (equal to ten cartloads;) they are made of green stone, or porphyry pebble, with single and double grooves, by which a withe was attached; such are not uncommon in other parts of the country; but a copper gad, with the head much battered, a copper chisel, with a socket for the handle, a copper knife, fragments of a wooden bowl to dip water, numerous levers of wood, used in raising the mass of copper to the surface; all denoting work performed by a people of whom there exists neither record nor tradition. Remnants of charcoal have been found in many places, and pits have been explored, which had formerly been sunk some fourteen feet

---

[1] Carver's Travels; Henry's Travels.

deep, following the course of copper veins; these pits have been discovered in extending continuous lines—at one place twelve miles, and at another, thirty miles; and upon a mound of earth, thrown out of one of them, grew a pine tree, ten feet in circumference; the annular growths of a hemlock, which was cut down, (growing on a mound, under similar circumstances,) counted three hundred and ninety-five years. A pit on Isle Royale, which had been filled up with surrounding earth, was opened; the old mine had been worked through solid rock nine feet, the walls being perfectly smooth; at the bottom was found a vein of native copper eighteen inches thick, including a sheet of pure copper lying against the foot-wall.[1]

It is well known, that copper rings, designed for bracelets, are frequently met with in the Western mounds. Are not these copper rings a strong link in the chain of evidence to connect the ancient mining of the Lake Superior region, with the earth-works of the Mississippi Valley? Who were the nations that peopled these regions? Whence did they come? How have they passed awáy, and left in the bosom of their mother Earth the only traces of their existence?—are questions that time and research have not yet solved, and we must be content to leave them in the mystery with which they are enveloped.

---

[1] Foster and Whitney's Report, 1850, passim.

# CHAPTER III.

## UNDER BRITISH DOMINION.

Treaty of 1763—England possesses all New France and Louisiana—Protection of eminent domain—Carver's Grant—Illinois and Wabash Companies—Classes of grants in the Territory of Michigan, and in Wisconsin—De Vaudreuil's Grant—French inhabitants under English rule—Indians unfriendly to the English—Pontiac's designs—His great confederacy—Calls a grand council, and states his plans to them—Unexpected attacks on the British posts—Black rain at Detroit—Surprise and capture of Michillimackinac—Henry's personal account of it—Fort at Green Bay abandoned—Fort at St. Joseph's captured—Situation of Detroit—Stratagem of Pontiac—Discovered and prevented—Siege of Detroit—Barbarities of the Indians—Reinforcements arrive—Captain Dalyell's sortie, defeat, and death—Siege abandoned by the Indians—Arrival of General Bradstreet—Concludes a peace with the Indian tribes—Pontiac does not consent—His death—His character—Absence of settlements in Wisconsin—Captain Carver's intentions and attempts—His travels and remarks—No Europeans on the Upper Mississippi, as settlers, in 1766—Evidence as to Carver's Grant—The Illinois country—Peaceable settlements of the French—Their mode of life—Their villages and general regulations of property—Tranquillity and happiness—Their religion—Changes under British rule—Settlements decline—Emigration to Spanish Louisiana—Population of the Illinois country—British occupy the forts—Col. Clark's Expedition—His plan adopted by Virginia—British influence over Indians the source of the depredations on the frontier settlements—Claims of Virginia to the Northwest, by her royal charters—Clark assembles his force—Descends the Ohio—Marches overland to Kaskaskia—Captures the town and fort—Fears of the inhabitants—They apply to Clark—His answer—Their rejoicings—Cahokia surrenders—Fort Sackville, or Vincennes, submits—Oath of allegiance taken—Clark establishes forts—County of Illinois established by Virginia—Indians make treaties with Clark—The British governor collects his forces—Resolves to make Clark prisoner—Governor Hamilton's character—He arrives before Vincennes—Captain Helm alone in the fort—Obtains honourable terms—Clark determines on retaking Vincennes—Marches from Kaskaskia—Hardships suffered by his forces—Arrive at the town and capture it—Attack the fort—Hamilton capitulates, and is sent prisoner to Virginia—Clark's views on Detroit—Captures a convoy of supplies—The result of Clark's enterprises—The five states of the Northwestern Territory—The Northwest during the Revolutionary War—Claims of States proposed to be relinquished—Plans devised and debated in Congress—Deeds of cession by States—Geographical boundaries of the new States not defined understandingly—Revision of deeds of cession proposed—New boundaries of States—Resolutions of Congress on this subject—Ordinance of 1787—Assent of Virginia to alteration of her deed of cession—Review of sixth article of ordinance of 1787.

A NEW era in the history of the West commenced with the year 1763. The capture of Quebec in 1759, and the subsequent capitulation of Montreal in 1760, extinguished the dominion of France in the basin of the St. Lawrence, and by the terms of the Treaty of Paris, in 1763, all the possessions in, and all the claims of, the French nation, to the vast countries watered by the Ohio and the Mississippi, were ceded to Great Britain. Thus, England held the sovereignty of Nova Scotia, Acadia, Canada, all, in fact, of New France, and the whole country from the Gulf of Mexico to the sources of the Mississippi, designated as Louisiana; of all the power of France over these vast regions, not an atom remained, except that which sprung from the deeply-seated affection and ever-enduring friendship of the Indian nations.

The definitive articles of the Treaty of Paris had been signed by the contracting parties, on the 3d of November, 1762, on which day, by a secret treaty, France ceded to Spain all Louisiana west of the Mississippi, and the island of Orleans. The Treaty of Paris was concluded on the 10th of February, 1763, by which Great Britain became possessed of the whole of New France, and of all that portion of the province of Louisiana lying on the east side of the Mississippi, except the town of New Orleans, and the island on which it is situated, which remained to France; the navigation of the Mississippi was to remain equally free to the subjects of Great Britain and France.

Among the first acts of the new masters of the country, was the protection of the eminent domain of the government, and the restriction of all attempts on the part of individuals to acquire Indian title to lands. By the king's proclamation, of 1763, the British governors were prohibited from issuing grants of land except within certain prescribed limits, and all private persons were interdicted the liberty of purchasing lands from the Indians, and of making settlements without those prescribed limits. The policy which dictated this governmental measure is unexceptionable; the indulgence of such a privilege as that of making private purchases of the natives, conduced to the most serious difficulties, and made way for the practice of the most reprehensible frauds. The same policy has ever been adopted, and acted upon, by the government of the United States, in respect to the extinguishment of the Indian title to lands in every quarter of the country. But, in the very face of the proclamation, and within three years after its promulgation, under a supposed purchase, or voluntary grant from the natives, a tract of country, nearly one hundred miles square, including a large portion of Northern Wisconsin, was claimed by Captain Jonathan Carver, and a ratification of his title solicited from the king and council. This, it appears, was not conceded, and the representatives of Captain Carver, after the change of government had brought the lands under the jurisdiction of the United States, for a series of years presented the same claims before Congress, and asked for their confirmation. Such a demand, under all the circumstances of Carver's case, could not justify an expectation of success, from a compliance on the part of the general government; and of course it has often been refused, and the claim rejected. But, notwithstanding the abundant means which the public had of informing themselves of the true nature and condition of Carver's claim, bargains and sales of portions of the tract have been made among visionary speculators, for half a century past, and up to the present time; and it is now only a short period, since the maps of the

United States have ceased to be defaced by a delineation of the "Carver Grant."[1]

Similar to this supposed grant, but in many respects entitled to a favourable consideration, was the purchase made by William Murray, in 1773, from the Illinois Indians, of a tract of country, contained in several parcels, amounting altogether to double the quantity of land embraced in Carver's grant. Murray's claim was known by the name of the Illinois and Wabash Company's purchase. For the several purchases from the Indians, more than fifty thousand pounds sterling was paid, and deeds were executed at places where solemn treaties were held, and every matter pertaining to the transfer of title was conducted with good faith between the contracting parties: the highest legal authorities in England had been consulted on the validity of the title; and Pratt, Yorke, and Dunning, (two of them afterward lord-chancellors,) gave their opinions in favour of the purchase. It was even questioned whether the King of England possessed the power to restrain the Indians from selling, and whether he possessed such a power to restrain British subjects from buying. The crown lawyers, being consulted by the king in council, in 1772, as to the legal effect of Indian grants, and royal patents, gave the following answer:

"In respect to such places as have been, or shall be acquired by treaty or grant, from any of the Indian princes or governments, your majesty's letters-patent are not necessary, the property in the soil vesting in the grantee, by the Indian grants, subject only to your majesty's right of sovereignty over the settlements as English settlements, and over the inhabitants as English subjects, who carry with them your majesty's laws, wherever they form colonies, and receive your majesty's protection, by virtue of your royal charters."

But, notwithstanding the many attempts made by the Illinois and Wabash Land Company to have their claims ratified by Congress, they have never yet succeeded. Although sup-

---

[1] Docum. History, Carver Grant.

ported by learned argument, and sometimes fortified by the favourable reports of committees, the policy of the proclamation of October 7th, 1763, prohibiting individuals from purchasing lands from the Indians, has always prevailed in the action of our national legislature. The claim of this company would cover a great portion of the most valuable lands in the centre of the state of Illinois.[1]

In the region of country which is now properly Wisconsin, there does not appear to have been any claims of the description alluded to, with the single exception of that of Captain Carver. At so early a period as 1806, when the general government was prosecuting its inquiries into the nature of the claims of the inhabitants of the Northwest, to lands in the territory of Michigan, the able report of the commissioners on this subject comprehended the titles to all the farms in six classes.

The first class consists of grants made by the French governors of New France and Louisiana, confirmed by the King of France.

The second class consists of grants made by the French governors, not confirmed by the King of France.

The third class consists of occupancies, by permission of French military commanding officers, without confirmation or even grant, and, perhaps, without any written evidence of the permission, but accompanied by long and undisturbed possession.

The fourth class consists of occupancies while France possessed the country, without any permission whatever, but still accompanied by undisturbed possession.

The fifth class is composed of similar titles, together with extinguishments of native right, by individuals, while the country belonged to Great Britain.

The sixth class is composed of occupancies, and extinguishments of native right, by individuals, since the country has appertained to the United States.[2]

---

[1] Land Laws, vol. ii. [2] For one of this class at Green Bay, see Doc. Hist

Of this latter class, the commissioners say that there were Indian grants, generally for a few hundred acres, though there are several for five, ten, fifteen, thirty, and fifty thousand acres, and some for even one hundred thousand acres. But the policy and principles of the royal proclamation of 1763, adopted and acted on by the United States government, at all subsequent periods, determined the total invalidity of such claims.[1]

Another class embraced claims founded on actual settlements and improvements, without other pretended title; and this class comprehended all the old claims to lands and lots at Green Bay and Prairie-du-Chien, which, at subsequent periods, were proved, and favourably reported on, by the United States commissioners, and finally confirmed by the general government.

In 1766, an application was made to Sir William Johnson, by the merchants of Canada, for the confirmation of a grant of an extraordinary nature, made by the Marquis de Vaudreuille, in October, 1759, and confirmed by the King of France in January, 1760, to Monsieur Rigaud and Madame de Vaudreuille, and afterward sold by them to a Mr. William Grant. This concession, or grant, was no less than "The fort at La Baye des Puants, in Lake Michigan, with an extensive territory, over which the grantee was to have the exclusive right of trade, with liberty to erect houses, and make establishments thereon." The period at which this grant was made, when the French possessions in Canada, and the West, were almost entirely lost to the French crown, affords a proof that it was intended as a mere perquisite to a favourite, and it need scarcely be added that the claim was rejected by the English Board of Trade.[2]

The mere transfer of the dominion over the country, from the French to the English government, and the consequent occupation of the military posts by the new masters, did not, in any great degree, alter the social condition of the inhabitants.

[1] Land Laws, vol. i. See Note A.

[2] See Note B.

By the terms of the capitulation of Montreal, the French subjects were permitted to remain in the country, in the full enjoyment of their civil and religious rights, and the fur trade was prosecuted upon the lakes with much energy by English companies, who employed French agents in conducting their trading transactions with the Indians. Agriculture was little attended to, or encouraged by the English, as few of their nation had, as yet, come into the country, except for the purposes of trade. The French settlements were made along the principal streams of the lakes, and in the immediate vicinity of the military posts; the farms scattered upon the banks of the rivers were of narrow form, surrounded by pickets, which yet continues to be the French mode of enclosure.[1] In all parts of New France and Louisiana, wherever settlements were made for the purposes of cultivation, on the borders of lakes and banks of water-courses, a general consent appears to have established a uniform system of claim. A few arpens in width along the water, with a varied depth over the adjoining prairie or wood, back to bluffs, or other boundaries, according to the moderation or cupidity of the claimant or proprietor, constituted a title, which has continued to be respected to the present day; and the shape of the lots or farms of the original proprietors, with narrow fronts and extended sides, still remains, along the lakes and waters of the regions settled by the French.

At the period of the surrender of the posts to the English, it is stated by a contemporary, that there were about fifty cottages on the strait of Detroit, with orchards by their side; they were constructed of logs, with roofs of bark, or thatched with straw; wheat was sown in rows; potatoes were first introduced by the English; corn began to be introduced under English jurisdiction, while peltries were chiefly the circulating medium: the first horses used in Detroit were introduced from Fort Duquesne, and these were taken from the English by the Indians, at Braddock's defeat.[2]

---

[1] Lanman's Michigan.

[2] Ibid., and MS. quoted.

The succession of authority over the North-west did not bring with it, to the English, the friendship of the Algonquin tribes in that quarter; the new masters were regarded as intruders by the Indians, and the long cherished affection which many of the tribes had for the French, produced an opposite feeling in them toward the new people, the enemies of their great French father, and of his representative Ononthio, which quickly ripened into a deadly hatred. This feeling was early exhibited by Pontiac, when he first met the detachment under Major Rogers on their way to take possession of the military posts: it was well understood by Henry, who was undoubtedly the pioneer of the English fur-traders in this region, when, on his first visit to the country, he was advised and obliged to disguise himself as a Frenchman, in order to avoid certain pillage, and impending death:[1] it was fully developed in the disastrous events which quickly followed the occupation of the posts by the English, known as the Pontiac war.

It has been observed of Pontiac, that no American savage has exhibited a more marked character in his power of mind to grasp great designs, or in his bold and strong arm in carrying them into execution. He had evinced great judgment and clearness of discrimination in his interviews with Major Rogers. He sought to inform himself of the discipline of the English forces, inquired the mode of manufacturing cloth and iron; and even, wishing to see England, offered a part of his country to the English commandant, if he would take him there. He also had stated to the English that he was willing to remain in subordination to the King of Great Britain, pay a yearly tribute in furs, and call him his *uncle*. After the surrender of the country, he intimated that he was also ready to encourage the settlement of the English in his country, so long as they treated him with respect; but that if they failed in this, he should exclude them from it, and "shut up the way." These remarks might have been merely policy, but, at all

[1] Henry's Travels.

events, it is clear that he did not consider himself conquered.[1]

Pontiac had conceived the great design of driving the English at once and effectually from the country, by a destruction of their forts and strongholds, which would not only deprive them of all present power in this quarter, but would also present very important obstacles to their future advance on the north-western waters. His plan was to unite the various tribes in one grand confederacy, and by a simultaneous attack, by stratagem if practicable, on all the English posts, to massacre the garrisons, take possession of these points, drive out the British from the land, and secure the return of the French, the ancient friend of the Indian race—their allies in war, and in many instances endeared to them by consanguinity.

The league formed by Pontiac in this great undertaking was more extensive than any which had ever been known upon the continent. All the tribes inhabiting the region extending from the lakes on the north, to the southern limits of Carolina, and west of this extensive frontier, back to the Mississippi, were engaged in it by the great chief, who seemed to exercise the power of an absolute dictator, and all the influence of an inspired leader. Well acquainted with the geography of the whole region, he had planned each attack, and had assigned to each band and leader their respective stations and duties.

After his plans and policy had been well matured in his mind, Pontiac called a grand council of warriors of the western tribes, the Miamies, the Ottawas, the Chippewas, the Wyandots, the Potawatamies, the Mississagas, the Shawanese, the Outagamies, and the Winnebagoes: he made an eloquent and powerful appeal to them against the advance of the British power, and showed them a belt which he pretended he had received from the French king, and declared that he was urged by him to aid in driving out the British and securing the return of the French. Taking advantage of the superstition which belongs to the Indian character, he stated that the

[1] Lanman's Michigan. Rogers's Account of North America.

Great Spirit had appeared to a Delaware Indian in a dream, in which the course of the Indians at this crisis was clearly prescribed. He told them that the Great Spirit had ordered them to abstain from ardent spirits, to cast away the manufactures of the white men, to return to the use of the skins of wild beasts for clothing, and to resume their bows and war-clubs. "Why," said the Great Spirit to the Delaware, "do you suffer these dogs in red-coats (the English) to enter your country, and take the lands I have given *to you?* Drive them from it! drive them! and when you are in trouble, I will help you." The speech of Pontiac had its full effect, for the motives urged appealed to the pride, interest, superstition, and nationality of the savages. Belts and messages were soon after sent to the Indians along the whole line of frontier, stretching a thousand miles on the lakes, in order to secure their co-operation. The above enumerated tribes were willing to join the confederacy, and when hostilities were commenced, every energy was bent to their effectual prosecution. Never did military commanders of any nation display more skill, or their troops more steady and determined courage, than did those red men of the wilderness in the prosecution of their gigantic plan for the recovery of their country from the possession of the English. It was a war of extermination on a large scale, where a few destitute savage tribes, in defence of their country and their homes, were arrayed against the colossal power and resources of the mistress of the civilized world; a contest where human nature, in its simplest state, was the antagonist of wealth, civilization, and arts, and where the wild man was obliged to call to his aid all the power of stratagem, treachery, revenge, and cruelty against the innocent, the helpless, and the unoffending. Such is the stern mode of savage warfare, which knows no mercy to the feeble, the aged, or the infant; where the youthful mother and her tender infant are alike doomed to the fate of the tomahawk and scalping-knife.[1]

---

[1] Doddridge's Notes. Lanman's Michigan. Monette, vol. i. Cass's Discourse. Thatcher's Lives of the Indians, vol. ii. Parkman, Hist.

Before any suspicion had been excited on the part of the English, the sanguinary war burst upon them like lightning from the overcharged thunder-cloud. In the month of May, 1763, the attack of the confederated Indians was made nearly at the same time on all the British posts, nine of which were captured, namely, Ouiatenon, Green Bay, Michillimackinac, St. Joseph's, Miami, Sandusky, Presqu'isle, Le Beuf, and Venango: some had been taken by open attack, others by stratagem and treachery; and in nearly all of them the garrisons had shared the fate of Indian victory, their bodies mangled in triumph, and their blood quaffed in rage. The posts of Presqu'isle, St. Joseph's, and Michillimackinac were taken, with a general slaughter of the garrisons.

Besides those posts which fell before the victorious savages, no less than six were beleaguered for many weeks or months, until they were finally relieved by reinforcements from the older settlements and from England. The principal of these were Detroit, Ligonier, Bedford, and Loudon, (all three in Pennsylvania,) and Cumberland, (in Maryland:) most of these were reduced to great extremities before relief reached them. Niagara was deemed impregnable to the savages, and was not attacked.[1]

In addition to the destruction of life and property at the forts, and in their immediate vicinity, the frontier settlements in the old States, from the Susquehanna to the Roanoke, were broken up with indiscriminate massacre where the inhabitants were unable to effect a timely escape, and the English traders among the Indians were the first victims in this contest; out of one hundred and twenty of them, it is said, only two or three escaped the general destruction; and to one of those traders, Alexander Henry, we are indebted for a vivid picture of his own severe sufferings, and the massacre of the garrison, on the disastrous surprise and capture, by Pontiac's bands, of the fort at Michillimackinac.[2]

At this period, prognostics of coming evil were found by

---

[1] Monette, vol. i.

[2] Docum. History.

the simple Canadians in the unexplained phenomenon of the fall of a rain of inky blackness in the vicinity of Detroit. Four years after its occurrence, Carver, who was on the spot, writes as follows: "In the year 1762, in the month of July, it rained on this town and the parts adjacent, a sulphurous water, of the colour and consistence of ink; some of which being collected into bottles, and wrote with, appeared perfectly intelligible on the paper, and answered every purpose of that useful liquid. Soon after, the Indian wars already spoken of, broke out in these parts. I mean not to say that this incident was ominous of them, notwithstanding it is well known that innumerable well attested instances of extraordinary phenomena happening before extraordinary events, have been recorded in almost every age by historians of veracity. I only relate the circumstance as a fact of which I was informed by many persons of undoubted probity, and leave my readers, as I have hitherto done, to draw their own conclusions from it."[1]

As the time approached for the accomplishment of Pontiac's great plan of attack on the posts, suspicions of the hostile intentions of the Indians were general, and even information of the approaching danger was given to the commandant at Michillimackinac, Major George Etherington, by several Canadians least hostile to the English. Mr. Laurent Ducharme distinctly informed him that a plan was absolutely conceived for destroying him, his garrison, and all the English in the upper country; but the commandant, believing this and other reports to be without foundation, proceeding only from idle, or ill-disposed persons, and of a tendency to do mischief, expressed much displeasure against M. Ducharme, and threatened to send the next person who should bring a story of the same kind, a prisoner to Detroit.

The garrison at this time consisted of ninety privates, two subalterns, and the commandant; and the English merchants at the fort were four in number. Thus strong, few entertained anxiety concerning the Indians, who had no weapons

[1] Carver's Travels.

but small arms. Meanwhile the Indians were daily assembling in unusual numbers, but with every appearance of friendship, frequenting the fort, and disposing of their peltries in such a manner as to dissipate almost every one's fears. Mr. Henry, however, observed to Major Etherington, that no confidence ought to be placed in them, and that no less than four hundred lay around the fort. The major only rallied him on his timidity, and neglected every admonition; but the same rash heedlessness in the midst of danger is acknowledged on the part of Henry himself: he also had received a mysterious warning from a friendly Indian, to which he had unfortunately turned a deaf ear. In the preceding year, a Chippeway, named, Wa'wa'tam, often came to Henry's house, showing him strong marks of personal regard. At one time he came with his whole family, bringing a large present of skins, sugar, and dried meat, and begged Henry to accept of them, as he had dreamed of adopting an Englishman as his son, brother, and friend, and from the moment he had seen Henry he had recognised him as the person whom the Great Spirit had been pleased to point out to him for a brother, and that he should ever regard him as one of his family. Henry accepted the present, gave the Indian one in return, and acceded to the proffered tie of friendship and brotherhood between them; Wa'wa'tam then went on his winter's hunt.

A year had now elapsed since the occurrence of this incident, and Henry had almost forgotten the person of his *brother*, when, on the second day of June, (two days before the massacre,) Wa'wa'tam came to Henry's house melancholy and thoughtful. Henry asked after his health; but without answering the question, Wa'wa'tam told him he was sorry to see that he had returned from Sault Ste. Marie; that he intended to go immediately from Michillimackinac to the Sault, and wished Henry to accompany him and his family the next morning. To all this he joined an inquiry, whether Henry's commandant had heard *bad news*, adding that he had himself been frequently, during the winter, disturbed with the noise of *evil birds;* and suggested that there were numerous Indians near the fort, many of whom had never shown themselves within it.

Henry told him he could not think of going to the Sault so soon, but would follow him there, after the arrival of his clerks. The Indian then withdrew, but came again next morning, accompanied by his wife, bringing a present of dried meat. He told Henry he had several packs of beaver to trade with him, expressed his apprehensions, a second time, concerning the numerous Indians around the fort, and earnestly pressed Henry to depart immediately for the Sault, stating as a reason, that all the Indians proposed to come in a body that day to the fort, to demand liquor of the commandant, and he wished him to be gone before they should grow intoxicated.

Unfortunately, Henry did not sufficiently comprehend the figurative language of the friendly Indian, nor take the hints which subsequent events rendered perfectly lucid; and having refused to go with Wa'wa'tam and his wife, after their long and patient efforts to persuade him, they departed alone with dejected countenances, and not before they had each let fall some tears.

In the course of the same day, Mr. Henry observed that the Indians came in great numbers into the fort, purchasing tomahawks, and frequently desiring to see silver arm-bands, and other valuable ornaments, of which he had a large quantity for sale. These ornaments, however, they in no instance purchased, but after turning them over, said they would call again the next day. Their motive, as it afterward appeared, was no other than the very artful one of discovering, by requesting to see them, the particular places of their deposit, so that they might lay their hands on them, in the moment of pillage,with the greater certainty and despatch.[1]

The next day, being the 4th of June, was the king's birthday; more memorable as the day on which the fort was surprised by a stratagem, doubtless contrived by the master-spirit of Pontiac, and successfully carried into effect under

---

[1] Henry's Travels, passim.

his direction, although at the time, he himself was near Detroit.

In order to do honour to the day, and to add to the festivities, it was proposed that the game of *baggatiway*, an Indian ball-play, generally called by the French *le jeu de la crosse*, should be played between the Chippewas and Sacs for a high wager. It was stated that the commandant was to bet on the side of the Chippewas; Mr. Henry, for the last time, expostulated with Major Etherington, and suggested that the Indians might have some sinister design in view, but his caution and advice were alike fruitless.

The game of la crosse, or baggatiway, is played with a bat and ball; two posts are planted in the ground, about a mile apart, and each party having its post, the object is to propel the ball, which is placed in the centre, toward the post of the adversary. In the ardour of contest, if the ball cannot be driven to the desired goal, it is struck in any direction by which it can be diverted from that designed by the opposite party. To view this game, Major Etherington, who had wagered on the side of the Chippewas, was not only present himself, but all the garrison who could be induced, were by some pretext drawn outside of the pickets, in order to weaken the defences of the fort. The stratagem of the Indians was soon developed.

The design was to throw the ball over the pickets, which was accomplished; and as in the heat of the game such an event was not liable to excite any extraordinary alarm, so the immediate and promiscuous rushing of the Indians into the fort, in pursuit of the ball, was, for a moment, regarded as a mere natural consequence. But in an instant, the war-yell was heard within the pickets, and the Indians were seen furiously cutting down and scalping every Englishman whom they could discover; the Canadians around the fort neither opposed the Indians, nor received any injury from them. Heaps of dead lay around the fort, scalped and mangled; the dying were shrieking and writhing under the tomahawk and scalping-knife, and the bodies of the English soldiers were gashed, and their blood was drank by the savages from the hollows of joined hands, amid demon-like yells.[1]

According to the testimony of the eye-witness, Mr. Henry, who escaped the general massacre in a miraculous manner, no less than seventy soldiers, together with Lieutenant Jemette, had been killed, and but twenty Englishmen, including soldiers, were still alive;[2] these were all within the fort, together with nearly three hundred Canadians, who belonged to the canoes, &c., and upon whom no reliance could be placed for any aid in the recovery of the fort, and maintaining its possession against the Indians.

The fort at Green Bay had received an English garrison in 1761, which consisted of seventeen men, under the command of Lieutenant Gorell: the prudent conduct of the commandant had secured the good-will of all the surrounding tribes; but although it escaped the fate of Michillimackinac, it was soon abandoned by orders of Major Etherington, and the garrison, with Lieutenant Gorell, afterward were escorted by a band of friendly Menominees to L'Arbre Croche, where they met with Major Etherington and the remnant of his command, who were still detained as prisoners. On the 18th of July they were liberated, and the whole party reached Montreal, by way of the river Ottawa, about the middle of August.[3]

A missionary post had been established at the mouth of the river St. Joseph, in 1712; it had also been erected afterward into a military post. This was also surprised and captured by Pontiac's bands, on the 25th of May, 1763; there was an officer and fourteen men stationed there at the time, eleven of whom were killed in the assault and capture by the Indians.

We have observed that La Motte Cadillac was the founder of Detroit; in 1701, he planted there the little military colony. Major Rogers tells us that at the close of the French

[1] Lanman's Michigan. Henry's Travels.

[2] See Bancroft, vol. v. 121, as to errors in Henry's account.

[3] See Note C.

war, the place contained two thousand five hundred inhabitants. Within the limits of the settlement there were three large Indian villages. On the western shore, a little below the fort, were the lodges of the Pottawatamies; nearly opposite, on the eastern side, was the village of the Wyandots; and on the same side, two miles higher up, Pontiac's band of Ottawas had fixed their abode. The settlers always maintained the best terms with their savage neighbours. The British took possession, in an evil hour for the Canadians, towards the close of the year 1760.[1]

Detroit was then deemed the most important of the northwestern posts, as it commanded an extensive region of navigation and trade upon the upper lakes, and stood at the very broad gate of the western waters. At the city, the Detroit River is about half a mile wide. The possession of this post would break the allegiance of the French inhabitants on the river, and form a chain of operations for the savages, from Lake Michigan to Buffalo and Pittsburg. Pontiac determined, therefore, to undertake its capture in person. His forces consisted of two hundred and fifty Ottawas, one hundred and fifty Pottawatamies, fifty Wyandots, two hundred Ojibwas under Wasson, one hundred and seventy under Sekahos; in all, eight hundred and twenty warriors. At this time, the town was garrisoned by one hundred and twenty-two men and eight officers, of whom Major Gladwyn, who had succeeded Captain Campbell, was commandant.[2]

The stratagem devised by Pontiac to gain possession of this important post exhibited much cunning, and promised success if the deception should not be discovered. His plan was to gain admission to the fort, for the pretended purpose of holding a council with the commandant; his chiefs and warriors, who were to accompany him to this council, were to have their rifles concealed under their blankets, and, at a preconcerted signal, which was the delivery of a belt of wampum in a certain manner, by Pontiac, in the course of his speech, to Major

[1] Parkman. [2] Cass's Discourse. Lanman's Michigan. See Note D.

Gladwin, they were to fire on the officers in the council-chamber, rush on the troops, and open the gates to the warriors on the outside of the fort, who were to be ready to co-operate with those within. To carry this plan into execution, he encamped at a little distance from Detroit, and sent word to Major Gladwyn, that he and his chiefs wished to hold a council with the English commandant, in order to "brighten the chain of peace." This was on the 8th of May, 1763; Major Gladwyn appointed the next day for holding the council. Pontiac in the mean time had ordered his warriors to saw off their rifles, so as the more readily to conceal them under their blankets, which was done.

On the evening of the 8th of May, an Indian woman, who had been employed by the commandant in making mocassins for him, feeling grateful for his kindness to her, brought home to him her work, and by her mysterious conduct, and unwillingness to depart from the fort, excited the curiosity of Major Gladwyn, who called the woman before him; and after interrogation as to the motives of her conduct, she disclosed to the commandant the details of Pontiac's stratagem to surprise the fort, with all the circumstances of the shortened rifles, and the concerted signal of massacre by the particular mode of delivering the belt of wampum. The woman was permitted to depart, with assurances of safety and reward.

On the following day, at ten o'clock, Pontiac and his warriors, with their concealed arms, were admitted to the council by Major Gladwyn, who had already taken every necessary precaution to frustrate the Indian stratagem, and given the proper direction to his officers and soldiers to be fully on their guard, and prepared to act at the moment when the Indian signal was expected to be given. Accordingly, when Pontiac, in the course of his speech, had arrived at that point when the belt of wampum should be delivered, Major Gladwyn and his officers laid their hands on their swords, half drew them, and the soldiers within and without the council-room made a martial clatter with their fire-arms. Pontiac immediately became disconcerted, and his preconcerted signal was not given; consequently his chiefs remained quiet in their places, looking at each other with astonishment. Major Gladwyn then addressed Pontiac, reproaching him with his premeditated treachery, and informed him that the English could not thus be circumvented, as they had knowledge of all things. Pontiac attempted to deny the charge made against him of treachery, but Major Gladwyn seized the blanket of the warrior next to him, and exposed the hidden and shortened rifle. He then ordered Pontiac and his chiefs to quit the fort immediately, telling him that his word had been pledged for their safety at the council, and he would not violate it. The Indians soon left the fort, and instantly set up their yells of defiance and fired at the stockades. The same evening they committed several murders and other depredations in the vicinity, and the siege of Detroit was from that time regularly commenced. The savages stationed themselves behind the buildings which were scattered outside the pickets, and from these as well as the pickets, they kept up a constant fire on the British, without, however, doing much damage.[1]

The post was regularly invested, and Pontiac demanded its surrender by capitulation, requiring the British to lay down their arms and march out, as the French had done. This having been refused, he renewed his attacks with increased vigour and frequency. So unremitted were they, that for several weeks neither the officers nor men within the fort were allowed to take off their clothes to sleep, all being constantly engaged about the ramparts.

Every stratagem that Indian cunning could devise was put in operation; parties were continually hovering near the fort, under some concealment, for the purpose of taking off, by their marksmen, any who might incautiously expose themselves; other detachments scoured the country around in every direction, to intercept every kind of aid or succour intended for the garrison; floating fire-rafts were constructed, and sent against

---

[1] See Note E.

the two vessels lying in the river, and they were with difficulty preserved from the flames. A strong detachment, sent from Niagara for the relief of the fort, was entirely cut off, and the supplies of provisions, arms, and ammunition, which they brought, were captured by the Indians. Nor was this state of things the sole source of annoyance to the beleaguered garrison; scenes of unparalleled barbarity were daily perpetrated in the vicinity of the fort, and it was a matter of almost daily occurrence for the garrison to behold the dead and mangled bodies of their countrymen floating past the fort. Every family and individual in the neighbourhood had been murdered in the most horrid manner, and every habitation destroyed by fire.

In July, a reinforcement of two hundred and sixty regular troops, under Captain Dalyell, arrived in safety at the fort, from Niagara. This was on the 29th; and, in the evening of the 30th, a sortie was made by two hundred and forty-seven chosen men, commanded by Dalyell, against the Indian breastwork, about a mile from the fort. It was a disastrous affair. They were met by a concealed fire from the Indians, accompanied by a furious assault; and notwithstanding the brave resistance of the troops, and their determined charge against unseen foes, in the darkness of night, they were compelled to retire toward the fort, fighting their way every step; nineteen men were killed, and forty-two wounded. Captain Dalyell was among the slain.

In August, some of the Indians, allies of Pontiac, becoming, perhaps, in some measure disheartened by the fruitless length of the siege, retired to their respective homes; but Pontiac remained, and continued to annoy the garrison from time to time until the spring of 1764. In the month of June, General Bradstreet arrived at Detroit, with a force of three thousand men, for the purpose of compelling a peace with the tribes of the Northwest. The Indians, representing twenty-two tribes, had already concluded a peace with the general at Niagara. Among these were eleven of the tribes of the Northwest, but Pontiac was not included. On the arrival of the English force at Detroit, the tribes of Pontiac laid down their arms, and, with the exception of the Delawares and Shawanese, concluded a treaty of peace; Pontiac, however, took no part in the negotiation, and soon after retired to the Illinois, where he was killed in 1767, by a Peoria Indian.[1] It may be remarked, that the Ottawas, the Pottawatamies, the Chippewas, and other northern tribes, united in a common cause to revenge his death, and nearly exterminated the Illinois.

We must regret that our knowledge of Pontiac and his war is very limited, although, of late years, literary research has brought to light many valuable manuscripts, detailing events of his extraordinary enterprises and career, and more is hoped for.[2] Among many instances of elevation of feeling, related of Pontiac, it is stated, that on one occasion Col. Rogers sent to him a bottle of brandy; Pontiac's warriors cautioned him not to taste it lest it might be poisoned; Pontiac rejected their advice, saying, "He cannot take my life, I have saved his!" In commenting on this anecdote, the Abbè Raynal remarks, "A hundred traits of equal elevation have fixed upon Pontiac the gaze of the savage nations. He wished to reunite all his tribes, for the purpose of making their territory and independence respected, but unforeseen circumstances prevented the project.[3] The terrific drama got up by this son of the forest stamps his name with greatness. The living marble and the glowing canvas may not embody his works; but they are identified with the soil of the Western forest, and will live as long as the remembrance of its aboriginal inhabitants—the Algonquin race.[4]

No Englishman, and few of any other nation, save the solitary French trader, or the devoted missionary, had hitherto ventured into the country of the Upper Mississippi, or beyond the western shores of Lake Michigan, and the mouth of Fox River at Green Bay. The restoration of peace between the new masters of the country and the Indian tribes, and the

---

[1] Monette, vol. i. and authorities.
[2] Parkman, Lanman, Nicollet.
[3] Raynal, Hist. Phil.
[4] Lanman.

very natural desire of the English to reap the advantages of their new possessions, doubly secured by them, first by conquest, and now by treaties of concession by the French, and of toleration and peace by the Indians—all contributed to the expectations of a gradual, if not speedy occupation and settlement of the fine country between the great Lakes and the Mississippi.

The projects and views of Captain Jonathan Carver, had they been carried into effect, would undoubtedly have resulted in beneficial effects, both to the colonial region and the mother country. Carver gives us his own plans, and states reasonable grounds for his expectations of their success. He wished to acquire, by personal observation and adventurous exploration, an accurate knowledge of the vast territory in the Northwest, so lately come into the possession of Great Britain. He proposed to correct all inaccurate maps and charts of the country and its waters, and to rectify and restore the proper nomenclature of the nations and tribes who inhabited it, and of the locations and objects within it. After gaining a knowledge of the manners, customs, languages, soil, and natural productions of the different nations that inhabit the back of the Mississippi, he contemplated to ascertain the breadth of that vast continent which extends from the Atlantic to the Pacific Ocean, in its broadest part between forty-three and forty-six degrees northern latitude. In case of his success in this, he intended to propose to the government to establish a post in some of those parts about the Straits of Annian, which, having been first discovered by Sir Francis Drake, of course belonged to the English. This (he was convinced) would greatly facilitate the discovery of a northwest passage, or a communication between Hudson's Bay and the Pacific Ocean. To accomplish these highly desirable results, he proposed to assume the character of trader as well as traveller; and accordingly we find him, in September, 1766, in the prosecution of his enterprise, at the remote post of Michillimackinac; and having been here supplied with a proper assortment of goods by Col. Rogers, the commandant, Carver proceeded, by way of Green Bay and the Fox and Wisconsin Rivers, to Prairie du Chien, where he arrived on the 15th of October.

In somewhat of the spirit of prophecy, Carver remarks, "To what power or authority this new world will become dependent, after it has arisen from its present uncultivated state, time alone can discover. But as the seat of empire from time immemorial had been gradually progressive toward the west, there is no doubt but that, at some future period, mighty kingdoms will emerge from these wildernesses, and stately palaces and solemn temples, with gilded spires reaching the skies, supplant the Indian huts, whose only decorations are the barbarous trophies of their vanquished enemies."[1]

At the time Carver was at Fort La Baye, at the mouth of Fox River, on the 18th of September, 1766, there was no garrison there, nor had it been kept in repair since it had been abandoned by Lieut. Gorell; a few families lived in the fort, and opposite to it, on the east side of the river, there were a few French settlers, who cultivated the land and appeared to live comfortably. The inhabitants of the coasts denominated the bay "Menominee Bay"—the French, "la Baye des Puants"—and the English, since they had obtained possession of this part of the country, "Green Bay," for the reason that on leaving Michillimackinac in the spring season, though the trees there have not even put forth their buds, yet the country around La Baye, notwithstanding the passage has not exceeded fourteen days, is found covered with the finest verdure, and vegetation as forward as it could be, were it summer.[2]

Proceeding up the Fox River, our traveller arrived at the island at the east end of Lake Winnebago, now known as Doty's Island. Here he found the great town of the Winnebagoes, over which tribe a woman held the chief power, and who received him kindly and entertained him with great hospitality during the three or four days he remained there.

[1] Carver's Travels. [2] Idem.

At this period, the Winnebagoes could raise about two hundred warriors, and their town here contained about fifty houses strongly built with palisades. Another town belonging to the same nation, but smaller than this one on the island, stood forty miles higher up the river. The traveller finally reached the carrying place, memorably signalized by the first adventurers, Marquette and Joliet, and having crossed over a morass of three-fourths of a mile in length, and a plain with some few oaks and pine trees growing thereon, of the same distance, Carver entered the Wisconsin.[1]

On reaching the point long familiarly known as the Portage, and more recently, in Wisconsin, as the site of "Portage City," Carver remarks, "I observed that the main body of the Fox River came from the southwest, and that of the Ouisconsin from the northeast; and also that some of the small branches of these two rivers, in descending into them, doubled, within a few feet of each other, a little to the south of the carrying place. That two such rivers should take their rise so near each other, and after running such different courses, empty themselves into the sea at a distance so amazing, (for the former, having passed through several large lakes, and run upward of two thousand miles, falls into the Gulf of St. Lawrence; and the other, after joining the Mississippi, and having run an equal number of miles, disembogues itself into the Gulf of Mexico,) is an instance scarcely to be met in the extensive continent of North America. I had an opportunity the year following, of making the same observation on the affinity of various head branches of the waters of the St. Lawrence and the Mississippi, to each other; and now bring them as a proof that the opinion of those geographers, who assert that rivers taking their rise so near to each other, must spring from the same source, is erroneous. For I perceived a visible, distinct separation in all of them, notwithstanding in some places they approached so near, that I could have stepped from one to the other."[2] This remark of Carver

---

[1] See Note F. [2] Carver's Travels.

does not appear to be strictly applicable to the Fox and Wisconsin Rivers; for although at this point of the Portage, their waters approach each other within two miles, yet it is well known that the main source of the Wisconsin is in Lac Vieux Desert, or Kattekittekon, some two hundred miles north of the Portage; and that the Fox River receives also from the north many large tributaries, one of which, Wolf River, has its source in Lac du Port, some one hundred and twenty miles north of its entrance into Lake Winnebago, which latter becomes for a time a common receptacle for all the streams running eastward, until the whole mass of waters is discharged by the Lower Fox River into Green Bay.

Proceeding down the Wisconsin River, Carver arrived at the great village of the Saukies, situate on what is now known as Prairie du Sac, or Sauk Prairie. Here it must be acknowledged that the fancy of the traveller appears to have greatly embellished his facts, as he describes streets regularly laid out, houses built of hewn plank, and having porches before the doors for the luxuriant indulgences of the inhabitants; that the town is considered as a great mart for furnishing provisions to traders, and that *lead* is so plentiful that large quantities of it were lying about the streets. It also states that he visited a lead region, about fifteen miles to the south, and ascended one of the mountains, whence he had an extensive view of the country: this was evidently at the Blue Mounds, as the locality is described with sufficient accuracy. Descending the river, he arrives at a deserted village of the Outagamies, and finally reaches Prairie du Chien, where their great business town was situated.[1]

The accounts of Carver, thus given, of the country through which he passed in 1766, furnish, at least, negative testimony relative to there being any occupancy or attempt at settlement, on the part of the whites, from Green Bay to the Mississippi; if such had been the fact, he undoubtedly would

---

[1] Note G. See chap. ii. ante.

have mentioned it. At this time he finds no European at Prairie du Chien; but, on the shore of Lake Pepin, he observed the ruins of a French factory, where, it is said, Captain St. Pierre resided, and carried on a very great trade with the Naudowessies before the reduction of Canada.

Having explored the country above the Falls of St. Anthony as high up the Mississippi as the river St. Francis, where only Hennepin had been before him, he ascended the St. Peter's River, or Waddapaw-Menesotor, about two hundred miles, and resided for many months with the Naudowessies of the Plains, with whom, and other tribes, he entered into a compact, confirmed in council at the Great Cave, on the first of May, 1767, that these Indian nations should be taken under the protection of the King of England henceforth, and that trading-posts should be immediately established, and traders sent among them. Carver says, that he was made a chief, and it has been claimed on his part afterward, that a tract of country more than one hundred miles square was then granted to him by the Naudowessies in consideration of his eminent services rendered to them in peace and war. But Carver makes not the slightest mention of such a grant, in his published book; and the greater probability is, that if any such grant or concession was made by the Indians, it was only for the purposes of trading-posts, and possibly for establishments for protection and defence. The intended action of the British Government in relation to this supposed grant, at a subsequent period, was frustrated by the American Revolution; but according to the evidence produced by the representatives of Carver before the Congress of the United States, in support of their claim under this grant, it appears that the king and council considered the concession by the Indians as conferring a right of occupancy by the British Government, and not as the gift of a principality to a private subject.[1]

It has been already remarked, that the whole country west

---

[1] Docum. History. Carver's Grant. Ante, chap. ii.

of Lake Michigan, and south of the Wisconsin River, to the junction of the Wabash (or Ohio) with the Mississippi, was generally designated as the Illinois country; the southern portion of this territory had for nearly half a century been devoted to agriculture and the Indian trade, and it now contained many flourishing settlements. The French, in making these settlements on the Illinois and Wabash Rivers, had adopted a wise and benevolent policy, well adapted to insure unity and harmony among themselves, and to secure the good-will and friendship of the numerous tribes in the North-west by which they were surrounded. While other colonies were continually embroiled with the natives in exterminating wars, they sought peace and friendship; lived in harmony and mutual confidence with their Indian neighbours; associated with them in their migrations and explorations of remote waters and hunting-grounds, like a band of brothers, and as equally the children of the same Great Father of all; they shared with the Indians their hospitality, and commiserated with their sufferings in distress; they readily accommodated themselves to their manners and customs, united their races by the ties of blood, and the offspring of such unions are among us at the present day; Providence smiled upon this happy and peaceable intercourse between the white man of Europe and the red man of the American wilderness.

Unlike most other European immigrants, who commonly prefer to settle in sparse settlements, remote from each other, the French manifested in a high degree, at the same time, habits both social and vagrant. They settled in compact villages, although isolated, in the midst of a wilderness a thousand miles remote from the dense settlements of Canada. On the margin of a prairie, or on the bank of some gentle stream, their villages sprang up in long narrow streets, with each family homestead so contiguous that the merry and sociable villagers could carry on their voluble conversation, each from his own door or balcony. Their mode of life approached the patriarchal; each village had its "common field," consisting of a large contiguous enclosure, reserved for the common use, and enclosed by one common fence for the benefit of all. In this field, which sometimes contained several hundred acres, each villager and head of a family had assigned to him a certain portion of ground, for the use of himself and family, as a field and garden. The extent of the field was proportionate to the number of persons or families in the village. The subdivisions were in due proportion to the number of members in each family. Each individual, or family, laboured and reaped the product of his own allotment for his own use. If the enclosure became ruinous or was neglected contiguous to the plat of any family, or individual, so as to endanger the general interest, that individual, or family, forfeited their claim to the use of the common field; and their interest was assigned to another person who would be less negligent. Each individual, or head of a family, so long as he conformed to the regulations and requisitions of the village, retained his interest in the common field in fee simple, transferable by sale, gift, or otherwise; liable, however, to the general regulations which might be adopted by the village. The season for ploughing, planting, reaping, and other agricultural operations in the "common field," was regulated by special enactments, or by a public ordinance, and to take place simultaneously in each village. Even the form and manner of door yards, gardens, and stable-yards, and other arrangements for mutual benefit, and the convenience of all, were regulated by special enactments of the little village senate. These were often in such shape and connection as to form a partial protection, like a picketed camp, against any hostile irruption of Indians, provided such event might ever occur.

Near the village, and around the common field, was an extensive open scope of lands reserved for "commons," or a common pasture-ground. This consisted of several hundreds, and often of thousands, of acres uninclosed, and free for the use of all as a common pasture, as well as for the supply of fuel and timber. Yet no one could take possession of any portion of it, or appropriate it to his own individual use, without the general consent of the villagers. To the indigent, however, who came to settle among them, and to newly-married pairs, appropriations were often made from portions of the "commons" contiguous to the common field, and situated so that it might subsequently be taken into it, by extending the enclosure, provided the individuals proved themselves acceptable members of their community.

In making grants of land for the use of a village or community, the commandant always took special care to cause a reservation to be specially designated for a "common field," and a "commons." These were deemed indispensable requisites for every large French village. The same custom was observed by the Spanish authorities after the dominion of Spain was extended over Louisiana.

Their houses were simple, plain, and uniform; each homestead was surrounded by its own separate enclosure of a rude picket-fence, adjoining or contiguous to others on the right and left. The houses were generally one story high, surrounded by sheds or galleries; the walls were constructed of a rude framework, having upright corner posts and studs, connected horizontally by means of numerous cross-ties, not unlike the rounds in a ladder. These served to hold the "cat and clay" with which the interstices were filled, and with which the walls were made, and rudely plastered with the hand. "Cat and clay" is formed by mud, or clay, made into soft mortar, which is then intimately blended with cut straw, or Spanish moss, cut fine, instead of hair. The chimney was made of similar material, and was formed by four long corner posts, converging toward the top to about one-half, or less, of the space below.[1]

Nothing was better calculated to improve the simple and benevolent feelings of unsophisticated human nature, to maintain the blessing of peace and harmony, and the prevalence of brotherly love, than the forms of life and the domestic usages which prevailed in these early French villages. Under this benign influence, peace and confidence smiled upon them;

---

[2] Flint's Geography, vol. i. Monette, vol. i.

joy and mirth beamed from every countenance; contentment sat on every brow. The natural affluence which pervaded the whole village was common to all. The prolific soil, solicited by gentle labour, as a mere matter of recreation, yielded abundance of all the necessaries of life, except those which were derived from the still more prolific waters and the chase. With all these advantages, and all these easy enjoyments, in a climate of great benignity, remote from the strife and conflicting interests of a dense population, what should prevent them from esteeming the "Illinois" a "terrestial paradise," as La Salle had termed it in 1682?[1]

In the early French settlements, the "commons" abounded with herds of domestic animals, with cattle, horses, sheep, swine, and others tamed from the forest, which wandered at large, and was used as a general store-house from which all were freely supplied; while care was a stranger in the village, and was banished from hearts as light as those of the animals that quietly roamed the fields. Amusements, festivals, and holydays, were frequent, and in the festive dance the young and the gay were active participants, while the serene and smiling countenance of the aged patriarch, and his companion in years, and even the "reverend father," lent a sanction and a blessing upon the innocent amusement and healthy recreation. The amusements past, all could cheerfully unite in offering up to God the simple gratitude of the heart for his unbounded mercies.

In religion, all were Catholics, and revered the Pope as the great head of the church, who held the keys of heaven and of purgatory, and dispensed his favours or his frowns through his priests, who were their friends and counsellors, and whom they esteemed as their "reverend fathers." They knew no difference of sects, no creed except the "Apostles' Creed," and ardently attached to their spiritual guides, and observing strictly all the outward rites and ceremonies of the Romish Church, religion became one of their great rules of social life,

[1] Flint's Geography, vol. i. Monette, vol. i.

and their lives corresponded with their professions. Such may not be considered as an overcharged picture of the condition of the inhabitants of the Mississippi Valley under the French dominion.[1]

After the Canadian provinces had been torn from the crown of France by the arms of England, and the English power had been extended over the Illinois country, which was in 1765, a change came over the happy and peaceful abodes of the French in New France and Louisiana. The inhabitants were repugnant to submission to England, their ancient national enemy, and many preferred to leave their homes and their fields, and to seek new dwelling-places under the dominion of France, which still prevailed west of the Mississippi. Consequently the French settlements began to decline, on the Illinois, and, in order to prevent an almost entire abandonment of them, the English government gave assurances to the inhabitants that their religion, their rights, and their property, should be protected, and remain inviolate under the dominion of Great Britain. Although many consented to remain, yet many retired to Western Louisiana, and French settlements began to extend on the west side of the Mississippi, within the limits of the present State of Missouri. But even here, their hopes of tranquillity were doomed to disappointment: it was soon rumoured that all Western and Southern Louisiana had been ceded to Spain, and such being the fact, they found themselves already subjects of the Spanish monarch. Still, although the Spanish authority was not extended over them for a period of five years, yet these were years of suspense, chagrin, and trouble, all of which was finally dispelled by the mild and paternal government of Spain, which differed not, in these respects, from that of France; their habits of tranquil life were not again disturbed until the Anglo-Americans began to approach the Mississippi; and finally an almost total change was effected in all their relations

[1] See Stoddard's Louisiana; Flint's Geography; Martin's Louisiana; Monette, and authorities.

of social and political life, by the cession of Louisiana to the United States, in 1803.

In the month of October, 1765, Captain Stirling, of the British army, arrived, by way of the Ohio, and established his head-quarters at Fort Chartres, as commandant of the Illinois country, under the orders of General Gage, commander-in-chief of his majesty's forces in America. At this time the French population of the whole Illinois country, from the Mississippi eastward to the Wabash, was probably not less than five thousand persons, including about five hundred negro slaves. The loss, by subsequent emigration, was not replaced by English settlers, and ten years afterward the population of Kaskaskia was estimated at but little over one hundred families; that of Cahokia, fifty families; and of Prairie Dupont, and Prairie du Rocher, each fourteen families. These were the great points of settlement in the country. Fort Chartres, subsequently called "Fort Gage," was a stockaded fort, on the east bank of the Kaskaskia River, opposite the town of Kaskaskia; Cahokia was a small post on the bank of the Mississippi, about three miles below St. Louis.

Pittman, who visited the Illinois country in 1770, in speaking of the soil and productions of this region, says, that a man in Illinois could have been fed and lodged the year round for two months' work; the one in seed-time, the other in harvest. At that time one man furnished the king's stores from his crop, 86,000 lbs. of flour;[1] in 1769, the Illinois produced one hundred and ten hogsheads of wine from the native grape.[2]

Under the new masters of this highly productive and salubrious portion of the North-west, for a series of years, embracing the period from 1763 to the capture of the British posts, by the forces under Colonel George Rogers Clark, in 1779, we find little account of improvements in settlements in the south part of Illinois, and still less, if any at all, in that portion lying immediately west of Lake Michigan. The expedi-

[1] Pittman, State of Eng. Sett. on Miss. p. 43, 55.
[2] Hutchin's Top. Descr. p. 43.

tion of Colonel Clark was in itself not only successful, and opened the way for the emigration of the Anglo-American population to the Mississippi Valley, but, at the close of the American Revolution, Great Britain, by the terms of the treaty of 1783, renounced all claim to the whole territory east of the Mississippi. Thus terminated forever the dominion of the English in the Illinois and Wabash countries, with the loss of three military posts which commanded the whole Northwestern territory of the United States.

At the commencement of the Revolution, from the first act of hostilities by the royal troops against the inhabitants of the colonies, the savages of the Northwest had been associated as allies of Great Britain, and employed by the British commanders to lay waste the whole frontier country; and a bloody partisan war ensued, and continued for two years, until Patrick Henry, then governor of Virginia, adopted the plan of Colonel George Rogers Clark for suppressing the terrible incursions of the Northwestern Indians.

The British posts on the Wabash, the Illinois, and the Upper Mississippi were considered properly within the chartered limits of Virginia; these posts, as subordinate to Detroit, were found to be the actual source of all the Indian incursions which had been sent against the exposed frontier of Virginia, west of the mountains, from Fort Pitt, southward to the Kentucky River. From these points the British officers and emissaries operated upon the Indian tribes, which were dispersed over the whole Northwestern territory, from the Ohio and the great lakes westward to the Upper Mississippi: from these points, also, were planned and supplied the numerous hostile incursions which had spread desolation and blood along the wide frontier east of the Ohio; and these were the points at which the savages were supplied with arms, ammunition, and clothing, to enable them to carry on their murderous warfare into the remote settlements. To these points, too, they carried their captives, torn from their families, and the scalps of their murdered victims, as trophies of their prowess and evidence of their industry. To dry up this fountain of evil, to cut up this death-bearing tree by the roots, a secret expedition was set on foot, for the reduction of the British posts on the Upper Mississippi and upon the Wabash Rivers; this expedition was prompted and guided by the genius and enterprise of Colonel George Rogers Clark, under the authority of the governor and executive council of Virginia. What the commonwealth lacked in men and means, was fully supplied by the courage, skill, and daring intrepidity of her frontier defenders.

The entire expedition was to consist of three hundred and fifty men, at most, or seven companies of fifty men each, or such portion of them as could be enlisted for the enterprise. Even this number could not be spared from the exposed frontier settlements, and Colonel Clark was at length compelled to undertake his hazardous enterprise with less than half the number authorized by the instructions of Governor Henry, and with no other means than twelve hundred dollars in depreciated paper currency of the time, and an order on the commanding officer at Fort Pitt, for transports and supplies of powder and ammunition: each private was also promised a bounty of three hundred acres of land.

By virtue of three royal charters, Virginia claimed all the territory within which the contemplated expedition was now to be directed were situate. The first charter, dated 10th of April, 1606, extended along the sea-coast, from the thirty-fourth to the forty-first degree of north latitude, but only fifty miles inland; the second charter, of May 23d, 1609, granted all those lands situate, lying, and being in that part of America called Virginia, from the point of land called Cape or Point Comfort, all along the sea-coast to the southward two hundred miles; and all that space and circuit of land lying from the sea-coast of the precinct aforesaid, up into the land throughout, from sea to sea, west and northwest; and also all the islands lying within one hundred miles along the coast of both seas of the precinct aforesaid. The third charter, dated March 12th, 1612, annexed to Virginia all the islands within three hundred leagues of the coast. Previous to the granting of these charters to the Company of Merchant Adventurers, Virginia was understood to extend from thirty-four to forty-five degrees of north latitude, bounded by the ocean to the east, Florida to the south, and Canada, or New France, to the north; but toward the west unlimited and unknown.[1] The three royal charters were vacated by writ of *quo warranto* in the year 1626, at which time a commission was issued for the government of Virginia, by officers immediately under the appointment of the king, without, however, making any alteration in boundaries.[2] The colony was afterward curtailed on the north by the grant to Lord Baltimore, and to William Penn; and on the south by that to the proprietors of Carolina. By the treaty of 1763, the river Mississippi was established as the boundary between British America and Louisiana.[3]

Surmounting great difficulties, and by extraordinary exertions, Colonel Clark assembled his force, consisting of six incomplete companies, at the Falls of the Ohio, about the middle of June, 1778. Selecting from his whole force, four companies of picked men, each armed with a rifle, tomahawk, and scalping-knife, he confided their respective commands to his captains—Montgomery, Bowman, Helm, and Harrod; the party commenced their voyage down the river, about the 24th of June, in keel-boats; their destination was Kaskaskia.

Reaching Fort Massac, Clark determined on crossing the country by land, and having sunk his boats, to conceal them, he commenced his toilsome and perilous march through a trackless wilderness, wading through swamps, and traversing unsheltered prairies, under the heats of a summer sun, for a distance of one hundred and twenty miles. At length, on the evening of the 4th of July, the party reached a point within two miles of Kaskaskia. Here they remained concealed until boats were collected to take them across the river, to surprise the town. In the dead of the night, two divisions crossed the river, and were instantly in possession of the town, the inha-

---

1 Keith's Virginia, part i. 53. 2 Idem. part i. 141.
3 Docum. Hist. Boundary Question.

bitants of which were aroused from their sleep by the wild Indian-like yells and cries of their conquerors, who, constantly, during the night, warned the affrighted inmates of the houses, not to appear in the streets, on pain of immediate death. Colonel Clark, in the mean time, was equally successful in his capture of the fort, on the opposite side of the river: he found the gates open, and not a sentinel was posted, nor an alarm given, until the commander, Rocheblave, found himself and all his force, prisoners to an unforeseen enemy. Lieutenant Rocheblave was captured while in bed with his wife, and she, with the tact of an intelligent woman, managed to secure her husband's public papers, which she concealed among her dresses in her trunks: these were not searched by the polite invaders, and Colonel Clark never obtained possession of them.

The fort was unconditionally surrendered by Rocheblave, and the inhabitants of the town having been disarmed, and forbidden to communicate with each other from their houses, their worst fears were naturally excited as to the treatment they might expect to receive from the dreaded Long Knives. British falsehood had transformed, in the eyes of the simple French, the American into the most obdurate and bloodthirsty savage, and the terror of the captured people was wrought up to the extreme. In the morning, the appearance of the victors, their sunburnt visages and tattered garments, so much at variance with the pomp and splendour of military command, was by no means calculated to allay the fears of the inhabitants. They looked for captivity and separation from their families, as one of the least of their dreaded evils, and a deputation waited on Colonel Clark, deprecating such events, and supplicating mercy for their wives and children. They solicited permission to meet, perhaps for the last time, in the church, there to take leave of each other; this was granted to them by Clark, but he would not listen to any thing further. After their melancholy meeting had taken place, the leading men renewed their application for food and clothing for their women and children, and begged that they might not be separated from them.

Clark now saw that the proper hour for leniency had arrived, and in a speech which he made to them, he disabused them of the false opinions they had entertained as to the character of the Americans; he told them that one cause of their war against the English in this region, was to protect their own wives and children from the tomahawk and knife of the merciless savage, who was incited to every such bloody deed by the English commanders; he also informed them of the alliance between the King of France and the Americans, (the news of which Clark had very lately heard,) and that they were now united in war against Great Britain, the hereditary enemy of France; he finally told them that they should be at liberty to take either side they chose, in the contest, and that they and their wives and children should be at liberty, their property protected, and any insult which should be offered to their religion should be immediately punished.

The joy produced by these announcements may well be conceived, and one natural result quickly followed: nearly all the population declared for the American cause, and acknowledged the jurisdiction of the United States and of Virginia over the country; and when a detachment was ordered next day to march against Cahokia, the Kaskaskians offered to go with it and secure the submission of their neighbours. In this also success was obtained, and on the 6th of July, the two chief posts in the Illinois had passed, and without bloodshed, from the possession of England into that of Virginia.

With the exception of Detroit, the most important western post was Fort St. Vincent, or, as named by the English, Fort Sackville, situate on the Wabash River, now known as Vincennes. This post remained as yet unconquered, and Colonel Clark could scarcely hope to obtain possession of it with his small force, as he must of necessity be for some time engaged near the Mississippi, in organizing a government for the territory he had taken, and in treating with the Indians of the Northwest. Under these circumstances, Colonel Clark accepted of the offer of M. Gibault, the priest of Kaskaskia, who assured him that by persuasion alone, he could lead the inhabitants of Vincennes to throw off their forced connection with England; and this he undertook to do. Accordingly, on the 14th of July, in company with another inhabitant of Kaskaskia, M. Gibault departed upon his mission of peace; and upon the first of August he returned with the intelligence that the oath of allegiance to the Old Dominion had been taken by the inhabitants of the post on the Wabash.

Colonel Clark having established courts, and placed garrisons at Kaskaskia, Cahokia, and Vincennes, directed a fort to be erected at the Falls of Ohio, which proved the germ of Louisville; in October of this year, the Legislature of Virginia established the county of Illinois, and John Todd was appointed lieutenant-colonel and civil commandant. The jurisdiction of Virginia was thus formally extended over all the settlements on the Wabash and the Upper Mississippi; and the Indian tribes in the vicinity of all the Northwestern British posts, panic-struck at the daring courage and success of the Virginia troops, hastened to enter into treaties of amity with their renowned leader, whose policy, dictated by long acquaintance with the Indian character, was to impress them with a sense of the power of the Americans, of their unalterable determination to punish their enemies, and to fight them until they should be compelled to sue for peace.

In the mean while the success of Colonel Clark justly alarmed the British commander at Detroit, Lieutenant-governor Henry Hamilton, who immediately collected all the force in his power, composed of regular troops, militia, and Indians, and determined to proceed to the Illinois country, recapture tho conquered posts, devastate the infant settlements of that region, and above all, to make prisoner of Colonel Clark, and bring him to Detroit as the chief trophy of the expedition.

The reputation of Colonel Hamilton for honourable warfare did not stand high in the estimation of the Americans; he had pursued, together with other coadjutors at Detroit and elsewhere, the abominable policy of urging the Indians to the extremes of barbarity, by offering rewards for scalps, but none for prisoners—a course which naturally resulted in wholesale and cold-blooded murder, as the Indians would often drive their captives within sight of the British forts, and then butcher them. Such an ultra-barbarous policy procured for the British lieutenant-governor the soubriquet of "the hair-buyer," by which name he was very generally known.

Hamilton's first efforts were directed against Vincennes, where he arrived in December, 1778, and summoned the garrison to surrender. Captain Helm, who had been left in command of the fort by Colonel Clark, but with no garrison to protect it, was nevertheless not disposed to yield without obtaining honourable terms. Therefore, loading his single cannon, he bade the enemy to halt, and desired to know what terms would be granted the garrison in case of a surrender. Governor Hamilton being, of course, unwilling to lose time, and risk the lives of his men, offered all the usual honours of war to the garrison; and his surprise may well be imagined, when he saw march out, Captain Helm, of Fauquier county, Virginia, and a private named Henry; these were the only regulars; there were also three others, volunteer citizens of Vincennes, who were dismissed, while the captain and his fellow-soldier were detained prisoners of war. The people of Vincennes were obliged to renounce their adhesion to the government of the United States and Virginia, and to resume a forced allegiance once more to Great Britain.

Governor Hamilton took up his winter quarters in the town and fort, and proceeded no further in his design of recovering Kaskaskia and Cahokia, and of capturing Colonel Clark; who, on his part, having learned late in the month of January, of the recapture of Vincennes, devised his plans to avoid being sent a prisoner to Detroit, by capturing Colonel Hamilton, and sending him a prisoner to the capital of Virginia.

Accordingly, Colonel Clark assembled his forces at Kaskaskia on the 5th of February, 1779; they consisted of one hundred and thirty men,[1] and including pack-horsemen, &c., one hun-

[1] Jefferson's Writings, i. 451. Clark's Letter.

dred and seventy;[1] with this little force he set forward to besiege the British governor, who had under him seventy-nine men as a garrison.[2] On the day previous, a batteau had been repaired, provisioned, manned, and armed with forty-six men, and was on her way down the Mississippi, in order to ascend the Ohio and Wabash, and co-operate with the land forces destined against Vincennes.

On the 7th of February, in rainy weather, the paths covered with mud and water, Clark's little band of brave souls commenced their toilsome way toward Vincennes, one hundred and fifty miles distant; and after the most indefatigable and almost incredible exertions, reached within a few miles of that post on the 21st of the same month. Drenched by daily rains, while traversing woods and prairies slippery with mud; crossing rivers by means of trees felled for their purpose; fording other deep streams, and often obliged to wade for miles over the low grounds which were now overflowed from the swollen rivers—often thus struggling, up to their necks in water, with an uncertain and unseen foothold beneath them; sometimes without sufficient provision, and at all times deprived of the means of rest, while almost sinking under accumulated fatigue, Colonel Clark and his heroic followers no sooner found themselves in sight of the goal of their enterprize, than, eager for an anticipated victory, they marched to the town, took possession of it without difficulty, and their leader immediately summoned the fort to surrender. The commander, Colonel Hamilton, found his post surrounded by Clark's forces, who met with a cordial reception from many of the inhabitants of the town, and under cover of the houses and fences, an almost incessant fire was kept up against the garrison, day and night; there was not much return made from the guns of the fort, as its defenders could scarcely open the port-holes without becoming a mark for the American backwoodsmen. Seven British soldiers were thus severely wounded, if not killed, while during the whole of the siege, only one of the Ameri-

---

[1] Bowman's MS. [2] Clark's Letter to Jefferson.

cans was wounded. At length, on the 24th of February, Colonel Hamilton capitulated, and surrendered the garrison as prisoners of war. He was sent with some others prisoners to Virginia, where the council ordered their confinement in jail, fettered, and alone, as a punishment for the barbarous policy he had pursued in relation to the scalps of prisoners. But as this rigid confinement, however just, was not in accordance with the terms of Hamilton's surrender, General Phillips protested in regard to it, and Jefferson having referred the matter to the commander-in-chief, Washington gave his opinion decidedly against it, in consequence of which the Council of Virginia released the Detroit "hair-buyer" from his irons.[1]

The capture of Vincennes placed Detroit within the reach of the enterprising Virginian, but as his force was too small to conquer and also to garrison the British posts, he concluded to wait for the reinforcements which had been promised him by Governor Patrick Henry. The people of Detroit had great rejoicings when they heard of Hamilton's capture; Clark, in his letter to Jefferson, says that with five hundred men when he first reached Illinois, or with three hundred after the conquest of St. Vincents, he could have taken Detroit; the garrison of the fort was but eighty strong.[2]

A few days after the surrender of Vincennes, Colonel Clark learned that a convoy of merchandise, including goods for the Indians and supplies for the army, was advancing by way of the Wabash, from Detroit, under an escort of forty men. Clark, with his accustomed secrecy and despatch, immediately took measures to capture the rich cargo and its escort, before the news of the fall of Vincennes could reach the advancing party. Captain Helm, the late British prisoner, was sent, at the head of sixty men, to intercept the convoy; in a few days he returned, completely successful, having captured the entire escort as prisoners of war, and their cargo, amounting to ten thousand pounds in value, without the loss of a man in this enterprise.

---

[1] Sparks's Washington, vi. 315. See also Note H.

[2] Jefferson's Writings, vol. i. 451.

The results of Clark's expedition against the Illinois posts must ever be viewed as of the greatest importance—difficult, indeed, of estimation. It has been ascertained that Hamilton had made arrangements to enlist the southern and western Indians for the next spring campaign, and it is believed that Brandt and his Iroquois were to act in concert with him.[1] Had Clark failed to conquer Hamilton, there is every reason to believe that the whole West, from the Mississippi to the Alleghanies, would have been swept and desolated; the union of all the tribes from Georgia to Maine, against the colonies, in their struggle with Britain, might have been effected, and the whole current of our national history changed! No doubt, this great measure of policy had been in contemplation by Great Britain from the outset of the American contest; and the vast and controlling influence which a military occupation of the whole country from Detroit to the mouth of the Ohio, and bounded westward by the Mississippi, would inevitably have over the Indian tribes, gave an immense and fearful power to England. During the struggles of the American Revolution, the most of those tribes either joined the forces of the English, remained neutral under their control, or were engaged in predatory and destructive warfare on every American settlement within their reach. It is true that distress and suffering were common to all the colonies during the trying period of the Revolution, and they were borne with fortitude by all; by none with more than by the settlers of the West. Had it not been for their bold resistance and partisan warfare on the frontiers of population, who will now undertake to say what might have been the result of a pouring out by England of her troops from Canada, in the whole rear of the settlements of the Atlantic States, assisted as she could command herself to be, by all the Indian nations of the West? One matter is very certain, that a great check was given to the power of the British over the Indians, and a vast extent of frontier country wrested from the possession of the

---

[1] Butler's Kentucky, p. 80. Stone's Life of Brandt, vol. i. 400.

enemy by the patriotism of Virginia in fitting out expeditions, and by the prudence, judgment, perseverance, and bravery of one of Virginia's sons, Colonel George Rogers Clark. In the result of his enterprise and success, Virginia obtained possession of her claimed territory, the great Northwest, at this day comprising five of our confederated States—Ohio, Indiana, Illinois, Michigan, and Wisconsin.

Independent of the predatory excursions of the Indians from this region of country, on the frontiers of the old States, the Northwest remained in a comparative degree of quietude during the progress of the Revolutionary war: it exhibits few events to engage the attention of the annalist, in regard to organized government, production, or commerce; and a total barrenness in relation to settlement and growth of population. We look in vain beyond the military stations, and the old French settlements in Southern Illinois, and the vicinity of Detroit, for the traces of the agriculturist; we find alone the path of the hunter, the accustomed route of the Indian trader, and the scattered Indian villages with their little cultivated patches of corn, squashes, and melons. But the time was approaching with slow and sure steps, although yet far distant, when this magnificent country was to receive a dense population of industrious citizens, and to yield certain returns for labour, unsurpassed in richness by those of any part of the world.

Several of the Eastern States, under their colonial charters, laid claim to portions of the land comprised in the territory northwest of the Ohio River; as those charters had been granted by the crown, these lands were denominated crown lands. After the peace of 1783, it was urged in argument in our political bodies, that as the Revolutionary war had been carried on for the defence and general benefit of the whole country, the several States claiming these lands, and who could not realize any special advantage from these possessions, ought to relinquish them as a common fund for the benefit of the United States, rather than to suffer the whole nation to sink under a burden of debt. A concession of these lands was in fact made an important object in establishing the confederation.

Soon after the treaty with France had rendered it highly probable that the war of the Revolution would eventuate in the foundation of an independent government on this side of the Atlantic, the anxiety of the Continental Congress increased, to adjust amicably all conflicting titles to the wild lands of the West. For that purpose, on the 6th of September, 1780, a resolution was passed, earnestly recommending to those States who had claims to the Western country, to pass such laws, and give their delegates in Congress such powers, as would effectually remove the only obstacle to a final ratification of the articles of confederation. On the 10th of October, Congress declared that the territory ceded should be disposed of for the common benefit of the Union, and be formed into republican States, possessing the same rights and privileges with the other States; and to be of proper extent of territory, not less than one hundred, nor more than one hundred and fifty miles square; and that the expense incurred by any State since the commencement of the war, in subduing any British post, or in maintaining and acquiring the title, should be reimbursed.

On the 2d of January, 1781, Virginia responded to this request, and passed a law offering to cede all right and title to the lands northwest of the Ohio, with certain conditions. One was, "that the territory so ceded shall be laid out and formed into States containing a suitable extent of territory, not less than one hundred, nor more than one hundred and fifty miles square." The other was, "that all the remaining territory of Virginia between the Atlantic Ocean, and the southeast side of the Ohio, and the Maryland, Pennsylvania, and North Carolina boundaries, shall be guarantied to the commonwealth of Virginia by the United States." To the first proposition Congress acceded, as it was in conformity with her own resolution previously passed; the other proposition was rejected, because "Congress wished to avoid all discussion of the territorial rights of individual States."[1]

In March, 1781, New York ceded to the United States all her claims to the lands northwest of the river Ohio. Massachusetts made her deed of cession in April, 1785, of all her right to lands west of the line fixed by New York. In September, 1786, Connecticut ceded all the lands included within her chartered limits lying one hundred and twenty miles west of the western boundary of Pennsylvania; and in August, 1787, South Carolina granted to the United States her right to land lying west of the chain of mountains which divide the eastern and western waters.

Notwithstanding the refusal of Congress to give the guaranty demanded by Virginia, this State, on the 1st of March, 1784, ceded all right and title which the commonwealth had to the territory lying northwest of the river Ohio, with conditions; one of which was, that it should be formed into states as proposed in the resolution of Congress of 1780. At the time this resolution was adopted, it is evident that Congress was very deficient in knowledge of the geography of the country for which they were legislating. After the close of the war, enterprising individuals traversed the whole country which had been ceded to the United States, and companies were formed to explore and settle the fertile and beautiful lands beyond the Ohio. From such sources, Congress soon collected sufficient information to show that the promise given to the States by the resolution of October, 1780, imposed inconvenient restrictions. Accordingly, on the 7th of July, 1786, they again took into consideration the resolution of 1780, and the conditions in the deeds of cession, which related to the boundaries of the States that were to be formed northwest of the Ohio. The proceedings of Congress on this occasion shed much light on the question of boundaries, which of late years has much agitated the public mind, in the States formed in the northwestern territory, on the true meaning

---

[1] Thomas's Report, North. Boundary, March 2d, 1836.

and construction of the fifth article of the ordinance of 1787.[1]

It was first proposed to apply to Virginia and Massachusetts, to revise and change their acts of cession, so as to empower Congress to make such division of the ceded territory into states as the situation of the country and future circumstances might require; with this limitation and condition, that all the territory of the United States lying northwest of the river Ohio, shall be formed into a number of states not less than two, nor more than five, to be admitted into the confederacy, on the principles and in the forms heretofore established and provided.

In lieu of this proposition, Mr. Grayson, seconded by Mr. Lee, (both of Virginia,) offered the following:—"That it be recommended to the States of Virginia and Massachusetts, so to alter their acts of cession as that the states in the Western Territory may be bounded as follows: There shall be three states between the Ohio and a line running due east from the Mississippi to the eastern boundary of the United States, so as to touch the most southern part of Lake Michigan.

"The State lying on the Mississippi shall be separated from the middle State by a line running north from the western side of the mouth of the Wabash River, till it intersects the said east line; the middle State shall be separated from the others by the aforesaid line, and a line running also due north from the western side of the mouth of the Big Miami, till the intersection thereof with the said east line; and the other State shall be divided from the middle State by the said line, the said east line, Lake Erie, the bounds of Pennsylvania, the other original States, and Ohio; there shall be a State between the said east line, Lake Michigan, Lake Huron, and the straits of Michillimackinac; and another between the said east line, the Lake Michigan and Superior, and the boundary line of the United States, and the river Mississippi."

For this proposition all the delegates of Virginia voted;

---

[1] Docum. Hist. Boundary Question.

Massachusetts voted against it. The question was lost; five States voting in the affirmative, five in the negative, and two States, New York and South Carolina, were each divided in their votes. Another proposition (offered by Mr. Pinckney) was adopted. This was, to strike out the words "with this limitation," &c., so as to leave the number of States discretionary with Congress. Finally the resolution, as modified, was adopted by Congress unanimously, twelve States voting in the affirmative. This resolution is as follows:—

"Resolved, that it be, and hereby is, recommended to the Legislature of Virginia, to take into consideration their act of cession, and revise the same, so far as to empower the United States, in Congress assembled, to make such a division of the territory of the United States lying northerly and westerly of the river Ohio, into distinct republican States, not more than five nor less than three, as the situation of that country, and future circumstances may require; which States shall hereafter become members of the Federal Union, and have the same rights of sovereignty, freedom, and independence as the original States, in conformity with the resolution of Congress of the 10th of October, 1780."

On the 13th of July, 1787, Congress passed the celebrated "commended and commendable" Ordinance for the government of the territory of the United States northwest of the river Ohio; the fifth article of this ordinance is in strict accordance with the above resolution as to the number of States to be formed in the territory, and the boundaries of three of them, are therein specially defined; subject however to be altered so far that if Congress shall hereafter find it expedient, they shall have authority to form one or two States in that part of said territory which lies north of an east and west line drawn through the southerly bend of Lake Michigan.

On the 30th of December, 1788, Virginia gave her assent to the resolution of Congress in relation to altering the terms of her act of cession, and ratified and confirmed the fifth article of the ordinance of 13th July, 1787; this being the only part of the compact between the original States and the people and States of the territory northwest of the Ohio River, to which the assent of Virginia was required to give it validity.[1]

Viewing the ordinance of 1787 as a solemn compact, entered into, after years of deliberation on its provisions, between the original States and the people and States of the great Northwestern Territory, one of its provisions prominently presents itself, considered then and now as of vital importance to the welfare of the whole country; important to the civil and political institutions of the several original States, as well as of those thereafter to be formed in the territory of the Northwest; important as the forerunner of one of the great compromises embodied in the Constitution of the United States, which had not yet been adopted, and which at that period was still under solemn deliberation; important as a sacred and inviolable agreement, made by the unanimous voice of eight States, being all that were present, and an equal number of slave and free States being represented; of immense importance, when considered as a political basis, on which has hitherto rested, in a great measure, the peace and harmony of the Union, the perpetuity of which might be greatly endangered by any rash attempt even to disturb it, much less to abrogate it.

This important provision is the following:

"Article 6th. There shall be neither slavery nor involuntary servitude in the said territory, otherwise than in the punishment of crimes, whereof the party shall have been duly convicted. *Provided always*, That any person escaping into the same, from whom labour or service is lawfully claimed in any one of the original States, such fugitive may be lawfully reclaimed and conveyed to the person claiming his or her labour as aforesaid."

---

[1] Old Journals, vol. iv. 373. Land Laws, p. 100, 338. Report on Northern Boundary, March 2d, 1836. Ordinance of 1787. Old Journal, iv. passim. Sparks's Washington, ix. 48. Perkins, 292. See, also, Note I.

This was the first great compromise made between the slaveholding and non-slaveholding States; it was made previous to the adoption of the Federal Constitution; paramount in point of time, it is at least equal, in its force and effect, to any of the compromises contained in that instrument. Legal enactments by Congress have at subsequent periods followed both the spirit and the letter of the compromise of 1787; one the Missouri compromise of 1820, another the act of 1850, generally called the Fugitive Slave Law. In our own day, 1854, the introduction of the so-called "Nebraska Bill" in the Houses of Congress, has once again not only agitated the whole Union on the subject of these compromises, but strikes at the very root of their validity and inviolable character. The fate of this "Bill," and of its effects throughout the length and breadth of our land, is yet in the womb of time.

During the past half century, five attempts were made, at five different times, by the people of the Northwestern Territory, to impair the slavery compromise of 1787; five times did Congress, without any distinction between Northern and Southern members, refuse to impair it. The territory of Indiana had been slave territory under the French government, and continued so under the American, until 1787. It extended to the Mississippi, and contained many slaves. Vincennes, Kahokia, Prairie de Rocher, Kaskaskia, were all slaveholding towns. The inhabitants were attached to that property, and wished to retain it, at least temporarily, and also to invite a slaveholding immigration, until an increase of population should form an adequate supply of free labour; and they petitioned Congress accordingly. The petition came from a convention of the people, presided over by Governor Harrison, and only asked for a suspension of the anti-slavery part of the ordinance for ten years, and limited in its application to their own territory. The petition received its answer in a report made by a select committee, of which Mr. Randolph was chairman: "The committee deem it highly dangerous and inexpedient to impair a provision wisely calculated to promote the happiness and prosperity of the Northwestern country, and to give strength and security to that extensive frontier. In the salutary operation of this sagacious and benevolent restraint, it is believed that the inhabitants of Indiana will, at no very distant day, find ample remuneration for a temporary privation of labour and immigration."

This report of the Select Committee, became the answer of the House of Congress to the Indiana petition of 1803, fifty years ago. The answer is a peremptory refusal to yield to a request even for a ten years' local suspension of this anti-slavery clause; "highly dangerous and inexpedient to impair that provision;" to *impair!* it is a refusal to weaken or lessen in the smallest degree, a "benevolent and sagacious act," which the committee recommend to remain "unimpaired," because it is calculated to increase the happiness and prosperity of the Northwest, and to give strength and security to its frontier.

But this was not an end to the petitions; the people of Indiana were not satisfied with one repulse. They returned to the charge, and four times more, in the course of as many years, renewed their application for the ten years' suspension of the ordinance. It was rejected each time: five times in as many years rejected by Congress, and the rejection the more emphatic, in some instances, because it was the reversal by the House of a favourable report from a committee.[1]

Wise statesmen, profound politicians, stern patriots, have ever regarded the anti-slavery clause in the ordinance of 1787 as an act equal in its force and effect with the Constitution of the United States. In March, 1784, the Virginia delegation in Congress, headed by Jefferson and Monroe, conveyed the Northwestern Territory to the thirteen United States. In April ensuing, Mr. Jefferson brought in an ordinance for the government of the territory so conveyed, with the anti-slavery clause as a part of it, to take effect in the year 1800, but without a clause for the recovery of fugitive slaves. For want

---

[1] Benton's Speech on the "Nebraska Bill," April 25th, 1854.

of this provision, the anti-slavery clause was opposed by the slave-holding States, and rejected. In July, 1787, the ordinance was remodelled, the anti-slave clause, with the fugitive slave recovery clause, as they now stand, were inserted in it, and in that shape the ordinance had the unanimous vote of every State present—eight in the whole—four slave, and four free States.[1]

[1] Note K.

# CHAPTER IV.

## THE NORTHWESTERN TERRITORY.

British retain the Western posts—Effect on the Indians—Land speculations in the West—Washington's opinion—Cession of title by the States—Retrospective view—Steuben sent to take possession of Western posts—He is refused the possession—Causes assigned—Boundary line not to be crossed—British strengthen the posts—Great council of Indian tribes—Treaties of Fort Harmar—Not adhered to—Brant and the Northern confederacy—St. Clair, governor of the Northwestern Territory—Indians deny the validity of his treaties—State of the case—Ordinance of 1787—Unwise proceeding of government—British policy and agency—Encouragement given to Brant—Influence of McKee, Elliott, and Girty—Mission of Gamelin to the Western tribes, and his report—Conduct of British agents—United States adopt war measures against the Indians—St. Clair's levies, and dissensions—Harmar's Expedition, and two defeats—Discord in his army—Indian villages destroyed—Indian account of the battles—Action of the government in relation to the Indian War—Peace messengers and warlike preparations—British agents and Indians dissatisfied—American policy explained—Scott's Expedition—Wilkinson's Expedition—St. Clair organizes his army at Fort Washington—Commences his march—Builds Forts Hamilton and Jefferson—Reaches the waters of the Wabash—Army encamps—Attacked by the Indians and entirely defeated—Great loss of the Americans—Causes of defeat—St. Clair exculpated—New army authorized by Congress to be raised—General Wayne appointed to its command—Peace still offered to the Indians—The chiefs of the nations are invited to the seat of government—Commissioners meet the Indians in council—Indians insist on the Ohio boundary—Attempts at peace fruitless—The causes—British erect a new fort on the Maumee—Spain offers assistance to Indians—Wayne assembles his forces at Fort Washington—Final report of the peace commissioners—Wayne moves his army—Establishes Fort Greenville—Goes into winter quarters—Buries the bones on the field of St. Clair's defeat—Fort Recovery built—Attack by the Indians on an escort—Wayne learns the movements of the Indians and the British agents

—Indians attack Fort Recovery, and are repulsed—Wayne marches from Greenville—Builds Fort Defiance—Sends a peace messenger to the Indians—The reply of the Indians—Wayne marches on—Leaves his heavy baggage—Moves down the Maumee—Battle, and complete victory—Wayne destroys Indian and British property—Effect of the victory on the Indians—The army returns—Fort Wayne built—Fort Loramie built—Army in winter quarters at Greenville—Indian spirit subdued—The tribes disposed to peace measures—Opposition made by the British agents—Great council held—Propositions made by the English governor of Detroit—Brant coincides—Indians do not consent—They send peace messengers to the Americans—The preliminaries of peace entered into—Great council held at Greenville, and treaty made—Terms of the treaty—Other events during the Indian War—Genet, French minister; his schemes to involve the United States in war—His attempts in the West; contemplated invasion of Louisiana and Florida—Separation of the Western States, and revolt in the Spanish provinces, projected—Genet issues commissions—Excitement among the Western people—Action of the United States government—Genet recalled by France, who disowns his acts—Free navigation of the Mississippi insisted on by the United States; denied by Spain—Governor Miro relaxes the stringent measures in relation to duties—He grants special privileges of trade on the Mississippi—Attempts of Spain to dismember the Union—Operations in relation to the navigation of the Mississippi—Unsuccessful attempts of government to treat with Spain—Baron Carondelet's policy and attempts to separate the West—Treaty of Madrid—Free navigation of Mississippi secured—New Orleans a free port of deposit—Yazoo speculation—Projected British invasion of the Spanish provinces, by way of the lakes and the Illinois—Spanish posts withheld from the Americans—The causes—Spanish perfidy and duplicity—Powers proceeds to Detroit, the head-quarters of Wilkinson—Conduct of Wilkinson—New Orleans ceases to be a port of deposit, unless duties are paid—The act of the Intendant reversed by the King of Spain—Jefferson sends ministers to France and Spain—Spain cedes Louisiana to France—Diplomacy of the American ministers relative to the purchase of Louisiana—All Louisiana purchased from France—Spain objects, but renounces opposition—Effectual agency of Mr. Livingston—Spanish and French claims to land—British evacuate the Western posts—Northwestern Territory—Ohio set off—Indiana created—Extent of the United States' possessions in the Northwest.

THE treaty of peace of September, 1783, was not accompanied by the immediate surrender of the British posts to the American authorities. Much recrimination occurred between the two governments, each charging the other with the non-performance and violation of certain articles of the treaty; and more than ten years of diplomatic controversy intervened, creating and cherishing bitter feelings on both sides of the Atlantic, before a great part of the disputes were in a measure settled, by Jay's treaty of 1794. In the mean time, the British retained possession of the posts on the American side of the great lakes, and, as those posts gave their possessors a decided influence over the warlike tribes of Indians in their neighbourhood, this was a subject to which the United States were peculiarly sensible.

The year 1784 had nearly passed away before the determination of the British cabinet not to evacuate the Western posts, was known to the government of the United States. To the detention of these posts on the lakes, was ascribed the hostile temper manifested by the Indians; for it unfortunately was soon apparent that the cessation of hostilities with England was not necessarily the cessation of warfare with the native tribes; and, while all hoped that the horrors of border war in the West were ended, it was not difficult to see the probability of a continued and violent struggle. Thus, to the indignity of permitting a foreign power to maintain garrisons within the limits of the nation, were superadded the murders perpetrated by the savages, and the consequent difficulty of settling the fertile and vacant lands of the West.[1]

Virginia, at an early period, (in October, 1779,) had by law discouraged all settlements, on the part of her citizens, northwest of the Ohio;[2] but the prospect of peace added fuel to a spirit of land-speculation that soon became stronger than law; and in what manner to throw open the immense region which lay west of the mountains, without driving the natives to desperation, was a problem for statesmen to solve. Washington, in a letter to James Duane, in Congress, in September, 1783,[3] writes upon the difficulties which lay before that body in relation to the public lands. He pointed out the necessity

---

[1] Marshall's Washington, vol. ii. [2] Rev. Stat. of Vir. vol. ii. 378.
[3] Sparks's Washington, vol. viii. 477.

which existed for making the settlements compact; and proposed that it should be made even felony to settle or survey lands west of a line to be designated by Congress, which line, he added, might extend from the mouth of the Great Miami to Mad River, thence to Fort Miami, on the Maumee, and thence northward, so as to include Detroit, or, perhaps, from the fort, down the river to Lake Erie. He proposed other stringent measures, in order to preserve the tranquillity of the Northwest; but, before Congress could take any efficient steps to that effect, it was necessary that those measures of cession which commenced in 1780–81 should be completed. Six days after the date of this letter, on the 13th of September, Congress stated the terms upon which they would receive the proposals of the Old Dominion for the cession to the United States of all their right in the territory northwest of the river Ohio.[1]

We have seen the result of the action of Congress, and of the several States claiming the lands of the Northwestern region, terminating in the adoption of the famous ordinance of July 13th, 1787: our view must now be turned to the condition of this portion of the Northwestern Territory, from the latter period to the time of the formation of a distinct territorial government in Wisconsin. A retrospective glance at existing affairs is, nevertheless, necessary.

In July, 1784, General Washington had sent Baron Steuben to Canada for the purpose of obtaining possession of the Western posts, under the terms of the treaty of 1783, with orders, if he found it advisable, to embody the French of Michigan into a militia, and place the fort at Detroit in their hands. The baron was received by General Sir Frederick Haldimand with politeness, but, at the same time, was told by him that he had received no orders to deliver up the posts along the lakes; and the necessary passports were refused.[2] The retention of the posts by the British was alleged to be for the purpose of preserving the peace of the frontiers, as the

---

[1] Old Journals, iv. 189.

[2] Sparks's Washington, vol. viii. 463.

Indian tribes scattered along the Northwestern Territory were alarmed at the prospect before them of the advance of the white population, and were daily showing undoubted signs of dissatisfaction, if not of hostility. The true ground of existing differences between the Indians and the United States was a question of boundary, and the encroachments of white settlements already made, together with the dread of future action in this respect. The Indians maintained that the Ohio River was the line, and was not to be crossed by the Americans; and, as the Indians were not included in the treaty, it became a nice legal question how far the United States had a right to advance upon the territory then occupied by the Indians. The posts in Michigan thus withheld from the possession of the United States were Detroit and Michillimackinac; and Great Britain, in order to guard against the incursions of the Americans, took immediate measures to garrison the fort of Detroit, under instructions from Lord Dorchester.[1]

In December, 1786, a grand confederate council of the Indians northwest of the Ohio, was held near the Huron village, at the mouth of the Detroit River, which was attended by the Six Nations, the Hurons, Ottawas, Miamies, Shawanese, Chippewas, Cherokees, Delawares, Pottawatamies, and the confederates of the Wabash. The council was pacific, providing that the United States did not encroach on their lands. It was finally proposed to call a grand council of the Indians, in which the whole ground of complaint between the savages and the United States should be discussed, and some final determination made.

This council was held, and, although no records of its proceedings have been discovered, yet it is believed that they were forwarded to Lord Dorchester. It is probable that there was a division in their deliberations, because two separate treaties were held at Fort Harmar, in January, 1789, which were attended by only a part of the Indians. These treaties were held by General St. Clair: in the first place with the

---

[1] Lanman's Michigan, p. 150. See Note A.

Five Nations, with the exception of the Mohawks; and the second was made with the warriors and sachems of the Wyandot, Delaware, Ottawa, Chippewa, Pottawatamie, and Sac tribes.[1] But these treaties, if meant in good faith, were not respected by those who made them; and, in a short time, the confederacy of Northern Indians, which had, three years before, been formed by the noted Brant, or Thayendanegea, exhibited their long-smothered feelings of hatred and hostility to the Americans; and, in their subsequent success in the defeats of Harmar and St. Clair, acquired not only a confidence in themselves, but spread terror over the frontier white settlements, and deep concern in the councils of the nation.

Major-general Arthur St. Clair had been appointed governor of the Northwestern Territory, in October, 1787. Among his first important acts was, making the treaties at Fort Harmar, in January, 1789; one of these treaties the confederated nations of the lakes especially refused to acknowledge as binding; their council, in referring to it afterward, in 1793, using these words:—

"Brothers: Your commissioner, (General St. Clair,) after having been informed by the general council of the preceding fall, that no bargain or sale of any part of these Indian lands would be considered as valid or binding, unless agreed to by a general council, nevertheless persisted in collecting together a few chiefs of two or three nations only, and with them held a treaty for the cession of an immense country, in which they were no more interested than as a branch of the general confederacy, and who were in no manner authorized to make any grant or cession whatever. Brothers: How then was it possible for you to expect to enjoy peace, and quietly hold these lands, when your commissioner was informed long before he held the treaty of Fort Harmar, that the consent of a general council was absolutely necessary to convey any part of these lands to the United States?"

Also, in 1795, at the Treaty of Greenville, Masas, a Chip-

---

[1] Lanman's Michigan, p. 149, 151.

pewa chief, who signed the treaty at Fort Harmar, said—"Elder Brother: I was surprised when I heard your voice, through a *good interpreter*, say that we had received presents and compensation for those lands, which were thereby ceded. I tell you now, that we, the Three Fires, never were informed of it. If our uncles, the Wyandots, and grandfathers, the Delawares, have received such presents, they have kept them to themselves. I always thought that we, the Ottawas, Chippewas, and Pottawatamies, were the true owners of those lands, but now I find that new masters have undertaken to dispose of them; so that, at this day, we do not know to whom they of right belong. I don't know how it is, but ever since that treaty, we have become objects of pity, and our fires have been retiring from this country."

In reference to this treaty at Fort Harmar, the truth seems to be, that the confederated nations as a whole did not sanction it, although the Wyandots, and some other tribes, acknowledged its binding force. The relations of the Indians and the United States, in 1789, appear to have stood thus:—Transfers of territory had been made by the Iroquois, the Wyandots, the Delawares, and the Shawanese, which were scarce open to any objection; but the Chippewas, Ottawas, Kickapoos, Weas, Piankeshaws, Pottawatamies, Eel River Indians, Kaskaskias, and above all, the Miamis, were not bound by any existing agreement to yield the lands north of the Ohio. If their tale is true, the confederated tribes had forbidden the treaty of Fort Harmar, and had warned Governor St. Clair that it would not be binding on the confederates. They wished the Ohio to be a perpetual boundary between the white and red men of the West, and would not sell a rod of the region north of it. So strong was this feeling that their young men, they said, could not be restrained from warfare upon the invading Long Knives, and thence resulted the unceasing attacks upon the frontier stations and the emigrants.[1]

---

[1] **Perkins's Annals.** American State Papers, vol. v. **Stone's Brant, vol. ii.**

If the treaty of Fort Harmar had been the sole ground whereon the United States could have claimed of the Indians the Northwest Territory, it may be doubted whether right would have justified the steps taken in 1790, '91, and '94: but before that treaty, the Iroquois, Delawares, Wyandots, and Shawanese had yielded the south of the Ohio, the ground on which they had long dwelt. It was not without reason that Washington expressed a doubt as to the justness of an offensive war upon the tribes of the Wabash and Maumee; he says (speaking of these tribes)—"In the exercise of the present indiscriminate hostilities, it is extremely difficult, if not impossible, to say that a war without further measures would be just on the part of the United States.[1]

By the third article of the Ordinance of 1787, it is declared "that the lands of the Indians shall never be taken from them without their consent." It may perhaps with great truth be said that the Federal government in taking those steps in 1790 and 1791, which resulted in such calamitous consequences, acted unwisely; and that in the outset, it should have done what it did in 1793, after St. Clair's disastrous defeat; that is, have sent commissioners of the highest character to the Lake tribes, and in the presence of their friends, the British, learned their causes of complaint, and offered fair terms of compromise. Such a step, government, by its subsequent action, acknowledged to be wise and just.[2]

The agency of the British in keeping up Indian hostility after the peace of 1783, has been thus summed up:—Most of the tribes adhered to England during the Revolutionary struggle. When the war ceased, however, England made no provision for them, and transferred the Northwest to the United States without any stipulation as to the rights of the natives. The United States, regarding the lands of the hostile tribes as conquered and forfeited, proceeded to give peace to the savages, and to grant them portions of their own land. This produced discontent, and led to the formation of the confederacy headed

---

[1] American State Papers, vol. v. 97. [2] Perkins, 328.

by Brant.[1] To assist the purposes of this union, it was very desirable that the British should still hold the posts along the Lakes, and supply the red men with all needful things. The forts they claimed a right to hold, because the Americans disregarded the treaty of 1783; the trade with the Indians, even though the latter might be at war with the United States, they regarded as perfectly fair and just. Having thus a sort of legal right to the position they occupied, the British did, undoubtedly and purposely, aid and abet the Indians hostile to the United States.[2] In 1785, Brant went to England to solicit aid for his confederacy; he stated the forgetfulness of England of her old allies, the Indians; the encroachments of the Americans; the probable consequences, war; and asked support and countenance, such as true and old friends expect. He received a non-committal answer from the British minister, and returned home; he met the confederated natives in November, 1786, and told them he could give them no distinct assurances of aid from England; but the Indian Superintendent, John Johnson, and the commandant at Detroit, Major Matthews, in their correspondence with Brant, gave him every flattering assurance of countenance and protection in his hostile movements, which might fall short of actual aid by arms.[3]

In May, 1787, Major Matthews writes to Brant, apparently with the sanction of the Governor of Canada, (Lord Dorchester, formerly Sir Guy Carleton,) as he says, "his lordship is sorry to learn," &c., as follows:—

"In your letter to me you seem very apprehensive that the English are not very anxious about the defence of the posts. You will soon be satisfied that they have nothing more at heart, provided that it continues to be the wish of the Indians, and that they remain firm in doing their part of the business, by preventing the Americans from coming into their country, and consequently from marching to the posts. On the other hand, if the Indians think it more for their interest that the Americans should have possession of the posts, and

---

[1] Heckewelder's Narrative. [2] Perkins, 332. [3] Stone, vol. ii.

be established in their country, they ought to declare it, that the English need no longer be put to the vast and unnecessary expense and inconvenience of keeping posts, the chief object of which is to protect their Indian allies, and the loyalists who have suffered with them. It is well known that no encroachments ever have, or ever will be made, by the English upon the lands or property of the Indians, in consequence of possessing the posts; how far that will be the case, if ever the Americans get into them, may very easily be imagined, from their hostile perseverance, even without that advantage, in driving the Indians off their lands, and taking possession of them."[1]

With such assurances on the part of British authority, together with the ever active influence of such wretches as Alexander McKee, Matthew Elliot, and Simon Girty, who were living disgraces on civilized society, in their transactions between the whites and the Indians, it is not a matter of surprise that the hostility of the confederated nations against the Americans should have been kept ever alive. Of the history of the lives and conduct of these Indian traders, English agents, and leaders of murderous war-parties of savages, (for they, each, combined these characters,) this is not the place to speak; but the whole history of the border warfare of the Northwest, is replete with the instances of their perfidy and cruelty, which in the scale of humanity, sunk them beneath the savage whose cause they had espoused.

In the spring of 1790, General Washington being desirous of learning the real sentiments of the Northwestern Indians, Governor St. Clair instructed Major Hamtramck at Fort Knox (Vincennes) to send some experienced person to ascertain the views and feelings of the Miamis and their confederates. The person chosen was Anthony Gamelin, who proceeded on his mission on the 5th of April. The Piankeshaws, Kickapoos, and Weas, all referred him to their elder brethren, the Miamis, so that he had to journey on to the point where the

---

[1] Stone's Brant, ii. 271.

Miamis, Shawanees and Delawares resided. He arrived there on the 23d of April, and on the 24th he assembled the Indians, with whom he held various conferences in public council, and in private interviews, during five or six days, the result of which may thus be summed up.

He gave to each nation two branches of wampum, and made his speech to them, in the presence of the French and English traders, who were invited to attend. He showed them the treaty at Muskingum (Fort Harmar) made between Governor St. Clair and sundry nations, which displeased them. He offered them peace, without proposing any conditions for them to submit to at this time. They told him they could give him no answer without hearing from their father at Detroit; the Shawanees and Delawares delivered him back his branches of wampum, and desired him to go to Detroit to hear the chief. Le Gris, the great chief of the Miamis, told him he might go back when he pleased; that he could not give him a positive answer until all the Lake nations, together with the commandant at Detroit, had been consulted on the subject of his speeches, of which he asked a copy in writing. He promised to send an answer to Vincennes in thirty days. Gamelin gave him a copy of his speech.

At the last council, Gamelin told him he had nothing to say to the commandant at Detroit, nor the commandant to him; that he had given them a copy of his speeches to be shown to him, and that he would not go to Detroit, unless they intended to take him there. Blue Jacket told him, that they did not intend to force him to go there, but only proposed it to him, thinking it for the best. An answer was promised in thirty days.[1]

On the 8th of May, Gamelin returned to Fort Knox; and on the 11th, news arrived that the northern savages had already gone to war upon the Americans, and that three days after Gamelin left the Miamis, an American captive had been burned in their village.[2] All these matters plainly foretelling

[1] Perkins, 329. Am. State Papers, v. 93. [2] Idem. 87.

trouble on the frontier, Governor St. Clair hastened to Fort Washington to concert with General Harmar a campaign into the country of the hostile tribes.

It has been justly remarked,[1] that at the time of Gamelin's mission, in the spring of 1790, before any act of hostility on the part of the United States had made reconciliation impossible, and before the success of the savages had made their demands such as could not be granted, it would have been true wisdom to have sent to the northern tribes, not an Indian trader, but such a representation as was sent three years later, composed of General Benjamin Lincoln, Beverly Randolph, and Timothy Pickering.

It is difficult to determine the extent of the aid, by advice or otherwise, which was furnished the Indians by the high and responsible officers of the British crown; but it is certain that by the means of such characters as McKee, Elliot, and Girty, who were the channels of intercourse between them, every peaceful message from such officers was stopped on its way to the excited children of the forest, while every word of a hostile character was added to and exaggerated.[2] "You invite us," said one of the war chiefs to Gamelin, "to stop our young men. It is impossible to do it, being constantly encouraged by the British."

The course adopted by the United States government toward the tribes of the Northwest, was no longer peaceable. Governor St. Clair, in virtue of the authority granted by Congress, by the act of 29th September, 1789, and in pursuance of the order of the President, dated 6th of October, called on Virginia for one thousand, and on Pennsylvania for five hundred militia; this call was made on the 15th of July, 1790, and the force was distributed as follows:—Three hundred were to meet at Fort Steuben, (Jeffersonville,) to aid the troops from Fort Knox, (Vincennes,) against the Weas and Kickapoos of the Wabash; seven hundred were to gather at Fort Washington, (Cincinnati,) and five hundred just below

---

[1] Perkins, p. 337.

[2] Am. State Papers, v. 196.

Wheeling; the two latter bodies being intended to march with the federal troops from Fort Washington, under General Harmar, against the towns at the junction of the St. Mary and the St. Joseph.[1]

About the middle of September, the militia began to arrive at Fort Washington, from Kentucky and Pennsylvania; they were ill equipped, destitute of camp kettles and axes, and with arms wholly unfit for service, and several without any; among them were old, infirm men, and young boys hardly able to bear arms, and many of whom had probably never fired a gun—and the numbers which came were far short of what had been ordered; to all these disadvantages must be added the disputes which arose among them in making the choice of their officers, many of the militia declaring they would return home unless certain individuals could receive the command of them.[2]

The aversion of the frontier men to act with regular troops had been anticipated as the cause of trouble, and it subsequently proved so; but every pains had been taken by General Harmar to avoid the apprehended evil, and notice had been given to the British, that the troops collected were to be used against the Indians alone, so that no excuse might be given to McKee and Co. for co-operation.[3] On the 30th of September, Harmar left Fort Washington with a force of one thousand four hundred and fifty-three men, and every step seemed to have been taken which experience or judgment could suggest, to secure the success of the expedition; the same seems to have been true of the march, as the court of inquiry held in 1791, approved of every arrangement.[4]

Having arrived within thirty or thirty-five miles of the Miami villages, information given by a captured Indian induced the general to send forward Colonel John Hardin with a detachment of six hundred militia and one company of

---

[1] Am. State Papers, v. 94.

[2] See Note B.

[3] Am. State papers, v. 96, 100.

[4] Idem, xii. 24, 33.

regulars, to surprise the enemy and keep them in their forts until the main body could come up with the artillery.[1]

This party marched forward on the 14th of October, and on the next day, about three o'clock, reached the villages, which they found deserted. On the morning of the 17th, the main army arrived, and the work of destruction commenced; so that by the 21st the chief town, five other villages, and nearly twenty thousand bushels of corn had been destroyed.[2]

On reaching the Maumee towns and finding no enemy, it was the design of General Harmar to push forward and attack the Wea and other Indian settlements upon the Wabash, but he was prevented by the loss both of pack horses and cavalry horses, which the Indians seem to have stolen in quantities to suit themselves, in consequence of the wilful carelessness of the owners, who made the United States pay first for the use of their nags, and then for the nags themselves.[3]

Dropping the plan of the march on the Wabash towns, General Harmar despatched Colonel Trotter, with three hundred men, to scour the woods in search of an enemy, as the tracks of women and children had been seen near by; this was on the 18th, but the utter want of energy in the officers, inattention to orders, and the absence of discipline in the army, rendered the expedition fruitless. The party returned in the night to the camp, after having discovered and killed two mounted Indians, who were doubtless sentinels of the enemy; and if this success had been properly followed up, there is every reason to believe that the Indians might have been surprised in their camp, and defeated.

Dissatisfied with the inefficient chase of the preceding day, on the 19th General Harmar sent another detachment, under the command of Colonel Hardin, in search of the enemy. This force proceeded in the route Colonel Trotter had taken the previous day, and found where the enemy had encamped. The same inefficiency on part of the commanding officer, amounting to every thing except cowardice, and the same

---

[1] See Note C. [2] Am. State Papers, xii. 25. [3] Idem, p. 21.

want of discipline in the troops which was exhibited the day before, appears to have accompanied this detachment, but with more disastrous consequences. The enemy was discovered, and his camp was approached by Colonel Hardin, without giving any orders or making any preparations for an attack upon it. He remarked to Captain Armstrong, when informed that the enemy's fires were seen at a distance, that "they would not fight!" and rode on in front of the advance, until fired upon from behind the fires. Hardin's loss of men was very severe, and he was compelled to retreat under all circumstances which constitute a defeat, although the affair was not so considered by the commanding general.

The jealousy between the regulars and the militia, which had been anticipated, began to work mischief. The regular troops disliked to be commanded by Trotter and Hardin; the army officers despised the militia; and the militia, hating them, were impatient under the control of Harmar and his staff. Again, the rivalry between Trotter and Hardin was calculated to make the elements of discord and disobedience yet more widely spread; so that all true confidence between the officers and men was destroyed, and with it, of necessity, all true strength.[1]

Although the troops had been defeated, and their sanguine hopes had been disappointed, still the villages and crops had been burned and wasted, and this may have been considered a sufficient success by Harmar, for the army commenced its homeward march on the 21st of October.[3]

It may well be supposed that Colonel Hardin did not feel easy after his defeat; therefore, the night of the 21st being favourable, he urged the general to send a detachment back to the villages, under the belief that the Indians had returned to the scene of devastation. Harmar was not much disposed to engage in any new experiment, but at length he consented, and Hardin obtained an order for three hundred and forty militia, forty of whom were mounted, and sixty regular troops.

[1] Perkins, 342.

[2] See Note D.

The militia were under the command of Colonel Hardin himself, and the regulars were commanded by Major Wyllys. The detachment reached the banks of the Maumee early in the morning of the 22d, and the spies reported that the enemy was discovered. A plan of attack was formed, by which the enemy was to be surrounded, and the battalions were to support each other, or to embody, as the occasion required, but in no case to separate. The attack commenced, and, as usual, disobedience of orders accompanied it; in place of being surprised, the Indians were prematurely alarmed; they fled in different directions, and the militia battalions pursued them in as many directions: the regulars, being thus unsupported, fell a sacrifice to the Indians, and a second defeat completed the disastrous campaign of General Harmar, from which so much had been expected by the country.[1]

From the reports to the secretary of war, and the general orders of the commanding general, it seems that the destruction of the villages and the corn was considered by him equivalent to a victory, and that the object of the campaign had been effected by such act; but the public were not of that opinion, nor were the Indians themselves, for their own account represents the expedition as an utter failure and defeat. They say—"There have been two engagements about the Miami towns, between the Americans and the Indians, in which it is said the former had about five hundred men killed, and that the rest have retreated. The loss was only fifteen or twenty on the side of the Indians. The Shawanees, Miamis, and Pottawatamies were the principal tribes who were engaged."[2] The commanding general, although not guilty of any breach of military duty, certainly exhibited a total inefficiency for the task intrusted to him, and the result of this expedition against the Northwestern Indians redounded neither to his honour nor to the credit and advantage of the country. When Colonel Hardin returned to camp

---

[1] Am. State papers, v. 104, 105. See Note E.

[2] Stone's Brant, vol. ii. 294.

after his second skirmish, he wished the general either to send another party, or to take the whole army to the battle-ground, but Harmar would not favour either plan. "He thought," he said, "the Indians had received a good scourging." On the morning of the 23d of October, the army took up the line of march for Fort Washington, (Cincinnati.) *Two* men, says Colonel Hardin, wished to have another tussle with the Indians. Of the whole army, only two![1]

The failure of General Harmar's expedition, and the consequent attacks by the Indians on the new settlements on the Ohio, made the government sensible that decisive and strong measures must immediately be adopted, whereby a peace should be obtained by force of arms, or secured by prudent and effective negotiation. The plan adopted was threefold: first to send a messenger to the Western Indians, with offers of peace, to be accompanied by some Iroquois chiefs, who were favourable to America; second, at the same time to organize expeditions in the West to strike the Wea, Miami, and Shawanee towns, in case it should be clear that the peace messenger should fail in his mission; and third, to prepare a grand and overwhelming force, with which to take possession of the country of the enemies, and build forts in their midst.[2]

Colonel Thomas Proctor was selected as the peace commissioner, who left Philadelphia on his mission, March 12th, 1791. Having reached Cornplanter's settlement, and with difficulty prevailed on certain Iroquois chiefs to accompany him, provided they obtained a water passage, the whole enterprise failed, as the British commandant at Niagara would not allow an English vessel to be hired to convey the ambassadors up Lake Erie; and no other could be obtained. This refusal of Colonel Gordon to grant the required permission, may, in a great measure, be accounted for in the fact that the governor-general, Lord Dorchester, Colonel Gordon, and Brant, (Thayendanegea,) who possessed so much influence over the

---

[1] Hardin's Deposition. Am. State Papers, xii. 34. Cist's Miscellany, i. 105.
[2] Am. State Papers, xiii. 36.

savages of the Northwest, were naturally offended at the entire disregard shown by the American government to such influence; and as those tribes were entirely under the control of the British agents, Dorchester, Gordon, and Brant might look for an appeal to them as mediators in the coming quarrel; or at least that their mediation would be accepted by the Americans, if asked for by the Indians; an acceptance of the kind given in 1793, after St. Clair's defeat, and not then considered dishonourable or degrading. Besides, the apparently inconsistent proceedings of the American government were calculated both to puzzle and excite the Indians and the English; the seeming, although not actual want of good faith on part of the States, consisted in commissioning General Scott to make war upon the Miamis, Colonel Proctor to treat of peace with them, Governor St. Clair to invade and take possession of their lands, and Colonel Pickering to hold a council with their brethren for burying the hatchet and quenching the destructive brand.[1]

The policy of the American government is exhibited and fully explained in the instructions of President Washington, given through General Knox, secretary of war, to General St. Clair, governor of the Northwestern Territory, on his appointment, in 1791, as commander-in-chief of the forces to be employed in the meditated expedition. The following is the language used:—"An Indian war, under any circumstances, is regarded by the great mass of the people in the United States as an event which ought, if possible, to be avoided. * * * The sacrifices of blood and treasure in such a war, far exceed any advantages which can possibly be reaped by it. The great policy, therefore, of the general government, is to establish a just and liberal peace with all the Indian tribes within the limits and in the vicinity of the territory of the United States. * * * But if all the lenient measures taken, or which may be taken, should fail to bring the hostile Indians to a just sense of their situation, it will be necessary that

---

[1] Stone, ii. 300.

you should use such coercive means as you shall possess for that purpose. * * * If the Indians refuse to listen to the messengers of peace sent to them, it is most probable they will, unless prevented, spread themselves along the line of frontiers, for the purpose of committing all the depredations in their power. To avoid so calamitous an event, Brigadier-General Charles Scott, of Kentucky has been authorized to make an expedition against the Wea or Ouiatanon towns, with mounted volunteers, or militia, not exceeding the number of seven hundred and fifty, officers included. * * * It is confided to your discretion whether there should be more than one of the said expeditions of mounted volunteers or militia. * * * All captives are to be treated with great humanity. It will be sound policy to attract the Indians by kindness, after demonstrating to them our power to punish them on all occasions. * * * If no decisive indications of peace should have been produced, you will commence your march for the Miami village, in order to establish a strong and permanent military post at that place.[1] * * * The Indians continuing hostile, you will seek the enemy and endeavour, by all possible means, to strike them with great severity."[2] * * *

No news of peace having arrived, General Scott's command, with Colonel John Hardin, as a volunteer without commission, accompanying him, moved on the Wabash towns, where they arrived on the 1st of June, 1791. The Indians abandoned their villages on the approach of the army; some slight skirmishing occurred at several points, but no decisive battle; several Indians were killed in attempting their escape across the river, and Colonel Hardin, with a detachment of sixty mounted infantry, and a troop of light horse under Captain McCoy, killed six warriors and took fifty-two prisoners. The village of Ouiatanon was destroyed: many of the inhabitants were French, and lived in a state of civilization. By the books, letters, and other documents found there, it is evident

---

[1] Junction of the St. Joseph's and St. Mary's rivers, forming the Maumee, or Miami of the Lake.

[2] Am. State Papers, v. 171.

that place was in close connection with, and dependent on Detroit. A large quantity of corn, a variety of household goods, peltry, and other articles were burned with this village, which consisted of about seventy houses, many of them well finished.[1]

Scott's expedition having succeeded, thus far, in destroying the settlements of the enemy, returned; and not having reached the higher towns on the Wabash, Governor St. Clair despatched a second expedition, under Colonel Wilkinson, against the villages on Eel River. Wilkinson left Fort Washington on the 1st of August, and on the 7th reached the Wabash just above the mouth of Eel River. Word having been brought to him that the enemy was alarmed and flying, he ordered a charge, plunged through the river, and found the enemy unable to make the smallest resistance. Six warriors, two squaws, and a child were killed, thirty-four prisoners taken, and a captive released, with the loss of two men killed and one wounded. This town, says Colonel Wilkinson, was scattered along Eel river for full three miles.[2]

This expedition had the same results as those of Harmar and Scott; villages were burnt, growing corn cut up, and settlements destroyed; but no victory had yet been obtained over the Indians, no strong post had yet been established in their midst, and the great object of the government in securing the tranquillity of the frontiers was yet as distant as ever.[3]

Governor St. Clair, having received his instructions, proceeded to organize his army, and on the 15th of May, 1791, he reached Fort Washington. At that time the whole United States troops in the West amounted to two hundred and sixty-four non-commissioned officers and privates fit for duty. By the 17th of September, the army was increased, by the arrival of recruits, to two thousand three hundred strong, exclusive of militia; it then commenced its forward movements, and on

[1] Am. State Papers, v. 131. [2] Idem, 134.

[3] See Note F.

the Great Miami built Fort Hamilton, the first in the chain of fortresses. This being completed, the troops moved on, forty-four miles further, and on the 12th of October commenced Fort Jefferson. On the 24th, the troops resumed their march, and on the 3d of November reached a branch of the Wabash, which General St. Clair supposed to be the St. Mary of the Maumee. Upon the banks of this creek the army encamped in two lines; it was now not more than fourteen hundred strong, owing to considerable desertion of the militia on the march, sixty at a time; sickness among the troops, and the absence of parties sent to arrest deserters. General St. Clair himself was suffering from a severe indisposition, by turns afflicting him in his stomach, lungs, and limbs.[1]

Here the general was attacked in his camp, about half an hour before sunrise, on the morning of the 4th of November, just as the men had been dismissed from parade. The attack was made by the Indians on the militia, who soon gave way, and rushed into camp, throwing the regulars into a disorder which was never altogether remedied, and the Indians closely following them. The attack was made instantly by the enemy on both of St. Clair's lines, and the great weight of it against the centre, where the artillery was placed, from which the men were repeatedly driven with great slaughter. The general ordered a charge with the bayonet; the Indians were repulsed, but soon returned to the attack, and the troops gave way. The camp was entered by the left flank, and the troops driven in; successful charges on the enemy were repeatedly made, but many men, and particularly officers, were lost; the artillery was silenced, all the officers killed, except one, who was badly wounded, and more than half of the army had fallen, when a retreat was ordered. This was accomplished; it was not only a precipitate retreat, but a flight; the camp and artillery were abandoned, as not a horse was left alive to draw off the guns, had it been practicable; arms and accoutrements were thrown away by the men, even after the pursuit

---

[1] St. Clair's Journal. Am. State Papers, v. 136.

had ceased. The Indians followed the retreating army about four miles, and the fugitives continued their flight until they reached Fort Jefferson, twenty-nine miles distant, a little after sunset. The action began about half an hour before sunrise, and the retreat was attempted at half an hour after nine o'clock.

The defeat of St. Clair was most disastrous in its consequences; the loss of life, both of officers and men, was exceedingly severe; it was in its effects a second Braddock's defeat; the plans and hopes of Washington, Knox, and St. Clair, in reference to the Indian campaign and its results, were in one hour overthrown. The causes which led to so fatal a termination of the expedition were at a subsequent period fully inquired into by a committee of the House of Representatives, which expressly declared the general free of all blame in relation to every thing both before and during the action.[1] The true causes of the defeat appear to have been the surprise by the Indians, who were in no degree expected by the army, and the confusion introduced at the outset by the flying militia. The savage forces were led with ability and valour, and in no recorded battle did the sons of the forest ever show themselves better warriors. The retreating army reached Fort Washington on the 8th of November: it is said (perhaps on the best authority) that something more than one thousand Indians were engaged in this battle: St. Clair's total force, we have seen, did not exceed fourteen hundred.[2]

The loss in this disastrous battle, on the part of the Americans, was very great, when compared with the numbers engaged. Thirty-eight commissioned officers were killed upon the field, and five hundred and ninety-three non-commissioned officers and privates were slain and missing. Twenty-one commissioned officers, several of whom afterward died of their wounds, and two hundred and forty-two non-commissioned and privates were wounded. Among the dead was the brave and lamented Major-General Butler. No estimate could be

---

1 American State Papers, xii. 38. 2 Perkins, 371. See also Note G.

made of the loss of the Indians, but the probability is that it bore no proportion to that sustained by the American army. However unfortunate St. Clair may have been, the report of the committee of inquiry explicitly exculpated him, and more satisfactory testimony in his favour is furnished by the circumstance that he still retained the undiminished esteem and good opinion of the President.[1]

Meanwhile the exigency of the times imperiously demanded that a new army should immediately be raised, and when Congress had authorized such measure, it became a difficult question with the executive to select a person in all respects qualified for its command. St. Clair had requested a court of inquiry to examine into the reasons of his defeat, and expressed his wish to resign his post as commander of the Western forces, so soon as the examination had taken place. This proposition was rendered nugatory, as under the existing system no court of inquiry could be constituted to adjudge his case, and Washington accordingly informed him that it was neither possible to grant him the trial he desired, nor to allow him to retain his position.[2] From the list of general officers spoken of to command the army, the President selected Major-general Anthony Wayne.

But previous to proceeding to the last extremity, it was the wish of Washington that every effort should be made to prevent bloodshed. Authorized agents were sent into the Indian country to learn from the several chiefs their views; invitations were extended to the different nations to send their deputations to Philadelphia to meet the Congress in session, and to take their newly adopted father by the hand; Brant was especially urged to be present in a peace-making council; but all efforts were fruitless. Although the great Mohawk did visit the Federal capital, and was treated with marked attention; although five independent embassies had been sent to the inimical tribes, asking for peace; although fifty Iroquois chiefs visited the city of Brotherly Love, and in the spirit of love

---

[1] Marshall's Washington, vol. ii. [2] Idem. Sparks's Washington, x. 227.

had transacted their business with the American rulers; although various councils were held by the American agents, and inchoate treaties were formed, but not ratified; and although the United States commissioners, Lincoln, Randolph, and Pickering, met the confederated tribes of the Northwest, in the presence of their English friends, at the Rapids of the Maumee, in grand council,—still, pacificatory measures were found to be wholly impracticable. The Indians insisted on the Ohio being the boundary between themselves and the Americans; they denied any right they possessed, by the treaty of peace with England, to purchase Indian lands, as the Indians had never made any agreement with the king, nor with any other nation, that they would give to either the exclusive right to purchase Indian lands; they considered themselves free to make any bargain or cession of lands, whenever and to whomsoever they pleased; they said the great point was that the Americans should consent that the Ohio should be the boundary line, and, without such consent, any further meeting would be unnecessary.[1]

At this great council, which was held at the foot of the Maumee Rapids, August 13th, 1793, were present the chiefs of the following nations:—Wyandots, Seven Nations of Canada, Pottawatamies, Senecas, of the Glaize, Shawanees, Cherokees, Miamis, Ottawas, Messasagoes, Chippewas, Munsees, Mohicans, Connoys, Delawares, Nantakokies, and Creeks. Doubtless, the victories they had gained, and the favourable whispers of the British agents, closed the ears of the red men, and all propositions were rejected in one form or another. This of necessity closed the attempts of the United States to make peace, and from the month of August the preparations for a decision by arms of the question pending between the white and red men went forward constantly.[2]

The causes which led to the rejection of the liberal terms

---

[1] American State Papers, v. 356 et passim. Stone's Brant, ii. 328. Sparks's Washington, x. 313. See Note H.

[2] Perkins, 381, 394.

offered by the United States, and the staking, as it were, by the Indians, of their very existence, on a renewed contest of arms, may be found in the expected aid of England, and also of Spain. Brant, some years afterward, uses this language: "For several years we were engaged in getting a confederacy formed, and the unanimity occasioned by these endeavours among our western brethren enabled them to defeat two American armies. The war continued without our brothers the English, giving any assistance, except a little ammunition; and they seeming to desire that a peace might be concluded; we tried to bring it about at the time that the United States desired it very much, so that they sent commissioners from among their first people to endeavour to make peace with the hostile Indians. We assembled, also, for that purpose, at the Miami River, in the summer of 1793, intending to act as mediators in bringing about an honourable peace, and if that could not be obtained, we resolved to join our western brethren in trying the fortune of war. But to our surprise, when upon the point of entering upon a treaty with the commissioners, we found that it was opposed by those acting under the British government, and hopes of further assistance were given to our western brethren, to encourage them to insist on the Ohio as a boundary between them and the United States."[1]

This confidence in English aid was excited among the Indians by such channels as Elliot, McKee, and Girty; but it was afterward strengthened by the governor-general of Canada, Lord Dorchester, who, in February, 1794, in addressing the deputies from the council of 1793, said, among other equally significant matters:—"Children: I flattered myself with the hope that the line proposed in the year eighty-three, to separate us from the United States, *which was immediately broken by themselves as soon as the peace was signed*, would have been mended, or a new one drawn in an amicable manner. In this I have been disappointed. Children: Since my return I find no appearance of a line remains; and from the manner

---

[1] Stone's Brant, ii. 358.

in which the people of the United States rush on, and act, and talk on this side, and from what I learn of their conduct toward the sea, I shall not be surprised if we are at war with them in the course of the present year; and if so, a line must then be drawn by the warriors. * * * I shall acknowledge no lands to be theirs which have been encroached on by them since the year 1783. They then broke the peace, and as they kept it not on their part, it doth not bind on ours. * * * Therefore all their approaches toward us since that time, and all the purchases made by them, I consider as an infringement on the king's rights. And when a line is drawn between us, be it in peace or war, they must lose all their improvements and houses on our side of it. Those people must all be gone, who do not obtain leave to become the king's subjects."[1]

One of the strongest assurances that England could give the confederates that she would espouse their cause, was sending Governor Simcoe, in April, 1794, to erect a fort at the Rapids of the Maumee, within the acknowledged territories of the United States; which was not only built and fortified, but its commander was well nigh coming to hostilities with General Wayne, on the day of his victory over the Indians at that place.[2] In May, 1794, a messenger from the Mississippi Provinces of Spain, also appeared in the Northwest, offering assistance. "Children," he said, "you see me on my feet, grasping the tomahawk to strike them. We will strike together. I do not desire you to go before me, in the front, but to follow me."[3] Spain had long been fearful and jealous of the Western colonists; she had done all in her power to sow dissensions between the Americans and the Southern Indians, and now hoped to cripple her Anglo-Saxon antagonist by movements at the North.[4]

General Wayne was now using all exertions to bring an army into the field—to grapple with this "Hydra," as he

---

[1] Perkins, 395. See Note I.
[2] Note A.
[3] Stone, vol. ii. 375.
[4] Am. State Papers, vol. v. 304, 308, 325.

termed it, of Indian, British, and Spanish enmity. We have seen that the policy of the government was to be prepared for war, while strenuously using all exertions for honourable peace; therefore, Wayne's "legion" having passed the winter of 1792–3 at Legionville, moved down the river to Fort Washington, in May, 1793, where it was encamped, and engaged in drilling and preparations, the executive having directed the commander-in-chief to issue a proclamation forbidding all hostile movements north of the Ohio, until the Northern commissioners were heard from.[1] The final messages between the American commissioners and the Indians, took place on the 16th of August, at the mouth of Detroit River, and information was immediately sent to General Wayne by three distinct channels, advising him of the issue of the negotiations.

On the 7th of October the legion left Cincinnati, and on the 13th encamped at a strong position selected by Wayne, about six miles in front of Fort Jefferson. This "fortified camp" he named Fort Greenville; it afterward became noted for the great treaty concluded there, and is near the site of the present town of Greenville, in Darke county, Ohio. Here the army wintered; one of the duties performed was of a humane and melancholy character: on the 23d or 24th of December, a detachment was sent forward to take possession of the field of St. Clair's defeat. They arrived on the spot on Christmas day. "Six hundred skulls," says one present, "were gathered up and buried: when we went to lie down in our tents at night, we had to scrape the bones together and carry them out, to make our beds."[2] At this place Fort Recovery was built and garrisoned.

One attack had been made by the Indians, and only one, previous to the troops going into winter quarters at Fort Greenville. On the 17th of October a detachment of ninety

[1] American State Papers, vol. v. 42.

[2] American Pioneer, vol. ii. 294. Will's Letter. Dillon's Indiana, vol. i. 360. American State Papers, vol. i. 458.

men, commanded by Lieutenant Lowry and Ensign Boyd, conducting a quantity of provisions and military stores from Fort Washington, was attacked, early in the morning, by a superior force of savages, seven miles in advance of Fort St. Clair. After a severe skirmish, both officers were killed, and the detachment retreated to Fort St. Clair, leaving thirteen of their number on the field, together with seventy horses, and the stores in twenty-one wagons, to the mercy of the enemy. The whole number killed was fifteen. The wagons and a large portion of their contents were subsequently recovered.[1]

During the spring of 1794, General Wayne was steadily engaged in making every necessary preparation for striking a sure blow at the proper time; and, by means of his spy company, kept himself well informed of the plans and movements of the savages. It appeared that the promise of aid from the British was still encouragingly given to them; two Pottawatamies, taken prisoners by Captain Gibson, of the spies, June 5th, in reply to various questions, answered to the following effect:—"The British had sent three chiefs—a Delaware, a Shawanee, and a Miami—to invite the Pottawatamies to go to war with the Americans. The British were on their way to war against the Americans; the number of their troops at Roche de Bout, for that purpose, was four hundred, with two pieces of artillery, exclusive of the Detroit militia. They had made a fortification around Colonel McKee's house, and stores in which they had deposited all their stores of ammunition, arms, clothing, and provision, which they promised to supply to all the hostile Indians in abundance. The British troops and militia that will join the Indians to go to war with the Americans will amount to fifteen hundred, agreeably to the promise of Governor Simcoe, who will command the whole. The British and the Indians will advance against the Americans about the last of this moon, or beginning of next."[2] (July.)

The conduct of the Indians was in conformity with a reli-

[1] Monette, vol. ii. 297. American State Papers, vol. i. 361.
[2] American State Papers, vol. v. 489.

ance on such aid, and a belief in all the reports brought to their ears by agents of the British, who were constantly stimulating them to acts of hostility. On the 30th of June, the chief "Little Turtle," at the head of one thousand to fifteen hundred warriors, made an assault on Fort Recovery, the advanced post of the Americans: although repelled, the assailants returned to the charge, and kept up the attack the whole of that day and part of the following. This assailing force was not entirely composed of natives, for General Wayne, in his despatch, says "that his spies report a great number of white men with the Indians; and that they insist there were a considerable number of armed white men in the rear, who they frequently heard talking in our language, and encouraging the savages to persevere in the assault; that their faces were generally blacked, except three British officers who were dressed in scarlet, and appeared to be men of great distinction, from being surrounded by a large body of white men and Indians, who were very attentive to them. These kept at a distance in the rear of those that were engaged."[1] In this attack the Americans lost twenty-five killed and missing, and thirty wounded.

General Wayne having been joined at Greenville by General Scott, on the 26th of July, with sixteen hundred mounted men from Kentucky, the "legion" moved forward on the 28th. On the 8th of August the army was near the junction of the Au Glaize and the Maumee, at Grand Glaize, and proceeded at once to build Fort Defiance where the rivers meet. While engaged in this work, Wayne received full and accurate accounts of the Indians, and the aid they would receive from the volunteers of Detroit and elsewhere; he learned the nature of the ground, and the circumstances favourable and unfavourable; and, upon the whole, considering the spirit of his troops, officers and men, regulars and volunteers, he determined to march forward and settle matters at once. But yet, faithful to the spirit of compromise and peace, so forcibly

---

[1] American State Papers, vol. v. 488.

taught by Washington, on the 13th of August he sent Christopher Miller, who had been naturalized among the Shawanees, and had been taken prisoner on the 11th by Wayne's spies, as a special messenger, offering terms of friendship.[1]

On the 15th the troops moved forward, and met Miller returning with a message that if the Americans would wait ten days at Grand Glaize, they (the Indians) would decide for peace or war. Wayne's reply to this was only by marching straight on. On the 18th the legion had advanced forty-one miles from Grand Glaize, and being now near the long looked-for foe, began to throw up some light works called Fort Deposite, wherein to place the heavy baggage during the expected battle. On the 20th, at seven or eight o'clock, all baggage having been left behind, the American force moved down the north bank of the Maumee.

Major Price's battalion of volunteers was kept sufficiently advanced in front, so as to give time for the troops to form in case of action, it not yet being known whether the Indians would decide for peace or war. When they had proceeded about five miles, Price's battalion received a severe fire from the concealed enemy, and were compelled to retreat. The legion immediately formed in two lines, in a thick wood, which rendered it impracticable for cavalry to act, as the ground was also covered with fallen timber. The enemy were formed in three lines, within supporting distance of each other, their left resting on the river, and their line extending nearly two miles at right angles with it; here their right rested in a dense thicket of brushwood. This extended front was intended to outflank the left of the American line; when General Scott was ordered to that quarter with General Todd's brigade, to charge and turn the enemy's right flank. Captain Campbell was ordered to charge the enemy's left; this order was promptly obeyed, but in the advance Captain Campbell was killed, and his command was driven back upon the infantry. The infantry were ordered to advance with trailed arms, and rouse

[1] American State Papers, vol. v. 490.

the Indians from their covert with the bayonet, and, when roused, to deliver a well-directed fire upon their backs, and follow it up immediately with a brisk charge, so as to give no time to reload, or to form their line again.

Such was the impetuosity of this charge by the first line of infantry, that the Indians and Canadians were driven from all their coverts so rapidly, that only a part of the second line of General Scott's mounted battalion could gain their position in time to take an active part in the battle. The Indians were driven through the thick woods and fallen timber more than two miles in the course of one hour, by less than half their number.[1]

The force of the Indians and their white allies was estimated at about two thousand combatants; the troops under General Wayne, who were actually engaged did not exceed nine hundred. The woods, for a considerable distance, were strewed with the dead bodies of the Indians and their white allies—the latter having been armed with British muskets and bayonets. The loss of the American army was comparatively small. Of the legion of cavalry, Captain Robert Mis Campbell, Lieutenant Henry B. Towles, and twenty-four non-commissioned officers and privates were killed, and eighty-seven officers and privates wounded. Of the dragoons and artillery, three were killed and eight wounded. Of the Kentucky volunteers, seven were killed and thirteen wounded. The total loss of killed and missing, including eleven who died of their wounds was forty-four: the whole number of wounded was one hundred.[2]

The battle was fought in view of the British post: the Americans encamped for three days on the banks of the Maumee, in sight of the fort: the troops burned all the houses and destroyed all property of every kind belonging to the Indians and Canadians, as well as the house and store

---

1 American State Papers, vol. i. 491. Butler's Kentucky, p. 237. Monette, vol. ii. 305.

2 American State Papers, vol. i. 491. See also Note K.

of the British agent—McKee. General Wayne reconnoitred the fort and its defences, by advancing with his staff within range of the guns: this gave occasion to the correspondence between Major Campbell, the British commandant, and General Wayne, which has been formerly mentioned.[1]

This was one of the most decisive battles ever fought with the Western Indians, and tended more than any other to humble the power and spirit of the hostile tribes. The name of General Wayne alone was more terror to them than an army, for they looked upon him as a chief who never slept, and whom no art could surprise.

The army returned to Fort Defiance, where it arrived August 27th, having laid waste all the adjacent country. The defences of the fort were completed, and the line of march was taken up for the "Miami Villages" at the confluence of the St. Joseph's and the St. Mary's Rivers, forty-seven miles above Fort Defiance. A site was here selected by General Wayne for another stockade fort, which was completed by the 23d of October, and named by Colonel Hamtramck "Fort Wayne," in honour of the commander-in-chief.

On the 18th of October the cavalry and a greater portion of the infantry set out from Fort Wayne on their march for Greenville. On their way a detachment was left at Loramie's Creek, seventy miles from Fort Wayne, where Fort Loramie was erected. On the 20th of November the regular troops went into winter quarters at Greenville. The campaign of 1794 put a close to the Indian hostilities in the northwest. The spirit and power of the savages had been subdued; their country had been ravaged with fire and sword; their houses and their fields were destroyed; their supplies consumed; their hopes of checking the advance of the white population had been blasted; and now, fearing the power of the United States, they soon began to evince a disposition to enter into amicable negotiations for a permanent

---

[1] See Note A.[1]

treaty of peace and friendship, notwithstanding the opposition urged by the British agents.[1]

Strong attempts were made by these agents, that their opposition should be effective; Governor Simcoe sent for the chiefs of the different hostile Indians, inviting them to meet him at the mouth of the Detroit River to hold a treaty. Simcoe, McKee, and Brant, together with Blue Jacket, Buckongahelas, the Little Turtle, Captain Jonny, and other chiefs of the Delawares, Shawanees, Miamis, Tawas, and Pottawatamies, and about one hundred Mohawks and Messasagoes who came with Brant, assembled at the appointed place about the first of October. Some of the chiefs desired to treat with Wayne, but Governor Simcoe insisted that the Indians should not listen to any terms of peace from the Americans, but to propose a truce, or suspension of hostilities, until the spring, when a grand council of all the warriors and tribes of Indians should take place for the purpose of compelling the Americans to cross to the east side of the Ohio; and in the interim, advised every nation to sign a deed or conveyance of all their lands on the west side of the Ohio, to the king, so as to give the British a pretext or colour for assisting them, in case the Americans refused to abandon all their posts and possessions on the west side of the river; and which the Indians should warn them to do immediately after they (the Indians) were assembled in force in the spring, and to call upon the British to guaranty the lands thus ceded in trust, and to make a general attack on the frontiers at the same time; that the British would be prepared to attack the Americans also in every quarter, and would compel them to cross the Ohio, and to give up the lands to the Indians.

Brant advised them to keep a good heart and be strong; to do as their father advised; said he would go home and return in the spring with an additional number of warriors, to fight, kill, and pursue the Americans, who could not possibly stand against the numbers and force which would be op-

---

[1] Monette, vol. ii. 307, 308.

posed to them; that he had always been successful, and would insure them victory.[1]

But notwithstanding these inimical councils, and the unusually large presents then made to the Indians, the chiefs and nations were much divided; many were inclined for peace; many preferred holding their lands under the Americans, as they did not like the *title* of the British, and in a short time the general wish of the natives to make peace became apparent.[2]

Messengers of peace from the Chippewas, Ottawas, Sacs, Pottawatamies, and Miamis, came to Colonel Hamtramck, at Fort Wayne, in the last days of December; and on the 24th of January, 1795, these nations, together with the Delawares, Wyandots, and Shawanees, entered into preliminary articles with the commander-in-chief at Greenville.[3] As contributing to this desirable result, may be considered the circumstances, that the red men were disappointed in the conduct of their white allies after the action of the 20th of August: Brant said "a fort had been built in their country under pretence of giving refuge in case of necessity, but when that time came, the gates were shut against them as enemies."[4] During the winter, (as Wayne had laid waste their fertile fields,) the savages were wholly dependent on the British, who did not half supply them; their cattle and dogs died, and they were themselves nearly starved.[5] They thus lost faith in the British, and after the carnage experienced at the hands of the "Black Snake," (as Wayne was called,) the various tribes by degrees made up their minds to ask for peace, and during the winter and spring they exchanged prisoners and made ready to meet General Wayne in June, at Greenville, for the purpose of forming a definite treaty, as was agreed should be done, by the preliminaries of 24th of January.[6]

The representatives of the northwestern tribes began to

---

1 Am. State Papers, vol. v. 548.

2 Ibid.

3 Idem, 559, 566, 567.

4 Stone, vol. ii. 390.

5 American Pioneer: i. 53.

6 See Note L.

gather at Greenville during the month of June; they continued to arrive until the 18th of July, and it appeared from their statements that most of them had been tampered with by McKee, Brant, and other English agents, even after they had agreed to the preliminaries of January 24th, and while Jay's treaty was still under discussion; but they had all determined to make a permanent peace with the "thirteen fires," and bury the hatchet for ever.[1]

The treaty of Greenville, "a great and abiding peace document," was finally agreed upon and signed on the 3d of August, 1795; it was laid before the Senate, December 9th, and ratified December 22d, and thus terminated the old Indian wars of the West. At the execution of the treaty there were present eleven hundred and thirty chiefs and warriors of the several nations and tribes of the Wyandots, Delawares, Shawanees, Ottawas, Chippewas, Pottawatamies, Miamis, Weas, Eel Rivers, Kickapoos, Piankeshaws, and Kaskaskias. It was signed by eighty-four chiefs, representing these nations and tribes, and by General Anthony Wayne, sole commissioner on part of the United States.

By the 3d article of this treaty, certain lands were relinquished to the United States by the Indian tribes, and among them the only portions west of Lake Michigan, are, one piece of land six miles square at the mouth of Chicago River, emptying into the southwest end of Lake Michigan, where a fort formerly stood—one piece twelve miles square at or near the mouth of the Illinois River, emptying into the Mississippi—one piece six miles square at the old Peoria's fort and village, near the south end of the Illinois Lake, on said Illinois River.

By the 4th article of the treaty, in consideration of the cessions and relinquishments aforesaid, the United States relinquished their claims to all other Indian lands northwestward of the river Ohio, eastward of the Mississippi, and westward and southward of the great lakes, and the waters

---

[1] Am. State Papers, vol. v. 566, 568. See Note M.

uniting them, according to the boundary line agreed on by the United States and the king of Great Britain in the Treaty of Peace made between them in the year 1783. But from this relinquishment was excepted 150,000 acres near the Rapids of the Ohio, which had been assigned to General Clark for the use of himself and his warriors; the post of Vincennes on the river Wabash, and the lands adjacent, of which the Indian title has been extinguished; the lands at all other places in possession of the French people and other white settlers among them, of which the Indian title has been extinguished, as mentioned in the 3d article; and the Post of Fort Massac toward the mouth of the Ohio; to all the above, the tribes relinquish all their title and claim.

By the 5th article of the treaty it was provided—That, to prevent any misunderstanding about the Indian lands relinquished by the United States in the fourth article, it is now explicitly declared that the meaning of that relinquishment is this: the Indian tribes who have a right to those lands are quietly to enjoy them, hunting, planting, and dwelling thereon so long as they please, without any molestation from the United States; but when those tribes, or any of them, shall be disposed to sell their lands, or any part of them, they are to be sold only to the United States; and until such sale, the United States will protect all the said Indian tribes in the quiet enjoyment of their lands, against all citizens of the United States, and against all other white persons who intrude upon the same. And the said Indian tribes again acknowledge themelves to be under the protection of the said United States, and no other person whatever.

It was during the period of the existence of the Indian wars, that events of great local importance to the West occurred, without in their effects producing the results which were intended and calculated on by the projectors and actors in the political dramas of the time. In May, 1793, Citizen Genet appeared in the United States as the representative of the French republic; his *secret* instructions were to induce the government, and if that could not be done, the *people* of the United States, to make common cause with France against all her enemies; although his *open* instructions spoke of the United States as being naturally neutral in the existing contest between France and the united powers of England, Holland, and Spain. In pursuance of his plan, Genet and his emissaries began a system of operations, the tendency of which was to involve the people of the United States in a war with the enemies of France, without any regard to the views of the Federal government.[1] It was sought, through the prejudices which had been roused against the Spaniards relative to the navigation of the Mississippi, to instigate an invasion of Louisiana and Florida by the people of the United States, and, if practicable, even a separation of the Western States, and an alliance with Louisiana, under the dominion and protection of France. Connected with this scheme, a revolt of the French population of Louisiana against the Spanish authority was contemplated.[2]

Genet and his emissaries moved boldly; they issued commissions to a number of persons as officers in the French service, with authority to raise troops in the United States for the contemplated invasion and revolution of Louisiana; and the field of their operations was the Western country, particularly in Kentucky and Tennessee. They succeeded so far as to persuade George Rogers Clark to become a major-general in the armies of France, and commander-in-chief of the revolutionary forces on the Mississippi. Public meetings were held; addresses were made to the people by democratic societies; representations and remonstrances were made to Congress; the governor of a sovereign State had expressed himself favourable to the views of, and unwilling to act against Genet and his coadjutors; the French population of Louisiana were elated with the prospect of emancipation from absolute monarchy, and were ripe for a rising against the Spanish authorities; but the wise and prudent measures adopted by

---

1 Marshall's Washington. American State Papers, i. 454.

2 Monette, vol. ii. 482, and authorities cited.

Washington and his cabinet, frustrated all the designs of the French minister. Governors Shelby and St. Clair and General Wayne were written to, and instructed; troops were prepared; Fort Massac was renewed, in order to stop by force any body of armed men who should proceed down the Ohio; just and correct views of existing affairs were disseminated among the people; and by request made of the French government that Genet should be recalled, the plans of that mischief-maker and his agents were effectually defeated; the rulers of France disowned his acts—he was ordered back to Europe, and the conclusion of the efforts of his agents was found in the proceedings of a meeting held at Lexington, Kentucky, which denounced Washington and all that adhered to him.[1] The dismemberment of the West was nevertheless prevented.

By the treaty of 1783, Great Britain relinquished to the United States all the territory on the east side of the Mississippi, from its sources to the 31st parallel of north latitude, which was to be the boundary of Florida on the north.

With this relinquishment, of course, was ceded all the previous rights of Great Britain to the free navigation of the river to its mouth, as derived from previous treaties with France and Spain. The United States therefore claimed the free navigation of the river to its mouth.

At the same time, Great Britain had ceded to Spain all the Floridas, comprising all the territory east of the Mississippi and south of the southern limit of the United States. Hence Spain possessed all the territory on the west side of the river, and Florida on the east; and the river for the last three hundred miles flowed wholly within the dominions of Spain. His Catholic Majesty, therefore, claimed the exclusive right to the use of the river below the southern limit of the United States.

In reference to the free navigation of the Mississippi, the United States asserted a natural right, independent of any

---

[1] Am. State Papers, xx. 931. Marshall, ii. 335. Butler, 234.

claim derived through Great Britain. The American people occupied and exercised dominion over the whole eastern portion of the Mississippi Valley, comprising all the country drained by its great eastern tributaries, and the east bank as low as the northern limit of Florida. This gave to them the natural right to follow the current of their rivers to the sea, as established by the admitted laws of nations.

The use of the river was necessary, and absolutely indispensable to the Western settlements, which were now fast rising into political importance. Situated as they were, no power on earth could prevent the final appropriation of the river below them to their use, when their numbers should enable them to maintain their rights by force.

Such was the question between the two governments, and concession on the one side, or war on the other, was the only alternative presented. For the whole West there was but one outlet, and that was through the province of Louisiana, and by way of the port of New Orleans. This circumstance alone must of necessity lead to difficulties between the Spanish authorities and the people of the United States. The Western people had, at a very early period after the treaty of 1783, begun to demand *as a right* the free navigation of the Mississippi.

In 1786, Spain occupied both banks of the Mississippi below the mouth of the Ohio, and no less than four military posts on the eastern bank of the former, confirmed her power to collect heavy duties on all imports by way of the river from the Ohio region. These duties were arbitrary, and often unjust; every boat descending the river was compelled to land and submit to the revenue exactions.

In 1787, when Governor Miro entered on the duty of his office over the province of Louisiana, he resolved, with the approbation of Don Gardoqui, the Spanish minister to the United States, to relax the import and transit duties on the river trade from the Western settlements. Many privileges of free trade were granted to favoured individuals; among these were the privileges granted to Colonel James Wilkinson, between the years 1787 and 1790, of a free trade in tobacco, flour, and other Western productions, besides the privilege of introducing several hundreds of American families into Louisiana and the West Florida districts.[1] By this new arrangement, the excitement of the Western people was greatly calmed, and Miro was esteemed as a friend and benefactor; but many of the people of Kentucky, although satisfied and pleased with the commercial privileges extended by Miro, were unwilling to submit to the species of vassalage implied by the *manner* in which the river commerce was enjoyed. They claimed these advantages not as special favours, but as common and indefeasible rights.

In 1791, the Spanish government boldly showed its designs to dismember the Union. Various inducements were held out to those who were willing to submit to the Spanish dominion. Grants of land were promised to such as desired to make their permanent residence in Louisiana. It was disseminated among the people that the Spanish government would grant to them as a *community, every commercial advantage and privilege* which could be desired, provided they were disconnected from the Federal government *east* of the mountains. The Spanish minister resident in the United States had declared unequivocally to his confidential correspondent, that unless the Western people, and especially those of Kentucky, would *declare themselves independent* of the Federal government, and establish for themselves an independent form of government, Spain would never allow them the free navigation of the Mississippi; "but upon those terms *he was authorized*, and would engage to open the navigation of the river for the exportation of their products and manufactures, on terms of mutual advantage."[2]

The American government, in the mean while, had been exerting itself by every means of honourable negotiation, to obtain the "free navigation of the Mississippi, from its source to its mouth;" but all efforts had been unsuccessful, and Gardoqui, the Spanish minister, had given what was considered a

[1] Butler's Kentucky, p. 154, 170. Monette, vol. i. 494 et passim.

[2] Idem. Butler, 177.

conclusive answer, that the Spanish king *would never permit any foreign power* to use that river, both banks of which belonged to him.[1]

The Baron de Carondelet succeeded Governor Miro in his office of governor and intendant of Louisiana and West Florida; but his policy in respect to granting commercial privileges was the reverse of that of his predecessor. Hence the people of Kentucky, and of that quarter of the West, were the more easily disposed to listen to the persuasions of Genet and his emissaries to join in the contemplated invasion of Florida and Louisiana, and thus by conquest obtain the desirable boon of the free navigation of the Mississippi, which the negotiations of government had hitherto failed to procure. The unsuccessful termination of Genet's plans, while it relieved Carondelet from the apprehension of such an invasion, did not deter him from pursuing a similar course in endeavouring to sever the people of the West from the general government of the United States: he entered with ardour and perseverance on a systematic plan of operations; his efforts were mainly directed on the people of Kentucky, with whom he proposed particularly to treat; and the opening of the navigation of the Mississippi, and the establishment of commercial regulations equally beneficial to both parties, and the Western people generally, was the old lure especially held out to induce them to enter into negotiations with his agent, Colonel Gayoso, who was to be sent by him to New Madrid in October, 1795, for that purpose.[2] He did not cease from his operations, or despair of success until after the treaty of Madrid, nearly three years afterward.[3]

By this treaty, which was signed October 20th, 1795, boundaries were defined between the territories of the United States and Spain; the middle of the Mississippi was to be the western boundary of the United States, from its source to the intersection of a line of demarcation, which was the thirty-first parallel of north latitude from the Mississippi, east-

[1] Jay's Life, i. 235. [2] Am. State Papers, xx. 926. [3] Monette, i. 505, ii. 185.

ward, &c. &c., being the north boundary of the Floridas. The King of Spain stipulates that the whole width of said river, from its source to the sea, shall be free to the people of the United States. He also stipulates that the people of the United States be permitted for the term of three years to use the port of New Orleans as a place of deposit for their produce and merchandise, and to export the same, free from all duty, &c. &c. Other commercial advantages were also held out as within the reach of negotation.[1]

The great Yazoo speculation was about this time set on foot; but of which it is here unnecessary further to speak than merely to observe, that in its concoction and projected operations it bid fair to rival the famous "Mississippi Scheme" of John Law. The act of the Georgia Legislature, which authorized this great scheme of speculation, was in the next annual session declared to be null and void, as having been obtained by fraud and corruption. Nevertheless, the seeds had been already sown which might be expected to produce a full harvest of public as well as private injury; and it was not until near twenty years afterward, that the "Yazoo Bubble" was finally set at rest, by the action of the national legislature on that subject.[2]

Spain, having entered into an alliance with France, had declared war against Great Britain in 1796; the British authorities in Canada had planned an invasion of Upper Louisiana, by way of the lakes and the Illinois River, whenever hostilities should be formally proclaimed. To prevent this invasion was one object to be gained by Spain in acceding to the treaty of Madrid, which would place the neutral territory of a friendly power in the way of military operations. But even under the terms of that treaty, the Spanish posts on the Mississippi were withheld from the possession of the American government, and their evacuation delayed, on account of the threatened invasion of Spanish territory, by British troops from Canada, by way of the Illinois River. The Spanish governor

---

[1] American State Papers, i. 547.

[2] Idem, 122, 128.

had reason to fear such event, as at this time there were persons of great influence in the United States, who would gladly have made common cause with the English of Canada, to expel the Spaniards from the Mississippi.[1]

But the failure to evacuate the military posts on the Mississippi, and the surrender of the Natchez district according to the line of demarcation established by the treaty, was an act of perfidy and duplicity on part of the Spanish government, which had for its foundation the still lingering hope that future events would so transpire, that Spain would still retain possession of this portion of Louisiana, and that the "Western people" might yet be induced to separate from their Atlantic brethren; but even those people who had favoured the overtures held out by the Spanish emissaries had become satisfied with the treaty of Madrid, and desired no other alliance than the Federal union. As late as September, 1797, the Spanish agent, Thomas Powers, having failed in his negotiations with Sebastian and other influential men in Kentucky, had penetrated on the line of northwestern posts as far as Detroit, the head-quarters of General Wilkinson, then commander-in-chief of the northwestern army.

The real object of Powers was to press General Wilkinson into the Spanish conspiracy, with the whole weight of his power and authority, in sustaining the separation of the western territory from the United States. Wilkinson was at Michillimackinac when Powers arrived at Detroit; he caused him to be arrested, on his return, and thus secured Baron de Carondelet's despatches; after which he hurried him off under an escort, by way of the Wabash, to Fort Massac, in order to avoid interception by the Federal authorities. In the mean time, government had been apprized of the embassy of Powers, and instructions had been issued to the governor of the Northwestern Territory to cause him to be arrested and sent a prisoner to Philadelphia.[2]

---

[1] See Note N.

[2] Martin's Louisiana, ii. 151. Wilkinson's Memoirs, ii. 214, and App. xlv.

General Wilkinson had previously proceeded to a great length in his treasonable intrigues and correspondence with the Spanish governor, and the suspicions of his own government rested on him. His brilliant hopes of becoming the head of a new confederation had vanished; he was now anxious to retain his command, and with it his standing as a patriotic citizen of the United States. Hence his cold reception of Mr. Powers: he informed him that the time for *separation* had gone by: that the Western people had gained all they desired by the late treaty, and they entertained no desire for an alliance with either Spain or France; and that all political ferment which existed four years before, had now entirely subsided.[1]

By the Spanish treaty, New Orleans, or "an equivalent establishment," was to be allowed the citizens of the United States as a place of deposit for property sent down the Mississippi, for a definite period; no change in relation to this place of deposit took place until October 16th, 1802; but on that day, Morales, the intendant of Louisiana, issued an order putting an end to this important privilege granted to the Americans. This led to instant excitement and remonstrance, and on the 7th of January, 1803, a resolution was adopted by the House of Representatives, affirming "their unalterable determination to maintain the boundaries, and the rights of navigation and commerce through the river Mississippi, as established by existing treaties."[2] But this act of the intendant was not acquiesced in by the governor, although the suspension continued until February 25th, 1803, when the port was opened to provisions paying a duty; and in April, orders from the King of Spain reached the United States, restoring the right of deposit.[3] In January, 1803, in consequence of this act of Morales, and to "effectually secure our rights and interests in the river Mississippi and in the territories eastward thereof," President Jefferson sent a message to the Senate, nominating Robert R. Livingston and James Monroe, ministers at the court of France, and Charles Pinckney and James Mon-

---

[1] See Note O. [2] American State Papers, ii. 469, 527, &c. [3] Idem.

roe, at that of Spain, with full powers to form treaties to effect those objects.

At this time the government had intimation that in some form, a treaty was on the carpet, or had been made, by which Spain had ceded or transferred her interest in Louisiana to France. In November, 1801, Rufus King, then our minister in London, sent a copy of the treaty signed at Madrid, March 21st, 1801, by which the Prince of Parma, son-in-law of the King of Spain, was established in Tuscany, and this had been the consideration for the grant of Louisiana to France, in the previous autumn, and that grant was now confirmed.

To secure the interests of the Union in relation to the Mississippi now became the all-important question, and the subject of sagacious diplomacy. Our ministers were instructed to procure a cession of New Orleans and the Floridas to the United States. All idea of purchasing Louisiana west of the Mississippi had been disclaimed by President Jefferson up to January, 1803. On the 10th of this month, however, Mr. Livingston proposed to the minister of Napoleon to cede to the United States, not only New Orleans and Florida, but also all of Louisiana above the River Arkansas. But such were not the views entertained by the cabinet; on the 2d of March, the instructions sent to Messrs. Livingston and Monroe gave a plan which expressly left to France "all her territory on the west side of the Mississippi." On the 11th of April, intimations in conformity with this plan were given to the French ministry, when Talleyrand suggested the cession of the *whole French domain* in North America, and asked how much would be given for it. Mr. Livingston intimated that twenty millions of francs might be a fair price; this the minister of Bonaparte said was too low, but asked the American to think of the matter.[1]

In an interview with the American minister, Napoleon frankly confessed his inability to retain Louisiana; it was a vast province sparsely inhabited and utterly unable to defend itself against the formidable power of the British navy, by

---

[1] American State Papers, ii. 524 to 552. Marbois's Louisiana.

which it might be devastated if known to be a province of France. Bonaparte declared "he was compelled to provide for the safety of Louisiana before it should come into his hands, and he was desirous of giving the United States a magnificent bargain, an empire for a mere trifle." He intimated a price of 125 millions of Francs.

On the 12th of April, Mr. Monroe arrived, and negotiations were renewed for the purchase of the whole of the vast territory upon and beyond the river first navigated by Marquette; the treaty was arranged on the 30th of April; the American Commissioners had gone entirely beyond their instructions, but their act, although unauthorized, and unexpected, was at once agreed to by the President; Congress was summoned to meet on the 17th of October, when the treaty was laid before the Senate, who ratified it on the 21st, and on the 20th of the following December the Province of Louisiana was officially delivered over to Governor Cairborne, of Mississippi, and General Wilkinson, who were empowered to assume the government.

The terms of sale as finally agreed on were, that the United States should pay sixty millions of francs in stocks bearing six per cent. interest, irredeemable for fifteen years, afterward to be discharged in three equal annual instalments; the interest to be paid in Europe.

To this transfer of Louisiana, Spain at first objected, as she alleged on "solid grounds;" but early in 1804 renounced her opposition.[1]

It will thus be seen, that beyond the approval of the unlooked-for act of his ministers in France, Mr. Jefferson had no agency in the purchase of Louisiana: if any person deserves to be remembered in connection with that great bargain, it is Mr. Livingston, whose efforts were constant and effectual. The person through whom Mr. Livingston obtained the ear of Napoleon, was Joseph Bonaparte.[2]

---

[1] Am. State Papers, vol. ii. 553 to 583.

[2] Am. State Papers, vol. ii. 525, 533. Perkins, 485.

Thus, in 1803, the United States became possessed of the great valley of the Mississippi, to the exclusion of the title of any foreign power; limited by the possessions of Spain, in Mexico, on the west and southwest, and in the Floridas, on the southeast: the Indian title to the lands in this vast region, alone remained to be extinguished. During the time the country was under the control of its French and Spanish rulers, very many extensive and valuable grants of land had been made to individuals, which, for a long series of years, became the subject of investigation by the governmental authorities, and called for the action of the national legislature, as well as the judicial determination of the high courts of the Union. Of such character were the claims of the Baron de Bastrop, the Marquis de Maison Rouge, the Baron de Carondelet, Julien Dubuque, and a host of others. It is only since the year 1853 that the claim of the latter to highly valuable lands in the State of Iowa has been decided, judicially, adverse to his representatives.

In 1796, the posts in the northwest were evacuated by the British, and delivered up to the Americans under the treaty stipulations. The Northwestern Territory then contained few white settlements beyond the boundaries of the present State of Ohio, within which was the seat of government of the territory; the present State of Michigan was within the county of Wayne; General Arthur St. Clair was the first governor of the territory, which was constituted August 7th, 1789. On the 7th of May, 1800, the territory was divided, and excluding the boundaries of Ohio, as then defined, the new Territory of Indiana embraced all the remainder of the Northwestern Territory, including on the east side of the Mississippi, the present States of Indiana, Illinois, Michigan, and Wisconsin, and the Territory of Minnesota; on the west side of the river, the Rocky Mountains might be considered as a barrier, but the Pacific Ocean alone was the limit of the possessions of the United States.

# CHAPTER V.

## INDIAN DISTURBANCES.

Principle which governs European title in America—Rights of original inhabitants—Rights of discoverers—Ultimate dominion over the Soil—Political condition of the Indians—Review of the character of Indian treaties—General Harrison appointed governor of Northwestern Territory—His first acts in treaties with the Indians—The Black Sparrow-hawk—His rank and place of residence—Treaty of St. Louis of 1804—Vast territory ceded—Afterward confirmed—Fort Madison built—Jealousy among the Sacs, Black Hawk's band—Attempts to surprise Fort Madison—Territory of Michigan erected—Governor Hull—Fire at Detroit—New town laid out—Lieutenant Pike ascends the Mississippi—Obtains cessions of lands from the Indians—Prospect of Indian disturbances—Tecumthe and the Prophet—Black Hawk—Indian talk of Le Marquois—Enterprise and efforts of Tecumthe and his brother—They attempt to deceive Governor Harrison—The governor prepares for emergencies—Indian hostility apparent—Black Hawk urged to join the confederacy—War parties sent out—Result of their acts—General outbreak expected—Tecumthe assembles a hostile force—Harrison convenes a council of Indians—Violent conduct of Tecumthe—Governor Harrison assembles an army—Marches to the Prophet's town—Indians temporize with Harrison—He encamps, and is attacked in the night—Battle of Tippecanoe—All the Western posts and settlements threatened—War of 1812—Conduct of the English traders—Robert Dickson, his great influence—Predatory warfare of the Indians—Dickson collects the Indians at Green Bay—Gives Black Hawk the command, and sends him to Detroit—Black Hawk remains a short time with the army, and returns to the Mississippi—News of the declaration of war does not arrive quickly in the West—Disastrous consequences—Mackinaw surrenders—Surrender of Detroit—Fate of the garrison at Chicago—Massacre of Captain Heald's forces—Alleged cause of Indian vengeance—Events of the war on the Mississippi—Fort at Prairie du Chien repaired—Captured by the British under McKay—The prisoners sent down the Mississippi—Indian rage—Major Campbell ascends the river from St. Louis—Is attacked by Black Hawk; is wounded and retreats with his boats—British send cannon and soldiers to Rock Island—Major Zachary Taylor ascends the river with a force—Great body of Indians at Rock Island—They attack Taylor, and after a severe fight he returns down the river—Forts Madison and Johnson burned—Peace with Great Britain and consequent peace with Indians by treaties—Fort Armstrong built at Rock Island—Settlements commence there—Keokuk and his band remove—Black Hawk remains—Illinois about to be admitted as a State—Boundary question—Increase of white settlements, and outrages committed—Lead trade with the Indians—Wisconsin a part of Michigan Territory—Settlements at Green Bay—Indian jealousy—Winnebagoes attack a party of Chippewas—Conduct of American commander at Fort Snelling—Red Bird's resentment—Murders near Prairie du Chien—Red Bird's people attack two boats on the river—Great excitement in the mining regions—General Atkinson ascends the river with his force—Red Bird and other Indians surrender themselves prisoners—General outbreak expected—Prompt action of Atkinson and the volunteers defeats it—Indians tried at Prairie du Chien—Convicted, and pardoned—Red Bird dies in prison—Other prisoners discharged—Country begins to settle—New disturbances on Rock River—Black Hawk returns to his village and threatens the whites—Governor Reynolds declares the State invaded—Applies for assistance to General Government—Raises volunteer force—General Gaines with United States troops proceeds up the river—Confers with the Indians—Is joined by the Illinois volunteers—They take possession of the Sac village, and Indians cross the river—The village destroyed—Treaty at Rock Island—Reflections.

An endeavour has thus been made to exhibit an outline of events that occurred in the valley of the Mississippi from the time of its first discovery, to the period when the sovereignty over it belonged to the United States, to the exclusion of the title of any foreign power. A proper understanding of the early history of any portion of the valley, required that a view should be taken of the prominent occurrences which in any degree affected the fortunes of the whole region; the space which has been allotted to such view, hitherto, may not, perhaps, be considered unprofitable or improper. Our attention may now with much propriety be turned to the more immediate consideration of such matters as pertain to the history of the Northwestern Territory, as organized and governed under the laws of the United States. In attempting this consideration, a partial review of occurrences which preceded the formation of Wisconsin into a distinct and separate Territory becomes necessary.

The acquisition, by the United States, of the exclusive title to the vast region of which we treat, required on her part the recognition and elucidation of the principle which has been received as the foundation of all European title in America; this principle was, that "discovery gave title to the government by whose subjects, or by whose authority it was made, against all other European governments; which title might be consummated by possession." The exclusion of all other Europeans necessarily gave to the nation making the discovery, the sole right of acquiring the soil from the natives, and establishing settlements upon it. It was a right with which no Europeans could interfere. It was a right which all asserted for themselves, and to the assertion of which by others, all assented. Those relations which were to exist between the discoverer and the natives, were to be regulated by themselves. The rights thus acquired being exclusive, no other power could interpose between them.

In the establishment of these relations, the rights of the original inhabitants were in no instance entirely disregarded, but were necessarily to a considerable extent impaired. They were admitted to be the rightful occupants of the soil, with a legal as well as just claim to retain possession of it, and to use it according to their own discretion; but their rights to complete sovereignty as independent nations were necessarily diminished, and their power to dispose of the soil at their own will, to whomsoever they pleased, was denied by the original fundamental principle that discovery gave exclusive right to those who made it.

While the different nations of Europe respected the right of the natives, as occupants, they asserted the ultimate right to be in themselves; and claimed and exercised, in consequence of this ultimate dominion, a power to grant the soil while yet in possession of the natives. These grants have been understood by all to convey a title to the grantees, subject only to the Indian right of occupancy.[1]

The United States have unequivocally acceded to that great and broad rule by which its civilized inhabitants now hold this country. They hold and assert in themselves the title by which it was acquired. They maintain, as all others have maintained, that discovery gave an exclusive right to extinguish the Indian title of occupancy, either by purchase or by conquest; and gave also a right to such a degree of sovereignty as the circumstances of the people would allow them to exercise.[2]

The condition of the Indians in relation to the United States is, perhaps, unlike that of any other two people in existence. In general, nations not owing a common allegiance, are foreign to each other. The term foreign nation, is with strict propriety applicable by either to the other. But the relation of the Indians to the United States is marked by peculiar and cardinal distinctions, which exist nowhere else. It may well be doubted whether those tribes which reside within the acknowledged boundaries of the United States can with strict accuracy be denominated foreign nations. They may more correctly, perhaps, be denominated domestic dependent nations. Their relations to the United States resemble that of a ward to his guardian. They look to our government for protection; rely upon its kindness and its power; appeal to it for relief to their wants; and address the President as their great Father. Nevertheless, the Indians are acknowledged to have an unquestionable, and heretofore unquestioned right to the lands they occupy, until that right shall be extinguished by a voluntary cession to the government.[3] The Indian nations have always been considered as distinct, independent political communities, retaining their original, natural rights, as the undisputed possessors of the soil from time immemorial: the term "nation" applied to

---

[1] Ch. Jus. Marshall, 8 Wheaton, 543. [2] Idem.
[3] 5 Peters's Rep. 1.

them means, "a people distinct from others." The constitution of the United States, by declaring treaties already made, as well as those to be made, to be the supreme law of the land, has adopted and sanctioned the previous treaties with the Indian nations, and consequently admits their rank among those powers who are capable of making treaties. The words "treaty" and "nation" are words of our own language, selected in our diplomatic and legislative proceedings by ourselves, having each a definite and well-understood meaning. We have applied them to Indians as we have applied them to other nations of the earth. They are applied to all in the same sense.[1]

The several treaties which had been made between commissioners on part of the United States and various nations of Indians, previous to the treaty of Greenville, were generally restricted in their objects to declarations of amity and friendship; the establishing and confirming of boundaries; the acknowledgment of the protecting power of the United States, and no other sovereign; the prohibition of settlement on Indian lands; regulations of trade; and small cessions of land for military establishments. In a few of those treaties small sums of money are given to the Indians as presents, and some annuities granted in consideration of former cessions of land, but no sale and purchase of any extensive district of country seems to have been made between the contracting parties. The second article of the treaty of January 31st, 1786, is as follows:—

"The Shawanee nation do acknowledge the United States to be the sole and absolute sovereigns of all the territory ceded to them by a treaty of peace, made between them and the King of Great Britain, the fourteenth day of January, one thousand seven hundred and eighty-four."

In this, as in all other of the like treaties, the sovereignty is recognised on the one side, while, by the several restric-

---

[1] 6 Peters, 515.

tions contained in them, the right of occupancy is acknowledged on the other.

The treaty of Greenville, made August 3d, 1795, contained the relinquishment of the Indian title to particular *tracts* of land in different quarters of the Northwest, for which a valuable consideration was paid by the United States; the United States also relinquishing their claims to all other Indian lands within the Northwestern Territory, with a few exceptions named in the treaty; herein also we find the principle of ultimate sovereignty and present occupancy acknowledged and acted on.

General William Henry Harrison was appointed, in 1801, the governor of the Northwestern Territory, and we find, in September, 1802, that he took the first step in those negotiations which, in their continuance through so many after years, contributed so much to the dominions of the United States. At Vincennes, he entered into an agreement with various chiefs of the Pottawatamie, Eel River, Piankeshaw, Wea, Kaskaskia, and Kickapoo tribes, by which were settled the bounds of a tract of land near that place, said to have been given by the Indians to its founder; certain chiefs were named who were to conclude the matter at Fort Wayne.[1]

Among the first acts of Governor Harrison in relation to the extinguishment of Indian title in the Northwest, we find the treaty of August 13th, 1803; by which the Kaskaskia tribe cede to the United States all their lands in the Illinois country, except a tract of three hundred and fifty acres near Kaskaskia, and a right to locate another tract of twelve hundred and eighty acres in Illinois, for a money consideration. On the 18th of August, 1804, Governor Harrison made a treaty with the Delaware tribe, by which the said tribe relinquish to the United States all their title to the country between the Ohio and Wabash Rivers, for a money consideration. On the 27th of August, 1804, the governor also obtained the relinquishment of title by the Piankeshaws to the same country,

---

[1] Dawson's Harrison, 27. See also Note A.

for a money consideration. But his most important treaty is that which he made with the Sacs and Foxes, as it not only became the foundation of various other treaties afterward made with the Indians of the Upper Mississippi, but its validity being denied by one band of the Sacs, the cession of land contained in its provisions became, twenty-eight years afterward, the alleged cause of the Black Hawk War.

About the time of the establishment of government in the Indiana Territory, Ma-ka-tai-me-she-kia-kiak, the "Black Sparrow-hawk," or "Black Hawk," as he is generally called, begins to appear prominent in the transactions on the Upper Mississippi. He was the chief of a band of the Sacs, and his village was at Rock Island, at the mouth of Rock River. To this beautiful and fertile spot he and his band were devotedly attached; it was the final resting-place of their forefathers, and the site of their own comfortable village, surrounded by their gardens and cultivated grounds. Black Hawk was not the great war-chief of the Sacs and Foxes, but merely the chief of his own band: he had always been opposed to the cession of the Indian lands to the Americans, and most particularly denied the validity of the treaty made at St. Louis, on the 3d of November, 1804, between William Henry Harrison, governor of the Indiana Territory and of the District of Louisiana, and the united tribes of Sac and Fox Indians.[1]

This treaty was made and signed by five individuals on part of the Indians, whose power to cede, sell, or grant lands, or whose authority to make any treaty whatever, at that time, is emphatically denied by Black Hawk in his own account of this important transaction,[2] but such denial must not be considered as conclusive of the fact alleged by him.

The boundaries of the land ceded by this treaty are thus described:—"Beginning at a point on the Missouri River opposite the mouth of the Gasconade River; thence in a direct course so as to strike the river Jeffreon at the distance of thirty miles from its mouth; and down the said Jeffreon to

---

[1] See Note B.

[2] Doc. Hist. Black Hawk War.

the Mississippi; thence up the Mississippi to the mouth of the Wisconsin River; and up the same to a point which shall be thirty-six miles in a direct line from the mouth of the said river; thence by a direct line to the point where the Fox River, (a branch of the Illinois,) leaves the small lake called Sakaegan; thence down the Fox River to the Illinois River, and down the same to the Mississippi.[1]

The consideration in money to be paid by the United States bears an insignificant proportion to the immense tract of country granted by the treaty; the boundaries embrace, it is said, more than fifty-one millions of acres;[2] while the purchase-money is "goods in hand to the amount of two thousand two hundred and fifty-four dollars and fifty cents, and a yearly annuity of one thousand dollars, of which six hundred dollars was for the Sacs and four hundred dollars for the Foxes, to be paid in goods valued at first cost."

It will be seen that within the boundaries mentioned in this treaty is embraced nearly the whole of the present State of Wisconsin, lying south of the Wisconsin River and west of the Fox River of the Illinois; also a great portion of Northern Illinois; and considerable portions of the States of Iowa and Missouri. This treaty was afterward ratified and confirmed by a treaty made at St. Louis, on the 13th of May, 1816, between the American commissioners and the chiefs and warriors of the Sacs of Rock River and the adjacent country: to this latter confirming treaty "the Black Sparrow-hawk" "touched the quill;" although he afterward alleged that he was ignorant of what he was then doing; in fact, it was a cession of his own village and the lands of his tribe to the United States.[3]

Soon after the treaty of 1804, Fort Madison was erected by the United States troops, within the ceded territory, and councils were held among the Sacs, particularly Black Hawk's band, in which much jealousy was expressed as to the inten-

---

1 See Note C. 2 Dawson's Harrison, 59.

3 Doc. Hist. Black Hawk War.

tions of the Americans in thus taking an armed possession of the country. An unsuccessful attempt was made at one time to take the fort by the stratagem of a dancing party of Indians endeavouring to enter it, in the same manner that the ball-play stratagem was practised at Mackinaw. Had they succeeded, the garrison would have been massacred: a reinforcement from St. Louis was soon afterward received at the fort.[1]

On the 11th of January, 1805, by an act of Congress, the Territory of Michigan was erected, and separated from the Indiana Territory, with William Hull as its first governor. In the month of June following, a most destructive fire at Detroit consumed all the buildings at that place, both public and private; and the first act of the governor was to arrange and settle conflicting claims to lots of land within the precincts of the ruined town, and to survey and lay out the site of a new and more extensive and commodious town, embracing the whole of the old one, and the public lands adjacent: the last act of the governor, some seven years subsequently, was to basely surrender the town and its fortress to a British enemy, without so much as striking a single blow in its defence.

On the 9th of August, 1805, Lieutenant Zebulon Pike left St. Louis with a detachment of soldiers under the orders of gove nment, on an exploring expedition toward the head-waters of the Mississippi. He passed up the river in boats, and conciliated the Indians with whom he met on his expedition, and at the same time impressed them with a knowledge of the power and strength of the government of the United States, of which they had always not only been kept in ignorance by the British traders, but against which their inimical feelings had also been constantly kept in a state of excitement. On the 23d of September, Lieutenant Pike held a council with the chiefs of the Mississippi bands at St. Peter's, and obtained a grant from the "Little Crow" and other

[1] Doc. Hist. Black Hawk War.

principal chiefs, of one hundred thousand acres of land, for the purpose of military posts at St. Peter's, the Falls of St. Anthony, and the mouth of the St. Croix.[1]

For more than two years it had been surmised that mischief was gathering among the tribes of the Northwest; some murders by the Indians had taken place in Indian country, and the conviction became more and more strong at the close of the year 1806, that hostilities were in meditation on an extensive scale. Two chiefs of great power and influence had, it is believed, for some years been exerting both, for two purposes; one of which was the reformation of the Indians, whose habits unfitted them for continuous and heroic effort, and the other was such a union of the tribes as would make the purchase of land by the United States impossible, and give to the aborigines a strength that might be dreaded. Both these objects were avowed, and both were pursued with wonderful energy, perseverance, and success: in the whole country bordering upon the lakes, the power of these chiefs, Tecumthe, and his brother, the Shawanese Prophet, was felt, and the work of reformation went on rapidly.[2]

We have the evidence of Black Hawk himself, that soon after his return from Fort Madison, runners came to his village from the Shawanese Prophet, (while others were despatched by him to the villages of the Winnebagoes,) with invitations for them to meet him on the Wabash, which was accordingly done by a party from each village.[3] This was probably about the year 1807, as at this time a *talk* was industriously circulated among the tribes of the Northwest, accompanied with belts of wampum. The object of the great Manitou, or second Adam, undoubtedly was to induce a general effort to rally and strike a desperate blow on the white settlements, under the pretence of restoring to the aborigines their former independence, and to the savage character its ancient energies.

---

1 Pike's Exp. 27, and Append. 6.

2 Drake's Tecumseh, 88, 103. Dawson's Life of Harrison, 83, 90.

3 Doc. Hist. Black Hawk War.

This talk was delivered at Le Maiouitinong, entrance of Lake Michigan, by the Indian chief Le Marquois, or the Trout, May 4th, 1807, as coming from the first man whom God created, *said to be now* in the Shawanee country, addressed to all the Indian tribes:—

"I am the Father of the English, of the French, of the Spaniards, and of the Indians. I created the first man, who was the common Father of all these people, as well as yourselves; and it is through him whom I have awakened from his long sleep, that I now address you. *But the Americans I did not make. They are not my children, but the children of the evil spirit.* They grew from the scum of the great water, when it was troubled by the evil spirit, and the froth was driven into the woods by a strong east wind. They are numerous, but I hate them.

"My children, you must not speak of this *Talk* to the whites. *It must be hidden from them.* I am now on the earth, sent by the Great Spirit to instruct you. Each village must send me two or more principal chiefs to represent you, that you may be taught. The bearer of this *Talk* will point out to you the path to my wigwam. I could not come myself to Arbre Croche, because the world is changed from what it was. It is broken and leans down, and as it declines, the Chippewas, and all beyond, will fall off and die. Therefore you must come to see me and be instructed. Those villages which do not listen to this *Talk* and send me two deputies, will be cut off from the face of the earth."[1]

From this time forward until the battle of Tippecanoe, in 1811, Tecumthe and the Prophet continued to extend their influence, professing no other end than a reformation of the Indians. They had removed from Greenville to the banks of the Tippecanoe, a tributary of the Upper Wabash, where a tract of land had been granted them by the Pottawatamies and Kickapoos. They were here strengthening themselves both openly and secretly, and the Prophet once sent a mes-

[1] Am. State Papers.

senger to Governor Harrison, begging him not to believe the tales told by his enemies. In August, 1808, he paid a visit to the governor, and spent two weeks at Vincennes. In this visit, his words and promises induced Harrison to change his opinion of him, and to believe that his influence might be beneficial rather than mischievous.[1] However, the governor had been led more and more, in the two succeeding years, to suspect the ultimate design of the wily brothers, and was preparing to meet an emergency whenever it might arise.[2] In 1810, the hostile intentions of Tecumthe and his followers toward the United States were placed beyond a doubt; the exciting causes were, the purchase made at Fort Wayne, in 1809, from the Delawares, Pottawatamies, Miamis, and Eel River tribes, which the Shawanese denounced as illegal and unjust; and the ever-existing British influence.

When Black Hawk's delegation returned to his village, a *prophet* came with them, who industriously kept alive his feelings of resentment on the subject of the Americans depriving them of their lands, and urged him to join the confederacy on the Wabash, as in case he did not, "the Americans would take his very village from him." Black Hawk, however, did not join him, and he returned to the Wabash, where a party of Winnebagoes had arrived, and preparations were made for war. A battle ensued, in which several Winnebagoes were killed; which, as soon as their nation heard of, they started war parties in different directions, one to the mining country, (Missouri,) one to Prairie du Chien, and another to Fort Madison. This latter, on their return by Black Hawk's village, exhibited several scalps which they had taken, whereby other-parties were induced to go against the fort. On the evening of Black Hawk's arrival there, a reinforcement of seventeen men had also arrived from St. Louis, in a keel-boat; the Indians remained three days in the vicinity, not being able, as Black Hawk says, to take it by stratagem, although he set it on fire by arrows, but it was soon extin-

---

[1] Dawson, 107. Drake's Tecumseh, 104 to 109. [2] Dawson, 130.

guished. His ammunition being expended, his party returned home, having killed three of the whites, and having had one Winnebago killed and one wounded.[1]

The Sacs and Foxes appear to have remained comparatively quiet until the fall of 1811, when a general outbreak was expected among all the Indians of the Northwest; information of an intended attack by the Sacs and Foxes, on the frontiers of Missouri, was sent to the commanding officer at St. Louis, by the means of one Antoine de Pense, a Frenchman. This information was communicated by Thomas Forsyth, who had been Indian agent for these tribes for many years, and had made some treaties with them.[2]

In the mean while hostilities appeared ripe for commencement in that part of the Northwest known as the Indiana Territory; here, the great chief Tecumthe, who had always opposed the sale and cession of lands to the United States, and who contended that the treaties and sales were null and void, and as such, refused to permit the occupancy of the lands by the whites, had assembled a large force of chiefs and warriors, with every hostile indication.

Late in the summer, General Harrison, governor of the Indiana Territory, and agent for Indian affairs, had convened a council of the Indians at Vincennes for the purpose of friendly negotiations; but owing to the violence and impetuous insolence of Tecumthe, no arrangement was made, and the council was broken up. The Federal Government, fearing the worst consequences of the rashness of the Indians, concentrated its forces in the neighbourhood of Vincennes, and as the threatening aspect of Indian affairs clearly indicated immediate hostilities, Governor Harrison advanced with his army toward the principal Shawanees towns on the Wabash, near the outlet of Tippecanoe creek.

General Harrison's force consisted of about twelve hundred men, including regulars, militia, and mounted volunteers. His

---

[1] Doc. Hist. Black Hawk War.

[2] Am. State Papers.

object was to demand satisfactory explanations for the hostile appearances, or to enforce the observance of existing treaties by force of arms.[1]

On the 6th of November, 1811, the troops were within a few miles of the prophet's town, near the mouth of Tippecanoe Creek. During this day's march the Indians hovered upon the flanks and in front of the army, in warlike array, eluding every attempt to approach them, and rejecting all overtures to meet in council. When the army reached within one mile of the Prophet's town, a delegation of warriors came to General Harrison, and proposed to meet in council next morning. Colonel Boyd urged the expediency of advancing immediately upon the town, to take possession of it, and to chastise them severely, when they would be able to dictate the terms of peace on their own ground. He knew the perfidious character of the savages, and was unwilling to afford them time to concert means of defence, or to mature any treacherous designs. But General Harrison had been instructed to avoid actual hostilities as long as possible, and he resolved to accede to the proposition for holding a council with them on the next day. The army accordingly halted, and took up a position for the night in a piece of woods on the margin of a prairie. The troops were ordered to repose upon their arms, with a numerous guard on duty within the line of sentinels. The order of encampment was designed to resist any sudden attack at night, so far as their unprotected situation permitted.[1]

In this condition they remained undisturbed until about four o'clock next morning, November 7th, when, the night being cloudy, and drizzly, the Indians made their attack in that part of the camp near the regular troops. They had crept on their hands and knees, unobserved, nearly to the sentinels, whom they designed to kill before any alarm could be given; but they were discovered, and the alarm was immemediately sounded. The Indians sprang to their feet, gave

---

[1] Breckenridge's Late War, 24. [2] Ibid. 25.

the terrible war-whoop, and rushed to the assault with the tomahawk, against the advanced guard of the militia on the left flank. The guard, panic stricken, fled in confusion upon the regulars under Colonel Boyd. The assault was first received by Captain Barton's company of infantry, and Captain Guiger's company of mounted riflemen, who maintained their position with great firmness. While the commander-in-chief was endeavouring to reinforce this point, and to dislodge the Indians from their covert by means of the cavalry, a furious attack was made on the right wing, which was received by two companies of United States infantry under Captains Spencer and Warwick. Captain Spencer and all his lieutenants were killed, and Captain Warwick was mortally wounded. This line was strengthened by Captain Robb's company, which maintained its position with great courage. While Governor Harrison was bringing up this company, his aid, Colonel Owen, was killed by his side. Colonel Daviess, of Kentucky, and Colonel White, of Indiana, were killed in leading a charge against the Indians on the left flank.

The camp fires had been extinguished, and the whole army was closely engaged in the action. The Indians, concealed behind logs and trees, and in the grass, kept up an incessant and galling fire upon the compact bodies of troops, who suffered severely until the savages were routed by a charge of cavalry led on by Captain Snelling.

The contest was now maintained with great valour on both sides, and on every part of the field. The Indians advanced and retreated alternately, fighting desperately, and with a fury seldom seen or equalled. Their yells, and the terrific rattling of deer hoofs and Indian drums, served to render the scene one of the most fearful import. Such it continued until about daybreak, when several companies were ordered to charge simultaneously from the right and left wings upon the enemy, aided by such of the dragoons as could be mounted. The savages fled in every direction, and were pursued by the horsemen into the wood as far as they could proceed. Thus terminated this sanguinary and unfortunate battle.[1]

According to the official return, the loss of the Americans in this engagement was 37 killed on the field, 25 mortally wounded, and 126 wounded: that of the Indians, about 40 killed on the spot, the number of wounded being unknown.[2]

In this battle the Americans had not more than 700 efficient men, non-commissioned officers and privates: the Indians are believed to have had at least 600, and the estimate has been made at from 800 to 1000 warriors.[3] This was the first blood spilt under public authority since the pacification of Greenville, in August, 1795: it was the beginning of the war declared against Great Britain, in the month of June following. The Indian tribes inhabiting the country south and west of the great lakes immediately flew to arms, and sought the aid of their allies, the English, in Canada. They had previously received assurance of aid from Great Britain in case of hostilities, and they now began to threaten all the American border population, and posts in the Michigan, Indiana, and Illinois Territories, as well as the northwestern confines of New York, Pennsylvania, and Ohio.

Previous to the war of 1812, the English traders in the Northwest were always active, whenever an occasion offered, in exciting the Indians against the American population, and most especially against the American traders. It can scarcely be supposed that this system of studied animosity had its source merely in the desire to prevent competition in the commerce with the Indians on the part of the traders: it is a reasonable conclusion, founded on indubitable facts, that it was the policy of the British government, in keeping alive the bitter feelings of the Indians against the Americans, to effect desired hostile results, through the means of such influential agents as the traders always were, without commit-

---

[1] Breckenridge, 26. Drake's Book of Indians, 103.

[2] Am. State Papers, v. 779.

[3] Am. State Papers, vol. v. 778. Dawson, 216. Drake's Tecumthe, 152.

ting the nation in its peaceable relations with our government, in an open and undisguised manner.

Among these traders was a talented Englishman who resided at Prairie du Chien, named Robert Dickson; he was a man of probity and of honourable conduct in his relations in life, and possessed great influence over the Indians of the Northwest. He had prepared, it is believed, between three and four thousand warriors, in the year 1811, ready to attack the frontiers of Illinois and Missouri; but these warriors were more needed in the early part of the year 1812, in Canada, and the West was probably thus saved. Dickson was unquestionably acting in concert with Tecumthe, the one in the North and the other in the South. Some few murders in the families of frontier settlers were committed by the Indians before war was declared, particularly in Illinois, and we find by information communicated to the secretary of war, among other depredations, that on the first of January, 1812, a party of Puants (Winnebagoes) arrived at the house of Mr. George Hunt, at the Lead Mines, (Missouri,) killed two Americans, and robbed Mr. Hunt of all his goods. This was at Fort Madison, on the Mississippi; the Foxes at this time promised to be friends to the Americans, and also promised to save all Mr. Hunt's goods that they could. Hunt's life was saved by being considered an Englishman. The Puants also killed a Mr. Pryor, and several others, at the same time, and the chief observed that the Americans had killed a great many of their people, and that they intended to kill all they saw. At this time, war parties were looked for every hour by the white inhabitants on the Mississippi, and the universal impression was that a general outbreak of the Indians would take place.[1]

Soon after the declaration of war, in June, 1812, Colonel Dickson, the English trader and agent, collected a considerable body of Indians at Green Bay, for the purpose of rendering assistance to the British forces in their operations on

---

[1] Am. State Papers.

the great lakes and in the Northwest. These Indians were principally Pottawatamies, Kickapoos, Ottawas, and Winnebagoes; to them was added Black Hawk's band, composed of two hundred Sac warriors, who had been specially sent for by Dickson, and whose leader was made commander-in-chief of all the Indians who then were at Green Bay. A silk flag, medal, and written certificate of good behaviour and attachment to the British, were then given by Dickson to Black Hawk, who was also complimented with the nominal rank of a brigadier-general in his majesty's service.[1] This certificate was found, at the battle of Bad Axe, twenty years afterward, having been carefully preserved by its owner, and a British flag was also found there, in all probability the same here spoken of.

Black Hawk was ordered to march with the Indian force to Detroit, but he wished to wage war on the Western settlements. It shows an honourable trait in Dickson's character, that he told him, this must not be; for he said, "he had been ordered to lay the country waste around St. Louis; that he had been a trader on the Mississippi many years; had always been kindly treated; and could not consent to send brave men to murder women and children. That there were no soldiers there to fight; but where he was going to send the Indians, there were a number of soldiers, and if they defeated *them*, the Mississippi country should be given up to them."[2]

The next day, arms, ammunition, and clothing were given by Dickson to the Sacs, and after a great feast in the evening, Black Hawk started the following morning with about five hundred Indians to join the British army. On their route they passed Chicago, which had been evacuated and the fort destroyed: the garrison left the post on the 15th of August, but were attacked by the Pottawatamies, within a mile and a half of the fort, and two-thirds of them, being from fifty to sixty were immediately massacred. One of the reasons for this murderous act, and perhaps the true one, is given by

[1] Doc. Hist. Black Hawk War.

[2] Idem.

Black Hawk: he says, "They had a considerable quantity of powder in the Fort at Chicago, which they had promised to the Indians, but the night before they marched they destroyed it. I think it was thrown into the well; if they had fulfilled their word to the Indians, I think they would have gone safe."[1]

Black Hawk was present during several of the operations of General Proctor on the borders of Lake Erie, but soon returned to his home at Rock Island, and found that Keokuk had been made a war-chief in his absence.[2] Henceforward his opposition was directed against the American settlements on the Mississippi.[3]

The declaration of war on part of the United States against Great Britain was made by act of Congress on the 18th of June, 1812. On the next day, proclamation of the contest was made. By some unaccountable neglect or mismanagement on the part of the officers of government, the information of this important event did not reach the Northwestern posts until some days after the British authorities in this region had full notice of the fact, and were enabled to act accordingly. Without commenting here upon what appears to be egregious blundering, or reprehensible omissions of duty on part of the officers of the General Government, it may suffice as a general matter pertaining to the history of this portion of the Northwest, merely to advert to the following facts.

On the day preceding the proclamation, Congress having passed the needful act, the secretary of war wrote to General Hull one letter saying nothing of the matter, and sent it by a special messenger; and a second, containing the vital news, which he confided to a half-organized post as far as Cleveland, and thence literally to accident. While the general of the Northwestern army was thus not uninformed merely, he had been actually misled. On the 24th of June, advices from the secretary of war dated on the 18th came to hand, but not a word contained in them made it probable that the long expected war would be immediately declared. Colonel McArthur

---

[1] Doc. Hist. Black Hawk War. [2] Idem. [3] See Note D.

at the same time received word from Chillicothe, warning him, on the authority of Senator Worthington of Ohio, that before the letter reached him, the declaration of war would be made public. This information McArthur laid before Hull, then on his way to Detroit; and when that commander proposed, at the Maumee, to place his baggage, stores, and sick on board a vessel, and send them by water to Detroit, McArthur warned him of the danger and refused to trust his own property on board. Hull refused to believe it possible that the Government would not give him information at the earliest moment that the measure of war was resolved on. He accordingly on the first of July embarked his disabled men and most of his goods on board the Cuyahoga packet, suffering his aid-de-camp in his carelessness to send by her even his instructions and army roll, and then proceeded on his way. The next day, July 2d, a letter of the same date with that received on the 24th of June reached him, and apprized him that the declaration of war was indeed, on that day made; and before his astonishment was over, word was brought of the capture of his packet off Malden with all his official papers. Nor is this all: letters franked by the secretary of the treasury of the United States bore the notice of what had been done, to the British post of St. Joseph near the northwestern shore of Lake Huron, and also to Malden, which place it reached on the 28th of June.[1]

It may well be supposed that Lieutenant Hanks, who commanded the post at Mackinaw, would not be better treated in the matter of timely notice of the declaration of war than was General Hull. The British commander at St. Joseph, on the receipt of his friendly communication, franked as we have observed by the American secretary of the treasury, lost no time, but on the 17th of July, with a force of British, Canadians, and savages, numbering in all 1021, made an attack on Fort Mackinaw, the key of the northern lakes. Lieutenant Hanks having received no notice of war from any source, and the garrison amounting to but fifty-seven effective men, felt

---

[1] Perkins, 526, and authorities cited. Hull's Defence, passim.

unable to withstand so formidable a body, and to avoid the constantly threatened Indian massacre, surrendered as prisoners of war, and were dismissed on parole.[1]

The crowing misfortune that befell the American cause, in this quarter of the seat of war, at this time, was the unparalleled act of the surrender of General Hull. The accounts of the several field-officers and others, of the whole of this disgraceful affair, the evidence produced on the subsequent trial of the general, on the accusation of treason and cowardice, and his own defence before the court martial, form a history of its own. It is enough here to say, that on the 16th of August, 1812, General William Hull, governor and general, without a blow struck, crowned his course of indecision and unmanly fear, by surrendering the town of Detroit, and Territory of Michigan, together with fourteen hundred brave men longing for battle, to three hundred English soldiers, four hundred Canadian militia disguised in red coats, and a band of Indian allies.[2]

Hull was afterward tried by a court martial, charged with acts of treason and cowardice; he was acquitted of the former and found guilty of the latter; sentenced to be shot; and afterward was pardoned by the President of the United States, but exiled from all military command.

The garrison of Fort Dearborn at Chicago had an unfortunate fate. General Hull had informed Captain Heald the commander of that post, of the loss of Mackinaw, and directed him to distribute his stores among the Indians and retire to Fort Wayne. Heald proceeded to do this, but it was soon evident that the neighbouring savages were not to be trusted, and he, in consequence, determined not to give them what they most of all wanted, the spirit and powder in the fortress; these articles he destroyed, and the Indians having learned the fact, it was this, as Black Hawk asserted, which led to the subsequent catastrophe. The orders to evacuate the post were received on the 9th of August, and on the 15th the garrison

[1] Perkins. McAfee, 72. See Note E.

[2] Perkins, 529

marched out, and had proceeded on their way, along the lake shore, little more than a mile, when they were attacked by the Pottawatamies under their chief, Black Bird. Captain Heald was escorted by a guard of about thirty Miamis, under the command of Captain Wells, who had been sent from Fort Wayne for that purpose. The force of Captain Heald was only fifty-four regulars and twelve militia; the Indian enemy numbered between four and five hundred. In a short conflict, more than half of Captain Heald's force was killed, and he surrendered to Black Bird under promise that the lives of the prisoners should be spared. Captain Wells and other officers were killed; Captain Heald and his wife were severely wounded; two women and twelve children were killed in the fight, in addition to twenty-six of the regulars, and all of the militia.

The prisoners were taken back to Fort Dearborn, which the Indians burned the next day, and then left the place, taking with them the prisoners, who had been distributed among the different tribes: Captain Heald and his wife were taken to the house of an Indian trader, where they remained some time, and finally reached Detroit.[1]

During the continuance of the war with Great Britain, Wisconsin presented but a small theatre for action; nevertheless the protection of this part of our frontiers was considered of as great importance to ourselves as its possession was to the British. Early in 1814, the government authorities at St. Louis had fitted out a large boat, having on board all the men that could be mustered and spared from the lower country, and despatched it up the Mississippi, to protect the upper country, and the few settlers that were then in it. This boat reached Prairie du Chien, and immediately on their arrival, the men commenced the work of putting the old fort in a state of defence, by repairing the outworks and fortifying it in the best manner they were able. Not long after they had taken possession of it, Colonel McKay, of the British army, descended the Wisconsin with a large force of British and In-

---

[1] Niles's Register, iii. 155. See Note F.

dians: they had reached Green Bay after the surrender of Mackinaw and Detroit, and had been piloted up the Fox River, as is generally well understood, by Joseph Rolette, afterward of Prairie du Chien. The fort was captured, after a determined resistance against an overwhelming force, and the utmost exertions of Colonel McKay were required to prevent an indiscriminate massacre of the Americans by the infuriated Indians. The lives of the prisoners were for some time in the most imminent danger, as the exertions of Colonel McKay in behalf of humanity were doubtful in their result. At length, after repeated and forcible remonstrances with the Indians, the colonel succeeded in getting the prisoners on board of the large boat which had brought the soldiers up the Mississippi, and she proceeded down the river. Apprehensive of danger, the colonel despatched some of his own force to protect the boat; and even then the Indians followed it, as if they had determined never to relinquish a prey which they saw thus rescued from their grasp. The boat passed Rock Island in safety, and in fact the pursuit by the Indians was abandoned when the boat reached the head of the rapids.

In the mean time, Major Campbell had ascended the river from St. Louis, with a squadron of boats and a detachment of United States troops, for the purpose of reinforcing the garrison at Prairie du Chien. When he arrived at Rock Island, he held some communication with Black Hawk, who was apparently neutral, at least not openly inimical; but a party of Indians came down Rock River with the news that Prairie du Chien had been captured, and as the boats of Major Campbell had by this time departed, they were immediately pursued by Black Hawk's band, and a severe fight took place, in which the Indians captured one of the boats, and Major Campbell himself was wounded; the expedition returned down the river, having lost several men killed, and others wounded in this fight.[1]

Some short time after this event, the British commander at

---

[1] Doc. Hist. Black Hawk War.

Prairie du Chien, then called Fort McKay, descended the river to Rock Island, bringing with him two field-pieces and a detachment of soldiers: these he placed in position to prevent, or at least annoy any force that might attempt to pass up the river.

On the 3d of August, 1814, an expedition of some three hundred men, under the command of Major Zachary Taylor, left St. Louis in boats, for the Upper Mississippi. When they arrived at Rock Island, they found the British there apparently in force, with a battery on shore, two field-pieces, and at least one thousand Indians, the greater part of whom were on the right bank of the river, while the large guns and battery were on the left bank. A severe fight took place, but after sustaining a loss of several killed and wounded, the American force returned down the river: on their way to St. Louis they burned Fort Madison and Fort Johnson.[1]

There was little of general interest that transpired after this time, in the Mississippi country, until after the peace of 1815. When this event was made known to the Indian tribes, many were willing and eager to make treaties of peace and friendship with the United States, and Black Hawk and his band were particularly urged to such a measure by all their friends. Several treaties were entered into at the Portage des Sioux in 1815, between the United States commissioners and various bands of Indians; and in May, 1816, by the Treaty of St. Louis, Black Hawk confirmed the treaty of 1804, thereby effectually ceding the lands on Rock River on which his village was located.

About this time, 1816, United States troops arrived at Rock Island and commenced the construction of Fort Armstrong, and a few settlers soon followed, who commenced making their improvements, although the Indians had not yet removed from this vicinity. It is true that Keokuk, and that portion of the Sacs and Foxes termed the American, or friendly band, had already removed to the west side of the

---

[1] Idem. Shaw's Narrative.

Mississippi: it is also true that Keokuk had repeatedly, although ineffectually, urged Black Hawk to remove his people to the west side of the river; his refusal to comply with such advice became daily more and more productive of ill consequences, as the restoration of peace with Great Britain and the Indians, and the contemplated admission of Illinois into the Union as a State, caused the Indian country to be immediately overspread by white people.

The Territory of Illinois was erected into an independent State, by act of Congress, in April, 1818, and its northern boundary was extended to the parallel of 42° 30′ north latitude. This line was far north of the line designated by the ordinance of 1787, and in subsequent times gave rise to much legislative controversy, and conflict of jurisdiction among constituted authorities. It may well be doubted whether the power of Congress, in the case of the boundary question between the States of Ohio and Michigan, and the settlement of boundary of the fifth State, (Wisconsin,) has not been exerted in defiance of right, and in direct contravention of the spirit and letter of the ordinance of 1787.[1]

The settlements of the whites continued to increase in the Indian country, and doubtless many outrages were committed by them on the persons and effects of the Indians, in order to hasten their voluntary departure from the country which they had ceded to the United States, and in which already government surveys had been made, and certificates of land entries had been issued; but these matters did not extend in any objectionable manner beyond the northern boundary of the State of Illinois. In 1818, a grist-mill was built at Fisher's Coulèe, at Prairie du Chien; and in the following year a saw-mill was built on Black River: these appear to be the first structures of the kind erected in Western Wisconsin. They were both constructed by Mr. John Shaw, now of Marquette county.

Immediately after the peace of 1815, a lucrative trade was

---

[1] Doc. Hist. Boundary Question. Note G.

carried on between the merchants of St. Louis and the traders and Indians of the Upper Mississippi. Goods were periodically sent up the river to the traders, who in return transmitted in payment, by the same boats, peltries and lead. The lead was smelted by the Indians at their primitive furnaces; and crude as was their mode of manufacturing the ore into a merchantable commodity, they were exceedingly jealous of permitting the whites to see the process, or even to approach the vicinity of the lead-mines. This jealousy, however, extended only toward the Americans, as Frenchmen had unlimited privileges of intercourse and trade among the Indians. In the period between 1815 and 1820, Mr. Shaw made eight trips in a trading-boat, from St. Louis to Prairie du Chien, and visited the lead-mines where the city of Galena is now situate. Here the Indians had about twenty furnaces, and Mr. Shaw at one time carried away seventy tons of lead, and left much still at the furnaces: the lead was smelted into *plats* weighing about seventy pounds each.[1]

In consequence of the admission of the State of Illinois into the Union, the upper country, now known as Wisconsin, was attached for all purposes of government to the Territory of Michigan, and although little of immigration yet appeared in the country, the few inhabitants began to feel that the laws of the United States had been extended over them, and that they were not altogether without the pale of protection, notwithstanding they were still surrounded by their savage neighbours. In the vicinity of Green Bay the settlements began to improve rapidly, and Fort Howard having been built in 1817, and Camp Smith (near Despères) having been occupied by a detachment of United States troops, in 1820, the banks of the Fox River soon assumed a cheerful and cultivated appearance. In a short period many new families were added to the old French settlements, and farms were commenced, villages located, and towns laid out and projected to

---

[1] Doc. Hist. Lead Trade with the Indians.

an extent that gave promise of a future prosperity, which at this day has been verified.[1]

In the western portion of the Territory, and particularly in the immediate vicinity of the lead-mines, immigration was rapidly on the increase, notwithstanding the jealousy of the Indians on the subject of what they deemed unauthorized intrusion on their lands, and the apparent danger of a speedy outbreak among them, in acts of hostility against the whites. The policy of the United States government had of late years been, to compel the Indian tribes to remain in peace with each other; and in some measure, to effect this object, the government in the treaties with the different tribes, entered into stipulations of protection for them, on its own part, and sought to enforce, on theirs, the preservation of peace with each other. But unfortunately in this respect, the stipulations were of little avail, and the interference of the United States government in the quarrels of the Indians, became a source of hostile feeling on their part, often terminating in the murder of the whites wherever they were found.[2]

In the early part of the year 1827, a party of twenty-four Chippewas, being on their way to Fort Snelling, at the mouth of St. Peter's River, were surprised and attacked by a war party of the Winnebagoes, and eight of them were killed. The commandant of the United States troops, at the fort, took four of the offending Winnebagoes prisoners, and, (certainly with great imprudence,) delivered them into the hands of the exasperated Chippewas, who immediately put them to death. This act was greatly resented by a chief of the Winnebagoes, named "Red Bird," and in addition to this source of enmity was to be added the daily encroachment of the whites in the lead region, for at this time they had overrun the mining country from Galena to the Wisconsin River.

In the spirit of revenge for the killing of the four Winnebagoes, Red Bird led a war party against the Chippewas, by

---

[1] Descriptive History, Brown County.

[2] Am. State Papers, vol. vi. 608.

whom he was defeated, and thus having been disappointed, he turned the force of his resentment against the whites, whom he considered as having not only invaded his country, but as having aided and abetted his enemies in the destruction of his people.

Some time previously, a murder by the Winnebagoes had been committed in the family of a Mr. Methode, near Prairie du Chien, in which several persons had been killed: it was apparent that a spirit of enmity between the Indians and the whites had been now effectually stirred up, and, for the first time since the war of 1812, disturbances were daily looked for by the settlers and the miners.

On the 28th of June, 1827,[1] a party of Winnebagoes entered a house at Prairie du Chien, murdered and scalped two men, Registre Gagnier and Solomon Lipcap, and scalped a child, Louisa Gagnier; a woman who was present made her escape. On the 30th of June, two keel-boats which had taken provisions to St. Peter's, were attacked by the Indians on their return down the river, about forty miles above Prairie du Chien. The Indians were in canoes, and boarded one of the boats, the Oliver H. Perry, and two of them were killed in the boat. They behaved with great intrepidity, and the engagement continued for three hours. Two men were killed and six wounded belonging to the boat; and it is supposed ten or twelve Indians were killed, and a great number wounded. The other boat, which was a few miles astern, was also attacked, though but little injury was done.[2]

The news of these depredations caused considerable alarm in all the frontier settlements, particularly in Galena, and in the lead-mines; this portion of the country then contained, as is supposed, about five thousand inhabitants: the militia of Prairie du Chien were called out; they did not exceed sixty men, badly armed and provided, but they took possession of the fort. The people of Fevre River organized them-

[1] This is according to Judge Doty's date. Niles's Register says June 24th.
[2] Niles's Register.

selves, and about one hundred volunteers marched to Prairie du Chien.

General Clarke, superintendent of Indian Affairs, at St. Louis, sent an express to Major Forsyth, agent of the Sacs, and Foxes, with orders to advise the chiefs to withdraw all their people from among the Winnebagoes, in order to prevent any disagreeable occurrences from taking place, by mistaking a Sac or a Fox for a Winnebago, by ranging parties; and to inform the upper Sac and Fox villages, that all their people residing or being with the Winnebagoes, must immediately retire from them, and remove to their lands west of the Mississippi.

The miners and settlers collected at Galena, on the first alarm of Indian hostilities, and organized themselves into a force of mounted volunteers, choosing Colonel Henry Dodge as their commander. Governor Edwards, of Illinois, sent a regiment of mounted men, under the command of General McNeale, from Sangamon county to Galena, which town was put in a state of defence. In the month of July, General Atkinson ascended the Mississippi, with six companies of the first, and the whole of the sixth regiment, comprising a force of six hundred infantry and one hundred and fifty mounted men, in order to obtain possession of Red Bird, and to put a speedy and effectual end to any further spread of Indian disturbances.

General Atkinson at once marched into the heart of the Winnebago country, and ascended the Wisconsin River; the Indians were awed into submission, and, without any blood having been shed, Red Bird, and six other Indians of his tribe voluntarily surrendered themselves prisoners, in order to relieve his people from the disastrous effects of a war with the whites. The prisoners were committed into safe keeping at Prairie du Chien, there to await their trial in the regular courts of justice for murder.

Notwithstanding these measures, and the apparent state of quietness in the Indian country, a close observer might have seen strong indications of coming disturbances. When

Governor Cass and Colonel McKinney had arrived, during this summer, at Green Bay, for the purpose of holding treaties with the Indians, it was ascertained that war messages and belts had been sent among the neighbouring tribes, and a general outbreak was feared. Governor Cass ascended the Fox River, and descended the Wisconsin, in order to ascertain the views and disposition of the Winnebagoes. They were evidently unfriendly: in descending the Wisconsin, their women and children fled into the woods, and the men were armed, and had prepared lodges of observation in secluded places upon the bank of the river. Governor Cass probably owed his safety to his coming unexpectedly upon them, and to the appearance of his birch-bark canoe, which was different from those of the traders, and which led them to suppose that there was a force accompanying it.

The treaty of Butte des Morts was made on the 11th of August, 1827, between the United States commissioners and the Menomonies, Midland Chippewas, and the removed bands of the Iroquois and Stockbridges, some Pottawatamies from the west shore of Lake Michigan, and one band of Winnebagoes. At this treaty, Schoolcraft says, "the replies of 'Four Legs,' the leading chief of the Winnebagoes, were evasive and contradictory. Circumstances indicated that they were ripe for a blow. They had fired into a boat descending the Mississippi, at Prairie du Chien, and committed other outrages."[1] The prompt and combined action of General Atkinson and the volunteers in the mining country, undoubtedly prevented the contemplated outbreak of the Indians at this time.

On the 25th of August, 1828, a special term of the United States District Court was held by Judge James D. Doty, at Prairie du Chien, for the trial of the Indians for the murders committed in June of the year preceding. In the mean time, Red Bird had died in prison: the delay of administering justice was to the Indians a matter not comprehended; they scarcely in any instance deny an act which they have com-

[1] Schoolcraft, Personal Memoirs.

mitted, and do not understand why punishment should not be immediately inflicted on the guilty. The imprisonment of the body is to them a most insufferable grievance, and they look upon the act as cowardice on the part of the whites, presuming that they dare not inflict such punishment as the crime demands.

On the first of September, Chick-hong-sic, or the Little Beuffe, and Wa-ni-ga, or the Sun, were indicted, tried, and convicted as accomplices of Red Bird in the murder of Registre Gagnier and Solomon Lipcap: they were sentenced to be hung on the 26th of December, 1828; but before that day, the President's pardon, dated November 3d, 1828, arrived at Prairie du Chien, and the two Indians were discharged. Two Indians, charged with the murder of the family of Mr. Methode, were discharged under a *nolle prosequi*, which was entered by the United States attorney, Mr. John Scott, of Missouri, who had been sent by the war department to conduct the trials. The marshal of the Territory, Mr. Thomas Rowland, came from Detroit, and accompanied Judge Doty, in a birch-bark canoe, from Green Bay to Prarie du Chien. The interpreters at these trials were Pierre Paquette and Amable Grignon for the Winnebago, and John Shaw, then a resident of Illinois, for the French language. Judge Doty remarks, "that there can be no doubt that this murder was intended by the Winnebagoes as a first act of hostility in the commencement of a war upon the whites."[1]

It is an error that many writers on these events have fallen into, in saying that some of these Indians were executed; this is not so, no one was executed. Black Hawk and Kanonekah, or the "Youngest of the Thunders," were among the prisoners charged with the attack on the boats, the preceding year, but the charge not being sustained for want of evidence, (although there was no doubt of their guilt,) they were discharged, as was also a son of Red Bird. During the disturbances occasioned by Red Bird, three men were also killed

[1] In letter to the compiler.

by some Indians, on Apple River, about twelve miles from the White-Oak Springs: this was about the beginning of July, 1827.

This outbreak was generally termed "the Winnebago war," and, as we have observed, was soon quieted: the restoration of tranquillity brought with it an influx of miners and settlers in the lead region, and an impulse was quickly given to a great portion of Western Wisconsin, which afforded every promise of future prosperity; the lake shore and the interior of the Territory did not as yet, in any considerable degree, receive the benefits of industrial immigration.[1]

In the mean time, the old causes of dissension between the Indians and the white settlers were again stirred up, as they had never been effectually allayed, by the restless Black Hawk. The Rock River country, and the vicinity of Rock Island, apparently was soon to become the seat of an Indian war; the whites were already in the possession of much of the country around Black Hawk's village, and even of the village itself; the chief was driven to desperation in his fruitless attempts to resist what he considered the lawless encroachments of the white settlers; and he once more, in the spring of 1831, crossed the Mississippi from the west, with his own band of about three hundred warriors, together with the women and children, determined to regain, if possible, the possession of the home of his people and the burial-place of his forefathers.

He applied in vain for redress to the Indian agent at Rock Island, and in desperate resentment he "ordered the white settlers away, threw down their fences, unroofed their houses, cut up their grain, drove off and killed their cattle, and threatened the people with death if they remained. The settlers made their complaints to Governor Reynolds. These acts were considered by the governor as an invasion of the State."[2]

---

[1] Doc. Hist. Lead Trade. Descriptive Hist.: the several counties.

[2] Ford's Illinois, p. 111.

Governor Reynolds consequently applied to General Gaines, of the United States army, and to General Clark, superintendant of Indian affairs, to afford such means on the part of the government as was in their power, to protect the citizens and remove the Indians. He informed General Gaines that he had called on seven hundred of the militia of the State to be mounted and ready for that service, and solicited his co-operation; this letter is dated at Belleville, then the capital of Illinois, on the 28th of May, 1831, and on the next day General Gaines said in answer, that he had ordered six companies of regular troops to proceed from Jefferson Barracks the day following, May 30th, for the Sac village, and, if necessary, he would add two companies more from Prairie du Chien; he also said that if the Indian force had been augmented by other Indians than the "hostile Sacs," he would correspond with Governor Reynolds, and avail himself of his offer of the seven hundred mounted volunteers.

General Gaines immediately proceeded with his force, in a steamboat, up the river to the disputed ground; on the 7th of June a council was held with the Indians, in which Black Hawk plainly told the general that he never would remove, asserted that he was a Sac, the descendant of Sacs, and that the village and grounds of his ancestors should never be abandoned or surrendered by him: he made some demonstrations of hostility by appearing at the council-house at the head of his band, armed and painted as if for war, but no hostile act was committed, neither party appearing willing to resort to extremities.[1]

The call of the Governor of Illinois for volunteers had been so well answered, that by the 10th of June about fifteen hundred men were assembled at Beardstown, who were organized into two regiments, an odd battalion, and a spy battalion. The first regiment was commanded by Colonel James D. Henry, the second by Colonel Daniel Leib, the odd battalion by Major Nathaniel Buckmaster, and the spy battalion by

---

[1] Doc. Hist. Black Hawk War.

Major Samuel Whiteside. The whole brigade was put under the command of Major-General Joseph Duncan, of the State militia.[1]

In four days, this volunteer army joined General Gaines on the Mississippi; he had already been at the Indian town, and was now at a place (since called Rockport) about eight miles below the mouth of Rock River; here the plan of future action of the forces was adopted, and the next morning the volunteers marched up the country, while General Gaines ascended the river in his steamboat. This was on the 26th of June, and when the Sac village was reached, no enemy was found there, as a great portion of the Indians had quietly departed the same morning, and in their canoes had crossed to the western side of the Mississippi. The Sac village was taken possession of without firing a gun, but the volunteers were determined to be avenged upon something. The rain descended in torrents, and the Indian wigwams would have furnished a comfortable shelter; but notwithstanding the rain, the whole town was soon wrapped in flames—and thus perished an ancient village which had once been the delightful home of six or seven thousand Indians.[1]

On the 27th, the army proceeded up the river to Rock Island, and encamped for several days on the site of the old town of Stephenson, now the town of Rock Island; here Black Hawk and the chiefs and braves of the hostile band sued for peace, doubtless stimulated thereto by the threats of General Gaines to pursue the Indians who had retreated across the river. A treaty was entered into June 30th, 1831, by which the Indians agreed to remain for ever after on the west side of the river, and never to recross it without the permission of the President or the Governor of the State; this treaty did not remain one year without an infraction.

In this attempt of Black Hawk to recover the possession of his village, hopeless as it in truth was, and as it certainly must have appeared to himself, if we allow him only a portion

---

[1] Ford's Illinois, 112.

[2] Ibid. 115.

of the judgment and discrimination attributed to him, he expected assistance from his friends the Winnebagoes, the Pottawatamies, and the Kickapoos; for this purpose they had been solicited by Black Hawk, and he had received promises of their compliance with his request. But the actual situation in which Black Hawk stood in his relations with the General Government, appears to have been comprehended by the neighbouring tribes of Indians; they had reason to dread the result of any contest with the American power, and although a few of them joined the Sacs, (about two hundred, according to the statement of General Gaines,) they did not long remain faithful to any hostile confederacy against the United States.

In his despatch to the secretary of war, General Gaines said he was of opinion that "the Sacs were as completely humbled as if they had been chastised in battle, and less disposed to disturb the frontier inhabitants;" and that Governor Reynolds was of the same opinion.[1] But in this they were both mistaken; for scarcely a year elapsed before Black Hawk's people again crossed the Mississippi under various pretexts, one of which was the starving condition of the Sacs, in consequence of the failure of the government authorities to supply them with corn according to contract, and therefore they went over the river to *steal corn from their own fields*.[2] Thus began a new series of troubles, ending in much bloodshed, and the final capture of Black Hawk, and the utter prostration of his power and influence.

In all his attempts to obtain redress for real or fancied injuries by a resort to arms, Black Hawk had been fed with the hopes of assistance, not only from his Indian allies, but from the British at Malden. Before he undertook his incursion in 1831, he had sent Ne-a-pope as an emissary to sound the neighbouring tribes on the subject of their co-operation with him against the whites, and he was grossly deceived by

---

[1] Gaines Report. Note H.

[2] Doc. Hist. Black Hawk War. Drake's Indians, 644.

the report which was made to him. Ne-a-pope informed him that his British father at Malden would aid him as soon as a blow was struck in war; and he also said that the Prophet had told him that the Ottawas, Chippewas, Pottawatamies, and Winnebagoes would join him; and if they were whipped they were to go to Selkirk's settlement, Was-sa-cum-mi-co, as the Prophet had received a friendly talk from the chief of that place, on the subject; but all this was false, and a fabrication of Ne-a-pope, as Black Hawk learned in the sequel.[1] Keokuk always told him he had been imposed upon by liars, and urged him to keep quiet; but his restless spirit could not be appeased; and notwithstanding all the experience which the events of 1831 should have taught him—notwithstanding all the assurances which he gave of his pacific determinations, at Rock Island—against all the remonstrances of his true friends, and with no probable prospect of ultimate success before him, we find Black Hawk, in 1832, again disturbing the peace of the Northwest, and opening a war-path that finally led to the destruction of his people, and his own degradation in rank, as a chief and a leader of his nation. We now proceed to view the chief incidents of the outbreak known as the Black Hawk war; many of which occurred in that part of Michigan which is now the State of Wisconsin, and within which the career of the obstinate and revengeful Indian terminated in irremediable defeat.

---

[1] Black Hawk's Life. Doc. Hist. Black Hawk War.

## CHAPTER VI.

### BLACK HAWK IN WISCONSIN.

The treaty of St. Louis—Settlers in Black Hawk's village—Obstinacy of Black Hawk—He again crosses the Mississippi—Governor Reynolds demands aid—General Atkinson ascends the river—Black Hawk refuses to go back—The army follows him—Volunteers at Dixon's Ferry—Major Stillman's attack, and flight of his men—First blood shed in the war—Governor Reynolds demands more aid—Sioux and Menomonies offer their services—Talk with the Winnebagoes—Alarm in the mining district—Colonel Dodge writes to Governor Reynolds—Authority of Colonel Dodge—Assembles volunteers—Marches to Rock River—Returns home and prepares for defence—Massacre at Indian Creek and capture of Misses Hall—St. Vrain, Hawley, and others killed—Affair at Buffalo Grove—Major Dement's battle—Attack at Apple River—Affair at Sinsinawa Mound—Dodge talks with the Winnebagoes—Forts and block-houses in Iowa county—The Misses Hall delivered up—Winnebagoes suspected—Aubrey killed at Mound Fort—Dodge's volunteers march—He addresses them—They bury St. Vrain, Hawley, and others—Reach the camp at Dixon—Proceed to General Atkinson's camp—Dodge receives his orders and returns—Murders at Spafford's farm—Dodge assembles a force—Proceeds to Fort Hamilton—Apple killed—Battle of the Pecatonica—Chippewas and Sioux come to Fort Hamilton and return—Force and Green killed at Mound Fort—Dodge joins General Posey's command—Disposition of the forces—March of a portion of the army—General Atkinson at Koshkonong—The White Crow offers to pilot the forces to Black Hawk's camp—His supposed treachery—General Atkinson sends to Fort Winnebago for provisions—General Henry and Colonel Dodge march in search of Black Hawk—They reach Rock River rapids—Discover the Indian trail, which is followed—Overtake Black Hawk—Battle of the Wisconsin Heights—General Atkinson breaks up his camp and marches in pursuit of Black Hawk—They cross the Wisconsin River and follow the Indian trail—Battle of Bad Axe—Winnebago chiefs bring Black Hawk in as a prisoner—General Scott's rapid movements with his forces—They are attacked with cholera—Loss of the Americans in this war—Subsequent notices of Black Hawk, and reflections—The volunteers of

**Wisconsin—Increase of population in the mining country—Important Indian treaties—Land speculations—Military road opened—Mail route up the Mississippi—Early private enterprise—Hamilton—Farnsworth—Transportation of troops—Early history of Prairie du Chien—Causes operating against the early settlement of the country—Michigan about to become a State—New Territory to be formed in the West—Jealousy as to the seat of government—Legislative proceedings—Final action of Congress establishing the Territory of Wisconsin.**

THE treaty of St. Louis, in November, 1804, and all subsequent treaties by which certain lands of the Sacs and Foxes were ceded to the United States, were ever denied to be valid and binding by Black Hawk and a few chiefs who adhered to his party; inasmuch as by the terms of those treaties, (as they asserted,) territory was described which the Indians never intended to sell; and the treaty of 1804, particularly, was made by parties who had neither authority in the nation, nor power to dispose of its lands. A quarter of a century had passed since this latter treaty had been made, and each year had brought with it the undying animosity of Black Hawk against the Americans.

The United States had found no good reason to doubt the reciprocal good faith in which the several treaties with the Sacs and Foxes had been entered into; and hence, could not anticipate an armed resistance on the part of the Indians, to a possession of the lands being taken by citizens emigrating from different parts of the Union into the newly acquired country. It was generally understood in the summer of 1830, that the Sacs had ceded all their land on the east side of the Mississippi, and soon a flowing tide of immigration set in for the neighbourhood of Rock River, and particularly for the fertile spot near its mouth, known as Black Hawk's village. The settlement of the whites, before the entire removal of the Indians, became, as might well be expected, a source of great annoyance, and of manifest danger to all parties. Black Hawk saw his grounds surrounding his village daily encroached upon by the white settlers; and his remonstrances, and representations of wrongs committed upon what he considered his unalienated rights and property, were alike disregarded by those whom he believed were able to protect him, and bound to give him redress. He had been repeatedly advised by Keokuk, and the chiefs of that party which acknowledged the validity of the treaties, to remove, as they had done, to the western side of the Mississippi; he had been informed of the consequences of a refusal to fulfil the treaties, and of the utter hopelessless of a resistance on the part of his band against the power of the United States, which would certainly be put in force to protect the immigrating settlers; he had not, according to his own account, been ignorant of his situation, but he always, as he says, expected redress for his wrongs from the General Government; in fine, when he saw before him no hope of retaining possession of the village and burial-place of his ancestors, his firmness of purpose degenerated into blind obstinacy, and his bitter hatred of the Americans assumed the features of a bloody revenge.

Of all these matters we have already partially spoken, and it now remains for us to view the final efforts of Black Hawk to recover the possessions of his ancestors; efforts in which he opposed the whole power of the General Government, combined with the aroused spirit of a hardy and active population of settlers from the States, who were thus compelled, immediately after their immigration to the mining region, to enter into all the vicissitudes of Indian warfare.

Notwithstanding the lessons of experience which Black Hawk and his band might have derived from the result of affairs in 1831, and in despite of the treaty then entered into at Rock Island, we find that this restless Indian, early in the spring of 1832, was again prepared to assert his rights to the disputed land at the mouth of Rock River, and apparently determined to obtain, and protect the same by the force not only of his own band, but by the aid which he had been induced to look for from his British father, as well as several of the neighbouring tribes: in both the latter, as we have observed, he was deceived.

Black Hawk commenced his last, and to him fatal expedition, in April, 1832; he moved up the Mississippi with his band, the women and children in canoes, his braves on horseback; the number of his force is not accurately known, but it is believed that at no period of the ensuing disturbances did his combined forces exceed five or six hundred. He was joined by the Prophet below Rock River, which, after crossing the Mississippi, he prepared to ascend, hoping to meet the Pottawatamies and Winnebagoes as his allies, when he arrived in their country.

As soon as Governor Reynolds was apprized of this matter, he again declared the State of Illinois invaded, and made a call for volunteers, as well as a demand for aid from the General Government; in a few days about eighteen hundred men assembled at Beardstown, and they were immediately organized into four regiments and a spy battalion, the whole being placed under the command of Brigadier-General Samuel Whiteside.

General Atkinson, with a body of United States troops, had ascended the Mississippi in steamboats: on their arrival in the neighbourhood of Rock River they were joined by the Illinois volunteers; and General Atkinson despatched several expresses to Black Hawk, ordering him in a peremptory manner to leave the country and return to the west side of the Mississippi; to these expresses Black Hawk as peremptorily answered "that he would not leave the country, that he was going up Rock River to the Prophet's village to *make corn*, to which he had been invited, and the whites might attack him if they dared; that they might come on if they chose, but they would not find him unprepared; yet he would not begin with them."[1] Black Hawk hoisted the British flag and proceeded up Rock River to the Prophet's village, below Kishwaukee, where he called his chiefs together and informed them that he had found that Ne-a-pope had deceived him in the expected aid which he had asserted he would receive, but that his people must not know this fact.

The regular troops under General Atkinson followed Black

[1] Drake's Indian Biog. p. 644. Doc. Hist. Black Hawk War.

Hawk up Rock River: they were preceded by the militia under General Whiteside, who on his march burned the Prophet's village, and made a halt at Dixon's Ferry, about forty miles higher up the river—having found that Black Hawk was still in the advance; and it became necessary to send out reconnoitering parties to ascertain his position, and also to wait for a junction with the United States forces, which was soon effected.

Previous, however, to the arrival of General Atkinson at Dixon's Ferry, the officers of the volunteers exhibited a willingness to be employed on active and dangerous service, and on the 12th of May a battalion of 275 mounted men, under the command of Major Stillman, marched up the left bank of Rock River to endeavour to find the locality of Black Hawk: on the 14th this force had reached a small stream (since called Stillman's Run) in the vicinity of Sycamore Creek, where they encamped, and in a short time discovered a small party of Indians about a mile from them, apparently approaching them.

Black Hawk had been aware of the approach of Stillman's detachment, and had sent out three of his young men with a white flag to invite a conference with the officers at his camp, and (as he says) if that was refused, then to say that he would himself go to the American camp: his desire, up to this time, if his declarations are to be credited, was to make peace, and at all events to offer no resistance, unless he should be attacked by the whites.[1]

These Indians were no sooner perceived by Stillman's men, than a party of them, eager for an Indian fight, mounted their horses without orders or officers, and rode in a disorderly manner upon the advancing party, who retreated displaying their flag, but they were taken prisoners and carried into camp. In the mean time, Black Hawk had despatched five other of his young men to ascertain what had become of his first party, and these having also been discovered approaching, were attacked by Stillman's men, who killed two of them,

---

[1] Doc. Hist. Black Hawk War, and references.

and the others escaped and reported the existing circumstances to Black Hawk. From all the facts of which we have any knowledge in this case, from his own declarations, and from the circumstance of his having at this time with him only forty of his men, it does not appear that Black Hawk expected any attack upon him; neither did he contemplate any attack on his part upon the whites; but when he learned the death of his braves, and believed that his white flag was not respected, but on the contrary that a war of extermination was determined on against him, he aroused his warriors, sounded the war-whoop, and rushed upon the advance of Stillman's horsemen, who immediately retreated in the hottest haste, carrying with them terror and dismay, into, and through the camp, where all attempts of Major Stillman to rally his men and make a stand were alike ineffectual, and the retreat of a few individuals soon became a most disorderly flight of the whole. The camp was abandoned to the Indians, who pursued the fugitives some ten or twelve miles: a few only were killed, owing to the extreme disorder of the flight, scarcely two men being together, and the fewness in number of Black Hawk's force. Major Stillman and his volunteers did not stop in their course of retreat until they came to Dixon's Ferry, at which place the stragglers were arriving at all times during the night, with the most exaggerated accounts of the numbers of the pursuing Indians, and the melancholy story, that all who had been left behind had been massacred by the savage foe. Black Hawk's force was magnified to fifteen hundred, and the most extravagant reports of their numbers, and of the bloody battle were made by the fugitives; but it was finally ascertained that the result of a flight of thirty miles on part of the terror-stricken whites, and a pursuit by some forty Indians, was the loss of eleven men, whose bodies were afterward found and interred: according to Black Hawk's own account, his loss was three men, and those were of the parties which he sent out to meet the whites before his pursuit commenced.[1]

[1] Doct. Hist. Black Hawk War.

It must be acknowledged that whether Black Hawk was sincere or not in his intentions of making peace and entering into amicable arrangements, when he first sent (as he asserts) his young men for that purpose to visit Stillman's camp, the first blood that was shed in these disturbances was shed by the whites. To the utter insubordination of Major Stillman's men, and the apparent desire exhibited by them of killing an Indian on the first favourable opportunity, may perhaps be attributed all the disastrous consequences of the subsequent Black Hawk war: at all events, the first blow was struck on the 14th of May, 1832, at Stillman's Run.

The alarm which had already spread through the country, was by no means lessened by the proclamation of Governor Reynolds, which was issued to the militia officers, and dated at Dixon's Ferry, on May 15th, in which he says—"The State is not only invaded by the hostile Indians, but many of our citizens have been slain in battle." He then alludes to Stillman's defeat, (275 mounted volunteers,) and states his belief that the Pottawatamies and Winnebagoes had joined the Sacs, and that *all* may be considered as waging war against the United States. To subdue those Indians and drive them out of the State, the governor makes a requisition of a force of two thousand mounted volunteers in addition to the troops already in the field. They were ordered to meet at Hennepin, on the Illinois River, in companies of fifty men each, on the 10th of June, to be organized into brigades.

In the commencement of the disturbances, there were very many of the Sioux and Menomonies, the implacable enemies of the Sacs, who, thirsting for an opportunity of wreaking vengeance upon them, freely offered their aid to the whites, which was then refused; but soon after the result of this first affair was made known, the services of these Indians were solicited, and Colonel William S. Hamilton was sent up the country above Prairie du Chien, to effect the desired end: several parties of Indians hostile to the Sacs were consequently soon on their march to join the army.

Late in the month of May, Mr. Gratiot, the Indian agent,

held a council with a number of Winnebago chiefs at the head of the Four Lakes, in order to secure their services, if possible, or at least to prevent them from joining the war party of Black Hawk. At this council, the chiefs all signified their desire to remain at peace with the white people, but did not testify any willingness to give their aid against the Sacs; but even this was gaining much, as, if they remained only neutral, the mining region would be in a state of comparative security, and its inhabitants thereby be enabled to act against the Indian foe in their front without being harassed by the Winnebagoes in their rear.[1]

As soon as the news of the disturbances between the Indians and the settlers on Rock River was made known in the mineral region, the utmost anxiety prevailed among the inhabitants; the greater portion of whom were miners and others engaged in the lead trade, who had been, in a proper view of the matter of their immigration, actually invited into the country by the agents of the General Government, and under its sanction, to work and explore the mineral lands. Such an immigration did not come within the category of those whose settlements in the country to which the Indian title had not been extinguished had been the source of Indian complaint and of Indian warfare. The immigrants in the mining country were citizens who had a peculiar claim on the immediate protection of the Government; many of them were the *lessees* of the Government, and all were contributing to its present advantage and ultimate benefit.

But these industrious pioneers were in a much exposed frontier country, in case of any sudden outbreak of the Indians, and were wholly without the necessary protection of the regular troops of the Government; it consequently became necessary to take every step within their power to protect themselves. The views and feelings of the settlers in Illinois acquired a double force in the mining country. "We knew," says Governor Reynolds, "that the hearts of all the

---

[1] See Note A.

Indians who resided within three hundred miles of the scenes of the Black Hawk War were with him in the quarrel, and wished him success. * * * If Black Hawk had succeeded in some skirmishes, and no efficient efforts been made against him, all the tribes around about him would unite with his band and harass the frontiers. To prevent this outbreak of the Indians it was necessary to act with despatch and efficiency."[1]

It was in the first week in May, 1832, that rumours reached the lead region that Black Hawk had crossed the Mississippi and taken possession of his village at Rock Island; also, that General Atkinson was ascending the river from St. Louis with troops, and that Governor Reynolds was to join him at Dixon's Ferry, (on Rock River,) with the Illinois militia, for the purpose of protecting the country, and to compel Black Hawk to leave the eastern side of the Mississippi. These reports being well founded, fears were justly entertained by the inhabitants of the mining region, that in the event of hostilities commencing with the Indians, they would fall back from Rock River on the settlers in the neighbourhood of Galena and south of the Wisconsin River. To express these views, and request assistance in such event, Colonel Henry Dodge addressed a letter to Governor Reynolds, on the 8th of May, 1832, and sent the same by a deputation.[2]

Henry Dodge was one of the early pioneers of the lead region, to which he had emigrated from Missouri, with a large family of sons and daughters, some six years previously: he was largely engaged in the lead business of mining and smelting, himself an industrious citizen. His public position at this time, in this part of the Territory of Michigan, was that of Colonel of the Michigan militia; to this command was added, immediately on the commencement of hostilities, the command of the mounted volunteers of Iowa county, and the Galena volunteers of the State of Illinois, when they served by companies in the Territory of Michigan, now the State of Wisconsin. He was under the orders of Brigadier-General

[1] Reynolds's Illinois

[2] See Note B.

Atkinson, of the United States army, from the commencement to the close of the Indian disturbances on this frontier. At the battles of Wisconsin Heights and Bad Axe, the officers and volunteers served under the orders of General Henry.

In virtue of his military authority, and in the judicious exercise of a wise precaution, Colonel Dodge assembled a few of the miners and settlers in the neighbourhood of Dodgeville and Mineral Point, in Iowa county, in number twenty-seven, among whom was the Colonel's second son, Augustus C. Dodge, now of Iowa. This little party of volunteers started about the eighth or ninth of May, on an expedition to Rock River, to ascertain the position and probable movements of Black Hawk and his followers.

Colonel Dodge proceeded by way of Apple River to Buffalo Grove, at which place an Indian trail was discovered, which was followed by his little company to Rock River, at a point nearly opposite the Kishwaukee, and within a few miles of the ground upon which Major Stillman, at the head of three hundred Illinois volunteers, was, on the same day, (May 14th,) with his whole command, disastrously beaten and put to flight by Black Hawk.[1] After the battle, Governor Reynolds sent an express, at night, to Colonel Dodge, informing him of the facts, and that his country in the Territory was in imminent danger from the attacks of the Indians.[2] Colonel Dodge immediately returned home, and gave notice and advice to the inhabitants of the mining country to fort themselves, and immediately organize for defence.

During the month of May, many depredations were committed by Black Hawk's bands in the Rock River country and within the State of Illinois.

At this time there was a small settlement at Indian Creek, a tributary of the Fox River of Illinois, some fifteen miles from the present town of Ottawa: one of the settlers, named Hall, had some time previously insulted and beaten a Pottawattamie Indian. On the 22d of May, the inmates of the

---

[1] Letter of A. C. Dodge, *penes me.*

[2] Reynolds's Illinois.

families of three of the settlers, Messrs. Hall, Davis, and Pettigrew, had assembled together in one of their dwellings, where they were attacked by a party of about seventy Indians, led on, it is said, by the outraged Pottawatamie; an indiscriminate massacre took place, and all who were in the house, in number fifteen persons, were killed, except two daughters of Mr. Hall, who were led away captive. These girls were taken by their captors to Black Hawk's camp, then near Lake Koshkonong, and, after a detention of a few days, they were delivered up to some Winnebago chiefs, who were induced to effect their liberation in consequence of a large reward offered by General Atkinson for that purpose.[1]

On the same day of this massacre, a party of four persons left Dixon's Ferry for the purpose of exploring the country in order to make settlements. Near Buffalo Grove they discovered the dead body of a man in their path: he was known to them, and had been killed and scalped by the Indians. They returned to the camp, and the next day, having been joined by others, among whom was Felix St. Vrain, Indian agent of the Sacs and Foxes, they proceeded to Buffalo Grove, and buried the body which had been found there. The party then went on their way toward Hamilton's settlement, Wiota, and on the following day they were attacked by a body of Indians, and four of them were killed; among them was the agent, St. Vrain; the others, after being closely followed for near two days by Indians, finally reached Galena in safety.[2]

St. Vrain had been peculiarly obnoxious in the eyes of Black Hawk's band, in consequence of the part he had taken in regard to their removal from their village at Rock Island: it is said that the party which murdered him was led by a chief called "The Little Bear," who had been a particular friend of the agent, and had adopted him as a brother; he had been an inmate of St. Vrain's household, and of course

---

[1] Doc. Hist. Miss Hall's Account.

[2] See Note C. Also Doc. Hist. Black Hawk War.

the agent might have had little cause to fear so fatal a termination of their meeting on the prairie. After the war, some unsuccessful attempts were made to bring the murderers to justice.[1]

Although the main body of Black Hawk's army, which is said to have been composed in all of about six hundred men, was stationed on Rock River, in the vicinity of Lake Koshkonong, yet a predatory war was still carried on by small detached parties in many parts of the country at considerable distances from each other. Hence arose the necessity of a constant vigilance on the part of the volunteer militia not attached to the army, and of every settler in the country; as the hour of an Indian attack could very seldom be anticipated, and the distance of the army from the scene of these predatory excursions of the Indians, rendered a personal defence almost the only reliable one. Of such attacks by Indian parties, were those at Mound Fort, Plum River, Apple River, Spafford's Creek, Hamilton's Fort, which resulted in the battle of the Pecatonica, Kellogg's Grove, Sinsinawa Mound, and other points, besides the several murders committed on individuals, found, unfortunately for themselves, alone and unprotected. In fact, as has been remarked, "the Indians had now shown themselves to be a courageous, active, and enterprising enemy. They had scattered their war-parties all over the North, from Chicago to Galena, and from the Illinois River into the Territory of Wisconsin: they occupied every grove, waylaid every road, hung around every settlement, and attacked every party of white men that attempted to penetrate the country."[2]

Early in June, a party of Indians made an attack on a block-house situate near the mouth of Plum River, below Galena, and after endeavouring for about an hour ineffectually to storm it, they retired without having effected any destruction of lives.[3]

---

[1] See Note C.

[2] Ford's Illinois, 128.

[3] Doc. Hist. Black Hawk War.

About the 18th of June, a party of volunteers from Galena, under the command of Captain James W. Stephenson, were on the look out for Indians, in the neighbourhood of the Pecatonica. A party of the enemy was discovered and pursued into a dense thicket in the prairie; the volunteers commenced a rapid fire upon them, but the Indians, having the advantage of the cover, succeeded in killing a few of Captain Stephenson's men, and he ordered a retreat. But neither he nor his men were willing to give up the fight, and they resolved to return and charge into the thicket upon the Indians. This was done promptly and courageously, the captain leading the way; but they had scarcely penetrated the cover twenty steps when they received the fire of the Indians, which was instantly returned; the charge was made a second and third time, each party giving and receiving the fire of his enemy, until three of Captain Stephenson's men being killed, and himself severely wounded, he found it necessary to retreat, having but a small part of his company then with him. This attack, although in a measure unsuccessful, was certainly one of daring courage: it is said that Black Hawk himself was present in the fight.[1]

Towards the last of June an attempt was made by a considerable body of warriors to surprise the fort at Buffalo Grove, a few miles to the north of Dixon's Ferry. It was guarded by a force of one hundred and fifty militia, who were prepared to meet them, and a sharp contest ensued. Sixteen of the Indians were killed before they retreated. Few of the whites were wounded, but the garrison was in great fear of being cut off, as their ammunition was expended before the arrival of a reinforcement, which had been sent for while the attack was going on.[2]

At this time also, about June 24th, Black Hawk, with a considerable body of Indians, believed to be near one hundred and fifty, made an attack on Apple River Fort, near the present village of Elizabeth, which was defended by twenty-

---

[1] Ford's Illinois, 128. Drake's Indian Biog. 648. [2] Idem.

five men, under Captain Stone. The attack was a fearful one, as the Indians had got possession of the log-houses, and from these opened their fire on the fort with much security, while they were committing every act of devastation on the provisions and property in the houses. The battle was kept up for about fifteen hours, when the Indians retreated, having lost several of their party, but the number was not known, as they carried all away with them; they also took with them a considerable quantity of provisions, and a number of cattle and horses: the loss of the whites was one man killed and one wounded.[1]

Major John Dement, who commanded a spy battalion attached to the army, had a severe contest with Black Hawk's band, on the 25th of June, near Kellogg's Grove. Major Dement had heard, on his arrival there, that a large trail had been discovered, and he set out in advance of his party with twenty men, at daylight next morning, to gain intelligence of the movements of the enemy. He soon discovered a small party of Indians, who were pursued by some of his men, but fearing an ambuscade, he endeavoured to call them back. But he still proceeded with caution, and being followed by some of his men from the camp, he formed about twenty-five of them into line on the prairie, to protect a retreat. Scarcely was this done when a force of three hundred Indians issued from the grove to attack him. They approached with their accustomed yelling and firing, and the major slowly and prudently retired to his camp, closely pursued by the Indians. Here his whole party took possession of some log-houses which answered for a fort, and they were here vigorously attacked by the Indians for nearly an hour. An express was sent to General Posey for relief, and he marched with his whole brigade for that purpose, but did not arrive until after the retreat of the Indians. There was great courage and prudent conduct displayed by Major Dement, in this affair;

[1] Doc. Hist. Black Hawk War. Ford's Illinois, 126. Drake's Indian Biog. 648.

it even called forth the decided applause of Black Hawk himself:[1] the loss of the Americans was five killed and three wounded; and on the part of the Indians, nine left dead on the field, and probably five others carried away. General Posey here awaited the arrival of his baggage-wagons, and afterward proceeded to Fort Hamilton, where he was joined by Colonel Dodge's command.

On the 29th of June, three men were attacked in a field near Sinsiniwa Mound, and two of them, John Thompson and James Boxley, were killed. Captain Stephenson marched from Galena in pursuit of the murderers, but they had reached the Mississippi, and escaped by crossing it in a canoe.

In the latter part of May, Colonel Dodge assembled a company of fifty mounted volunteers, commanded by Captains James H. Gentry and John H. Rountree, and proceeded with them to the head of the Four Lakes, where on the 25th of the month he held a talk with the Winnebagoes. He desired to know their intentions as to the Sacs; whether or not they would aid, counsel, or harbour them in their country; if they would, it would be considered as a declaration of war on their part. He told them that the Sacs had lied to them and given them bad counsel, wishing to draw them into the same situation with themselves; and that if they (the Winnebagoes) were unfaithful to their treaties, they must expect to share the fate of the Sacs.[2]

The Winnebagoes made all fair promises to be faithful to their treaties and remain at peace. This was the same council of which we have spoken as held by the agent Gratiot.

In the mean time the inhabitants of the mining region (Iowa county) had erected the following forts, block-houses, and stockades for the protection and defence of their families, and into which they removed:

---

[1] Doc. Hist. Black Hawk War. Ford's Illinois, 129. [2] See Note A.

Fort Union .... Head Quarters. Colonel Dodge's residence, near Dodgeville.

Fort Defiance .. At the farm of Daniel M. Parkinson, about five miles south-east of Mineral Point.

Fort Hamilton .. At William S. Hamilton's lead diggings, now Wiota.

Fort Jackson ... At Mineral Point.

Mound Fort .... On the high prairie, about a mile and a half south of Ebenezer Brigham's residence, at the Blue Mounds.

Parish's Fort ... At the residence of Thomas J. Parish, now Wingville.

Forts at Cassville, Platteville, Gratiot's Grove, Diamond Grove, White-Oak Springs, Old Shullsburg, Elk Grove at the farm of Justus De Seelhorst.

About the first of June, Captain Sherman, who commanded at Mound Fort, fearing an attack from the Indians, sent word of his apprehensions to Colonel Dodge, who immediately collected from the several posts some two hundred mounted men. These proceeded to Mound Fort on the 3d of June, on which day the two girls who had been captured by the Sacs, were delivered up by the Winnebagoes, in consequence of a reward having been offered by General Atkinson for their recovery.[1] Colonel Dodge did not place the utmost reliance on the faith of these Winnebagoes, believing they were acting as spies; and he therefore advised them to cross the Wisconsin to the northern side, for their safety, as the whites could not distinguish the red men, and knew not a Winnebago from any other Indian. They promised to follow his counsel, but did not. The detachment of volunteers returned to Fort Union, and the next day proceeded to Gratiot's Grove, where they were joined by Captain Stephenson's company of volunteers from Galena.

On the 6th of June, one James Aubrey, an intimate of

---

[1] Doc. History.

Colonel Brigham's family, at the Blue Mounds, was killed by the Sacs, while getting water at the spring near the dwelling-house: this was about one mile and a half north of the Mound Fort, but in sight of it. It has been since well ascertained that the Sacs had been piloted to this place by certain Winnebagoes; suspicion ever attached to this treacherous people.

From Gratiot's Grove, Colonel Dodge's command proceeded on their march, and at Kirker's farm, where they camped, the Colonel delivered a very spirited address to the volunteers, recommending to them union, vigilance, discipline, and obedience to orders. He advised them to have full confidence in the Government and its officers, but that its assistance might arrive too late; therefore it well became them not to wait the arrival of the enemy at their doors, but to advance and fight them, watch them, and hold them in check; to lie down with their arms in their hands, and to rise ready to form the line. His address was received by the volunteers with its deserved effect.[1]

The command proceeded to the scene of the murder of St. Vrain, Fowler, Hale, and Hawley; they buried the bodies of the three former; the body of Hawley was never found. Here Captain Stephenson's company separated and returned to Galena; Colonel Dodge with the remainder of the command proceeded to the camp of the regular troops at Dixon's Ferry on Rock River. General Hugh Brady was here in command, who was escorted by Colonel Dodge and twenty-five of his volunteers to the rapids of the Illinois River, now Ottawa, which was General Atkinson's head-quarters, and where the general then was engaged in organizing three brigades of Illinois volunteers: this was on the 11th of June, and at this time, doubtless, the plan of the campaign was agreed upon, and Colonel Dodge received his orders.[2]

From head-quarters, Colonel Dodge returned to Gratiot's Grove, where his whole command were dismissed to their posts: this was on the 14th of June, and on the same day the

---

[1] See Note D.

[2] See Note E.

murder, by the Sacs, of the men at Spafford's farm occurred.[1]

The news of these murders was brought by express to Colonel Dodge, on the same evening that he had arrived at home; and he despatched an express that night to Captain Gentry to muster immediately what men he could, and meet him at Hamilton Fort. The next morning the Colonel proceeded with two companions, Major Thomas Jenkins, and John Messersmith, Jr., by way of the Blue Mounds, to Wiota. They camped at night at Fretwell's diggings, and the next morning by eight o'clock they were within half a mile of Hamilton's Fort. Here they were met by a German, named Apple, who said he was going to his cabin, some small distance off, to get his blanket, in order to join Gentry and his volunteers, who had arrived at the fort the previous evening. The German left them, and Dodge proceeded to the fort. In an instant, firing was heard, and the horse which the German rode came galloping back, bloody, and without the rider. The Indians had been in ambush near the path which Colonel Dodge had taken, but on the main road to the fort, and, in all probability, his having taken the nigher path saved his life, and the German became the victim.

On the day previous, a number of the volunteers from Fort Defiance, having heard of the murders at Spafford's farm, had proceeded to the scene, and buried the dead bodies; they had returned in the evening to Fort Hamilton, and Captain Gentry and his men having arrived, they were now at this early hour in the morning awaiting the arrival of Colonel Dodge, to go in search of the enemy. The simultaneous arrival of their commander, with the report of the rifles and the return of the German's horse in a bloody condition, caused an instant excitement. All immediately mounted, and, under the lead of their colonel, they rode from the fort: they soon found the mutilated body of Apple lying in the road, while in the hazel thicket skirting the road, they discovered the

---

[1] Doc. Hist. Battle of Pecatonica. Bracken's Account.

ground where the Indians had been lying in ambush. Their trail was soon found and followed, with the Indians sometimes in sight, until the colonel and his party reached the banks of the east branch of the Pecatonica, about five miles from Fort Hamilton.

Although the Indians were not then seen, it was pretty certain that they were concealed in the thickets and behind the sand-banks, on the opposite side of the stream. Colonel Dodge here ordered his men to dismount, linked the horses together, and detailed seven of his men to take charge of them; he had previously ordered four men to take post on the high grounds, for the purpose of watching the course of the Indians, in case they attempted flight. With the remainder of his men, twenty-one in all, Colonel Dodge prepared for a charge on the concealed foe: he first addressed them, pointing out where the murderers of their fellow citizens were then lying, ready to deal death among those who should venture to attack them; and he requested those only to follow him in whom should be found no disposition to turn and flee; if any such were there, now was the time to retract, but never while engaged with the enemy. His address was answered by the instant forward movement of the whole party, following their brave and energetic leader, wading through the Pecatonica River, and with difficulty gaining the firm ground on the opposite bank.

The party were then ordered to trail arms and keep a look out for the Indians: in less than five minutes, the enemy, who were lying concealed behind the sand-banks and in the cavities caused by the floods of the river, delivered their fire, by which three of the volunteers fell, two mortally wounded, the third seriously; the battle was then literally fought hand to hand, and the desperate conflict was short and decisive; not an Indian escaped to tell the tale of the defeat. Seventeen of the Sacs were in the fight, and at its close eleven dead bodies were found on the ground, while six other dead bodies were some time afterward found in the immediate vicinity: the wounded Indians had crawled and secreted themselves in the thickets, where they soon died. Black Hawk is said to have remarked, after the war, that there was one band of seventeen of his braves, of whose fate he had never heard. Of Colonel Dodge's men, three were killed, one wounded.

Some idea of the length of time occupied in this desperate hand-to-hand conflict, may be gathered from the words of one of the volunteers:—"I fired my yager; let it drop—drew out my left pistol; fired it at an Indian—let the pistol fall—drew out my right pistol; fired at another Indian—was pouring powder in my hand to reload, when one of our company said, 'They are all dead!' "[1]

Before this time, Colonel William S. Hamilton had gone up the Mississippi to endeavour to procure assistance from the Sioux and the Chippewas against the Sacs and Foxes. On the morning of the battle of Pecatonica, he had arrived at his fort, together with Mr. Levi Marsh, of Prairie du Chien, having under their charge two hundred Indians of the two nations Sioux and Chippewas. When Colonel Dodge returned to the fort, the Indians no sooner heard of the fight than they hastened to the battle-ground, and held a pow-wow over the dead bodies, which they actually cut to pieces. These Indians, for some cause, perhaps want of means on the part of Colonel Dodge to subsist them, or unwillingness without further orders to employ them, became dissatisfied, and returned up the Mississippi the next day.[2]

On the 20th of June, some Indians were discovered in the vicinity of Mound Fort; and Lieutenant Force, and one Green, whose family was in the fort, mounted their horses and rode out to reconnoitre. In a short time they fell into an ambush of the Sacs, about two miles in front, and in immediate view from the fort: the unfortunate men were plainly seen endeavouring to escape to the fort, but they were both soon surrounded and killed by the savages, who mutilated the bodies in a most horrible manner. The information was sent

---

1 Doc. Hist. Bracken's account of the battle of Pecatonica. See Note F.

2 Doc. Hist. Colonel Dodge's official account.

to Colonel Dodge, who immediately assembled a detachment of volunteers, and made a night march, by way of the Blue Mounds, as far as Sugar River, in search of the Sacs. At Sugar River their trail appeared to be scattered, as if they had dispersed, and the volunteers returned to Fort Union; on their way they buried the body of Lieutenant Force by the side of the road, under one of the few trees growing on the edge of the prairie: the body of Green had been buried two or three days before by the people at Mound Fort. This expedition of Colonel Dodge was about the 24th of June.[1]

Immediately after this, in pursuance, no doubt, of the plan of the campaign, as formed at head-quarters, Colonel Dodge, with his immediate command, met Brigadier-General Posey with his brigade at Fort Hamilton: these commands composed the left wing of the army. General Alexander's command formed the centre; General Atkinson, with General Henry's brigade, formed the right wing, and advanced up Rock River. The left wing marched across the country by the way of the Pecatonica battle-ground and Sugar River, to the first of the Four Lakes. At Sugar River, they were reinforced by the Galena company of volunteers, and at the First Lake they were joined by the "White Crow," and about thirty Winnebago warriors, who avowed their purpose of showing the army the path of the Sacs and Foxes.

General Atkinson was at this time encamped, with his portion of the army at the outlet of Lake Koshkonong, where he had been joined by General Alexander's brigade. Some cause of dissatisfaction having occurred between Colonel Dodge's command and General Posey's brigade, a change of position was effected, whereby General Alexander's command was associated with that of Colonel Dodge, while Posey's brigade assumed the station which Alexander's had occupied. Colonel Dodge then moved up the right bank of Rock River,

---

[1] Doc. Hist. Beouchard's Narrative.

accompanied by the White Crow and his band, who professed to guide them to the camp of Black Hawk.

The march was continued for two days, until Rock River was reached, a short distance above the mouth of Bark River, at which point the White Crow was anxious that Alexander and Dodge should turn their march up Rock River. But an express had arrived from General Atkinson requiring support from this portion of the army, in consequence of some alarms from the enemy near his own station. In pursuance of these orders Alexander and Dodge retraced their steps and crossed Rock River immediately below the mouth of Bark River, and found General Atkinson encamped about three or four miles up Bark River.

It appeared subsequently, by discovery of the trail and other evidences by the scouting parties, that a considerable ambush had been formed on the east bank of Rock River, at a point where the detachment under Alexander and Dodge would have been obliged to cross the river, at a very rocky ford, dangerous of course for horses. It was not without reason supposed that the "Blind, or White Crow" was acting in concert with Black Hawk, and was treacherously guiding the army to this point, when they received General Atkinson's orders by the express, and returned to Bark River. The White Crow had been suspected by Colonel Dodge when he was at the Blue Mounds: he had at that time promised to cross the Wisconsin, but had not complied.

General Atkinson finding his camp straitened for want of provisions, despatched about two hundred and fifty men, under the respective commands of Alexander, Posey, Henry, and Dodge, to Fort Winnebago for supplies. The detachment were ordered to return by the same route which they went, but with permission, in case the Indian trail was discovered, to follow it. The command reached Fort Winnebago, and having received the supplies, a consultation was had by the officers, on the route of return. Colonel Dodge suggested the idea of crossing Rock River higher up, so as to throw the Indians, if they were in the vicinity, between themselves and the rest of the army under General Atkinson. In the propriety of this movement General Henry and his officers agreed, while Generals Posey and Alexander dissented, who therefore retraced their steps in pursuance of orders.

Henry's and Dodge's commands marched eastward and struck Rock River at the Rapids, (near Hustisford,) from which an express was sent to General Atkinson's camp; but the express quickly returned with information that the enemy's trail was discovered. Pursuit commenced immediately, and the trail was followed down the river, until it diverged from it, westward. The detachment crossed the Crawfish River near Aztalan, and followed the trail, which bore to the west of Keyes's Lake, (Rock Lake;) it was still followed westward until the ground between the Third and Fourth Lakes was reached, now the site of Madison; thence it was followed around the southern end of the Fourth Lake, where it appeared that an admirable position for a battle-ground, with natural defences, and places of ambush, had been chosen by the enemy, and here they had apparently lain the previous night; this place was near Slaughter's farm. The pursuit continued this day, July 21st, with occasional glimpses of straggling Indians, some of whom were killed, until about five o'clock in the afternoon, when the highlands or bluffs of the Wisconsin River were reached; and here was Black Hawk with his retreating band, supposed to be five or six hundred in number, preparing to cross the Wisconsin River, with their women and children. At the time of the arrival of the army, the Indians had descended the bluffs and were in the low grounds which skirt the river.

In the ardour of pursuit, the immediate commands of Colonel Dodge and Colonel William L. D. Ewing had outstripped the rest of General Henry's brigade, and on their arrival at the bluffs they were met by the spy company which had preceded them, and were now driven in, with information that the enemy was in sight. Dodge's command, with Ewing's in its centre, having dismounted, immediately formed the line and advanced to the edge of the bluffs, where they were met by the enemy, who were in pursuit of the spy company: the battle began, and the Indians were repulsed. The position of Colonel Dodge was maintained under a heavy fire for about an hour, when General Henry's brigade arrived, which deploying to the right and left, formed the line of battle, leaving Dodge's command in the centre.

The battle began about five o'clock in the afternoon, and about sundown the firing had ceased, as a general matter, on both sides; a rain had fallen, and the high grass in the bottom-land being thus wet, it was found impracticable for the men to keep their arms dry in passing through it. The loss of the enemy must have been very severe compared with that of the Americans: it has never been accurately known what number Black Hawk lost, but it is believed that more than sixty were killed in the battle, and a great number of dead bodies were afterward found on the northern side of the Wisconsin River on the route to Bad Axe: these had, many of them, doubtless died from wounds received in the battle. The American loss was one killed and eight wounded.

The White Crow and his Winnebagoes, together with Pierre Pacquette their interpreter were in the battle; they had accompanied the detachment from Fort Winnebago to the Rock River Rapids, and also on the pursuit of the trail from its discovery until this time. After the battle, they all left the army in the night, and returned to Fort Winnebago: perhaps this was an unfortunate movement for Black Hawk's band, for during the night the voice of an Indian was heard hailing the American camp, and speaking in an Indian tongue which was not understood; it was afterward learned that he was speaking in the Winnebago language, under the belief that the "White Crow" and his chiefs were still in the camp, and the purport of the speech was an offer on the part of Black Hawk to surrender, which he wished to be made known to the American commander. The absence of the White Crow and of Pacquette may thus have been unfortunate, as there is no doubt of the wretched situation in which Black Hawk's deluded followers were then placed. Sickness, debility, and absolute starvation pervaded his whole band; the women and children were of course the greatest sufferers; the difficulty of getting them across the Wisconsin in the face of a pursuing foe, was only a forerunner of the multitude of evils which lay in his path of retreat to the Mississippi; and the fatal consequences of another battle, either on such retreat, or on an attempt to cross the broad and deep Mississippi, when its banks were reached, by a crowd of helpless fugitives, all must have presented themselves to the mind of Black Hawk in their true light, or have by this time been forced there, even if his delusive hopes of ultimate success still continued. It is therefore highly probable that an attempt to communicate his willingness to surrender was made in the manner mentioned.

In the morning after the battle, it was ascertained that all the Indians had crossed the Wisconsin during the night-time, and they now had disappeared. This day the country was scoured all around; expresses were sent to General Atkinson and to the commanding officer at Prairie du Chien, with information of the battle and retreat of the enemy; and litters were prepared for the wounded. On the day following, the army marched to the Blue Mounds, where Colonel Dodge's command, including Captain Stephenson's Galena company were dismissed.[1]

In the mean time, General Atkinson broke up his camp at Bark River, and marched by way of the Blue Mounds to Helena, on the Wisconsin River. Here the volunteers under Colonel Dodge were again assembled, and the whole army crossed the Wisconsin, and discovered the trail of the retreating Sacs, under the bluffs on the northern side of the river. The trail was marked by the bodies of Indians who had died of wounds and of disease; perhaps of debility produced by want of adequate food; perhaps of absolute starvation; the march was thus rendered in all respects very offensive and distressing to the feelings of the brave and humane soldier. On the evening of the first of August, signs

[1] See Note G.

of the enemy were discovered, and some stragglers were killed.

The line of march was taken up on the morning of the 2d of August, at two o'clock, Colonel Dodge's command forming the advance, supported by the regular troops under Colonel Zachary Taylor. About sunrise the spy company reported that they were up with the enemy; orders were given for an immediate advance and attack, and the line having been formed, it was advanced about a mile to the bluffs of the Mississippi, near the mouth of the Bad Axe River, where the battle took place. At this point was collected Black Hawk's retreating band of Sacs, men, women, and children, endeavouring to make their escape from their justly exasperated, and now highly excited enemy; and here was to terminate the ephemeral career of Black Hawk, together with the disturbances, massacres, and depredations consequent to his obstinate, headlong, and revengeful course. This was to be the last of the bloody battles and loss of human life of which the miserable delusion of Black Hawk had been the occasion.[1]

On the morning after the battle of Wisconsin Heights, Captain James B. Estes had been despatched with information to Prairie du Chien, at which place he arrived by noon of the 23d of July. Colonel Loomis, then in command of Fort Crawford sent the steamboat Enterprise, of Galena, up the Mississippi to Black River. At Black River they found forty Winnebagoes with twenty-eight canoes, collected there doubtless to aid the retreating Sacs to cross the Mississippi. These Winnebagoes and their canoes were seized and brought down to Fort Crawford on the 30th of July. The Enterprise being a slow boat, Colonel Loomis hired the steamboat Warrior to go up the river a second time. On the first of August this boat ascended the river (about forty miles) to the mouth of Bad Axe River, and here found the Indians on the east bank of the Mississippi, who commenced firing on the boat; the fire was returned from the boat with a six-pounder, and the

[1] Doc. Hist. Bracken's Account, passim. See Note G.

Indians fled into the woods. The boat returned the same night to Prairie du Chien for wood, and, having procured it, started back about midnight and arrived at the lower end of the large island below the mouth of Bad Axe, about ten o'clock in the morning of the 2d of August; they heard firing before they reached the island: the battle had already begun.[1]

There are two islands in the Mississippi near the mouth of Bad Axe; many of the Indians had been driven on to these islands by our troops; the steamboat opened a fire upon them with her six-pounder, and Captain Throckmorton sent two small boats ashore to bring our troops over to the islands. Four trips were made, and Colonel Zachary Taylor with his regulars, about one hundred and fifty men, were landed on the large island, and nearly all the Indians found upon it were killed.

The distance from the main shore to the islands is about one hundred and fifty yards: it appeared that the Indians had but one canoe with them, and they had to swim across the slough, so that many of them were drowned, as their bodies were found next day below the islands.

Toward the close of the battle, General Atkinson, who had now arrived with the main body of the army, came on board the steamboat and remained there until the close of the conflict, which soon terminated in the total destruction of a very large portion of Black Hawk's followers, men, women, and children, and the capture and dispersion of the remainder.[2]

Black Hawk after the battle fled to the Winnebago village at Prairie la Crosse, where he surrendered himself to the chiefs Cha-e-tar and the One-eyed Decorra, who brought him and the Prophet afterward to Prairie du Chien, and delivered them up as prisoners to General Street, the agent of the Winnebagoes, on the 27th of August, 1832.

A number of Black Hawk's people, men, women, and children, who had descended the Wisconsin River in canoes, after the battle on the Wisconsin Bluffs, were taken prisoners above the mouth of the river: it has also been ascertained that a

---

[1] Doc. Hist. Battle of Bad Axe. Este's Account. [2] Idem. See Note H.

number of the women and children who had got safely across the river at the battle of Bad Axe, were pursued and killed by a large body of Sioux, the implacable enemy of the Sacs.

The dread of a protracted warfare with Black Hawk had caused active measures on part of Government. In addition to the regular forces under General Atkinson, in the latter part of June, General Scott with nine companies of artillery, hastened from the seaboard, by way of the lakes to Chicago. The rapidity of his military movements is worthy of notice; passing from Fortress Monroe on the Chesapeake, to Chicago at the southern end of Lake Michigan, he landed his forces at Fort Dearborn on the 8th of July, having transported them eighteen hundred miles in eighteen days. But the conflict was over before he reached the scene of action. In July and August, Scott and his force contended with a more fatal foe than the Indians: the cholera had found its way from Canada up the St. Lawrence, by Detroit, where it first seized on Scott's men, and thenceforth his camp became a hospital. It was late in August when he reached the Mississippi, and so great were the ravages of the disease, that the aggregate of his losses at Detroit, at Fort Gratiot, on Lake Michigan, at Fort Dearborn, and at Rock Island, exceeded four hundred men.[1]

The loss on part of the Americans in this Indian outbreak, independent of the ravages of the cholera, and the murders committed in various quarters on the settlers by the Indians, is believed to be about fifty, perhaps some less than, but not exceeding that number. The loss of the Indians cannot well be known, but at Pecatonica it was seventeen; at Wisconsin Heights about sixty, and at Bad Axe about one hundred and fifty killed, besides thirty-nine women and children taken prisoners.

Black Hawk was afterward sent as a prisoner to Jefferson Barracks, and thence was taken, together with some of his family, to Washington, where he arrived on the 22d of April, 1833. After an interview with President Jackson, and the

---

[1] See Note I.

assurance given to him by the President that the Government would compel the red men to be at peace, he was sent to Fortress Monroe. The prisoners remained here until June 4th, 1833, when they were liberated by order of the President. They were sent home, under officers appointed to conduct them through the principal cities of the Union, in order to impress them with a proper sense of the power of the whites, and the utter hopelessless of any permanent organized resistance against the United States Government, on part of the Indians. In this, there is every reason to believe that success was obtained; Black Hawk ever after remained quiet: he died October 3d, 1840, in Iowa Territory, and was buried on the banks of the Mississippi.[1]

Black Hawk always alleged that the cause of his hostility against the Americans, was the invalidity of the treaty of 1804, by which his own village and grounds were ceded by individuals of the Sac and Fox tribes, who had no authority for the act; but he also said, when, at a subsequent treaty, (May, 1816,) he himself had "touched the quill," and by which treaty the same territory was ceded, that he knew not what he was signing, and that he was therein deceived by the agent and others, who did not correctly explain the nature of the grant. Doubtless, the indiscriminate, and to a great extent, lawless spread of immigrating population, over the newly acquired country on Rock River, and the actual occupation of his own village by the Illinois settlers, accompanied by the forcible ejection of his own family and others of his band from their happy homes, created a rankling wound, which nothing less than the shedding of the blood of the whites could even cicatrize, much less effectually cure. Yet he denied that he had gone to war willingly, and asserted that when his flag of truce was fired upon by Stillman's men, his intention had been to surrender; but as he was forced into a combat, he said to his people, "Since they will fight us, let us fight."[2]

---

[1] Doc. Hist. Black Hawk War.

[2] Related by John Shaw, of Marquette county.

He could scarcely have a hope of success in his warlike enterprise, as he was not supported by Keokuk, nor by many other chiefs of the Sacs and Foxes west of the Mississippi: his expected aid (according to his own account) from the British and the Pottawatamies had totally failed him; and even the Winnebagoes, who were certainly his friends, but who were kept in salutary check by the energies of the inhabitants of the mining country, could render him no effectual assistance, however treacherously they were inclined. His cause was hopeless from the commencement of his obstinate and deluded career; still, his short course was vindictive and bloody, and his chastisement, heavily as it fell upon his people, was merited, and became necessary, although its infliction caused the expenditure of much national treasure, and was obtained at the priceless cost of the lives of many valuable citizens.

Although his own village was at the mouth of Rock River, yet it appears that his band were not much acquainted with the country high up the river and westward of it; as he acknowledges that the Winnebagoes guided him to a place of refuge for his followers, in the neighbourhood of the Four Lakes; and it has been ascertained that the Sacs who committed the murders at the Blue Mounds, had been shown the path thither by some Winnebagoes. After the first affair of the war at Sycamore Creek, generally called "Stillman's Run," the depredations of Black Hawk were committed altogether in the mining region, with the exception of the murders at Indian Creek, and the capture of the two Misses Hall. But in that quarter of the country, brave hearts quickly united in the common defence against savage hostility; constant vigilance, unceasing activity, unflinching courage, strict conformity to prudent counsels, and obedience to the orders of wise and energetic leaders, were the effectual means of protecting the sparse settlements of Iowa county and the neighbourhood of Galena. Black Hawk has been known to have often made this observation: "If it had not been for that chief, Dodge, the hairy face, I could easily have whipped the whites: I could have gone anywhere my people pleased, in the mining country."

The merit of defending this quarter of the country must not, in strict justice, be limited to those individuals alone who had the fortune to meet the enemy in actual combat. Many unavailable efforts were made in search of the enemy at various times, by the volunteers of the mining region: in the dangers and difficulties all were willing and ever ready to participate; and most certainly the meed of approbation cannot justly be withheld from those who, perhaps less fortunate than their companions in arms, did not encounter the foe in deadly fight. The constant vigilance and activity in scouring the country, evinced by the volunteers upon all occasions when called upon by their commander, very naturally imparted a confidence to the families of the inhabitants, who of necessity were congregated in little stockade posts, block-houses, and places of defence: such conduct also afforded them an efficient protection against the predatory incursions of the Indians, and certainly contributed to exciting the fears of a foe, whose principal hope of success is in the attack by surprise. Many journeys of much danger were cheerfully undertaken and performed by the volunteers, when acting as expresses; and in fine, where all were willing and all were ready, although not all were found in the actual battle-field, the slightest discrimination is improper and wholly unnecessary.

The companies of volunteers under the immediate command of Colonel Dodge at the battle of the Wisconsin Heights, were Captain Stephenson's, from Galena; Captain Clarke's, from White-Oak Springs; Captain Gentry's, from Mineral Point; Captain Parkinson's, from Fort Defiance; Captain Jones's, from Blue River, and Captain Dickson's, from Platteville. Lieutenant Charles Bracken was adjutant of the battalion and aid to Colonel Dodge.

The close of the Indian disturbances brought with it a rapid increase of immigration, not only in the mining country, but in various other parts of the territory west of Lake Michigan, more especially in that portion bordering the lake shore; the interior was as yet sparsely occupied. Within a few years past, several treaties had been made with different tribes of Indians, by which the boundaries of their several lands were defined, and much territory ceded to the United States. Among these the treaties of Prairie du Chien, of July 29th and August 1st, 1829, and of Rock Island, of September 15th and 21st, were highly important to the interests of the western portion of Michigan Territory, as opening a wide field for the enterprising and industrious emigrant; the advantages held out to him were in very many instances seized and improved; but the establishment of the United States land-offices at a subsequent period, in 1835, and the facilities thereby afforded to the speculating land monopolist, had an injurious effect on the settlement of this fine region of country, which is severely felt even to the present day, and unfortunately with a prospect of continuance.[1]

Much enterprise was already exhibited by the inhabitants of Green Bay, not only in the improvement of the vicinity by buildings and cultivation, but by calling public attention to the propriety and necessity of the erection of a separate Territory in this part of Michigan. It is true that courts of justice were already established here, and that members of the legislative council were elected to represent this portion of the Territory; but as the seat of government was at Detroit, months were employed by the legislator in travelling to transact the business of a few days; and, as if the country east of the Mississippi and west of Lake Michigan was not sufficiently remote for the protecting arm of the existing Territorial Government, Congress, by the act of June 28th, 1834, attached to Michigan all the country west of the Mississippi and north of the Missouri, comprising much more than the whole of the present State of Iowa.

In order to facilitate the intercourse between the two remote military posts at Green Bay and Prairie du Chien, three companies of United States soldiers were detached, by the orders of the adjutant-general, from Fort Howard, under the command of Lieutenant Alexander, to open a military road

[1] Doc. Hist. Indian Treaties. Descriptive Hist.: the several counties.

from Fort Howard to Fort Crawford, that is, from Green Bay to the Mississippi at the mouth of the Wisconsin River. They entered on duty June 1st, 1835, and the route, as laid out by them, still continues as one of the great thoroughfares between the East and the West, with little other deviations than those caused by the gradual settlement and cultivation of the country. An instance of persevering endurance of fatigue, in this connection, may well be recorded. In 1832, Colonel Zachary Taylor, then in command at Fort Crawford, established a regular communication by mail between that place and Fort Snelling, at the mouth of St. Peter's River: James Halpin, then a soldier in the United States army, now a citizen of Madison, was the bearer of the despatches. He travelled the most of the time on foot, and continued to carry his mail for one year: the time spent in going and returning was fourteen days, and the distance between the two places was about three hundred miles. He crossed the Mississippi at Prairie du Chien, and travelled on the western side of the river; the upper Iowa River was crossed by means of a canoe which he found on the bank, having been left there by some Indian, or perhaps by some traveller or explorer. There was no stream, except this one, of any consequence, to cross, until he came to St. Peter's River, near Fort Snelling. There was no cabin, tent or shelter for him in the whole distance, but sometimes he would come across a temporary Indian encampment, where he was always well treated, but he seldom found the encampment in the same place a second time.

At a much earlier period, the absence of white inhabitants presented no great obstacle to individual enterprise in passing through the country. In 1823, Colonel William S. Hamilton, late of Iowa county, had entered into a contract with the General Government to supply the garrison at Fort Howard with provisions. He left the lower part of Illinois with several hundred head of cattle, and came by the way of Chicago, coasting the lake past the points where Milwaukee, Sheboygan, and Manitoowoc now are, to Green Bay, with the whole of his drove. At Milwaukee River he found Mr. Solomon

Juneau alone; at another point he found Colonel Ebenezer Childs with a fishing party, and having accomplished his desired end, he returned to Illinois by his nearest route across the yet altogether unsettled country.[1]

The route of Father Marquette from Green Bay to the Mississippi was followed so early as 1818, in a manner well deserving a passing notice. Mr. William Farnsworth, now of Sheboygan, left Michillimackinac in a boat, accompanied by more than twenty other individuals, for the purpose of proceeding to St. Louis by water. The party ascended Green Bay and the Fox River, crossed the portage at Fort Winnebago, and descended the Wisconsin River to its mouth; thence proceeded down the Mississippi to St. Louis, and transacted their business. The same party, in the same boat, returned up the Mississippi to the mouth of the Illinois River; ascended the Illinois to a portage, where they carried their boat over to the Chicago River, which they descended to Lake Michigan; they then coasted the lake to its most southern extremity, and all returned in health to Michillimackinac.[2]

This course of water travel was by no means uncommon between Green Bay and Prairie du Chien: the instance above given is remarkable for the number of individuals in one boat, and also for the return voyage. In 1826, we find that a notice is made in the St. Louis Herald of the 8th of November, of the arrival at that place, a few weeks before, of thirty-five boats direct from Green Bay, bringing the third regiment of infantry. This flotilla, at the dryest season of the year, made but twenty-five hundred yards of portage between the Fox and Wisconsin Rivers. The voyage down the Mississippi from Prairie du Chien to St. Louis ranged from six to ten days; in ascending, the time occupied was from twelve days to one month.

It is difficult to ascertain the precise date of the first establishment of the French at Prairie du Chien: it is certain that when Carver was here in 1766, there was a considerable

---

[1] Doc. Hist. Early Adventure.

[2] Idem.

village of the Fox Indians, and that it was a place of annual resort of Indians and traders for the purpose of trade in peltries and the products of the chase, for the merchandise, arms, and ammunition furnished the Indians by the whites. But Carver furnishes at least negative testimony that at this period there were no white persons, either settled or residing there, for he says that he and his party left the village, and proceeded a few miles up the river, where they encamped on the western side of the Mississippi: this, it may reasonably be supposed, they would not have done, had there been any white persons at the village. Besides, there is no evidence that the Jesuit Fathers, or other missionaries, ever had in early days any establishment at the Dog Prairie; which alone, is a powerful circumstance against the idea of an early white settlement. In fact, when the United States commissioners were examining the land claims of the old settlers at Prairie du Chien, in 1820, the oldest claim by settlement, that of Michael La Pointe, dated back to 1784: the greatest portion of the claims were in virtue of settlements made within thirty years.[1]

Mr. Isaac Lee, the United States agent to receive testimony concerning the claims at Prairie du Chien, reports "that among the most aged of the inhabitants of the Prairie, none could be found who could recollect or who had any knowledge of the first establishment of the French there, nor could any satisfactory account be obtained by any traditions among them touching this point. The remains of what is commonly called the old French fort are yet (1820) very distinguishable. Though capacious and apparently strong, it was probably calculated for defence against musketry and small arms only. None can recollect the time of the erection of this fort—it was far beyond the memory of the oldest; nor can the time of its erection be determined by any evidence to be obtained. Some difference of opinion appears to exist there, as to the question whether it was originally built

---

[1] Am. State Papers, vol. iv. 872.

by the French or by the Spanish government. It is evidently very ancient."[1]

Michael Brisbois gave evidence before Mr. Lee, in 1820, that he then had been thirty-nine years in this country, and was sixty years of age; that from his own knowledge, and the best information he could obtain, Prairie du Chien, from the mouth of the Wisconsin to the upper part of the prairie, had been occupied and cultivated in small improvements, both before and since his arrival in the country; that about eighteen years since, the French became somewhat apprehensive as to their title; which fact having been made known to the Indians, one of the first chiefs of the Fox nation, named Nan-pouis, ratified at Cahokia, near St. Louis, an ancient sale of said prairie to the French; that in the year seventeen hundred and eighty-one, Governor Sinclair bought the Island of Michillimackinac, Green Bay, and Prairie du Chien. That the prairie derived its name from a large family called "Des Chiens" who formerly resided here, and some of the same family, and so called "Des Chiens," were here when he arrived.

Pierre la Pointe also, at the same time, gave evidence before Mr. Lee, that he was seventy years of age, and had been forty-four years in the country, and had resided thirty-eight years at Prairie du Chien. That in the year seventeen hundred and eighty-one he was at Michillimackinac, and acted as interpreter at the treaty held by Governor Sinclair with the Indians, for the purchase of the island of Michillimackinac, Green Bay, and Prairie du Chien; and that he was present at the Prairie, and saw the goods delivered to the Indians, by Basil Girard, Pierre Antya, and Augustin Angè, in payment for the purchase of the said prairie, according to the stipulations of the treaty with Governor Sinclair.[2]

It has been said that the old fort was destroyed by fire in the first years of the Revolutionary War: the village was renewed in 1783—that is, if one had existed there before that

---

[1] Am. State Papers, vol. iv. 867.

[2] Idem. 866.

time, which is extremely doubtful when the evidence in relation to land claims is considered. At what time any other fort or defences were built here by the French or English does not appear; but we learn, from a congressional report, that the village and *fort* were *formally* surrendered to the Americans in the month of June, 1796.[1] The *formal* surrender of the *fort*, is doubtful; the *general* surrender of the Western posts should have been made in June, but did not take place until July.

In 1805, when Lieutenant Pike was on his expedition up the Mississippi, he computed the fixed white population of the place, in the absence of the traders, and those connected with them, at 370, and the total number at from 500 to 600: there were then, thirty-seven houses. In 1812, the principal families there, were Dubuque, Antya, Brisbois, Boilvin, &c.: in 1814 the farms were in a high state of cultivation.

We have repeatedly had occasion to remark, that independent of the settlements of the whites around fortified posts and trading points, and the few old missionary stations, in the vicinity of the great lakes and the Upper Mississippi, no attempts at agricultural immigration, and the establishment of farming industry, had been made for more than a century after the first arrival of the Jesuit Fathers, and the early explorers in the country. A combination of causes was always presenting an insuperable barrier to an agricultural occupation of the great Northwest; until the time had arrived when such an occupation of it could only be checked by absolute and overpowering force, because the onward progress of American enterprise had at length reached this region. It is a certain fact, well established in the history of the occupation of all new countries, that industrial settlements cannot be forced; such never attain more than an outward show of prosperity, but are pregnant with the seeds of disease, which time soon ripens, and dissolution ensues. Natural causes will produce like effects, and perhaps no artificial

[1] Am. State Papers, vol. iii. 341.

efforts could have contributed to the settlement of Wisconsin one hour earlier than when the barrier of remoteness from civilized life had been removed, by the onward and steady march of agricultural emigration from the Eastern and Southern States. Such was a natural cause, and the effect was soon perceived in the rapid progress in improvements spread over the whole country. No colony established by a government, no settlement induced by the plausible representations of a body of land speculators, can justly hope for success in the absence of a natural demand for their action. The one may be kept alive by extravagant expenditures, and the other may linger in a sickly appearance of prosperity until it perishes from debility. Both are artificial, and neither of them can compare with that occupation and settlement of a country which, when the proper time has arrived, springs from a persevering and industrious immigration; and which is naturally withheld until the arrival of such time.

But there was a combination of causes always acting, so as to prevent the settlement of the country known now as the Northwestern Territory, by a body of agriculturists. In the first place, the Jesuit Fathers, the precursors of all succeeding population, were constantly occupied in the duties of religion, in the conversion of the savage, and in the spread of the Word of God over an immense country, inhabited by various nations and tribes of Indians, and in which their few missionary stations were often hundreds of miles apart. They gave no attention to agriculture; it was not their vocation, nor was it their design to encourage it; all the objects of this world, and even its obvious demands, were disregarded, when placed in competition with the fulfilment of the duties of their religion. The amelioration of the social condition of man may have appeared to them to be of less importance than the conversion to the true faith of a human soul; and the Jesuit Fathers were not the less in the faithful discharge of their holy calling, although the settlement of the country which they had discovered did not immediately follow in their footsteps.

Again: while this region was in the possession of the

French, for more than a century, up to the peace of 1763, scarcely the least encouragement was given to agriculture. The French Government made no grants of land—gave no attention to settlers or agriculturists; the occupation of the country was strictly military, from the time of the establishment of the forts at Michillimackinac and Detroit. It is true that a few grants of land were made, by French governors and commanders, previous to the year 1750, to favoured individuals, some of which were afterward confirmed by the King of France;[1] others which did not require confirmation, being made by Antoine de la Mothe Cadillac, commandant at Detroit, under special authority from the king:[2] of this latter kind, one for a small piece of about thirty acres, bears with it so many conditions, restrictions, imposition of duties, regulations of trade, rent charges, reservations, prohibitions of sale, and a whole cavalcade of feudal duties to be performed by the grantee, that in itself it would be a host, in opposition to the agricultural settlement of any country.[3] .

Again: these grants, such as they were in effect, were very few in number. Three were made by the French governor, commandant of Louisiana and the Canadas, in the year 1740; and ten by the like officer in 1750.[4] And whatever may have been the nature of the grants, or titles of the inhabitants, the whole number of settlements within the American title, in the neighbourhood of Detroit, in the year 1763, when the country was ceded by treaty to England, was only 77.[5]

Again: it is well known that immediately after the acquisition by Great Britian of the possessions of France on the continent of North America, by the terms of that treaty of 1763, the King of England issued a proclamation restricting the further extinguishment of native title; and although a

---

[1] Six, says Judge Woodward. Am. State Papers, vol. i. 247.

[2] Two of this kind. Idem.

[3] See Note K.

[4] Jouett's Report. Am. State Papers, vol. i. 175.

[5] Woodward's Report. Idem. 247.

number of claims to land, under pretended grants of commanding officers at Detroit, subsequent to 1763 and previous to 1783, were made, they were not confirmed by Government; nor did the English Government confirm any of the grants or purchases claimed to have been made by, and from the Indians.[1]

Again: the American Government has ever acted on the policy, and according to the effect of the proclamation of the king of Great Britain, of October 7th, 1763, whereby purchases by individuals from the Indians were strictly prohibited. And although the treaty of 1783 gave to the United States all that part of Louisiana lying east of the Mississippi, which France had ceded to England by the treaty of 1763; and although Virginia had ceded her claims to the Northwestern Territory to the United States, in 1787; yet an insuperable difficulty stood in the way of settlement of the country, so far as the encouragement, or even countenance of the Government could be given to it, for the Indian title to the soil had not yet been extinguished.

Again: the determined hostility of nearly all the Indian nations of the great lakes and of the Mississippi, of the Illinois and of the Wabash, to the new masters of the country, the Americans, added to the long protracted delivery of the Western posts by the British, and the constant state of excited enmity in which the Indians were kept against the people of the United States, by the agents of Great Britain, of course retarded the settlement of the country, even by those who might be disposed to move into a district to which the Indian title had not yet been extinguished.

Again: the interruption of the war of 1812, which stirred up all old enmities with the Indians, threw obstacles in the way of settlement of the country, which the lapse of many years did not overcome.

Again: the remoteness of Wisconsin, in particular, from any of the frontier settlements of the States whence emigra-

---

[1] Am. State Papers, vol. i. 249.

tion principally proceeds, and situated as she was, on the very verge of civilized life, and on one part of the extreme frontiers of the United States, was not the least obstacle in the path of her early settlement. But when all these opposing circumstances, although not co-existent, yet each forcibly operating with like effect on one subject, had gradually dissolved and disappeared, it was found that a natural tide of emigration was flowing westward, and the many attractions which Wisconsin presented to the enterprising and industrious labourer, were quickly rewarded in her acquisition of an active and productive population.

That portion of the territory lying east of Lake Michigan was now ripe for State government; and under authority of an act of the legislative council of Michigan, the inhabitants met on the first Tuesday in October, 1832, and expressed an affirmative opinion on the question, "whether it be expedient for the people of this territory to form a State government."

The idea of a new Territory in the western portion of Michigan was started in 1826, and in 1831 a bill to that effect passed the House of Representatives, but was lost in the Senate; in 1832 another bill to the like effect was reported in the House of Representatives, and remained over, among the unfinished business.[1]

On the 14th of December, 1833, a public meeting was held at Navarino; resolutions were adopted in favour of a new Territory, and a memorial to Congress on such subject was prepared. This memorial remonstrated against the action of the Western people with regard to the 13th section of the bill reported in Congress, January 6th, 1832, by which the seat of government was fixed at Menomineeville, on Fox River: the memorial also asked for the establishment of two land-offices west of Lake Michigan, and for appropriations for the improvement of the Fox and Wisconsin Rivers.

At this period a great jealousy existed between the people of the mines and those of the Green Bay country, as to the

---

[1] See Note L.

location of the seat of territorial government; whether it should be at Mineral Point, or at Menomineeville, three miles from Navarino. The counties of Brown, Mackinaw, and Chippewa were thrown into the political scale against those of the west, including the lead-mines (Dubuque's) on the west side of the Mississippi.

In 1834, Mr. Doty, from the committee on territorial affairs, reported to the legislative council (of Michigan) a memorial to Congress on the subject of forming the new Territory, (of Wisconsin,) in which the claims of the same to be separated from Michigan are set forth and strongly urged, together with her claims to a rigid adherence to the *letter* of the ordinance of 1787, in regard to boundaries and limits.

On the 14th of February, 1834, a bill establishing the Territory of Wisconsin was reported in the Senate. It differed from the bill reported in 1832 in the House of Representatives—the location of the seat of government being left to the decision of the governor and legislative council, and thus the conflicting interests of the counties of Brown and Iowa were equitably compromised.

As respects the unreasonableness of the continuance of the connection of the western counties with Michigan, the following paragraph exhibits the general public opinion and feeling.[1]

"The legislative council adjourned on the 8th ultimo, to meet again on the first of January, 1835. Mr. Martin is expected in the first vessel, which is now on the way. James D. Doty, one of the members from this district, has returned to this place, after an absence of nearly *five months*, to attend a *session of sixty days*, and having travelled through a considerable part of two States, and the whole of the Territory of Michigan, to get to the seat of government at Detroit. It is strange that Congress cannot see in such facts the inconvenience resulting to the people west of Lake Michigan, from this unnatural union with Michigan; how slender must be our participations in the benefits of her government; and conse-

[1] Navarino Intelligencer, April 16, 1834.

quently how great the necessity for the immediate passage of the bill to establish the Territory of Wisconsin."

As if to increase these inconveniences, as has before been observed, Congress, on the 28th of June, 1834, passed an act to attach the territory of the United States west of the Mississippi River, and north of the State of Missouri, to the Territory of Michigan.

In January, 1833, and in February, 1834, memorials were presented in Congress for the admission of Michigan into the Union, but in consequence of the difficulties existing and arising out of the boundary question, Michigan was not admitted as a State until January 26th, 1837, and then on the conditions prescribed by act of June 15th, 1836.

On the 9th of January, 1836, the first session of the seventh legislative council of Michigan Territory was held at Green Bay, at which place it had been convened by Secretary John S. Horner, then acting governor of the Territory of Michigan. Little business was transacted: Governor Horner did not attend, and the most essential matter taken in consideration by the council was the condition of that part of the territory which would be left after the State of Michigan had defined and accepted her boundaries; such remaining part being all the country on the east side of the Mississippi River, and not only the whole of the present State of Iowa, but also a very great portion of the present Territory of Minnesota.

At this session a memorial was adopted, asking Congress for the formation of a new Territory west of Lake Michigan, to consist of all the residue of Michigan Territory not embraced in the limits of the State of Michigan. The memorial holds this language: "Thrown off by Michigan in the formation of her new State, without an acting governor to enforce the fragments of laws under which we still live; without a competent civil jurisdiction to give security to our lives and our property, we have deemed it our last and best policy to ask the intervention of the national aid, to give us a new efficient political existence." * * * "It had been decided by the Federal courts that the population west of the Mississippi are not within its jurisdiction, and presuming such decision to be correct, the monstrous anomaly was presented, that ten or twelve thousand freemen, citizens of the United States, living in its territory, should be unprotected in their lives and their property by its courts of civil and criminal jurisprudence, which was unparalleled in the annals of republican legislation."

This memorial was presented March 1st, 1836, and on the 20th of April, 1836, an act establishing the Territorial government of Wisconsin was passed and approved. Hereafter we shall trace the history of Wisconsin as a distinct Territory, and view her progress through protective government, until she assumes upon herself the dignity of an independent member of the Union, possessing in herself every element calculated to render her one of the most important States in the confederacy.

# NOTES.

## Note A. Page 38.

### AN ACCOUNT OF NEW FRANCE.

M. Joliet, who was sent by Count Frontenac to discover a way into the South Sea, brought an exact account of his voyage, with a map of it; but his canow being overset, at the foot of the Fall of St. Louis, in sight of Montroyal, his chest and his two men were lost; therefore the following account contains only what he has remembered.

I set out from the Bay of Puans, in the latitude of 42 degrees 4 minutes, and having travelled about 60 leagues to the westward, I found a portage; and carrying our canows over land for half a league, I embark'd with six men on the river Misconsing, which brought us into the Meschasipi in the latitude of 42 degrees and a half, on the 15th of June, 1674.[1] This portage is but 40 leagues from the Mississippi. This river is half a league broad; its stream is gentle to the latitude of 38 degrees; for a river from the west-northwest, which runs into it, increases so much its rapidity, that we cou'd make but five leagues a day in our return. The savages told us that the current is not half so great in winter. The banks of that river are cover'd with woods down to the sea; but the cotton trees are so big, that I have seen some canows made of those trees, eighty foot long and three broad, which carry thirty men. I saw 180 of those wooden canows in one village of the savages, of 300 cabins. They have abundance of holly-trees, and other trees, the bark whereof is white; grapes, apples, plums, chesnuts, pomegranates, mulberries, besides other nuts unknown to Europe; plenty of turkey-cocks, parrots, quails, wild oxen, stags, and wild goats. These savages are affable, civil, and obliging; and the first I met with, presented me with a pipe or calumet of peace, which is a protection even in a fight. Their women and old men take care of the culture of the ground, which is so fertile as to afford three crops of Indian corn every year. They have abundance of water-melons, citruls, and gourds. When they have sown their corn they

[1] Error in date, perhaps typographical. See Marquette's Journal.

go a-hunting for wild oxen, whose flesh they eat, and the skin serves for their coverings, having dress'd the same with a sort of earth which serves also to dye them. They have axes and knives from the French and Spaniards, in exchange of their beavers and skins of wild goats. Those who live near the sea have some fire-arms.

The Mississippi has few windings and turnings, and runs directly to the south, and having follow'd its course till the 33d degree of latitude, I resolv'd to return home, seeing that river did not dischage itself into Mar Vermejo, which we look'd for, as also because the Spaniards observ'd our motions for six days together. The savages told me that the Spaniards live within thirty leagues to the westward.

The said M. Joliet adds, that he had set down in his journal an exact description of the iron-mines they discover'd, as also of the quarries of marble, and cole-pits, and places where they find saltpetre, with several other things. He had also observ'd what were the fittest places to settle colonies, &c. The soil is very fertile, and produces abundance of grapes, which might make delicious wines.

The river of St. Lewis,[1] which hath its source near Missichiganen, is the biggest and the most convenient for a colony, its mouth into the lake being very convenient for an harbour. It is deep and broad, and well stock'd with sturgeons and other fishes. The stags, oxen, wild goats, turkey-cocks and other game, are more plentiful on the banks of the said river than anywhere else. There are meadows, ten or twenty leagues broad, incompass'd with fine forests; behind which are other meadows, in which grass grows six foot high. Hemp grows naturally in all that country.

Those who shall settle themselves there, shall not be oblig'd, as we are here, to bestow ten years for felling down the trees and grubbing up the land, before it is fit for corn, whereas the ground is ready for the plough in that fortunate country, where they may have good wine. Their young wild oxen may be easily learned to plough their land; and their long curled hair, or rather wool, may serve to make good cloth for their wearing. In short, that soil wou'd afford any thing necessary for life, except salt, which they might have another way.

---

NOTE.—The above account is the only one I have seen, in the name of Joliet: there were doubtless others, for the editor of Joutel's Historical

[1] The Mississippi; it is so called in Crozat's Patent of Monopoly of Trade, granted in 1712.

Journal (the Sieur de Mitchel) speaks of "fables that were then published by the name of a Voyage of the Sieur Joliet." The main facts stated in this short account, corroborate Père Marquette; and it is worthy of notice, that it was published by Hennepin as an addition to the English edition of his "New Discovery," in 1698, and contains the assertions of Joliet, (after his journal and map had been lost in the river St. Lawrence,) that he had descended the Wisconsin and the Mississippi to the 33d degree of latitude, seven years before Hennepin claims to have been on the river at any point. As this account of Joliet was published in Hennepin's second edition of his "New Discovery," wherein his interpolations in regard to his having descended the Mississippi are very evident, we also give the following extract from pages 169, 170, of the first part of Hennepin's book, edition of 1698, as an instance of the unscrupulous mendacity of the author.—W. R. S.

"While I was at Quebec, I understood that M. Joliet had been upon the Meschasipi, and oblig'd to return without going down that river, because of the monsters I have spoken of, who had frighted him, as also because he was afraid to be taken by the Spaniards; and having an opportunity to know the truth of that story from M. Joliet himself, with whom I had often travelled on the river St. Lawrence, I ask'd him whether he had been as far as the Akansas? That gentleman answer'd me, that the Outtaouats had often spoken to him of those monsters; but that he had never gone farther than the Hurons and Outtaouats, with whom he had remain'd to exchange our European commodities with their furrs. He added, that the savages had told him that it was not safe to go down the river, because of the Spaniards. But notwithstanding this report, I have found nowhere upon that river, any mark, as crosses, and the like, that could persuade me that the Spaniards had been there; and the savages inhabiting the Meschasipi would not have express'd such admiration as they did when they saw us, if they had seen any European before."

---

NOTE.—Hennepin says, (page 169, New Discovery, 1698,) "I had quite forgot to relate that the Illinois had told us, that towards the cape, which I have called in my map St. Anthony, near the nation of the Messorites, there were some tritons and other sea-monsters painted, which the boldest men durst not look upon, there being some enchantment in their face. I thought this was a story; but when we came near the place they had mention'd, we saw, instead of these monsters, a horse and some other beasts painted upon the rock, with red colours, by the savages. The Illinois had told us likewise that the rock on which these dreadful monsters stood, was so steep that no man could climb up to it; but had we not been afraid of the savages more than of the monsters, we had certainly got up to them. There is a common tradition among that people, that a great number of Miamis were drown'd in that place, being pursu'd by the savages of Matsigamea; and since that time, the savages going by the rock, use to smoak and offer tobacco to those beasts, to appease, as they say, the Manitou, that is, in the language of the Algonquins and Acadians, an evil spirit, which the Iroquois call Okon; but the name is the only thing they know of him."

In Joutel's Journal, (Lintot's edition, 1719, page 165,) under the date of September 2d, 1687, he writes as follows:—"The second, we arrived at the place where the figure is, of the pretended monster spoken of by Father Marquette. That monster consists of two scurvy figures drawn in red, on the flat side of a rock, about ten or twelve foot high, which wants very much of the extraordinary height that relation mentions.[1] However, our Indians paid homage by offering sacrifice to that stone, tho' we endeavoured to give them to understand that the said rock had no manner of virtue, and that we worshipped something above it, pointing up to heaven; but it was to no purpose, and they made signs to us that they should die if they did not perform that duty. We proceeded, coasting along a chain of mountains, and at length, on the 3d, left the Mississippi, to enter the river of the Illinois."—Joutel ut supra.

The following note to Marquette's account of these "monsters," is by my friend Cyrus Woodman, Esq., of Mineral Point, Wisconsin.

"These painted rocks are at Alton, Illinois. I examined them with Edward Keating, Esq., in September, 1847, and found only some faint traces of the paintings."

Marquette describes the two monsters painted on the rock as follows: "They are drawn as big as a calf, with two horns like a wild goat; their looks are terrible, tho' their face has something of human figure in it; their eyes are red, their beard is like that of a tyger, and their body is cover'd with scales. Their tail is so long, that it goes over their heads and then turns between their fore-legs, under the belly, ending like a fish tail. There are but three colours, viz. red, green, and black."

---

[1] Marquette merely says "very high and steep." No extraordinary height is mentioned by him.—W. R. S.

## NOTE B. Page 39.

The labours of the Jesuit Missionaries had scarcely entitled the country lying west of Lakes Michigan and Superior to recognition as a part of "New France," before the discovery of the Upper and Lower Mississippi caused it to be included in that extended region designated by De la Salle as "Louisiana," and formally taken possession of by him, in the name of his master, Louis the Fourteenth, on the ninth of April, 1682. Apart from the accounts of the face of the country, its inhabitants, and its productions, as given by the early explorers in their journals, and contained in those letters of the reverend Jesuit Fathers, known as "Memorable Relations," &c., there is little in detail, in the history of Wisconsin, of interest to a general reader. Nevertheless, the vast importance of the discoveries of Marquette, De la Salle, Joutel, Hennepin, Tonti, and La Hontan, imparts to their respective narratives, where their truth can be relied on, as published, an interest which amply compensates for the absence of local incident or personal adventure.

We say where their truth can be relied on; but such is not always the case. The narrative of Marquette has been garbled in an English translation; spurious publications have been put forth in the names of Joliet, and of Tonti; Hennepin has voluntarily falsified himself, to assume the merit belonging to De la Salle, and perhaps for the purpose of laying the foundation of a claim on the part of England to discoveries in the Mississippi Valley; La Hontan generally exaggerates, and too often deals in absolute fable; Joutel is faithful and veracious—he relates what he saw, and gives good authority for what he heard and learned; and the "Relations" of the missionaries may safely be relied on, as containing truthful reports of their acts, their discoveries, their proceedings, and their consequent effects.

Although British writers mention a discovery of the Mississippi in 1564, by an Englishman named Wood, yet no proofs have been exhibited, no authority produced for this assertion; and this person must not be confounded with the Colonel Wood, of Virginia, who is mentioned by Coxe as having discovered several branches of the great rivers Ohio and Meschasebe.[1] Marquette and Joliet were undoubtedly the first Europeans who are known to have discovered and explored the Great River of the West. No doubt can be entertained of the genuineness of the narrative of Marquette: the manuscript was sent to France, where it was printed by Thevenot, at Paris, in 1681, accompanied with a map: this publica-

[1] Long's Expedition, vol. i. 236.

tion can be relied on, but the translation (I believe the only English one extant) published at London, in 1698, as a supplement to Hennepin's "New Discovery," is (as has been well remarked by Sparks) defective, erroneous, and thrown into the shade by the pretended discoveries of that mendacious traveller, who, several years after the death of La Salle, falsely assumed to himself the merit of having descended the Mississippi to its mouth. The evidences of the authenticity of Marquette's narrative have thus been summed up by his biographer:—[1]

"Marquette's map, attached to the narrative, in Thevenot's 'Recueil' is unquestionably the first that was ever published of the Mississippi River. In this light it is extremely curious; but it is also valuable as confirming the genuineness of the narrative. It was impossible to construct it without having seen the principal objects delineated. The five great rivers, Arkansas, Ohio, Missouri, Illinois, and Wisconsin, in regard to their relative positions and general courses, are placed with a considerable degree of accuracy.[2] Several names are entered on the map which are still retained, and near the same places, with slight differences in the orthography. The Wisconsin (or as the French write it, *Ouisconsin*) is written 'Mississing' in the map. It is 'Mescousin' in the narrative, perhaps by a typographical mistake for 'Mesconsin.' The Missouri, it is true, is named in the narrative 'Pekitanoni,' which it may at that time have been called by the natives; but in the map, a village is placed on the bank of that river, called 'Oumissouri.'"

"The Ohio is called 'Ouabouquigou' in which we may see the elements of 'Ouabache,' which name it retains in all the early French maps, the river itself being denominated by what is now regarded as one of its principal branches.

"The Arkansas is not named on the map, but in the narrative we are told of the village of 'Akamsca,' near the banks of that river, which is evidently the same name.

"To the northward of the Arkansas is a place on the map called 'Matchigamea;' the same name is found to this day, on French maps, applied to a lake very near the same place and a little to the northward of the River St. Francis.

"It should be kept in mind that this map was published at Paris, in the year 1681, and consequently the year before the discoveries of La Salle on the Mississippi, and that no intelligence respecting the country it represents could then have been obtained from any source subsequently to the voyage of Marquette. There is a slight error in the map,

1 Sparks's Life of Marquette.

2 Rock River is also marked on the map.—W. R. S.

in regard to the dotted line marked "Chemin de Retour," because the narrative is very explicit in stating that the voyagers returned up a river, which from the description given of it, could be no other than the Illinois. This dotted line therefore, must have been a conjectural addition."

These internal evidences of authenticity are satisfactory, and they have lately acquired a most powerful addition of strength. At a meeting of the New York Historical Society, on the 7th of April, 1852, Mr. Moore presented and read a communication from John G. Shea, accompanying the *original map* of Father Marquette, detailing the results of his discovery and exploration of the Mississippi River, in the year 1673, from which we make the following extracts:—

"Meanwhile, Father Marquette, broken in health, was reposing for a while at the Mission of St. Francis, awaiting the moment when his health should permit, to revisit his Mission of the Immaculate Conception, in Illinois, which he had founded as he was returning from the Mississippi. It was not till September that he felt strong enough to undertake the journey, and he accordingly set out soon after. Before his departure, he transmitted, as his autograph journal shows, copies of his journal down the Mississippi, or Conception River, and doubtless the map, which is this evening offered for the inspection of the Historical Society, and which now belongs to the archives of St. Mary's College, Montreal.

"He (Marquette) did not seek to publish his discovery, and if his superiors did, at the time, the court probably prevented it for fear of exciting the jealousy of Spain. It was never published by the Jesuits as a continuation of their relations, and when issued by Thevenot, was pruned so as to say nothing of the object in view.[1] The map in Thevenot, when compared with the autograph, shows, however, still greater discrepancy. The likeness is too little to be easily discerned, while the unlikeness is apparent. I have now but to add a word as to the history of the map, which thus comes before the world, nearly two hundred years after it was penned. The last published volume of the Jesuit Relations is that for 1671–2. This was published by Father Claude Dablon, the Superior of the Canada Mission, at the time. He prepared for the press the volume of the ensuing year, but for some reason, now unknown, the publication was stopped. The obstacle was apparently a temporary one, for he next drew up a relation embracing a period of six

[1] To explore the Great River, to see whether it ran to the Gulf of California, and opened the way to China, or passed itself by the realm of Quivira, which teemed with gold. Shea's Com.

years, to 1679, and also an account of the voyages and death of Father Marquette. None of these were ever published, and the collection was apparently abandoned. These manuscripts, with some others, including the last journal and map of Marquette, various papers copied under the direction of Father Ragueneau and Father Poncet, remained in the archives of the College of Quebec, unheeded and unknown, till the French war, as we on this side call that, which ended in the conquest of Canada. When the British flag had replaced the lilies of France at Quebec, the English Government excited in her former colonies a burst of indignation by an act maintaining the Catholic Church of Canada in its actual state. It made one sacrifice however to prejudice; the two religious orders of men then in Canada, were peculiarly obnoxious to the colonists: these were the Jesuits and the Recollects. As to them, it was decreed that no new members were to be admitted, and that when the last surviving priest expired, the property of the order should revert to the crown. The last survivor of the Jesuits died in 1800; but previous to his death he took from the archives the more valuable papers, including those we have named, and committed them to the care of the Hospital Nuns. The other papers were seized by the sheriff, at his death, and are now chiefly lost or scattered. Those thus saved by Father Cazot remained in the Hotel Dieu till 1844, when they were presented by their faithful guardians to the Jesuits, who but two years before had entered that land so rich in historical reminiscences, to a fellow-religious of a Jogues, a Brebeuf, and a Marquette. We are indebted for its presence here, to the kindness of the President of St. Mary's College, the Reverend F. Martin, who has agreed to its publication in New York, in the historical collections of Mr. French."[1]

---

## Note C. Page 41.

### ACCOUNT OF THE TAKING POSSESSION OF LOUISIANA.

BY M. DE LA SALLE. 1682.

rocès verbal of the taking possession of Louisiana, at the mouth of the Mississippi, by the Sieur de la Salle, on the 9th of April, 1682:—

"Jacques de la Metairie, notary of Fort Frontenac in New France, commissioned to exercise the said function of notary during the voyage

---

[1] See Transactions of New York Historical Society, 1852. Marquette's map has, since, been published, by Mr. J. G. Shea, in a volume accompanying the Narratives of Marquette, Allouez, Membrè, Hennepin, Douay, &c., a highly valuable addition to the documents of Western history.

to Louisiana, in North America, by M. de la Salle, Governor of Fort Frontenac for the King, and commandant of the said discovery, by the commission of his Majesty, given at St. Germain, on the 12th of May, 1678.

"To all those to whom these presents shall come greeting:—Know that having been requested by the said Sieur de la Salle to deliver to him an act, signed by us, and by the witnesses therein named, of possession by him taken of the country of Louisiana, near the three mouths of the river Colbert[1] in the Gulf of Mexico, on the 9th of April, 1682.

"In the name of the most high, mighty, invincible, and victorious Prince, Louis the Great, by the Grace of God, King of France and of Navarre, fourteenth of that name, and of his heirs, and the successor of his crown, We, the aforesaid Notary, have delivered the said act to the said Sieur de la Salle, the tenor whereof follows.

"On the 27th of December, 1681, M. de la Salle departed on foot to join M. De Tonty, who had preceded him with his followers, and all his equipage, 40 leagues into the Miamis country, where the ice on the river Chekagou, in the country of the Mascoutens, had arrested his progress, and where, when the ice became stronger, they used sledges to drag the baggage, the canoes, and a wounded Frenchman, through the whole length of this river, and on the Illinois, a distance of 70 leagues.

"At length all the French being together, on the 25th of January, 1682, we came to Pimiteoui. From that place, the river being frozen only in some parts, we continued our route to the river Colbert 60 leagues, or thereabouts, from Pimiteoui, and 90 leagues or thereabouts, from the village of the Illinois. We reached the banks of the river Colbert on the 6th of January and remained there until the 13th, waiting for the savages, whose progress had been impeded by the ice. On the 13th, all having assembled, we renewed our voyage, being 22 French carrying arms, accompanied by the Reverend Father Zenobe Mambrè, one of the Recollet Missionaries, and followed by 18 New-England savages, and several women, Ilgonquines, Otchipoises, and Huronnes.

"On the 14th, we arrived at the village of Maroa, consisting of a hundred cabins without inhabitants. Proceeding about a hundred leagues down the river Colbert, we went ashore to hunt on the 26th of February. A Frenchman was lost in the woods, and it was reported to M. de la Salle that a large number of savages had been seen in the vicinity. Thinking that they might have siezed the Frenchman, and in order to observe these savages, he marched through the woods during two days, but without finding them, because they had all been frightened by the guns which they had heard, and had fled.

[1] Mississippi.

"Returning to camp, he sent in every direction French and savages on the search, with orders, if they fell in with savages, to take them alive without injury, that he might gain from them intelligence of this Frenchman. Gabriel Barbiè, with two savages, having met five of the Chikacha nation, captured two of them. They were received with all possible kindness, and after he had explained to them that he was anxious about a Frenchman who had been lost, and that he only detained them that he might rescue him from their hands, if he was really among them, and afterwards make with them an advantageous peace, (the French doing good to every body;) they assured him that they had not seen the man whom we sought, but that peace would be received with the greatest satisfaction. Presents were then given to them, and, as they had signified that one of their villages was not more than half a day's journey distant, M. de la Salle set out the next day to go thither; but, after travelling till night, and having remarked that they often contradicted themselves in their discourse, he declined going farther without more provisions. Having pressed them to tell the truth, they confessed that it was yet four days' journey to their villages; and perceiving that M. de la Salle was angry at having been deceived, they proposed that one of them should remain with him, while the other carried the news to the village, whence the elders would come and join them four days' journey below that place. The said Sieur de la Salle returned to the camp with one of these Chikachas; and the Frenchman whom we sought having been found, he continued his voyage and passed the river of the Chepontias, and the village of the Metsigameas. The fog, which was very thick, prevented his finding the passage which led to the rendezvous proposed by the Chikachas.

"On the 12th of March, we arrived at the Kapaha village of Akansa. Having established a peace there and taken possession, we passed, on the 15th, another of their villages, situate on the border of their river, and also two others farther off in the depth of the forest, and arrived at that of Imaha, the largest village in this nation, where peace was confirmed, and where the chief acknowledged that the village belonged to his Majesty. Two Akansas embarked with M. de la Salle to conduct him to the Talusas, their allies, about fifty leagues distant, who inhabit eight villages upon the borders of a little lake. On the 19th we passed the villages of Tourika, Jason, and Kouera; but as they did not border on the river, and were hostile to the Akansas and Taensas, we did not stop there.

"On the 20th, we arrived at the Taensas, by whom we were exceedingly well received and supplied with a large quantity of provisions. M. de Tonty passed a night at one of their villages, where there were about 700 men carrying arms, assembled in the place. Here again a peace was concluded. A peace was also made with the Koroas, whose chief came there from the principal village of the Koroas, two leagues distant from that of the Natches. The two chiefs accompanied M. de la Salle to the banks of the river. Here the Koroa chief embarked with him to conduct him to his village, where peace was again concluded with this nation, which, besides the five other villages of which it is composed, is allied to nearly forty others. On the 31st, we passed the village of the Oumas without knowing it, on account of the fog and its distance from the river.

"On the 3d of April, at about 10 o'clock in the morning, we saw among the canes thirteen or fourteen canoes. M. de la Salle landed, with several of his people. Footprints were seen, and also savages a little lower down, who were fishing, and who fled precipitately as soon as they discovered us. Others of our party then went ashore on the borders of a marsh formed by the inundation of the river. M. de la Salle sent two Frenchmen, and then two savages to reconnoitre, who reported that there was a village not far off, but that the whole of this marsh, covered with canes, must be crossed to reach it; that they had been assailed with a shower of arrows by the inhabitants of the town, who had not dared to engage with them in the marsh, but who had then withdrawn, although neither the French nor the savages with them had fired, on account of the orders they had received, not to act unless in pressing danger. Presently we heard a drum beat in the village, and the cries and howlings with which these barbarians are accustomed to make attacks. We waited three or four hours, and as we could not encamp in this marsh and seeing no one, and no longer hearing any thing, we embarked.

"An hour afterward we came to the village of Maheouala, lately destroyed, and containing dead bodies and marks of blood. Two leagues below this place we encamped. We continued our voyage till the 6th, when we discovered three channels by which the river Colbert (Mississippi) discharges itself into the sea. We landed on the bank of the most western channel, about three leagues from its mouth. On the 7th, M. de la Salle went to reconnoitre the shores of the neighbouring sea, and M. de Tonty likewise examined the great middle channel. They found these two outlets beautiful, large, and deep. On the 8th, we reascended the river a little above its confluence with the sea, to find a dry place beyond the reach of inundations. The elevation of the north pole was here about 27°. Here we prepared a column and a cross, and to the said column were affixed the arms of France with this inscription:—

"Louis Le Grand, Roi De France, Et De Navarre, Règne;
Le Neuvième Avril, 1682.

"The whole party under arms chaunted the *Te Deum*, the *Exaudiat*, the *Domine salvum fac Regem*; and then after a salute of fire-arms and cries of *Vive le Roi*, the column was erected by M. de la Salle, who, standing near it said, with a loud voice, in French, "In the name of the most high, mighty, invincible, and victorious Prince, Louis the Great, by the grace of God, King of France and of Navarre, fourteenth of that name, this ninth day of April, one thousand six hundred and eighty-two, I, in virtue of the commission of his Majesty, which I hold in my hand, and which may be seen by all whom it may concern, have taken, and do now take, in the name of his Majesty and of his successors to the crown, possession of this country of Louisiana, the seas, harbous, ports, bays, adjacent straits; and all the nations, people, provinces, cities, towns, villages, mines, minerals, fisheries, streams, and rivers, comprised in the extent of said Louisiana, from the mouth of the great river St. Louis, on the eastern side, otherwise called Ohio, Alighin, Sipore, or Chukagona, and this with the consent of the Chaouanons, Chikachas, and other people dwelling therein, with whom we have made alliance; as also along the river Colbert, or Mississippi, and rivers which discharge themselves therein, from its source beyond the country of the Kious or Nadouessious, and this with their consent, and with the consent of the Montantees, Ilinois, Mesigameas, Natches, Koroas, which are the most considerable nations dwelling therein, with whom also we have made alliance, either by ourselves, or by others in our behalf;[1] as far as its mouth at the sea, or Gulf of Mexico, about the 27th degree of the elevation of the north pole, and also to the mouth of the River of Palms; upon the assurance which we have received from all these nations, that we are the first Europeans who have descended or ascended the said river Colbert; hereby protesting against all those who may in future undertake to invade any or all of these countries, people, or lands above described, to the prejudice of the right of his Majesty, acquired by the consent of the nations herein named. Of which, and of all that can *be* needed, I hereby take to witness those who hear me, and demand an act of the Notary as required by law."

"To which the whole assembly responded with shouts of *Vive le Roi*, and with salutes of fire-arms. Moreover, the said Sieur de la Salle caused to be buried at the foot of the tree to which the cross was at-

---

[1] There is an obscurity in this enumeration of places and Indian nations, which may be ascribed to an ignorance of the geography of the country; but it seems to be the design of M. de la Salle to take possession of the whole territory watered by the Mississippi from its mouth to its source, and by the streams flowing into it on both sides.—Note by Jared Sparks.

tached, a leaden plate, on one side of which were engraved the arms of France with the following Latin inscription:—

LVDOVICVS MAGNVS REGNAT.
NONO APRILIS CIↃ IↃC LXXXII.

ROBERTVS CAVELIER, CVM DOMINO DE TONTY, LEGATO. R. P. ZENOBIO MEMBRÈ, RECOLLECTO, ET VIGINTI GALLIS, PRIMVS HOC FLVMEN, INDE AB ILINEORVM PAGO, ENAVIGAVIT EJVSQVE OSTIVM FECIT PERVIVM, NONO APRILIS ANNI CIↃ IↃC LXXXII.

"After which the Sieur de la Salle said that his Majesty, as eldest son of the church, would annex no country to his crown without making it his chief care to establish the Christian religion therein, and that its symbol must now be planted; which was accordingly done at once by erecting a cross, before which the *Vexilla*, and the *Domine salvum fac Regem* were sung. Whereupon the ceremony was concluded with cries of *Vive le Roi.*

"Of all and every of the above, the said Sieur de la Salle having required of us an instrument, we have delivered to him the same, signed by us, and by the undersigned witnesses, this ninth day of April, one thousand six hundred and eighty-two.

"LA METAIRIE,
"Notary.

"DE LA SALLE,
"*P. Zenobe*, Recollet Missionary
"*Henry de Tonty.*
"*Francois de Boisrondet.*
"*Jean Bourdon.*
"*Sieur D'Autray.*
"*Jacques Cauchois.*
"*Pierre You.*
"*Gilles Meucret.*
"*Jean Michel,* Surgeon.
"*Jean Mas.*
"*Jean Dulignon.*
"NICOLAS DE LA SALLE."

This document was procured by Mr. Sparks, the biographer of De la Salle, from the archives of the Marine Department at Paris.

## Note D. Page 45.

The sources of information whence is drawn the account of De la Salle, and of his labours, his discoveries, his misfortunes, and his death, are few, but may be relied on as accurate. They consist of the memorials and reports of De la Salle to his government; the Memoir of the Sieur de Tonti, and his petition to the Count de Pontchartrain, recommended by Frontenac; the letters-patent granted by the King of France to De la Salle, dated 12th May, 1678, authorizing him "to endeavour to discover the western part of New France, through which it is probable a road may be found to penetrate to Mexico;" Joutel's journal of his voyage to Mexico,[1] and so far as the truth can be extracted therefrom, in Hennepin's New Discovery, edition 1684, Paris, and edition 1698, London.

The report and memorial of De la Salle are addressed to Monsieur De Seignelay, the son of his patron Colbert, now deceased, and in which he states his great discoveries, and urges the importance of an expedition by sea to the Mississippi; he also speaks of the facility of seizing on the rich mines of St. Barbe, and alludes to the possibility of discovering a passage to the South Sea. His propositions were acceded to by the king, De la Salle was authorized to build forts and plant colonies in the new country, and a fleet was fitted out, which sailed from Rochelle, on July 24th, 1684, on the expedition which terminated so fatally, and of which Joutel became the historian.

The Memoir of the Sieur de la Tonty is entitled "Memoir sent in 1693, on the discovery of the Mississippi and the neighbouring nations, by M. de la Salle, from the year 1678 to the time of his death, and by the Sieur de Tonty, to the year 1691." This memoir forms the basis of a spurious work printed at Paris in 1697, entitled "Dernier's Decouvertes dans l'Amerique Septentrionale, de M. de la Salle, par Chevalier Tonti, Gouverneur du Fort St. Louis, aux Illinois, Paris, 1697." It has been since reprinted under the title of "Relation de la Louisiane ou de Mississippi, par le Chevalier de Tonti." This work was disavowed by Tonti.[2] His petition to the minister of marine to be employed in actual service, was written probably about the year 1700; it is without date, and the last that is known of this brave and generous man is that he joined Iberville at the mouth of the Mississippi about the year 1700,

---

[1] These documents are given at length in Sparks's Life of De la Salle, and also in French's Historical Collections of Louisiana.

[2] Charlevoix, tom. iii. 385.

and that two years afterward he was employed on a mission to the Chickasaw nation. No notice has ever been taken of his death;[1] of his life it has been justly said—"All the facts that can be ascertained concerning De Tonty are such as give a highly favourable impression of his character, both as an officer and a man. His constancy and his steady devotion to La Salle are marked not only by a strict obedience to orders, but by a faithful friendship and chivalrous generosity. His courage and address were strikingly exhibited in his intercourse with the Indians, as well in war as in peace; but his acts were performed where there were few to observe, and fewer to record them. Hence it is that historians have done him but partial justice."

The journal of Joutel has always been considered a valuable and authentic work. He accompanied the unfortunate De la Salle from the sailing of the fleet at Rochelle until his assassination on the banks of Trinity River. He has faithfully recorded the unfortunate adventures of La Salle and his devoted colony, from their first settlement at Fort St. Louis in Texas, until the death of La Salle, which occurred almost within his own presence. He afterward returned to France by way of the Mississippi, Illinois River, the Great Lakes, and Quebec, and reached Rochelle on the 9th of October, 1688. His journal was published under the supervision of Sieur de Mitchel, first at Paris, and afterward at London in 1719. Charlevoix says that "he saw, and conversed a long time with Joutel, at Rouen, in 1723."[2]

---

## NOTE E. Page 51.

The internal evidence given by Hennepin himself of the falsity of his pretended voyage *below* the Illinois River, is in part to be found as herein noted; the exposition may be considered as entirely superfluous, except to point out to the curious reader, the little pains that Hennepin has taken to conceal his fabrications, by referring to the glaring absurdities and contradictions in his relations and his dates: his own narrative as published in the volumes entitled "A New Discovery," &c. &c., and the "Continuation," edition of 1698, furnishes the evidence and the proofs of the mendacity and imposture with which he has been charged.

In chapter xxxvi. page 148, Hennepin has parted with De la Salle, at Fort Crèvecoeur, on the 29th of February, 1680, and on the 12th of March he is at the mouth of the Illinois River, with his companions, Du

---

[1] French's Hist. Col. 80.

[2] Charl. Nouv. France, tom. iii. 56.

Gay and Ako. From this point his destination was northward, toward the heads of the Mississippi, according to the directions of, and his previous arrangements with De la Salle.

In chapter xliv. page 180, the rivers falling into the Mississippi, the Lake of Tears, (Lake Pepin,) and the Falls of St. Anthony of Padua, are described, and Hennepin says that he and his companions were made prisoners by the Issati, or Nadouessians, at the river of St. Francis, eight leagues above the Falls of St. Anthony.

In chapter xlv. page 185, Hennepin describes his voyage from the Illinois River toward the sources of the Mississippi, as agreed upon between De la Salle and himself, and stated in chapter xxxvi.; and the succeeding chapters state that (page 186) he was taken prisoner on the 12th of April, and that his capture took place (page 193) one hundred and fifty leagues up the River Mississippi, above the Illinois River. All these matters were published in the edition of his book in 1684, dedicated to the King of France.

The edition of 1698 is dedicated to the King of England, and in this book all the chapters between chapters xxxvi. and xliv. are interpolations, and fabrications founded on the Relations of Marquette, Le Clerc, and Father Anastasius. The last paragraph of chapter xxxvi. (page 149) is as follows—"I am resolved to give here an account of the course of that river, (Mississippi,) which I have hitherto concealed, for the sake of M. la Salle, who would ascribe to himself alone the glory, and the most secret part of this discovery. He was so fond of it that he has exposed to visible danger several persons, that they might not publish what they had seen, and thereby prejudice his secret designs."

In chapter xxxvii. Hennepin says that he and his companions, Du Gay and Ako, after having agreed to go *down* the river, embarked in "our canoe on the 8th of March, 1680." In six hours rowing they came to a river as big as the Mississippi, coming from the westward; (no doubt the Missouri, or Pekitanoni, of Marquette.) On the 9th of March he continues his voyage, and on the 10th comes to a river near which is a nation called Ouadebache, (Wabash, or Ohio River.) Here he stays until the 14th of March. (Page 152.) On the 15th he sees three Chickasaw Indians, and two days (17th) afterward meets with the Akansas. On the 18th they embarked again (page 154) and having "hid their commodities" and well-marked the spot, passed another village of the Akansas, (page 155,) went into the country of the Taensas on the 21st, and left them on the 22d, having understood from them that it was only seven days' journey to the sea. They continued the voyage on the 24th, and accomplished a distance of more than 35 leagues. (Page 159.) The next day, March 25th, came to three channels of the Mississippi, took the middle one, and eight leagues rowing enabled them to discover the sea. (Page 160.)

From the 8th of March to the 25th is eighteen days inclusive; eight of which is accounted for in *stoppages*, and other causes of detention; ten days only are allotted to a voyage in a canoe rowed by three men from the mouth of the Illinois River to the sea! By his own computation, Hennepin says it is about 340 leagues from the Illinois to the sea; this would require the incredible speed of 34 leagues, more than 100 miles, per diem. But let us see his account of the return voyage.

On the 1st of April they embarked to return toward the source of the river, (page 162,) and arrived at Koroa on the 4th. (Page 164.) At Taensas on the 7th; on the 9th at the place where "they had hid their commodities," and came to the village of the Akansas. (Page 165–6–7.) They had ascended the river as rapidly as they had descended—seven days going down, and only eight in coming up. "We left the Akansas," says Hennepin, (page 168,) "on the 24th of April;" and ascending the river, passed the mouth of the Illinois, without stopping at Fort Crèvecoeur, proceeded northward; "my men," says Hennepin, (page 179,) "being afraid to meet with their comrades, for fear of punishment for having disobeyed orders; and "I was afraid that by these means our voyage toward the sea would be discovered, (there being some reasons to keep it secret as I shall observe in another place,) and our further discovery stopt." This observation is made in the 43d chapter, (the last of the interpolation from the 36th,) and in the very first line Hennepin reiterates, "We embarked," (from the Akansas,) "as I have already said, on the 24th of April." According to his true account, he was taken prisoner by the Sioux on the 12th of April, above the Falls of St. Anthony; what irreconcileable statements!

In these fabrications all merit of the discovery is not only taken away from De la Salle, and denied to him, but even Joliet is asserted by Hennepin (page 169) to have denied that he had ever descended the Mississippi. Marquette's Journal was published by Thevenot in 1681. Hennepin's first "Account of Louisiana" was published in 1684; he could readily take sufficient facts from Marquette, on which to build his own fictions.

Charlevoix, in speaking of Hennepin's narrations, says—"It is even sufficiently difficult to comprehend how they could go to its mouth, (the Mississippi,) descend it, and reascend it up to the forty-sixth degree, remain during many months prisoners among the Sioux, and all this in less than a year. Besides, has it not always been believed in Canada that they had done nothing else but return to Fort Crèvecoeur by the same route which they had taken in going up as far as the Falls of St. Anthony."[1]

With regard to the effect produced in England by the pretended discoveries of Hennepin, we make the following extracts from Charlevoix:[2] "Iberville returned to Biloxi the 18th of January, 1700. On arriving there, he learned that towards the end of September the preceding year, an English corvette of twelve guns had entered the Mississippi; that Monsieur Bienville, who had gone to sound the mouths of this river, had met with this vessel twenty-five leagues from the sea,[3] and had declared to her commander that if he did not withdraw, he was in condition to compel him; that this menace had had its effect; but that the English in retiring, had told him that they would soon return with greater force; that it was more than fifty years since they had discovered this country, and that they had greater right than the French."

"Iberville learned at the same time that other English, come from Carolina, were among the Chicachas, with whom they carried on a commerce in furs and slaves, and that they had been known to have solicited the savages to kill an ecclesiastic, who was in reality massacred among the Tonicas."

"The Chevalier Tonti arrived with about twenty Canadiens, settled at the Illinois, and M. d'Iberville having spoken to him of the *Relation* which went under his name, he protested that it was not himself, but a Parisian adventurer, who had composed it on bad narratives, and had attributed it to him to give it circulation and to gain money."

"It was not possible that Father Hennepin did as much as this with his third *Relation*, since we know that he was himself the editor of it. Nevertheless we can scarcely doubt that it was upon these memoirs that the English entered the Mississippi. "I have learned," wrote M. de Callieres to M. de Pontchartrain, the 12th of May, 1699, "that they are preparing vessels in England and in Holland, to take possession of Louisiana, upon the *Relation* of Père Louis Hennepin, a Recollect, who has made a book of it, dedicated to King William."

"In a second letter, written a month after the first, the general tells the same minister that he had been assured that the King of Great Britain, in the embarrassment in which they were in England to subsist the French refugees, had sent, the preceding autumn, a great number of them in three ships, to take possession of the Mississippi; and that twenty Englishmen from New York, had left, to go to the Illinois, under pretence

[1] Charlevoix, tom. ii. 271. [2] Idem. tom. iii. 384–5–6.

[3] The river at this point makes a great bend, which since that time has been named English Turn.

that all the country to the south belonged to them. In fact, since the month of October, 1698, three ships had sailed from London for Louisiana, but they had put into Carolina, from whence some time afterward two sailed, one of twenty-four guns and the other of twelve."

"They went to the head of the Gulf of Mexico to search for the Mississippi, because their charts there placed the great river. Not having found it, they retook their route to the east, following always the coast in sight, until they at last discovered what they sought for. The smallest of these two ships entered the river, and it was this one that M. de Bienville had caused to retire. The other returned to the west, and penetrated as far as the Province of Panuco in New Spain. Thus the French colony of Louisiana, still in its cradle, found itself menaced by two powerful neighbours equally jealous of the establishment, the Spaniards and the English."

The claims of discovery, and the assumption of rights founded on travellers' falsehoods, and interpolations in books and documents, find a parallel in our own times, in the history of the claims of England to the Columbia River.

# NOTES TO CHAPTER II.

## NOTE A. Page 58.

### VALLEY OF THE MISSISSIPPI.

The following note is extracted from La Harpe, Journal Historique de d'etablissement des Francais à La Louisiane.

On December 7th, 1699, Messrs. Iberville and La Surjère arrived with the Renommèe of 50 guns, and the Gironde of 46 guns, with several officers from the garrison, and also with M. le Sueur, and thirty workmen. He was sent by Mr. L'Huillier, a farmer-general, to form an establishment at the source of the Mississippi. The design of the enterprise was to explore a mine of green earth which Le Sueur had discovered, and this is what gave rise to the enterprise. In 1695, Le Sueur, by order of the Count de Frontenac, governor-general of Canada, caused to be constructed a fort on an island in the Mississippi, more than 200 leagues above the Illinois, in order to effect a peace between the Sauteurs, (Leapers,) nations who dwell on the borders of a lake more than 500 leagues in circumference, situate 100 leagues to the east of the river, and the Sioux, located near the heads of the Mississippi.

Le Sueur in the same year took to Montreal, Chin-gou-abè, chief of the Sauteurs, and a Sioux chief named Ci-os-cate, who was the first of the nation who had seen Canada. Amity was established, and, in 1696, Le Sueur purposed to return to the Mississippi, when the Sioux chief died after thirty days' suffering at Montreal. Le Sueur was thus relieved from his promise to reconduct the chief to his own country, where he had discovered mines of lead, copper, and blue and green earth, and he resolved to go to France and obtain permission of the court to open them: this permission he obtained in 1697. He sailed from Rochelle, but was taken prisoner by the English on the banks of Newfoundland, and taken to Portsmouth. After the peace he returned to Paris to obtain a new commission, having thrown his former one overboard for fear the English should obtain knowledge of his project. He obtained a new commission in 1698, and afterward came to Canada, where he met with obstacles which obliged him to return to France. Amid all these disappointments, a part of the people whom he had left to guard the fort which he had built in 1695, not hearing any thing of him, went down to Montreal.

On the 10th of February, 1702, Le Sueur arrived (at Biloxi) with 2000 quintals of blue and green earth from the Sioux country. He gave an account of his voyage up the Mississippi, of which the following are extracts: they are made, to give the early names of the rivers and distances.

The 13th of July, 1700, he left the mouth of the Missouri; at six leagues farther, the Illinois; at twenty-two leagues above the Illinois River, he passed a little river which he named "Aux Boeufs." Nine leagues farther, he met seventeen Sioux on a war excursion against the Illinois, to avenge the death of three Sioux, one of whom had been burned. He appeased the Sioux by telling them that the King of France wished that the river no longer should be stained with blood, and that he had been sent to tell them, if they would obey his word, he would in the end give them all things that were necessary for them. The chief accepted his presents, and promised to do as he desired. From the 30th of July to the 25th of August, Le Sueur advanced fifty-two leagues to a little river which he named "The River of the Mines."[1] It comes from the north at its mouth, and flows from the northeast. Seven leagues to the right, there is a lead-mine in a prairie, a league and a half inland. This river, except the first three leagues, is only navigable in times when the waters are high, that is to say, from spring to the month of June.

From the 25th to the 27th he made ten leagues, passed two rivers,[2] and took notice of a lead-mine, at which he supplied himself. From the 27th to the 30th he made eleven and one-half leagues. On September 1st, he passed the Ouisconsin; it comes from the northeast at its mouth, and flows from the east; it is about one-half league wide. About forty-five leagues up the river, to the right, is a portage a league in length; one-half of this distance is boggy (trembling) ground; at the termination there is a little river which descends to a bay, called the "Bay des Puans," inhabited by a great number of nations who take their peltries to Canada. It was by this river, Wisconsin, that Le Sueur came for the first time to the Mississippi in 1693, to go to the Sioux country, where he lived at different times for seven years. From September 1st to the 5th, he advanced fourteen leagues; he passed "Canoe River" which comes from the northeast, and afterward "Quincapous," so named from a nation who formerly lived on its borders. From the 5th to the 9th, made ten and a half leagues, and passed the rivers "Cachèe," and "Aux Ailes." Three leagues farther, passed a little river on the western side, and afterward a much larger one on the east of the Mississippi; this is navigable at all times. From the 10th to the 14th, made seventeen and

---

[1] Fevre River.

[2] Platte and Grant Rivers.

a half leagues; passed the river "Raisins" and "Des Paquillinettes." The same day, he left to the east a large and beautiful river, which descends from far north, and is named "Bonne Secours," from the great number of buffalo, stags, bears, and roebucks which are found there. Three leagues on the river there is a lead-mine, and seven leagues above, on the same side, we find another river of *long course*, near which there is a copper-mine, from which he had taken a piece of sixty pounds weight in his preceding voyage. A league and a half from this neighbourhood, to the northwest, begins a lake six leagues long, and more than a league wide, called "Lake Pepin." Saltpetre caves are found in the mountains which border this lake to the west. Seven and a half leagues above the lake, passed another river called "Hiambouxeatè Onataba," which signifies the River of Flat Rocks.

Fifteenth, passed a small river; sixteenth, left to the east a large river called "St. Croix," because a Frenchman of that name was shipwrecked at the mouth of it. It comes from N.N.W.; at four leagues higher up, ascending it, we find a small lake, at the entrance of which is a very large mass of copper. It is on the bank of the water, in a little shore of sandy earth, to the west of the lake. From the 16th to the 19th, advanced thirteen and three-fourths leagues. Since he left Tamarois, two hundred and seven and a half leagues. At this place he left the Mississippi and entered the St. Peter's River on the west. On this, to the first of October, he made forty-four and a half leagues; then entered the Blue River, so named on account of the mines of blue earth which are found at the mouth of the river. Here he was told by nine Sioux whom he met, that this river was the country of the Sioux of the West, of the Ayavois (Iowas) and of the Otoctatas, a little farther distant. Here he has established himself in 44 degrees 13 minutes north latiiude, and built a fort, which he called "Fort L'Huillier."

---

## Note B. Page 59.

A synopsis of the 16th letter of La Hontan, extracted from vol. i. p. 174 to 260, is here given. This letter is dated "Michillimackinac, 28th May, 1689."

This letter, written after his return from his expedition to the "Long River," states, that he left Michillimackinac, September 24th, 1688, with twenty soldiers, and five Outagamie Indians, in canoes, with provisions and merchandise proper to traffic with the Southern savages. Having traversed Green Bay, they entered the River of the Puants, passed the

Falls of Kakalin, the village of the Kikapous, and on the 11th of October reached the little lake of the Malominies. Here he obtained three sacks of wild rice flour, from the Malominies, which, as he had made them a present of "three fathoms of tobacco," he says was no great stretch of generosity, as that grain is with them almost as common as water, their lake being covered with it. On the 13th, they arrived at the Fort of the Outagamies, who received them in a most hospitable manner. Penetrating the suspicions of the chief, that he was going to traffic with his enemies, La Hontan told him not to fear, for he would not go within a hundred leagues of the Nadowessious, as his intention was to explore the "Long River" to its source, and he asked the chief to give him six warriors to accompany him. The chief was delighted to hear that he was not about to supply his enemies the Nadowessious with arms and ammunition, but advised him to take care of himself and not go too high up the "Long River," as he would find a great number of people by whom he might be *overcome*, if not in open war, yet by stratagem and surprise. Nevertheless the chief gave him not only six, but ten warriors, who were acquainted with the Eokoros, knew their language and the chart of the country. Having made several valuable presents to the chief and his family, he left them on the 20th, and in the evening of the same day disembarked at the point where they were to leave the River of the Puants, (Fox River.) In three-quarters of a league of difficult portage they reached the Wisconsin.

In four days they reached the Mississippi River, "into which this hateful Wisconsin discharges itself,"[1] and commenced ascending it. On the 7th of November they arrived at the mouth of the "Long River," which they entered and found themselves in a kind of lake, almost wholly covered with reeds, but just about the middle there was a narrow channel. This sort of navigation among rushes continued for twenty leagues, but they finally emerged in a fine stream, bordered with lofty woods and wide prairies. Meeting with many and numerous tribes of Indians on their route, on the 27th they came to the first village of the Essanapès, where their arrival was expected, and measures had been taken to receive them in grand style of savage hospitality. About five hundred men received them on landing with dancing, loud cries, and frequent prostrations, similar to adoration. The strangers were then taken to the village by the Indians, where they were received by a deputation of the regency of the place, consisting of six hundred men, each holding

[1] This river (Ouisconsin) is cursed and shameful, (maudite, et abandonnèe). Its waters revolve a filthy and villanous slimy mud: on both sides of its channel we see only steep hills, frightful rocks, or barren marshes.—Vol. i. 192.

a bow in one hand, and an arrow in the other. Somewhat alarmed at this hostile appearance, the Outagamies told the Essanapès to throw aside their arms, and La Hontan and his party commenced retiring to the river, until this demand was complied with, when they all entered the village triumphantly. Leaving this place and passing many other villages, after a voyage of eighteen days, and being accompanied by crowds of Indians on the banks, they arrived at the principal village, situated on a kind of lake, at a distance of fifty leagues from the first one. Here dwelt the great chief, who received him kindly and with great attention. This chief offered him an escort of three hundred men to conduct him to the Gnacsitares, and told him they were a good nation, allied to the Essanapès, but were obliged to inhabit *islands* to be in greater safety from the Mozemleeks, their common enemies. Having obtained four pirogues from this chief, and astonished the natives by exhibiting the use of the gun, and the hatchet, he left his canoes and embarked in his pirogues, on the 4th of December, having on board his own pirogue no less than ten soldiers, ten Miamis, four Ottawas, and four Essanapès slaves, who were ordered by the great chief to accompany him. Passing many islands in the lake, after fifteen days of navigation, they landed, and the four Essanapès slaves were despatched to gain information of the inhabitants. They returned in a few hours, and stated that they had run a great risk of their lives, as the Gnacsitares had taken their new visitors to be Spaniards, whose name was in bad odour among them, on account of their cruelties in the new world. La Hontan and his companions encamped on an island in the lake, and the Gnacsitares sent couriers off, twenty-four leagues to the south, for some savages whose commerce with New Mexico would enable them to determine whether or not the new visitants were Spaniards. The arbitrating deputies having arrived in great numbers, they crossed over to the isle where the new-comers were encamped, and after having examined them from head to foot with great circumspection, and having taken into consideration their clothing, their guns, their swords, their air, their complexion, their tone of voice and accent, these judges pronounced that the visitors were not Spaniards. This verdict having been confirmed by the declarations of La Hontan, the Gnacsitares invited him to encamp on the great isle, and sent him a supply of provision. Two days afterward, on the 19th of January, the great chief paid him a visit, accompanied by four hundred men. La Hontan perceived among the attendants four men who appeared to be Spaniards from their clothing, their beards, the manner of wearing their hair, their complexion, and their polished manners. On inquiry they were found to be Mozemleeks, who dwell along a river which has its source in a chain of mountains, in which also the Long River has its source. The country of this nation is adjoining that of the Gnacsitares, which causes continual war between them. The mountains which separate them are five or six leagues in breadth, and high in proportion; so rugged and steep as not to be crossed except by long and winding paths, and inhabited only by bears and other ferocious beasts. From these Mozemleek slaves La Hontan learned that at a distance of one hundred and fifty leagues from where they then were, the Great River discharges itself by a mouth two leagues wide, into a vast lake of salt water, which is three hundred leagues in circumference.

Toward the termination of this river are built six fine towns, the walls of which are of stone, cemented with potter's clay. Around the lake are more than a hundred other villages great and small, which suffices to show the power and grandeur of this nation. The great salt lake is the field of their commerce; they cultivate the arts, and the mechanics flourish among them as with us. They fabricate stuffs, copper hatchets, and a multitude of other works. The government is monarchical, and the great chief is absolute in power. This nation, La Hontan was informed, was not Mozemleek, but was called Ta-hug-lauk. The Mozemleek slaves showed him a large copper medal engraved on the one side with characters, and on the other with four animals resembling bears in couples, and other devices. This medal was manufactured by the Ta-hug-lauks. La Hontan, being unable to visit these people, endeavoured to learn more of them from the four Mozemleek slaves, but his interpreters were very ignorant, and he was obliged to relinquish his inquiries. All he could learn was, that the Ta-hug-lauks were as numerous as the leaves on the trees. The Mozemleeks took to their villages wild calves of the buffalo, captured among the mountains, which the Ta-hug-lauks used partly for food, some for drawing in wheeled carriages, and their skins for clothing and shoes. This people wear the beard two fingers in length; their habit is a tunic descending to the knees; they wear a high pyramidal-shaped bonnet; they have buskins which cover the whole leg, and they are always armed with a long club, ironed at the end, like those of our peasants and foot travellers. Their women are secluded from sight, as in Italy and Spain. The nation is fond of war, but in seeking their enemies at a great distance, if they meet on the road any wandering tribes inferior to themselves, they believe it a crime to attack them. The river of the Mozemleeks and the Ta-hug-lauks runs always toward the west, and the salt water lake into which it discharges itself, and which is three hundred leagues in circuit, is thirty leagues in width, its mouth being very far to the south.

Having taken formal leave of the great chief of the Gnacsitares, La

Hontan descended the Long River: the Indians had made a map of the whole country for him, embracing all the rivers from Lake Superior to Tahuglauk. He conjectured the Long River to be at least two thousand miles in length, and at its head to communicate with a second great river which discharged itself into the South Sea; and thus the much-desired passage to China was a problem solved and a discovery achieved. On the 12th of March, La Hontan re-entered the Mississippi, descended it, and afterward arrived at Fort Crèvecoeur on the Illinois, where he found Tonti in command of the garrison left there by De la Salle.

---

## NOTE C. Page 63.

It is necessary to remark, that in the early relations respecting the French settlements in the Mississippi Valley, *two* Kaskaskias are mentioned. After the return of Father Marquette from his exploring voyage, he was detained at the mission of St. Francis Xavier, in Green Bay, during the whole summer of 1674. On his homeward journey he had promised the Illinois, called Kaskaskias, to return among them as their religious teacher, but the hardships of his first voyage had greatly enfeebled him, and he had almost lost the hope of fulfilling this great design of his heart. His malady having given way, he obtained permission of his superiors to return to the Illinois to found his projected mission, and on the 25th of October, 1674, he set out with two men, named Pierre Porteret and Jacques ———. They crossed the peninsula which forms the eastern side of Green Bay, and began to coast along the shore of Lake Michigan, accompanied by some Illinois and Pottawatamies. They advanced slowly; the good missionary was again seized with his malady, the dysentery, but he pushed on, and on the 4th of December had reached the Chicago, which connects by portage with the Illinois. The river was frozen, and the pious missionary resolved to winter at the portage, as his illness increased; he was deprived even of the consolation of saying mass on his patronal feast, the Immaculate Conception. His Indian companions now left him, and, though aided by some French traders, he suffered much during the following months. Of this however he says nothing. "The blessed Virgin immaculate," says his journal, "has taken such care of us during our wandering, that we have never wanted food; we have lived very comfortably—my illness not having prevented my saying mass every day." How little can we realize the faith and self-denial which could give so pleasant a face to a winter passed by a dying man in a cabin open to the winds!

Despairing at last of human remedies, the missionary and his two pious companions began a novena, or nine days devotion to the blessed Virgin immaculate. From its close he began to gain strength, and on the 29th of March, the river being open, he set out on his long interrupted journey; his last entry on his journal is on the 6th of April, when the wind and cold compelled them to halt: he never found time to continue his journal, and his last words are a playful allusion to the hardships undergone by the traders, in which he sympathized, while insensible of his own.[1]

Having reached the town of Kach-kach-kia on the 8th of April, he was received there as an angel from heaven, by the chiefs, the old men, and the whole people. A beautiful prairie near the town was chosen for the great council; it was spread with mats and bear-skins, and the reverend Father having hung on cords some pieces of Indian taffety, attached to them four large pictures of the blessed Virgin, which were thus visible on all sides. The auditory was composed of five hundred chiefs and old men, seated in a circle around the Father, while the youth stood without, to the number of fifteen hundred, not counting women and children, who were very numerous, the town being composed of five or six hundred fires.[2] The father explained to the multitude the mysteries of our religion; he preached to them Christ crucified, for it was the very eve of the great day on which he died on the cross for them, as well as for the rest of men; he then said mass.

Three days after, on Easter Sunday, things being arranged in the same manner as on Thursday, he celebrated the holy mysteries for the second time, and by these two sacrifices, the first ever offered there to God, he took possession of that land in the name of Jesus Christ, and gave this mission the name of "the Immaculate Conception of the Blessed Virgin." In a few days Marquette left this people, much to their regret, and died on his return voyage, on the east shore of Lake Michigan, where he was buried by his two sorrowing companions, who had thus far accompanied him, from the time of his departure from Green Bay. The Indian name of the river, at the mouth of which he died and was buried, according to some is Notispescago, and to others is Aniniondibeganining. It is a very small stream, being the outlet of a small lake, and has since been called Marquette River.[3]

In April, 1677, Father Allouez visited the large Illinois town of Kach-kach-kia, and found it composed of three hundred and fifty-one cabins, easily counted, he says, for they are mostly ranged on the banks of the river. He fixes the latitude of the location at 40° 42′, and this is in correspondence with its designation on the Illinois River, on the autograph map of Marquette, first published by Mr. Shea in 1852. This

[1] Shea, Discov. and Expl. (in note.) p. 53. [2] Idem. p. 55. [3] Idem. p. 59.

would bring it near Rock Fort, making allowance for the old latitude. The Kaskaskia of which later writers speak, is the Kaskaskia of our own day, and is situate in latitude 38°.

Bancroft writes, "The oldest permanent European settlement in the valley of the Mississippi, is the village of the Immaculate Conception of the Holy Virgin, or Kaskaskia, the seat of a Jesuit mission, which gradually became a central point of French colonization. We know that Father Gravier was its founder, but it is not easy to fix the date of its origin." Marquette had been followed by Allouez, who in 1684 may have been at Rock Fort, but who was chiefly a missionary to the Miamis, among whom he died. Gravièr followed Allouez, but in what year is unknown. Sebastian Rasles, after a short residence among the Abenakis, received orders to visit the west, and from his own narrative it is plain that after passing a winter at Mackinaw, he, in the spring of 1693, repaired to Illinois, where he remained two years. When the founder of Kaskaskia was recalled to Mackinaw, he was relieved by two missionaries, Pinèt, who became the founder of Cahokia, and Binnetau, who left his mission among the Abenakis, to die on the upland plains of the Mississippi. Before his death, Gabriel Marest, the Jesuit, joined the mission at Kaskaskia, and for a season, after the death of Binnetau and Pinèt, had the sole charge of it. Very early in the eighteenth century he was joined by Mermet, who, with the commandant Juchereau from Canada, had collected a village of Indians and Canadians, and thus founded the first French post on the Ohio, or as the lower part of the river was then called, the Wabash.[1] The gentle virtues and fervid eloquence of Mermet made him the soul of the mission at Kaskaskias.

The object of this note is to show that there has been an apparent confusion of accounts as given of Kaskaskia: it is evident that the Kaskaskia visited and written of by Marquette and Allouez, and dedicated by the former to the Immaculate Conception of the Holy Virgin, is not the Kaskaskia of Southern Illinois, founded by Gravier and dedicated in the same manner: the lately discovered manuscript and map of Father Marquette have shed light on this subject. But perhaps this extended note may not be considered as yielding information worth the research, as the whole country south of the Illinois River to the Mississippi, and mouth of the Ohio, may have been considered in early days as embraced in the Kaskaskia mission.

---

[1] See Bancroft, vol. 3, p. 195.

## NOTE D. Page 74.

### THE LETTERS-PATENT GRANTED BY THE KING OF FRANCE TO M. CROZAT.

Louis, by the grace of God, King of France and Navarre: To all who shall see these present letters, Greeting. The care we have always had to procure the welfare and advantage of our subjects having induced us, notwithstanding the almost continual wars which we have been obliged to support from the beginning of our reign, to seek for all possible opportunities of enlarging and extending the trade of our American colonies, we did, in the year 1683, give our orders to undertake a discovery of the countries and lands which are situated in the northern part of America, between New France and New Mexico: and the Sieur de la Salle, to whom we committed that enterprise, having had success enough to confirm a belief that a communication might be settled from NEW FRANCE TO THE GULF OF MEXICO BY MEANS OF LARGE RIVERS; this obliged us immediately after the peace of Ryswick to give orders for the establishing a colony there, and maintaining a garrison which has kept and preserved the POSSESSION we had taken in the very year 1683, of the lands, coasts, and islands which are situated in the Gulf of Mexico, between Carolina on the east, and Old and New Mexico on the west. But a new war having broken out in Europe shortly after, there was no possibility till now of reaping from that colony the advantages that might have been expected from thence, because the private men who are concerned in the sea trade were all under engagements with other colonies, which they have been obliged to follow: and whereas, upon the information we have received concerning the disposition and situation of the said countries known at present by the name of the Province LA LOUISIANA, we are of opinion that there may be established therein a considerable commerce, so much the more advantageous to our kingdom, in that there has hitherto been a necessity of fetching from foreigners the greatest part of the commodities which may be brought from thence, and because in exchange thereof we need carry thither nothing but commodities of the growth and manufacture of our own kingdom; we have resolved to grant the commerce of the country of Louisiana to the Sieur Anthony Crozat, our councillor, secretary of the household, crown, and revenue, to whom we intrust the execution of this project. We are the more readily inclined hereunto, because his zeal and the singular knowledge he has acquired in maritime commerce, encourage us to hope for as good success as he has hitherto had in the divers and sundry enterprises he has gone upon, and which have procured to our kingdom great quantities of gold and silver in such conjunctures as have rendered them very welcome to us.

For these reasons being desirous to show our favour to him, and to regulate the conditions upon which we mean to grant him the said commerce, after having deliberated this affair in our council, of our certain knowledge, full power, and royal authority, We by these presents signed by our hand, have appointed and do appoint the said Sieur Crozat *solely* to carry on a trade in *all* the lands possessed by us, and *bounded* by New Mexico, and by the lands of the English of Carolina; all the establishments, ports, havens, rivers, and principally the port and haven of the Isle Dauphine, hertofore called Massacre; the river of St. Lewis, heretofore called Missisipi, from the edge of the sea as far as the Islinois; together with the river of St. Philip, heretofore called the Missourys, and of St. Jerome, heretofore called Ouabache, with all the countries, territories, lakes within land, and the rivers which fall directly or indirectly into that part of the river of St. Lewis.

*The Articles.*

I. Our pleasure is, that all the aforesaid lands, countries, streams, rivers, and islands, be and remain comprised under the name of the Government of Louisiana, which shall be dependent upon the General Government of New France, to which it is subordinate; and further, that all the lands which we possess from the Illinois be united, so far as occasion requires, to the General Government of New France, and become part thereof, reserving however to ourselves the liberty of enlarging as we shall think fit, the extent of the government of the said country of Louisiana.

II. Grants to Crozat the exclusive trade of the whole country for the term of fifteen years.

III. Allows Crozat to search for, open, and dig all sorts of mines, veins, and minerals, throughout the whole extent of the said country of Louisiana; and to transport the profits thereof into any port in France during the said fifteen years. Also grants in *perpetuity* to him and his heirs, the property of, in, and to the mines, veins, and minerals which he shall bring to bear, paying us, in lieu of all claim, the fifth part of the gold and silver, and the tenth part of what effects he shall draw from the other mines, veins, and minerals; the said dues to be transported to France at the expense of Crozat. Also permission to search for precious stones and pearls, paying the fifth part as dues; and if Crozat, his heirs, or those claiming under him or them the perpetual right, shall discontinue the work during three years, the propriety of the mines, veins, and minerals shall be forfeited, and the same shall be fully reunited to the royal domain.

The remaining articles grant and prescribe privileges of buying, selling, manufacturing, and transporting all commodities and effects of the said country ; also the property in and to all settlements and manufactories, mansions, mills, and structures, and the lands which he shall cause to be cultivated, is secured to Crozat and his heirs, and those claiming under him or them ; and all his commerce from and to the mother country to be free of imposts and duties.

Article XIV. is as follows:—If for the cultures and plantations which the said Sieur Crozat is minded to make, he finds it proper to have blacks in the said country of the Louisiana, he may send a ship every year to trade for them directly upon the coast of Guinea, taking permission from the Guinea company so to do ; he may sell those blacks to the inhabitants of the colony of Louisiana; and we forbid all other companies and persons whatsoever, under any pretence whatsoever, to introduce blacks or traffic for them, in the said country, nor shall the said Sieur Crozat carry any blacks elsewhere.

Given at Fontainbleau, the fourteenth day of September, in the year of Grace 1712, and of our reign the 70th.

Signed, Louis.

By the King—Philipeaux, &c.

Registered at Paris in the Parliament, the four-and-twentieth of September, 1712.

---

## Note E. Page 82.

The relations which existed between the supposed wealth of the Valley of the Mississippi in its mines, precious stones, agricultural value, and projected commerce, and the wild infatuation which attended the grant of monopoly to the Western Company, the establishment of the Bank of France, and the union of both, under the auspices of John Law, may excuse the length of this note.

The speculative mania of the "Mississippi Scheme" was at its great height at the end of the year 1719, and beginning of the year 1720. Such was the confidence entertained in the system of Law, and such was the avidity for wealth, that the shares of the Company of the Indies rose with unexampled rapidity, every one taking it for granted that the speediest way to realize a prodigious fortune was to become a shareholder to as large an amount as possible in the India Company. The frenzy extended to all ranks and classes. "Clergy and laity, peers and plebeians, statesmen, princes, nay even ladies who had, or could procure money for that purpose, turned stock-jobbers, out-bidding each other." The shares soon rose to 5000 livres each. Prudent shareholders now began to sell out, and with the enormous fortunes which they had realized, to purchase houses and estates. The sight of opulence thus rapidly acquired, increased the popular delirium, each man saying, "Why may not I realize a fortune, and purchase houses and estates too?" The state creditors, likewise being paid in bank notes, such a quantity of paper was thrown into circulation, that it could be disposed of in no other way than by the purchase of East India stock; and the competition of these purchasers against each other increased the price of shares still more rapidly. In November, 1719, they were sold at 10,000 livres each, or at twenty times their original price.

Innumerable anecdotes are told illustrative of the eagerness of all classes to become shareholders in the company, of the intense anxiety which prevailed, arising from every fluctuation in the value of shares, and of the strange vicissitudes of fortune which were brought about during the frenzy. The street (in Paris) in which the stock-jobbers met, at first was the Rue de Quinquempoix; and the crowds which used daily to assemble there were so great, that accidents were constantly occurring. The occupiers of this street reaped a golden harvest from the general excitement by letting their houses to the speculators. Houses whose rent was 800 livres a year, were let at 6000 or 10,000 livres a month; and even single apartments were let for a pistole a day. A cobbler earned 200 livres a day, by allowing ladies and gentlemen to sit in his stall, furnishing them with chairs and writing materials; nay, one hump-backed man is mentioned as having acquired a fortune of 150,000 livres by allowing the jobbers in the street to use his hump as a writing-desk. M. Chirac, physician to the Duke of Orleans, was on his way to visit a lady, one of his patients, when he was informed that the price of shares was falling. His mind was so engrossed with the news, that while feeling the lady's pulse, he exclaimed in agony, "Oh it falls, it falls continually!" and the lady, alarmed, began to shriek, till he reassured her by telling her it was the Mississippi shares, and not her pulse, he referred to. No one was able to withstand the infatuation. Two of the ablest scholars and most learned men in France, the Abbè Tenasson and M. de la Mothe, were lamenting together the madness of the nation, and congratulating themselves on the fact, that being scholars, they had escaped the contagion. A few days after, the Abbè, pushing through the crowd at the Rue de Quinquempoix, met M. de la Mothe pushing through it also—both having come to bargain in the stocks. In the whole court, only five persons refrained from speculation, and those who did so were regarded as cowards, or fools.

The Rue de Quinquempoix being found too narrow for the immense crowds who congregated daily for the purpose of speculating in the India stock, the traffic was transferred to the Place Vendôme. In a short time, however, this open space was also found inconvenient; and Law, at an enormous price, purchased the Hôtel de Soissons, in whose gardens pavilions were erected for the accommodation of the public. Here the business was daily carried on.

Mr. Law, as the author and dispenser of all the wealth for which the nation was struggling, became beyond comparison the principal personage in the kingdom. The levee of the regent was forsaken; and princes, dukes, peers, bishops, and judges crowded in the retinue of the Scottish projector. His ante-chambers were constantly full of ladies, waiting for an interview, that they might prevail on Mr. Law to sell them a portion of stock. Troubled by such numbers of applicants, Law conducted himself with the utmost haughtiness, and would keep a peer of the realm waiting five or six hours before admitting him to an interview. Enormous bribes were given to his servants, on condition merely that they should announce the name of the person waiting. It was to the French aristocracy that Mr. Law behaved in this haughty way; to his own countrymen, and to persons coming on ordinary errands, he appears to have been exceedingly affable. "The Earl of Hay, afterward Duke of Argyle, going to wait upon Mr. Law, by appointment, found the ante-chambers filled with many of the highest quality in France; but being, by special orders, admitted into his private apartments, beheld the great man writing what from the number and rank of those left to wait his leisure, he naturally concluded to be despatches of the utmost consequence. Upon mentioning these surmises to his old friend, it was with no small surprise his lordship learned that he was only writing to his gardener at Lauriston (Scotland) to plant cabbages in a particular spot. After this important epistle was concluded, he desired the earl to play a game at piquet, at which they continued for a good while, till at length the great man thought proper to give orders for the admission of his humble supplicants." Many amusing anecdotes are told of the stratagems fallen upon by the ladies to procure an interview with Mr. Law. A Madame de Boucher being extremely anxious to possess some India stock, made every effort to procure an invitation to meet Mr. Law at dinner at the house of Madame de Simiani, where she knew he was to be present; but as it was known that Mr. Law did not wish to see her, Madame de Simiani could not comply with her friend's request. Resolved, nevertheless, to gain her point, the lady ordered her carriage to be driven past the house; and when exactly opposite to it, she gave the alarm of fire! The guests, Mr. Law included, rushed into the street.

The lady jumped out of her carriage, and was hurrying up to him; but perceiving her design, he took to his heels and escaped. Another lady gave orders to her coachman to be on the watch for Mr. Law in the streets, and the moment he saw him close at hand, to overturn the carriage. It was several days before the longed-for opportunity arrived; and then, the lady being the first to perceive the approach of the great man, called out to the coachman, "Upset me now, you rascal!—upset me now!" The man did as he was ordered; Law flew to the lady's relief, and had her conveyed into the Hôtel de Soissons. Here the lady confessed her trick; and Law, as a reward for her ingenuity, was obliged to enter her name as a purchaser of stock.

So sudden and rapid was the rise of the price of shares, that enormous fortunes were made in the course of a few days. Many instances are recorded of persons in the lowest ranks of life suddenly realizing immense wealth. One night at the Opera, all eyes were attracted by a lady in a magnificent dress, sitting in a very conspicuous position; and no one could make out who she was, till a young lady whispered to her mother, "Why, it is our cook, Mary!" And it proved to be so; Mary had been speculating, and become rich. A footman had speculated so successfully, as to be able to set up a carriage of his own; but when entering it for the first time, the force of habit was so strong, that he mounted into his accustomed place behind—excusing himself as he jumped to the ground again, by saying, he was trying how many lackeys would have room to stand on the board. Mr. Law's coachman had made such a fortune, that he asked his discharge, which Mr. Law gave him, on condition that before going, he should supply him with another coachman as good as himself. The man brought two coachmen next day, recommended both as excellent drivers, and asked his master to choose one, as he meant to engage the other himself. Another speculator, finding himself a rich man, gave orders to a coachmaker for a magnificent new Berlin, leaving 4000 livres as a deposit. The coachmaker inquiring what *arms* were to be put on the carriage, "Oh, the finest—the finest by all means!" said the fortunate man. One Brignaud, a baker's son, having acquired an enormous fortune, and wishing to have a superb service of plate, went into a goldsmith's shop, and purchased the whole collection of articles exposed for sale, at 400,000 livres.

Up to this time, Law's system had produced nothing but the most wonderful outward prosperity; and when the state of the nation was compared with what it had been at the death of Louis XIV., it appeared that the man to whose exertions the change was owing, could be nothing less than a demi-god. Money circulated in profusion, people in the lowest ranks indulged in luxuries previously unattainable, and the price of commodities rose without any injury to the people. The ell of cloth which had sold for fifteen livres, now sold for fifty; and the pound of coffee rose from fifty sols to eighteen livres. Wages rose correspondingly. In the course of three months, the silversmiths of Paris had received orders for, and manufactured above £7,000,000 sterling worth of plate—about $35,000,000. Paris was crowded with foreign visitors who had come to speculate in the stocks. No fewer than 305,000 strangers are said to have been living in Paris in November, 1719, and many of these were obliged to live in granaries and lofts, there not being sufficient house accommodation for them all. The promenaders in the streets were clothed in velvet and gold; and the winter of 1719–20 was more brilliant than the finest summer ever seen before.

Law was now the idol of the country, and the enthusiasm in his favour was greatly increased by his making a public profession of the Roman Catholic religion, in December, 1719. The only obstacle to his admission to political dignity being thus removed, he was declared comptroller-general of the finances, in January, 1720, a situation equivalent to that of prime-minister of France. Literary and other honours were showered upon him; venal poets and parasites complimented him as the saviour of France; he had realized an enormous fortune and had purchased fifteen or sixteen large estates, together with houses and mansions, amounting to the value of 7,000,000 livres; yet his generosity was equal to his wealth. On the occasion of professing himself a Catholic he gave 500,000 livres to assist in completing the church at St. Roch; he distributed another sum of 500,000 among the English who were impoverished in following the fortunes of the exiled house of Stuart, and his private liberalities were constant and munificent. His native city, Edinburgh, transmitted him its freedom in a gold box, proud of having given him birth; English and Scottish noblemen boasted of being acquainted with Mr. Law, although his return to England would have been attended with danger, in consequence of an appeal being still pending, against a pardon which had been granted to him in 1695, after he had been found guilty of murder in killing one Wilson in a duel, and sentenced to death. He had escaped from prison to the continent, and notwithstanding the rewards offered for his apprehension in the "London Gazette," he had hitherto remained undisturbed on the continent, and had risen to his present extraordinary elevation. The fugitive from England, the speculator and gambler of Holland, Belgium, Italy, and France, had become the greatest man of the age, and the future sovereign (George II., then Prince of Wales) to whom he might be indebted for his life, which had been forfeited, was a dabbler in his famous Mississippi stock.

The bubble however was already full blown. The credit of the Bank and of the India Company was at its height in the months of November and December, 1719, and January, 1720, when shares in the company were selling at 10,000 livres each. Such was the abundance of money in the Bank that it offered to lend sums of any amount, on proper security, at an interest of only two per cent. Now, however, a drain of specie from the Bank began to be discernible. Numbers of persons possessed of stock in the company, either foreseeing disaster or haunted with a vague suspicion that so prosperous a state of things could not last long, began to sell out, and convert their shares into gold and silver and other precious commodities, which they either hoarded up or sent secretly out of the country. The Prince de Conti, offended at being refused a quantity of fresh shares, for which he petitioned, sent to the Bank to demand specie for so enormous a mass of notes, that three wagons were required to carry the money from the bank to his house. Vernesobre de Laurieu, a Prussian, whom Mr. Law had appointed a cashier in the bank, remitted nearly 40,000,000 livres to foreign countries, and then disappeared. Various stock-jobbers remitted hundreds of thousands of louis-d'ors to England. These examples were imitated by others, for nothing is more contagious than fear; and in a short time 500,000,000 livres in specie were sent out of France.

To put a stop to this run upon the Bank, which, from the immense quantity of notes in circulation, would be ruinous, a series of edicts were issued by the regent in February and March, 1720. By these edicts, payments in specie were restricted to small sums, (not exceeding 100 livres in gold, and 10 livres in silver,) while at the same time efforts were made to secure a preference for paper over specie, by declaring the value of the former to be invariable, while that of the latter fluctuated. People were prohibited from converting their wealth into gold and silver plate without a royal license, the demand for plate having been one of the principal means of withdrawing the precious metals from circulation. The exertions thus made were for some time effectual; and numbers, seeing notes passing current at 5 or 10 per cent. above specie, hastened to convert all the specie in their possession into paper. There is, however, in the minds of men at such a time, a natural preference for the metals over paper; and accordingly it was found that many were busy in secret hoarding up gold and silver, and cautiously disposing of their paper in anticipation of the coming crash. Fresh edicts of a more stringent and arbitrary character were issued; one, forbidding the use of specie altogether in payment, another forbidding any person to have in his possession more than 500 livres of coin, under the penalty of having the sum confiscated and the payment of a fine in addition.

In an instant, so suddenly in fact, that it is impossible to trace the steps of the process, the nation, which had been glorying in its good fortune, was struck with dismay and despair. The use of specie had been prohibited, but this could not restore confidence in Law's paper, and nobody would accept it willingly. It was felt universally that Law's scheme had been a *bubble*, and that it had now burst. Complaints and execrations arose everywhere against Law, the Regent, and all who had been concerned in originating the project. Law was attacked by all who had envied his prosperity, and who had only been restrained from showing their ill will, by his success, and he was accused of plotting the ruin of France; even the Regent, who had hitherto been his intimate friend, and at whose solicitations Law had adopted some of his most questionable measures, turned against him.

All efforts to arrest the progress of the panic were in vain. Fresh issues of notes had taken place in consequence of the decree ordering all payments to be made in paper, and in May, 1720, the notes issued amounted to 2,600,000,000 livres, while the quantity of specie in the kingdom was estimated at 1,300,000,000, or only half as much. To equalize the paper with the specie, there were two plans: either to double the value of the specie, or halve the value of the paper. Law advised the former, as being a thing to which the people were quite accustomed; but his advice was overruled; and on the 21st of May, an edict was published reducing the value of the paper by a gradual process till it should be exactly half its present value—a note for 10,000 livres passing current for only 5000, and so on. This reduction was a violation of the original constitution of Law's Bank; and if paper had been disliked before, the promulgation of this edict made matters a thousand times worse; bank notes were regarded as waste paper, and a person might have starved with 100,000 livres of paper money in his pocket.

On the 27th of May the Bank stopped payment in specie, and on the same day Law was dismissed from his office as minister of finance. Riots and mobbings took place; troops occupied Paris to prevent insurrections from breaking out; Law's life was in danger, and the Regent gave him a guard as he drove through the street; but at length, not being safe in his own house, he took refuge in the Palais Royal.

Various ineffectual expedients were adopted to sustain some certain value for the notes; the funding of them in annuities, and their redemption by other issues of a distinct character were proposed, but still the holders of them hesitated to accept the propositions offered by the government; decrees passed declaring that the notes would be good for no purpose whatever after the first of November, 1721. Numbers however kept their notes until after the specified time, in the vain hope of better terms, and the consequence was that large quantities of Law's notes remained in houses as family lumber, down even to the date of the French revolution, when they were produced as curiosities, to be compared with the assignats.

With the Bank, fell the India Company; no efforts could keep its credit alive; the management of the Mint and the administration of the revenues of government were taken out of its hands; and it was degraded to a mere trading body. Such was the end of the famous Mississippi bubble.

Law obtained leave to quit France—his life was not safe in it. His enormous fortune he had invested in French lands and securities, which were confiscated the moment he left the country. The sole property he carried with him was a diamond worth about £5000 sterling. After travelling through various parts of the continent, he returned to England, where he resided four years, supporting himself by his talents for gambling. He died at Venice, in 1729, in very embarrassed circumstances. (See Chambers's Miscel. Wood's Life of Law of Lauriston. Mackay's Popular Delusions.)

---

## Note F. Page 88.

For the gratification of the curious we give a more particular account of this principal French fortress on the Mississippi. It was begun in 1720, and completed eighteen months afterward. It was erected in the vicinity of Prairie du Rocher, and was originally one mile and a half from the river bank. Its form was quadrilateral, with four bastions, built of stone, and well cemented with lime. Each side was three hundred and forty feet in length; the walls were three feet thick and fifteen feet high. Within the walls were spacious stone barracks, a spacious magazine, two deep wells, and such buildings as are common at such posts. The port-holes or loups were formed by four solid blocks of freestone properly shaped. The cornices, and casements about the gates, were of the same material. It was greatly repaired and enlarged in 1750.

In 1770 the river broke through its banks, and formed a channel near one of the bastions, and in two years afterward, two bastions being undermined, the English abandoned it in 1772. It was then suffered to fall to decay, and in 1809 it was a splendid ruin, grown over in its area with forest trees, vines, and weeds. Some of the trees then were from seven to twelve inches in diameter. (Stoddart's Sketches, p. 234.)

A good description of this fort, as it appeared in 1765 and 1829, may be seen in Hall's Sketches of the West, vol. i. 154–157.

## NOTE G. Page 96.

Extract from the Voyages of the Rev. Father Emanuel Crespel, in Canada, and his shipwreck in returning to France, in the years from 1723 to 1742.

### LETTER FIRST.

On the seventeenth day of March, in the year of my departure from Quebec, (1726,) M. de la Croix de St. Valier, bishop of that city, conferred upon me the degree of priest, and gave me shortly afterward a mission, or curacy, called Forel, situated south of the river St. Lawrence, between the City of the Three Rivers, and Montreal.

I was withdrawn from my curacy, where I had already remained two years, and appointed Almoner to a party of four hundred Frenchmen, that the Marquis de Beauharnois had joined to eight or nine hundred savages, of all manner of nations, but principally Iroquois, Hurons, Nepissings, and Outaouacs, to whom M. Peset, priest, and Father de la Bertonnière, Jesuit, served as Almoners. These troops, commanded by Monsieur de Lignerie, were commissioned to go and destroy a nation called the Foxes, whose principal habitation is distant from Montreal about four hundred and fifty leagues.

We commenced our march on the 5th of June, 1728, and ascended nearly a hundred and fifty leagues the great river which bears the name of the Outaouacs, and which is filled with falls and portages. We quitted it at Mataoüan to take the one which empties into Lake Nepissing: it is about thirty leagues in length, and is obstructed by falls and portages, like that of the Outaouacs. From this river we entered into the lake, the width of which is about eight leagues, and from this lake, French River very soon conducts us to Lake Huron, into which it empties, after traversing more than thirty leagues with great rapidity.

As it is not possible for many persons to travel together on these small rivers, it was agreed that those who first passed, should wait for the others at the entrance of Lake Huron, at a place called the Prairie, and which is, indeed, a most beautiful prairie. It is there that I saw, for the first time, the rattlesnake, whose bite is mortal: when I shall have the pleasure of seeing you, I will speak to you more particularly about these animals; it will suffice for the present to tell you that none of our party were incommoded by them.

The twenty-sixth of July, being all reunited, I celebrated mass, which I had deferred until that time, and the next morning, we started for Michillima, or Missillimakinac, which is a station situated between

Lakes Huron and Michigan. Although we had a hundred leagues to travel, the wind was so favourable that we arrived in less than six days. We remained there for some time, in order to repair all damages incurred at the portages and falls; while there, I consecrated two flags, and buried several soldiers who had been carried off by fatigue or sickness.

The tenth of August we left Michillimackinack and entered Lake Michigan. As we had been detained there two days by the wind, our savages had had time to take a hunt, in which they killed several moose and elk, and they were polite enough to offer to share with us. We made some objections at first, but they compelled us to accept their present, saying, that since we had shared with them the fatigues of the journey, it was right that they should share with us the comforts which they had found, and that they should not consider themselves as men, if they acted in a different manner toward others. This discourse, which one of our men rendered into French for me, affected me very much. What humanity in savages! and how many men might be found in Europe, to whom the title of barbarian might much better be applied than to these inhabitants of America.

The generosity of our savages merited the most lively gratitude on our part; already for some time, not having been able to find suitable hunting grounds, we had been compelled to eat nothing but bacon; the moose and elk which they gave us, removed the disgust which we began to have for our ordinary fare.

The fourteenth of the same month we continued our journey as far as the Detour de Chicagou, and as we were doubling Cap à la Mort, which is about five leagues across, we encountered a gust of wind, which drove ashore several of the canoes that were unable to double a point in order to obtain a shelter; they were broken by the shock; and we were obliged to distribute among the other canoes the men, who, by the greatest good fortune in the world, had all escaped from the danger. The next day we crossed over to the Folles Avoines, in order to invite the inhabitants to come and oppose our landing; they fell into the trap, and were entirely defeated.

The following day we camped at the mouth of a river called La Gasparde; our savages went into the woods, but soon returned, bringing with them several roebucks: this species of game is very common at this place, and we were enabled to lay in several days' provisions of it.

About mid-day on the 17th, we were ordered to halt until evening, in order that we might reach the post at the bay during the night; as we wished to surprise the enemy, whom we knew were staying with their allies the Saquis, whose village lies near Fort St. Francis. At twilight we commenced our march, and about midnight we arrived at the mouth of Fox River, at which point our fort is built. As soon as we had arrived there, M. de Lignerie sent some Frenchmen to the commandant to ascertain if the enemy were really at the village of the Saquis, and having learned that we ought still to find them there, he caused all the savages and a detachment of French troops to cross over the river, in order to surround the habitation, and then ordered the rest of our troops to enter the village. Notwithstanding the precautions that had been taken to conceal our arrival, (!!) the savages had received information of it, and all had escaped with the exception of four: these were presented to our savages, who, after having diverted themselves with them, shot them to death with their arrows.

I was much pained to witness this horrible spectacle; and the pleasure which our savages took in making these unfortunate persons suffer, causing them to undergo the horrors of thirty deaths before depriving them of life, I could not make accord with the manner in which they had appeared to think some days before. I would willingly have asked them if they did not perceive, as I did, this opposition of sentiment, and have pointed out to them what I saw condemnable in their proceedings; but those of our party who might have served me as interpreters were on the other side of the river, and I was obliged to postpone until another time the satisfaction of my curiosity.

After this little coup-de-main we went up Fox River, which is full of rapids, and is about thirty-five or forty leagues in length. The 24th of August we arrived at the village of the Puants, much disposed to destroy any inhabitants that might be found there; but their flight had preceded our arrival, and we had nothing to do but to burn their wigwams, and ravage their fields of Indian corn, which is their principal article of food.

We afterward crossed over the little Fox Lake, at the end of which we camped, and the next day, (day of St. Lewis,) after mass, we entered a small river which conducted us into a kind of swamp, on the borders of which is situated the grand habitation of those whom we were in search of. Their allies, the Saquis, doubtless had informed them of our approach, and they did not deem it advisable to await our arrival, for we found in their village only a few women, whom our savages made their slaves, and one old man, whom they burnt to death at a slow fire, without appearing to entertain the least repugnance towards committing so barbarous an action.

This appeared to me a more striking act of cruelty than that which had been exercised towards the four savages found in the village of the Saquis. I siezed upon this occasion and circumstance to satisfy my curiosity, about that of which I have just been speaking. There was in our company a Frenchman who could speak the Iroquois language. I entreated him to tell the savages that I was surprised to see them take so much pleasure in torturing this unfortunate old man—that the rights of war did not extend so far, and that so barbarous an action appeared to me to be in direct opposition to the principles which they had professed to entertain towards all men. I was answered by an Iroquois, who in order to justify his companions, said, that when they fell into the hands of the Foxes and Saquis, they were treated with still greater cruelty, and that it was their custom to treat their enemies in the same manner that they would be treated by them if they were vanquished. * * *

* * * I was about to give him some further reasons, when orders were given to advance upon the last stronghold of the enemy. This post is situated upon the borders of a small river which empties into another called the Ouisconsin, which latter discharges itself into the Mississippi, about thirty leagues from there. We found no person there, and as we had no orders to go any farther, we employed ourselves several days in destroying the fields, in order to deprive the enemy of the means of subsisting there. The country here is beautiful, the soil is fertile, the game plenty, and of very fine flavour; the nights are very cold, and the days extremely warm. In my second letter I will speak to you about my return to Montreal, and of all that has happened to me up to the time of my embarking for France. * * *

Your affectionate brother,

EMMANUEL CRESPEL, Recolet.

NOTE.—I am indebted to the library of Cyrus Woodman, Esq., of Mineral Point, for the perusal of this very small volume. Not being aware of any historical notice of the expedition spoken of, I was at first doubtful of the truth of the relation; but through the kindness of Governor Cass, I have obtained a full corroboration of the facts of which Crespel speaks. It is somewhat singular to observe the writer's remark on the "precautions" taken by a body of 1500 men sailing in canoes, and marching some 450 leagues to *surprise* a tribe of Indians; and it is equally amusing to see what a horror he has at the instances of cruelty in Indian warfare, and at the same time the coolness with which he describes the utter destruction of the villages and the cornfields of the absent Foxes.

The following is an abstract from an official report made for the use of the French council and ministers, agreeably to the uniform usage. It was procured from the archives at Paris by the American Minister, General Lewis Cass, and by him communicated to me.—W. R. S.

## CANADA.

*From Messrs. De Beauharnois and De Argemait, 1st September,* 1728.

### ENTERPRISE AGAINST THE FOXES.

It having been signified to them that his Majesty wished that they had waited his orders before commencing this undertaking:—

They answer that the information which they received from every quarter, of the secret wampums which the English had sent among the nations in the upper country, to cut the throats of the French in all the posts, and the war parties which the Foxes were raising every day, did not allow them to defer this expedition for a year, without endangering the loss of all the posts in the upper country.

They learned with regret that the Foxes had fled before the army had arrived in their country. They will do all they can to prevent any results from this, and will attentively observe all the movements which any of those nations who could enter into the interests of the Foxes might make, so as to prevent any surprise.

The Marquis de Beauharnois, by a private letter of the same day, sends the instructions which he had given to M. de Lignery for this expedition, and the letter which this officer entreated to enclose in his despatches, and by which he attempts to justify himself.

This letter states that he made use of all his skill to succeed in the expedition, but it was impossible for him to surprise the enemy, not being able to conceal from them, any further than the bay, the knowledge of his march.

He took at this post, before day-break, three Puants of the Foxes, and one Fox, who were discovered by some Sakis whom he had brought from Mackinac. These four savages were bound and sent to the tribes, who put them to death the next day. He afterward continued his march, composed of 1000 savages and 450 French, as far as the village of the Puants, and afterward to the Foxes. They all fled as soon as they heard we were at the bay, of which they were informed by some of their own people, who escaped by swimming. They captured, however, in the four Fox villages, two women, a girl, and an old man, who were killed and burnt. He learnt from them that the tribe had left four days before; that it had a collection of canoes, in which the old men, the women, and children had embarked, and that the warriors had gone by land: he urged the other tribes to follow in pursuit of them, but there was only a portion of them who would consent, the others saying the enemy had got too far for them to be able to catch them up. The French had nothing but Indian corn to eat, and this, added to the advanced season, and a march of 400 leagues on their return, by which the safety of half the army was endangered, decided them upon burning the four Fox villages, their forts, and their huts, to destroy all that they could find in their fields, Indian corn, peas, beans, and gourds, of which they had great abundance. They did the same execution amongst the Puants. It is certain that half of these nations, who number 4000 souls, will die of hunger, and that they will come in and ask mercy.

Major de Cavagnal, who has been in the whole expedition, and has perfectly performed his duty, is able to certify to all this.

In returning, having passed by a fort of the Sakis, these savages told him in a council of our tribes, that they no longer wished to stay with them, from fear of the Foxes, and that they were going to retire to the river St. Joseph. It was impossible to reassure them, which obliged him, seeing this post abandoned, to burn the fort, lest the Foxes or their allies should take possession of it, fortify themselves, and make war upon our nearest allies, the Folles Avoines.

In a second letter of M. de Beauharnios, of the 8th of September, 1728, he states that neither the glory nor the arms of the King were at all interested in this expedition, the Foxes having abandoned every thing and retired to the Ajaouès.[1]

All the army attributes the failure to M. de Lignery's stay at Mackinac which was considerable. But the climax was, that a Potowatamy, who had come to the army with four others, three of whom did not appear, was sent back to his comrades by M. de Lignery to say that he had come to talk with the tribes, and even with the Foxes, who were only two days off. This savage warned the latter of all he had seen in the army, and instantly they prepared to take flight. The French and savages wished to march upon them, but M. de Lignery would not hasten his departure, under the idea that the Potowatamy would return. The murmur was very general against him in the army: the savages in their speeches have not spared M. de Lignery, and have asserted that the people from the upper country ought to come in the spring, and state their complaints to him.

M. de Lignery performed another manœuvre on his return to the bay, which no one could understand. Because the Sakis said they were afraid of the Foxes, and that they wished to establish themselves at the river St. Joseph, without well examining the consequences of the step he was taking, he decided upon destroying the fort, though he had people and ammunition, and could wait for orders until the next year; and surely the Sakis would not have left, and would not have dared to do so.

---

[1] Iowas.

In this business M. de Lignery was the man in power in all the colony, and French and savages would have marched under his orders with great pleasure.

M. de Beauharnois is sorry to be obliged to state things as they are, but there will be many letters which will say the same thing, and he thinks it better that Monseigneur should know the truth of the matter. He might add that they say that M. de Lignery was ill, and that he did not wish that any other should reap any glory from the undertaking. M. de Beaujeu, who was second in command, would have admirably acquitted himself. Messrs. de Artagnal, Dubuisson, and all the other officers, would have desired nothing better than to have gone ahead. Every one wished it, but M. de Lignery would not listen to any representations.

The following marginal notes are appended to the above paper :—

"M. de Lignery allows the Foxes to escape."

"It is to be regretted that this enterprise did not have the success which was expected from it, both from the expense of it, and from the consequences it might have had. It is certain that M. de Beauharnois took all possible measures that it should have no evil results. There is every reason to believe that the Foxes who suffered much from the destruction of their villages and plantations, will ask for peace, and that is extremely to be desired."

---

## NOTE H. Page 111.

The following notice of Major Rogers is found in Parkman's History of the Conspiracy of Pontiac, and reference is made to authorities, MS. papers, &c., therein cited. See History, chap. vi.

"Major Robert Rogers was a native of New Hampshire, an associate of Putnam and Stark's; he commanded a corps of rangers, whose services during the French war rendered them famous throughout America; the name of Rogers's Rangers was never mentioned but with honour. Six years after his expedition to Detroit to receive possession of the posts from the French, he was tried hy a court-martial for a meditated act of treason, the surrender of Michillimackinac into the hands of the Spaniards, who were at that time masters of Upper Louisiana. Having afterwards passed over to the Barbary States, he entered the service of the Dey of Algiers, and fought two battles under his banners. At the opening of the war of independence he returned to his native country, where he made professions of patriotism, but was strongly suspected by many, including Washington himself, of acting the part of a spy. In fact he soon openly espoused the British cause, and received a colonel's commission from the crown. His services, however, proved of little consequence. In 1778, he was proscribed and banished under the Act of New Hampshire, and the remainder of his life was passed in such obscurity that it is difficult to discover where and when he died. Rogers's published works consist of the "Journals of his Ranging Service," and his "Concise Account of North America." To these may be added a curious drama, called "Ponteach, or the Savages of America," which appears to have been written, in part at least, by him. The steep mountain called Rogers's Slide, near the northern end of Lake George, derives its name from the tradition, that during the French war, being pursued by a party of Indians, he slid on snow shoes down its precipitous front for more than a thousand feet, to the frozen lake below. On beholding the achievement, the Indians, as well they might, believed him under the protection of the Great Spirit, and gave over the chase. The story seems unfounded; yet it was not far from this mountain, that the Rangers fought one of their most desperate winter battles against a force of many times their number."

---

## Note I. Page 113.

The following note is extracted from M. L. Martin's discourse before the Historical Society of Wisconsin, 1851:—

"About the year 1750, Sieur Augustin du Langlade became the principal proprietor of the post at Green Bay, and his descendants are there at the present day. He was a man of education and character, and the pure idiom of his native tongue and the polished manners brought hither from the French court have been transmitted uncorrupted to the generations which succeeded him. A distinguished French traveller within the last few years expressed his surprise at hearing from a native citizen of our country, and who had never been beyond the limits of our State, the purity and elegance of expression which distinguishes the refined circles of the French metropolis. His son, Charles de Langlade, a native of the country, bore a conspicuous part in the French war, and we find him acting in the capacity of lieutenant, afterward of captain, under the orders of Vaudreuil at Mackinac, St. Joseph, and at Duquesne. He also was a man of great energy, active and persevering in enterprises, and possessed in a high degree the confidence of the King and Government. In 1760 he was commissioned by Louis XV., and was appointed second in command at Michillimackinac, at which place he still remained on the 4th of June, 1763, when the Indians surprised and massacred the troops stationed at that post. In 1760, Vaudreuil informs him that he was under the necessity of surrendering Montreal to a superior force under General Amherst, and that the English had thus become masters of Canada. Major Etherington soon afterward took possession of Fort Mackinac and its dependencies, and in April, 1763, we find him giving authority to the Messrs. Langlade to take up their permanent residence at Green Bay. In 1782, Lieutenant-governor Sinclair repeats the permission in favour of the widow of Langlade senior, and thus the infant settlement of our State, which had been commenced and continued under French auspices, is sanctioned and encouraged under the more rigorous and arbitrary rule of the British crown. Of the great-grand-children of Augustin Langlade, the only one now surviving is Augustin Grignon of Butte des Morts, Winnebago county, aged 74 years."

Nevertheless the conduct of Langlade towards Mr. Henry during the massacre by the Indians at Michillimackinac, exhibits much of inhumanity. See Doc. Hist., Henry's Narrative.

---

## Note K. Page 120.

Parkman, in his History of the Conspiracy of Pontiac, (chap. xii. p. 233,) in a note, has the following remarks:—

"The annals of these remote and gloomy regions are involved in such obscurity, that it is hard to discover the precise character of the events to which Pontiac here refers; (events of 1746.) The only allusion to them which the writer has met with, is the following, inscribed on a tattered scrap of soiled paper, found among the McDougal manuscripts.

"'Five miles below the mouth of Wolf River is the Great Death Ground. This took its name from the circumstance that some years before the old French war, a great battle was fought between the French troops, assisted by the Menominees and Ottaways, on the one side, and the Sac and Fox Indians on the other. The Sacs and Foxes were nearly all cut off; and this proved the cause of their eventual expulsion from that country.

"The McDougal manuscripts above referred to, belonged to a son of the Lieutenant McDougal who was the fellow-prisoner of Major Campbell; (detained by Pontiac at the siege of Detroit.) On the death of the younger McDougal, the papers, which were very voluminous, and contained various notes concerning the Indian war, and the captivity of his father, came into the possession of a family at the town of Palmer, in

Michigan, who permitted such of them as related to the subjects in question, to be copied by the writer."

Schoolcraft, in his "Historical Discourse," speaking of the Sac and Fox Indians, says—"The Outagamies were driven from Old Toronto, through the Straits of Niagara to Detroit, where they played a conspicuous part in the Pontiac war. They afterward concentrated their remaining force at Green Bay, where they formed a close alliance with the Sauks, and for a while sustained themselves. But they were pursued by the French, with the aid of the Chippeways and Menominees. They were beaten in two sanguinary battles on the St. Croix and Fox Rivers, fled to the Ouisconsin, and finally sought refuge west of the Mississippi."

There is, in the above extract, evidently a blending of dates, or a use of the term "Pontiac war," for a war under "Mackinac the Turtle," against the French, in 1746. For certainly, *after* the Pontiac war against the English, in 1763, there was no expedition of the French against the Outagamies which caused two sanguinary battles—such battles were undoubtedly fought by the French, assisted by their allies the Chippeways and Menominees, but at a period long anterior to the so-called "Pontiac war." W. R. S.

# NOTES TO CHAPTER III.

## NOTE A. Page 128.

### UNDER BRITISH DOMINION.

Before the execution of Jay's Treaty of 1794, a project was devised between two or three adventurers of the States, and a number of merchants and traders of Detroit, which, had it succeeded, would have produced great injury to Michigan. In 1795, Robert Randall, of Pennsylvania, and Charles Whitney, of Vermont, were taken into custody by order of the House of Congress, for an unwarrantable attempt to corrupt the integrity of its members. Randall had visited Detroit in pursuit of some object in which he had failed, and he soon adopted a comprehensive plan to improve his fortune. In connection with Charles Whitney and another individual, he entered into an agreement with seven merchants residing at or near Detroit, through which the parties bound themselves to obtain a pre-emption right from the United States of a certain territory therein defined, which was to be purchased from the Indians. The tract contained, it is supposed, nearly twenty millions of acres, and was embraced by Lakes Erie, Huron, and Michigan. It was given in evidence before Congress, that Randall and Whitney had unfolded to several members their scheme, and by this it appeared that the territory was to be divided into forty-one shares, five of which were to belong to the traders of Detroit, who were parties to the agreement—six were to be appropriated to Randall and his coadjutors, and the rest were to be divided among the members of Congress who might give their influence to the measure. The amount proposed to be paid for the right to make this purchase, was from a half to one million of dollars. These merchants, it was maintained, exercised so great influence over the Indians, as to make an advantageous purchase practicable. It was maintained in opposition to this measure, that there was a bar in the fact that the treaty gave an exclusive pre-emption right to the United States. But it was urged on the other side, that the Indians were dissatisfied with this treaty, and would not be bound by it; and that this plan would, by appeasing the savages, restore tranquillity to the country. Having been brought before the House, Whitney was discharged, while Randall received a public reprimand, and was obliged to pay the fees which had accrued in the trial of his cause. (Whiting's Historical Discourse. Lanman.)

---

## NOTE B. Page 128.

The following is an extract of a letter of Sir William Johnson, to the Board of Trade, dated March 22, 1766. It is among the "London (MS.) Documents," preserved in the State Library at Albany, and is found in vol. xxxix. p. 42. The extract has been furnished me by Lyman C. Draper, Esq.:—

In this letter, Sir William Johnson, in speaking of the "Illinois," says, "Just now I have heard that Major Farmer, who proceeded by Mississippi, arrived there the 4th of December, and relieved Captain Sterling." This was at Fort Chartres. Sir William proceeds—

"I have been applied to by the merchants of Canada concerning a purchase lately made by Mr. William Grant from Monsieur Rigaud, and Madame de Vaudreuille, of the fort at La Baye de Puants, in Lake Michigan, with an extensive territory, over which he is to have an exclusive right of trade, with liberty to erect houses and make establishments thereon, to the infinite loss and detriment of the trading people, and likewise to the general dissatisfaction of the Indians, who cannot fail being greatly alarmed at such an establishment beyond our provincial limits.

"This grant to Mr. Rigaud and his lady was from the Marquis de Vaudreuille, in October, 1759, and confirmed by the King of France in January, 1760, at a very critical period, when Quebec was ours, and Montreal only wanting to complete the conquest of Canada, and therefore evidently intended as a perquisite, well knowing some of our unwary people might be drawn in to give a valuable consideration for it, as it would be highly impolitic for them to make such a grant or permit such settlements if they continued masters of the country, since it would alienate the affections of the Indians, and of friends, make them bitter enemies, which they will doubtless prove to us, if the 'grant' is attempted to be enforced.

"These considerations, supported by the request of the traders of Canada, induce me to lay these general heads before your lordships," &c.

In another letter, (London Documents, vol. xl. p. 230,) Sir William Johnson writes of "the importance of re-establishing the post of La Baye, and of Rigaud de Vaudreuille's claim; some steps had been ordered to be taken to render it invalid," &c.

This same Rigaud de Vaudreuille commanded an army of about nine hundred French and Indians, in an attack on Fort Massachusetts, in August, 1746. Colonel Hawks, who commanded the fort, which contained but 33 persons, men, women, and children, and was badly provided with ammunition, yet defended himself 28 hours, and then offered terms of capitulation, which were accepted. (Holmes's Annals, vol. ii. 32.)

---

## Note C. Page 138.

The following extracts from Parkman's "History of the Conspiracy of Pontiac," chap. 17, give lucid details on the subject of Lieutenant Gorell's command at Green Bay, deriving their authenticity from "Gorell's Manuscript Journal," deposited in the library of the Maryland Historical Society, and other reliable sources.

The posts of Green Bay and Sault St. Marie did not share the fate of Michillimakinac. St. Marie had been partially destroyed by fire in the preceding winter, and had been abandoned; many of the garrison had retired to Mackinaw, and perished there in the massacre. The fort at Green Bay had received an English garrison in 1761, consisting of seventeen men commanded by Lieutenant Gorell. At this time the Menominees lived at the mouth of Fox River, close to the fort. The Winnebagoes had several villages on the Lake Winnebago, and the Sauks and Foxes were established at a large village on the Wisconsin River.[1]

"The English commander had the task of securing the peace of the surrounding tribes, and to regulate the fur trade among them. Much intercourse existed between him and the Indians, as he appears to have conducted himself with judgment and prudence. Gorell explained to the tribes in bold and decided language the power of the King of England, and reproached the Menominees with their having taken part with France in the late war; threatened them, and finally obtained the good-will of all.

On the 15th of June, 1763, an Ottawa chief brought a letter to Gorell from Captain Etherington.

Michillimackinac, June 11th, 1763.

Dear Sir—This place was taken by surprise on the fourth instant by the Chippeways, at which time Lieutenant Jamet and seventy men were killed and all the rest taken prisoners; but our good friends the Ottawas, have taken Lieutenant Lesley, me, and eleven men out of their hands,

---

[1] Probably Sauk Prairie.

and have promised to reinstate us again. You'll therefore on the receipt of this, which I send by a canoe of Ottawas, set out with all your garrison, and what English traders you have with you, and come with the Indian who gives you this, who will conduct you safe to me. You must be sure to follow the instruction you receive from the bearer of this, as you are by no means to come to this post before you see me at the village twenty miles from this. * * * I must once more beg you'll lose no time in coming to join me; at the same time be very careful, and always be on your guard. I long much to see you, and am, dear sir

Your most humble servant,

GEO. ETHERINGTON.

*J. Gorell*, Royal Americans.

On the receipt of this letter, Gorell summoned a council of the Menominees, told them what the Ojibwas had done, and that he and his soldiers were going to Michillimackinac to restore order; that in his absence he commended the fort to their care. Great numbers of Winnebagoes, and of the Sacs and Foxes afterward arrived, to whom he addressed nearly the same words. Presents were given and the greater part of the Indians appeared well disposed to the English, though a few were inclined to prevent their departure, and even to threaten hostility. A fortunate incident occurred at this time; a Dahcotah chief arrived with a message from his people to this effect: that they had heard of the bad conduct of the Ojibwas; they hoped that the tribes of Green Bay would not follow their example, but on the contrary protect the English; unless they did so, the Dahcotah would fall upon them and take ample revenge. This interference must doubtless be ascribed to the hatred with which the Dahcotahs had long regarded the Ojibwas; the espousal of one side of the quarrel by the latter, was abundant reason to the Dahcotah for adopting the other. Some of the Green Bay Indians were also at enmity with the Ojibwas, and all opposition to the departure of the English ceased: some of the more friendly offered to escort the garrison on its way, and on the 26th of June, Gorell's party embarked in several batteaux, accompanied by ninety warriors in canoes. Approaching Beaver Island near the mouth of Green Bay, an alarm was given that the Ojibwas were lying there in ambush; on which the Menominees raised the war-song, stripped themselves, and prepared to do battle in behalf of the English. The alarm proved false, and having crossed Lake Michigan in safety, the party arrived at L'Arbre Croche on the 30th. The Ottawas came down to the beach to salute them with a discharge of guns, and on landing they were presented with the pipe of peace. Captain Etherington and Lieutenant Leslie with eleven men were in the village, detained as prisoners, though treated with kindness. It was thought that the Ottawas intended to disarm the party of Gorell also, but the latter gave out that he would resist such an attempt, and his soldiers were permitted to retain their weapons.

Several days were occupied by the Indians in holding councils. Those from Green Bay requested the Ottawas to set their prisoners at liberty, and the latter at length assented. On the 18th of July, the English, escorted by a fleet of Indian canoes, left L'Arbre Croche, and reaching without interruption the river Ottawa, descended to Montreal, where they arrived on the 13th of August. Except the garrison of Detroit, not a British soldier now remained in the region of the lakes.

---

## Note D. Page 139.

The post of Detroit was environed by three rows of pickets forming nearly a square. At each corner and over the gates there were erected block-houses; and between the houses and pickets there was a circular space, called *le chemin du ronde*, which formed a place of deposit for arms. Anchored on the river in front of the town, were two armed vessels, one called the Beaver, for the purpose of its defence; and the fort was protected by three mortars, two six-pounders and one three-pounder. These, however, were badly mounted, and seemed to be better calculated to terrify the Indians than for substantial defence. In the limits of the town there were also about forty-two traders and persons connected with the fur trade, who were provided with provisions and arms, besides the few families who were settled within the palisade. Most of the houses were enclosed within the pickets, for the purpose of securing them by the protection of the fort, while only a few French farms were scattered along the banks of the river. (Cass's Historical Discourse.)

---

## Note E. Page 141.

The schemes of Pontiac in the surprise and attack on the post of Michillimakinac, and other forts, were not so successful in their results at Detroit; this being a place of the greatest consequence, and well guarded, required great resolution and consummate art to overcome its defences, or obtain the possession of it by stratagem. Pontiac took the management of the expedition against this post on himself, and drew near it with the principal body of his troops. He was however prevented from carrying his designs into execution by an apparently trivial and unforeseen circumstance.

Carver, who was contemporaneous with the events, and whose account may be relied on as accurate, relates as follows:—

The town of Detroit, when Pontiac formed his plan, was garrisoned by about three hundred men, commanded by Major Gladwyn, a gallant officer. As at that time every appearance of war was at an end, and the Indians seemed to be on a friendly footing, Pontiac approached the fort without exciting any suspicions in the breast of the governor or the inhabitants. He encamped at a little distance from it, and sent to let the commandant know that he was come to trade, and, being desirous of brightening the chain of peace between the English and his nation, desired that he and his chiefs might be admitted to hold a council with him. The governor, still unsuspicious, and not in the least doubting the sincerity of the Indians, granted their general's request, and fixed on the next morning for their reception.

The evening of that day, an Indian woman who had been employed by Major Gladwyn to make him a pair of Indian shoes, out of curious elk-skin, brought them home. The major was so pleased with them, that, intending these as a present for a friend, he ordered her to take the remainder back, and make it into others for himself. He then directed his servant to pay her for those she had done, and dismissed her. The woman went to the door that led to the street, but no farther; she there loitered about as if she had not finished the business on which she came. A servant at length observed her, and asked her why she stayed there; she gave him, however, no answer.

Some short time after, the governor himself saw her, and inquired of his servant, what occasioned her stay. Not being able to get a satisfactory answer, he ordered the woman to be called in. When she came into his presence, he desired to know what was the reason of her loitering about, and not hastening home before the gates were shut, that she might complete in due time the work he had given her to do. She told him, after much hesitation, that as he had always behaved with great goodness toward her, she was unwilling to take away the remainder of the skin, because he put so great a value upon it; and yet had not been able to prevail upon herself to tell him so. He then asked her, why she was more reluctant to do so now, than she had been when she made the former pair. With increased reluctance she answered, that she never should be able to bring them back.

His curiosity being now excited, he insisted on her disclosing to him the secret that seemed to be struggling in her bosom for utterance. At last, on receiving a promise that the intelligence she was about to give him should not turn to her prejudice, and that if it appeared to be beneficial she should be rewarded for it, she informed him, that at the council to be held with the Indians the following day, Pontiac and his chiefs intended to murder him; and after having massacred the garrison and inhabitants, to plunder the town. That for this purpose all the chiefs who were to be admitted into the council-room, had cut their guns short, so that they could conceal them under their blankets; with which, at a signal given by their general, on delivering the belt, they were all to rise up, and instantly to fire on him and his attendants. Having effected this, they were immediately to rush into the town, where they would find themselves supported by a great number of their warriors, that were to come into it during the sitting of the council, under pretence of trading, but privately armed in the same manner. Having gained from the woman every necessary particular relative to the plot, and also the means by which she acquired a knowledge of them, he dismissed her with injunctions of secrecy, and a promise of fulfilling on his part with punctuality the engagements he had entered into.

The intelligence the governor had just received, gave him great uneasiness; and he immediately consulted the officer who was next to him in command, on the subject. But that gentleman considering the information as a story invented for some artful purposes, advised him to pay no attention to it. This conclusion, however, had happily no weight with him. He thought it prudent to conclude it to be true, till he was convinced that it was not so; and therefore without revealing his suspicions to any other person, he took every needful precaution that the time would admit of. He walked round the fort during the whole night, and saw himself that every sentinel was on duty, and every weapon of defence in proper order.

As he traversed the ramparts which lay nearest to the Indian camp, he heard them in high festivity, and, little imagining that their plot was discovered, probably pleasing themselves with the anticipation of their success. As soon as the morning dawned, he ordered all the garrison under arms; and then imparting his apprehensions to a few of the principal officers, gave them such directions as he thought necessary. At the same time he sent round to all the traders, to inform them, that as it was expected a great number of Indians would enter the town that day, who might be inclined to plunder, he desired they would have their arms ready, and repel every attempt of that kind.

About ten o'clock, Pontiac and his chiefs arrived, and were conducted to the council-chamber, where the governor and his principal officers, each with pistols in their belts, awaited his arrival. As the Indians passed on, they could not help observing that a greater number of troops than usual were drawn up on the parade, or marching about. No sooner were they entered, and seated on the skins prepared for them, than Pontiac asked the governor on what occasion his young men, meaning the soldiers, were thus drawn up and parading the streets. He received for answer, that it was only intended to keep them perfect in their exercise.

The Indian chief-warrior now began his speech, which contained the strongest professions of friendship and good-will toward the English; and when he came to the delivery of the belt of wampum, the particular mode of which, according to the woman's information, was to be the signal for his chiefs to fire, the governor and all his attendants drew their swords halfway out of their scabbards; and the soldiers at the same instant made a clattering with their arms before the doors, which had been purposely left open. Pontiac, though one of the boldest of men, immediately turned pale and trembled; and instead of giving the belt in the manner proposed, delivered it according to the usual way. His chiefs, who had impatiently expected the signal, looked at each other with astonishment, but continued quiet, waiting the result.

The governor in his turn made a speech; but instead of thanking the great warrior for the professions of friendship he had just uttered, he accused him of being a traitor. He told him that the English, who knew every thing, were convinced of his treachery and villanous designs; and as a proof that they were well acquainted with his most secret thoughts and intentions, he stepped toward the Indian chief that sat nearest to him, and drawing aside his blanket, discovered the shortened firelock. This entirely disconcerted the Indians and frustrated their design.

He then continued to tell them, that as he had given his word, at the time they desired an audience, that their persons should be safe, he would hold his promise inviolable, though they so little deserved it. However, he advised them to make the best of their way out of the fort, lest his young men, on being acquainted with their treacherous purposes, should cut every one of them to pieces. Pontiac endeavoured to contradict the accusation, and to make excuses for his suspicious conduct; but the governor, satisfied of the falsity of his protestations, would not listen to him. The Indians immediately left the fort, but instead of being sensible of the governor's generous behaviour, they threw off the mask, and the next day made a regular attack upon it.

Major Gladwyn has not escaped censure for this mistaken lenity; for probably, had he kept a few of the principal chiefs prisoners, while he had them in his power, he might have been able to have brought the whole confederacy to terms, and have prevented a war. But he atoned for this oversight, by the gallant defence he made for more than a year, amid a variety of discouragements. (Carver's Travels.)

---

From the Historical Discourse of Governor Cass, and Lanman's History of Michigan and authorities therein cited, the following note has been compiled, as exhibiting an interesting and authentic account of some prominent events during the siege of Detroit by Pontiac.

At the commencement of the siege, so weak did the commandant consider his own position, that he had nearly determined to evacuate the fort, embark in the armed schooner on the river, and retire to Niagara, as he feared a direct assault; but he was assured by the French inhabitants that such a course would not be undertaken by the Indians, and he gave up the project. Measures were immediately taken to burn the buildings which could furnish covert to the Indians, by hot shot, and occasional sorties from the fort. Shells were discharged, and the Indians practised running toward these shells, and blowing out the matches before they had exploded, with exulting yells. The wilderness poured forth its ferocious bands of savages, like vultures around the dead. Pontiac, although he was the chief actor in this siege, was aided by several Chippewa and Ottawa warriors, who maintained a subordinate part. Among these were Mahigam, the wolf; Wabanamy, the white sturgeon; Kittacoinsi, he that climbs; Agouchiois, a friend to the French, all of the Ottawa tribe; and also Gayashque, Wasson, Macataywasson, and Pashquior, Chippewa chiefs. When the buildings around the fort had been demolished, the Indians approached a low ridge which overlooked the pickets, and from this they kept up a fire upon the garrison.

During the Pontiac war, Detroit was stored with a large quantity of valuable goods, alleged to amount to the value of five hundred thousand pounds; and in addition to that, its demolition would unite the chain of operation among the Indians, which was broken by the establishment of the English at that post. Its actual position during the siege may be inferred from the following letter, dated Detroit, July 6th, 1763:—

"We have been besieged here two months by six hundred Indians. We have been upon the watch night and day, from the commanding officer to the lowest soldier, from the 8th of May; and have not had our cloaks off, nor slept all night since it began, and shall continue so till we have a reinforcement up. We then hope to give a good account of the savages. Their camp lies about a mile and a half from the fort; and that is the nearest they choose to come now. For the first two or three days we were attacked by three or four hundred of them, but we gave them so warm a reception, that they don't care for coming to see us; though they now and then get behind a house or garden, and fire at us about three or four hundred yards distance. The day before yesterday we killed a chief and three others, and wounded some more. Yesterday went up with our sloop, and battered their cabins in such a manner that they are glad to keep farther off."

The following letter is dated the 9th of July:—

"You have long ago heard of our pleasant situation, but the storm is blown over. Was it not very agreeable to hear every day of their cutting, carving, boiling, and eating our companions? To see every day, dead bodies floating down the river mangled and disfigured. But Britons, you know, never shrink. We always appeared gay, to spite the rascals. They boiled and eat Sir Robert Devers; and we are informed by Mr. Pauli, who escaped the other day from one of the stations surprised at the breaking out of the war, and commanded by himself, that he had seen an Indian have the skin of Captain Robertson's arm for a tobacco-pouch.

"Three days ago a party of us went to demolish a breastwork they had made. We finished our work and were returning home; but the fort espying a party of Indians coming up as if they intended to fight, we were ordered back, made our dispositions and advanced briskly. Our front was fired upon warmly, and returned the fire for about five minutes. In the mean time, Captain Hopkins, with about twenty men filed off to the left, and about *twenty French volunteers* filed off to the right, and got between them and their fires. The villains immediately fled, and we returned, as was prudent, for a sentry whom I had placed, informed me he saw a body of them coming down from the woods; and our party being but about eighty, was not able to cope with their united bands. In short, we beat them handsomely, and yet did not much hurt to them, for they ran extremely well. We only killed their leader, and wounded three others. One of them fired at me, at the distance of fifteen or twenty paces, but I suppose my terrible visage made him tremble. I think I shot him."

All the means which the savage mind could suggest, were employed by Pontiac to demolish the settlement of Detroit. Blazing arrows were shot into the chapel by his warriors, for the purpose of burning it, and this would have been effected, had not a French Jesuit convinced Pontiac that its conflagration would call down the judgments of the Great Spirit. During the siege the savages endeavoured to make a breach in the pickets, and aided by Gladwyn, who, as a stratagem, had ordered his men to cut also on the inside; this was soon accomplished, and the breach was soon filled with Indians. At this instant a brass four-pounder was discharged upon the advancing savages, which made a destructive havoc. After that period the fort was merely invested; supplies were cut off, and the English were reduced to great distress from the diminution of their rations.

Major Rogers had given the command of the Fort of Detroit to Major Campbell, and he had held it since the surrender of the country, although he had been once superseded. This officer was well known to the Indians, and was esteemed for his kindness both by the French and savages. It was made a point of policy by Pontiac to get this officer into his possession, as a pledge for the surrender of the fort; and for that object he requested some of the principal French inhabitants to seek an interview with Major Campbell, and inform him that Pontiac wished him to come to his camp, in order that they might terminate the war and smoke the pipe of peace. Godfroy and Chapoton, two estimable French citizens, advised this interview, on the solemn promise by Pontiac that he should return to the fort in safety. In order to bring the war to a peaceful termination, if possible, he consented; and accompanied by Lieutenant McDougall, he repaired to the Indian quarters, and was at first well received. The crafty chief, however, did not comply with his promise, and the English officers were at length detained at the house of M. Melvehi, near Bloody Bridge. Campbell was offered his life for the surrender of the fort, but the unprincipled conduct which Pontiac had before manifested, weakened all confidence in his word. The prisoners were permitted to walk out from time to time, but little chance seemed offered for escape, as they were surrounded by Indians. Lieutenant McDougall proposed to attempt it, but as his sight was somewhat affected, Campbell declined the proposition. McDougall, however, afterward made his escape and reached the Fort of Detroit without injury. The fate of Major Campbell was of unfortunate termination. An Ottawa chief of note had been killed at Michillimackinac, and his nephew, who was in that siege, had hastened for revenge to Bloody Bridge. Here he found Major Campbell, and immediately despatched him with his tomahawk, and the savage then fled to Saginaw to escape the vengeance of Pontiac, who was justly indignant at this act.

While the siege was in progress, and on the 21st of May, the smaller vessel which had been anchored in the river was despatched to Niagara to hasten the arrival of a reinforcement with arms and provisions, which had been expected. Twenty batteaux, which had been sent from that place with a detachment of troops and army stores, arrived at Point Pelee, apprehending no danger, and there they encamped. The detachment consisted of Green's Rangers, amounting to ninety-seven men, with Lieutenant Cuyler. The Indians who were stationed at that place had watched their movements, and had marked their place of encampment, and about the dawn of day they were attacked and massacred. All the men in this expedition were either taken or killed, excepting one officer, who rushed to a boat with thirty men, and crossed Lake Erie to Sandusky Bay. These barges were guarded by the Indians, who compelled the British prisoners to navigate the boats, while they were escorted toward Detroit by the Indians on the Canadian bank of the river. When they arrived near the fort, four British soldiers in the first batteau determined to effect their liberation or die in the attempt; and by suddenly changing the course of the boat, they made their intentions known to the crew of the armed schooner near the shore by loud cries. The Indian guards on board this boat leaped overboard, and one of them dragged a soldier with him into the water, where they were both drowned. The fugitives in their escape were fired upon by the Indians in the other boats, and also by those on the bank; but no injury was done excepting the wounding of one soldier, as the Indians were soon dispersed by the fire from the armed schooner on the Detroit side. The other soldiers escaped to the shore in the boat, which soon reached the vessel. In order to prevent their escape, the remaining prisoners were immediately landed and marched up to Hog Island, where they were massacred and scalped. On the 30th of May the sentinel had first announced that the fleets of boats was coming round the point of the Huron church, and the English had assembled on the ramparts to witness the arrival of their friends; but they were only greeted by the death-song of the savages, which announced their death. The light of hope flickered on their countenance, only to be clouded with the thick darkness of despair. It was these barges; but they were in possession of the savages, and filled with the scalps, and prisoners of the English detachment.

During the siege, the body of the French people maintained a neutral relation toward the Indians and the English, although a few Canadians had aided their cause, who were held in contempt by their countrymen. They had taken the oath of allegiance, and were prisoners of war under capitulation. This neutrality was necessary to be preserved, unless they chose to place themselves in the attitude of revolution. The fact that they did not take side with the Indians, roused a feeling of disaffection in the minds of the savages; and their doors were broken open, their provisions plundered, and their cattle killed by the forces of Pontiac. Some remuneration was, however, subsequently made by the Ottawa, in levying upon the French for his supplies. He appointed a commissary, and issued bills of credit made of bark, with an otter, the *totem* of his tribe, drawn upon them, and delivered these to the French people. These bills, when payable, were faithfully redeemed.

But the Indians soon discovered that their power was insufficient for the reduction of the Fort of Detroit, and they were anxious to form a league with the French for that object. Pontiac therefore called a council of his warriors and the principal French inhabitants near Detroit, on the 23d of May, 1763, and addressed to them the following speech:—

"My brothers," (these were his words,) "I have no doubt but this war is very troublesome to you, and that my warriors, who are continually passing and repassing through your settlements, frequently kill your cattle and injure your property. I am sorry for it; and hope you do not think I am pleased with this conduct of my young men. And as a proof of my friendship, recollect the war you had seventeen years ago (1746) and the part I took in it. The northern nations combined together, and came to destroy you. Who defended you? Was it not myself and my young men? The great chief Mackinac (the turtle) said in council, that he would carry to his native village the head of your chief warrior, and that he would eat his heart and drink his blood. Did I not then join you, and go to his camp and say to him, if he wished to kill the French, he must pass over my body and the bodies of my young men? Did I not take hold of the tomahawk with you, aid you in fighting your battles with Mackinac, and driving him home to his country? Why do you think I would turn my arms against you? Am I not the same French Pontiac who assisted you seventeen years ago? I am a Frenchman, and I wish to die a Frenchman.

"My brothers," said Pontiac, throwing a war-belt into the midst of the council, "I begin to grow tired of this bad meat which is upon our lands. I begin to see that this is not your case; for instead of assisting us in our war with the English, you are actually assisting them. I have already told you, and I now tell you again, that when I undertook this war, it was only your interest I sought, and that I knew what I was about. This year they must all perish. The Master of life so orders it. His will is known to us, and we must do as he says. And you, my brothers, who know him better than we do, wish to oppose his will! Until now, I have avoided urging upon you this subject, in the hope that if you could not aid, you would not injure us. I did not wish to ask you to fight with us against the English, and I did not believe you would take part with them. You will say you are not with them. I know it; but your conduct amounts to the same thing. You will tell them all we do and say. You carry our counsels and plans to them. Now, take your choice. You must be entirely French like ourselves, or entirely English. If you are French, take this belt for yourselves and your young men, and join us. If you are English, we declare war against you."

His solicitations, however, did not prevail; and the French continued steadfast in their neutrality. Many were, however, in the confidence of the Indians; and a French citizen, M. Beaufait, had been shown the shortened rifle, and informed of the plot, on the morning in which it was to be executed, by one of the warriors, the last in the party of Pontiac, and a particular friend whom he had met with the band, during that morning upon Bloody Bridge. But the news arrived on the 3d of June, of the treaty of peace of 1763, by which the country was ceded to England, and thus furnished a double bond to maintain their neutrality. When, therefore, Pontiac solicited them to join his cause against the English, one of the principal citizens was authorized to speak in the name of that people. Exhibiting the articles of peace between the French and the British governments, he replied, "My brother, you see that our arms are tied by our great father, the king; untie this knot, and we will join you. Till that is done, we shall sit quietly upon our mats."

About this time the vessel which had been despatched to Niagara, arrived at the mouth of the Detroit River, with sixty troops, and supplied with provisions and arms. The Indians had made every attempt to capture this vessel, which had been impeded from sailing up the river by the course of the wind. For the purpose of boarding her as she ascended, the forces of Pontiac left the siege of Detroit, and repaired to Fighting Island, which is just below the city. At the mouth of the river the Indians had annoyed her in their canoes, but she soon left, under a brisk wind, and reached the point of that island, where it failed, and she was there obliged to anchor. For the purpose of concealing the strength of the vessel, the captain had concealed his men in the hold; and as soon as evening came on, the Indians proceeded in silence to board the vessel from their canoes, while the men on board were secretly ordered up to take their stations at the guns. The Indians approached near the side, when the signal for a discharge was given by a blow upon the mast with a hammer. The power of the discharge killed and wounded many, the rest escaped in their canoes; and on the next morning the vessel dropped down the river, and remained six days waiting for a fair wind. On the 30th (June) she arrived without accident, at Detroit.

It now became an important object with Pontiac to destroy the vessels which were anchored before the town of Detroit, because they tended to protect the shore, and also furnished means of communication by water to the other English posts on the lakes. For that purpose the barns of many of the inhabitants were torn down, and the materials made into a raft, filled with pitch and other combustibles, which should burn with great rapidity and intenseness. The whole mass was then towed up the river, and fire was added, under the supposition that the stream would carry it down in contact, and set fire to the vessels. The attempt was made, but without success. The English, aware of this attempt, had anchored boats above the vessels, connected by chains, so as to ward off this blazing mass. The plan was successful, and the burning rafts floated down the river without doing any damage.

On the 29th of July, a fleet of gun-boats sailed up the Detroit River, each containing four swivels, two mortars, and the whole, a detachment of three hundred regular troops under the command of Captain Dalyell, an aid-de-camp of Sir Jeffrey Amherst, the commander-in-chief of the British forces in Canada. When this fleet appeared in sight, a gun was fired from the fort, and it was answered from the boats. They soon arrived in safety. Supposing that Pontiac might be surprised in his camp, a plan was concerted on that evening to march against him for that object. Accordingly, on the morning of the 31st of July, about two o'clock, Captain Dalyell, with a force of about two hundred and forty-seven men, marched up, two deep, along the Detroit River toward Pontiac's camp; while two gun-boats in the river were pushed against the stream to cover the retreat and take off the wounded and the dead. Information of this contemplated attack had been in some mode communicated to the Indians, and they removed their women and children, and prepared for the reception of the British troops. A party of warriors was stationed behind the pickets upon a neighbouring farm, (M. Dequindre's,) and another at Bloody Bridge, which is about a mile and a half from Detroit, on the main road. Here they were concealed in the high grass, behind pickets and heaps of cord-wood. The British party had reached the bridge, when a sudden and destructive fire was poured upon them from the cord-wood and the grass. This threw them into the utmost confusion. The attack in the darkness, from an invisible force, was critical. At the first fire, Captain Dalyell fell. The British fought with desperation, but were attacked on all sides, and a vigorous charge was made by the bayonet upon the positions of the Indians; but a scattering fire was kept up by the savages from every place that could furnish them a cover. At length, finding that their situation was perilous, the British were ordered to retire, which was effected without serious loss in this manœuvre, under the direction of Captain Grant, aided by that energetic and patriotic officer, Major Rogers. This retreat was covered on the shore of the Detroit River by the armed gun-boats; and the whole party arrived at the fort about eight o'clock. It was only effected, however, by driving the Indians from house to house, and field to field, until a line of defence could be made toward the fort. In this action, according to the official returns, there were nineteen killed and forty-two wounded. The place of its occurrence is called Bloody Bridge.

The whole number of troops lost during the siege of Detroit was but little short of three hundred, besides individuals unconnected with the army; the exact number, however, has never been correctly ascertained.

The Indians had appeared before the post on the 8th of May; their force was seldom less than one thousand men, and the siege, with innumerable attacks, was continued until the last of August, and, with occasional relaxations only, from that time until next spring, altogether about twelve months. After the last of August, many of the allies and warriors of Pontiac, wearied with the toil and privations of the siege retired to their towns and families.

In the mean while the operations of Pontiac in this region called for efficient aid on the part of the British government: accordingly, early in the spring of 1764, active preparations were in operation throughout the provinces for the chastisement of the hostile Indians, and for the protection of the frontiers from the merciless fury of savage warfare. Troops were fast concentrating upon the remote posts near the lakes, and upon the Ohio region. Early in June, 1764, General Bradstreet, with three thousand troops, reached Niagara on his route to reinforce the garrisons in the western posts. Overtures for peace having been made by the Indians of the Northwest, the general demanded of them a grand council, to confirm their professions of amity. At length nearly two thousand Indians were assembled at Fort Niagara, and among them were representatives and chiefs from twenty-two nations, and embracing those from eleven of the remote Northwestern tribes. A treaty was soon after concluded between his Majesty's Superintendent of Indian Affairs, Sir William Johnson, on the part of Great Britain, and the chiefs, sachems, and warriors of the respective tribes. The treaty stipulates for peace and friendship, and a cession of certain lands to Great Britain, lying south of Lakes Ontario and Erie; but Pontiac was not there, nor would he sanction the treaty.

General Bradstreet at length, (having narrowly escaped shipwreck with his whole army on Lake Erie, off the present city of Cleveland,) arrived safely at Detroit. After making several incursions against hostile towns, and chastising several bands of Indians who were opposed to the late treaty, he received overtures of peace from them. Negotiations for a truce were opened, which soon after resulted in a peace with all the Northwestern tribes, except the Shawanese and Delawares of the Scioto. Pontiac would take no part in the treaty, and remained adverse to peace. He retired to the Illinois, where he was assassinated about the year 1767, by an Indian of the Peoria tribe. (Monette, vol. i.)

## Note F. Page 146.

When Carver visited this region in the year 1766, the Winnebagoes had their great town on an island lying at the east end of Lake Winnebago. Here, he says, the queen who presided over this tribe instead of a sachem, received him with great civility, and entertained him in a most distinguished manner during the four days he continued with her. He states that—

"The day after my arrival, I held a council with the chiefs, of whom I asked permission to pass through their country in my way to more remote nations on business of importance. This was readily granted me, the request being esteemed by them as a great compliment paid to their tribe. The queen sat in the council, but only asked a few questions, or gave some trifling directions in matters relative to the state; for women are never allowed to sit in their councils, except they happen to be invested with the supreme authority, and then it is not customary for them to make any formal speeches as the chiefs do. She was a very ancient woman, small in stature, and not much distinguished by her dress from several young women that attended her. These her attendants seemed greatly pleased whenever I showed any tokens of respect to their queen, particularly when I saluted her, which I frequently did to acquire her favour. On these occasions, the good old lady endeavoured to assume a juvenile gayety, and by her smiles showed she was equally pleased with the attention I paid her.

"From all I could learn of the origin, language, and customs of this people, I conclude that the Winnebagoes originally resided in some of the provinces belonging to New Mexico; and being driven from their native country, either by intestine divisions, or by the extension of the Spanish conquests, they took refuge in these more northern parts about a century ago.

"My reasons for adopting this supposition are, first from their unalterable attachment to the Naudowessie Indians, (Sioux,) who they say gave them the earliest succour during their emigration, notwithstanding their present residence is more than six hundred miles distant from that people.

"Secondly, their dialect totally differs from every other Indian nation yet discovered; they converse with other nations in the Chippeway tongue, which is the prevailing language throughout all the tribes, from the Mohawks of Canada to those who inhabit the borders of the Mississippi, and from the Hurons and Illinois, to such as dwell near Hudson's Bay.

"Third, from their inveterate hatred to the Spaniards. Some of them informed me that they had made many excursions to the southwest, which took up several moons. An elderly chief more particularly acquainted me, that about forty-six winters ago, (1720) he marched at the head of fifty warriors towards the southwest for three moons. That during this expedition, while they were crossing a plain, they discovered a body of men on horseback, who belonged to the black people, for so they called the Spaniards. As soon as they perceived them, they proceeded with caution, and concealed themselves till night came on; when they drew so near as to be able to discern the number and situation of their enemies. Finding they were not able to cope with so great a superiority by day-light, they waited till they had retired to rest; when they rushed upon them, and after having killed the greatest part of the men, took eighty horses loaded with what they termed white stone. This I suppose to have been silver, as he told me the horses were shod with it, and that their bridles were ornamented with the same. When they had satiated their revenge, they carried off their spoil, and being got so far as to be out of the reach of the Spaniards that had escaped their fury, they left the useless and ponderous burthen with which the horses were loaded, in the woods, and mounting themselves, in this manner returned to their friends. The party they had thus defeated I conclude to be the caravan that annually conveys to Mexico the silver which the Spaniards find in great quantities on the mountains lying near the heads of the Colorado River; and the plains where the attack was made, probably, some they were obliged to pass over, in their way to the heads of the river St. Fee, or Rio del Nord, which falls into the Gulf of Mexico to the west of the Mississippi." (Carver's Travels.)

At this time, the town of the Winnebagoes contained about fifty houses, which were strongly built, with palisades; the island and land adjacent to the lake was very fertile, and the Indians raised on it a great quantity of Indian corn, beans, pumpkins, squash, and water-melons, with some tobacco. The nation was then able to raise about two hundred warriors; about forty miles up the Fox River from the great town stood a smaller town of the same people, the population of which Carver does not give, but his estimate of the number of warriors, if including all, shows the Winnebagoes at that time to have been weak in comparison with the neighbouring nations.

## Note G. Page 147.

On the 8th of October we got our canoes into the Ouisconsin River, which at this place is more than a hundred yards wide, and the next day arrived at the great town of the Saukies. This is the largest and best built Indian town I ever saw. It contains about ninety houses, each large enough for several families. These are built of hewn plank neatly jointed, and covered with bark so compactly as to keep out the most penetrating rains. Before the doors are placed comfortable sheds, in which the inhabitants sit, when the weather will permit, and smoke their pipes. The streets are regular and spacious, so that it appears more like a civilized town than the abode of savages. The land near the town is very good. In their plantations, which lie adjacent to their houses, and which are neatly laid out, they raise great quantities of Indian corn, beans, melons, &c., so that this place is esteemed the best market for traders to furnish themselves with provisions, of any within eight hundred miles of it.

The Saukies can raise about three hundred warriors, who are generally employed every summer in making incursions into the territories of the Illinois and Pawnee nations, from whence they return with a great number of slaves. But those people frequently retaliate, and in their turn destroy many of the Saukies, which I judge to be the reason that they increase no faster.

While I stayed here I took a view of some mountains that lie about fifteen miles to the southward, and abound in lead ore. I ascended one of the highest of these, and had an extensive view of the country. For many miles, nothing was to be seen but lesser mountains, which appeared at a distance like hay-cocks, they being free from trees. Only a few groves of hickory and stunted oaks covered some of the valleys. So plentiful is lead here, that I saw large quantities of it lying about the streets in the town, belonging to the Saukies, and it seemed to be as good as the produce of other countries. (Carver's Travels.)

---

## Note H. Page 163.

The following account of Clark's expedition is compiled from Monette, Perkins, Hall's Sketches of the West, Butler's Kentucky, and other authorities.

About the last of June the expedition arrived at the "Old Cherokee

Fort," below the mouth of the Tennessee, and about forty miles above the mouth of the Ohio. At this point Clark received two important pieces of information: one item, was the alliance of France with the colonies; this at once made the American side popular with the French and Indians of Illinois and the lakes; France having never lost her hold upon her ancient subjects and allies, and England having never secured their confidence. The other item was, that the inhabitants of Kaskaskia and the other old towns had been led by the British to believe that the Long Knives, or Virginians, were the most fierce, cruel, and blood-thirsty savages that ever scalped a foe. With this impression on their minds, Clark saw that proper management would readily dispose them to submit from fear, if surprised, and then to become friendly from gratitude, when treated with unlooked for clemency.

Having obtained experienced guides through the wilderness, Colonel Clark determined to march through by land, and take Kaskaskia by surprise. He sunk his boats for concealment, and plunged into the pathless wilderness, across extensive marshes and low grounds, through woods and over prairies, each man bearing upon his back his scanty rations, baggage, and camp equipage, but encouraged by the dauntless energy of their commander. At length they arrived, unperceived, in the vicinity of Kaskaskia, on the evening of the 4th of July. To avoid discovery, the troops remained concealed in the woods on the east side of Kaskaskia River, within two miles of the town, until night had obscured their movements from observation. Having procured boats for crossing the river, about midnight Colonel Clark prepared to advance against the enemy. A portion of the troops under command of Captain Helm crossed the river to the town, and having taken it by surprise, the principal street was secured while the inhabitants were asleep in their beds. Every avenue was guarded before they were apprized of their captivity.

On the opposite side of the river, Fort Gage was secured in like manner by the remainder of the force under Colonel Clark himself. The garrison and the sleeping commandant, Lieutenant-governor Rocheblave, were awakened from their peaceful slumbers only to find themselves prisoners of war. Apprehending no danger at this remote point, not even a sentinel was on duty, nor a gate secured. Colonel Clark, leading his column, was conducted silently by a guide, (whom he had taken prisoner during the evening,) through a postern gate into the open fort, and while with his sturdy warriors he surrounded the sleeping garrison, and controlled the defences of the post, the fearless Simon Kenton, at the head of a file of men, advanced softly to the apartment of the commander. While quietly reposing by his wife, he was aroused by a gentle touch only to behold his own captivity, and to order the unconditional surrender of the fort and its defenders.

The town of Kaskaskia, containing about two hundred and fifty houses, was completely surrounded, and every avenue securely guarded to prevent escape or intercourse; runners were sent to warn the people, in the French tongue, that every enemy found in the streets would be instantly shot down; at the same time they were convinced, by the terrible shout and yelling of the troops around the town, that they were all prisoners of war. A strict patrol was kept on duty during the night, throughout the town, and a sergeant's guard passing through the streets, and entering every house, succeeded in completely disarming the inhabitants in the course of two hours. The troops in the suburbs of the place were directed to keep up, during the remainder of the night, a continued tumult and whooping, after the Indian fashion, while the inhabitants were required to observe the most profound silence. All intercourse from house to house was strictly prohibited, and the terror inspired was general and appalling. At the same time Colonel Clark had full possession of the fort and its artillery, which commanded the whole town from the opposite side of the river.

Such was the work of the first night, during which this handful of brave backwoodsmen accomplished one of the most important conquests in the west without the shedding of a drop of blood, or committing the slightest outrage upon the conquered people. The wife of Mr. Rocheblave artfully concealed his public papers, which Colonel Clark did not succeed in obtaining, no search having been made among the luggage of the lady.

On the next day, Colonel Clark proceeded to organize the affairs of the conquered post. Having obtained ample intelligence of the state of the defences in the vicinity, and having properly secured his prisoners and all suspicious persons, he ordered the troops to be withdrawn from the town, behind an eminence in view. All communication between suspicious persons and the troops was strictly prohibited, and several militia officers in the British service were unceremoniously placed in irons. An air of stern severity and prompt decision was assumed by the colonel, which struck terror into the citizens: every movement was made with the most rigid military discipline, enforced by the severest penalties; the most unqualified submission was required from every individual in the town, which was placed under strict martial law; his words were few and stern; and a general gloom appeared to gather over every countenance. They were now prisoners of war to that inexorable enemy whom they had been taught to view as the most terrible of the "Bostonais," and all their fears and apprehensions were about to be realized.

At length the village priest, Father Gibault, at the head of six principal men of the town, was deputed to wait upon the American commander, to supplicate his mercy and to deprecate his vengeance. They were introduced to him at his quarters, where he and his officers were seated. At the first sight of the sturdy warriors, Father Gibault and his associates for some minutes were almost speechless; all their fears and prejudices were more than realized in the rough and severe features of the men, no less than in their tattered and soiled apparel. The reverend father at length spoke, and stated that they had one small request to make of the American commander, which they desired as a special favour.

As the people expected to be torn from each other, and probably separated forever, they begged, through him, to be permitted first to assemble in their church, to take a farewell of each other. Their request was granted, but they were warned not to attempt to leave the town. The colonel's replies were laconic and austere. The deputation were disposed to continue the interview, but with a wave of the hand they were informed that he had no leisure for further intercourse, and they retired. The whole village attended at church, and at length retired to their houses. The deputation again waited upon Colonel Clark, and tendered "their thanks for the indulgence they had received." They further continued, "they were sensible that theirs was the fate of war, and they could not well submit to lose their property;" but they prayed not to be separated from their wives and children, and that something might be allowed for their support. They declared that heretofore, in their conduct, they had only obeyed their commandants, as their duty required; that they were ignorant of the nature of the contest between the United States and Great Britain; and that many of them felt more favourably inclined toward the people of the United States than they dared avow.

At this time, when their anxiety and fears were most excited, they were thus sternly addressed by the commander:—"Do you mistake us for savages? From your language, surely you do. Do you think Americans will strip women and children, and take the bread out of their mouths? My countrymen disdain to make war upon helpless innocence. To prevent the horrors of Indian butchery upon our own wives and children, we have taken arms, and penetrated to this remote stronghold of Indian and British barbarity, and not for despicable plunder. The King of France has now united his powerful arms with those of America, and the contest will soon be ended. The people of Kaskaskia may side with either party; their property and families shall be safe; their religion shall not be molested by Americans. To verify my words, go tell your fellow citizens they are at liberty to do as they please, without apprehension of danger from me. I know they are convinced, since my arrival, that they have been misinformed by British officers as to the character of Americans. Your friends shall be released from confinement."

The deputation attempted to apologise for the imputation implied against the American character, but it was unnecessary; they were desired to communicate his declaration to the people. In a few moments the gloom and dejection of the whole town was changed into the extravagance of joy. The bells rang their loudest peals, and the church was crowded with grateful hearts, offering up to God their devout thanks for their unexpected deliverance from all the horrors they had anticipated.

Thus relieved from their state of fearful anxiety, the people expressed their admiration of the generous conduct of the commander and his troops, and professed their firm attachment to the cause and government of the United States, and of the commonwealth of Virginia especially.

On the evening of the same day, Colonel Clark despatched a detachment of troops under Captain Bowman to surprise and capture the post and village of Cahokia, on the banks of the Mississippi. The capture of this post was effected with the same secrecy and celerity which characterized the movements upon Kaskaskia. In this measure Captain Bowman was aided by many citizens of the latter place, who volunteered to serve as guides, and to lend their friendly influence with their countrymen at Cahokia, to ensure the successful issue of the enterprize. The people gladly espoused the American cause.

Every post and settlement on the Upper Mississippi having been secured, Colonel Clark proceeded to reorganize the civil government by placing in office chiefly those who were citizens of the country. The people rejoiced at the change, and acknowledged themselves a colony dependent on Virginia, well pleased with the protection of the United States, which were now at war with the hereditary enemy of France.

On the 18th of July, the inhabitants of Vincennes, at the recommendation of Father Gibault, parish priest of Kaskaskia, threw off their allegiance to the King of Great Britain, and voluntarily declared themselves citizens of the United States, and of the State of Virginia. The commandant of the Wabash, Captain Abbott, being absent at Detroit, and the post at Vincennes being protected by only a small garrison, Colonel Clark, early in August, having appointed Captain Helm commandant of Fort Sackville, and "Agent for Indian Affairs in the department of the Wabash," despatched him with a small garrison to take possession of the post of St. Vincent, and to await the arrival of reinforcements from Virginia. The new commander, under the instructions of Colonel Clark, soon succeeded in convening an Indian council of influential warriors, and the great Wabash chief, Tobacco, or "Grand Door;" with whom a treaty was effected, which conciliated the Wabash tribes as far north as Ouiatenon and the Wea towns.

September came, and but few recruits from Virginia had arrived; many of Clark's men had been enlisted for only three months; seventy of them returned to Kentucky, the remainder were re-enlisted by Colonel Clark, and with an additional company of resident inhabitants under their own officers, he organized two garrisons, one under Captain Williams at Kaskaskia, and one under Captain Bowman at Cahokia.

Before the middle of December all appearance of Indian hostility had vanished; the people of Vincennes remained firmly attached to the cause of the United States, and in their allegiance to the commonwealth of Virginia. Captain Helm was left with only two soldiers, and a few volunteer militia to protect the fort at Vincennes. The whole regular force at Kaskaskia and Cahokia was reduced to less than one hundred men.

This state of things was soon made known to Governor Hamilton, the British commander at Detroit. The success of the Virginia troops, and the disasters of the British arms had both alarmed and mortified him, and he determined to make an energetic invasion of the Illinois country, retrieve the honour of his Majesty's arms by the recapture of all the posts on the Wabash and Illinois, and lead Clark and his followers captive to Detroit.

Having assembled six hundred Indian warriors, in addition to his force of eighty regular soldiers, and some Canadian militia, he set out upon the expedition to Vincennes, and approached that post about the middle of December. Captain Helm and his few associates were upon duty, and witnessed the savage host which swarmed around the approaching column of red-coated Britons. The British commander, having determined to carry the fort by assault, advanced to the attack.

Captain Helm preserved the presence of mind of a backwoods warrior; with an air of confidence, and as if supported by hundreds of defenders in the fort, he sprang upon a bastion containing a well charged six-pounder, ranged to the advancing enemy, and with a voice of thunder, as he brandished his match in the air, commanded the column to "halt," or he would blow them to atoms. Surprised at such daring, and fearing a desperate resistance by the garrison, which possibly might far exceed his expectation, the British commander ordered a halt until a parley was opened. To the demand for the surrender of the fort, Captain Helm replied, that with the full "honours of war," he would surrender the post, but otherwise he would resist while a man lived to shoulder his rifle. The Briton agreed to allow him all the "honours of war;" and when the fort was thrown open, Captain Helm and five, others with due formality, marched out and laid down their arms before the astonished commander.

The people of Vincennes of course were obliged again to acknowledge the authority of England, and renounce that of the United States and Virginia. Captain Helm and one other American were retained as prisoners of war; the other three being volunteer citizens of Vincennes. Here ended the efficient operations of Colonel Hamilton toward the discomfiture of Colonel Clark. Winter having set in, he determined to postpone the recapture of Kaskaskia and its dependencies until the opening of spring, when he expected a reinforcement of two hundred warriors from Michillimackinac, and five hundred Cherokees and Chickasas from the south. With these forces, in addition to his present command, he had made his calculations of capturing Colonel Clark and his handful of backwoodsmen, and of prostrating the American settlements on the Ohio, by "sweeping Kentucky and Virginia," on his route to Fort Pitt.

Late in January, 1779, Colonel Clark received intelligence that Colonel Hamilton was at Vincennes, with only eighty soldiers under his command, and was uusupported by his savage allies, yet contemplated the reduction of the post of Kaskaskia in the spring. To avoid the very disagreeable alternative of being captured and led a prisoner to Detroit, Clark determined to make an energetic movement with such forces as he could raise, and anticipate his rival's movements, by capturing Fort Sackville, and sending Colonel Hamilton a prisoner to the capital of Virginia.

Accordingly, he prepared to make a sudden and unexpected march upon Vincennes with his whole disposable force, which was increased by two companies raised in Kaskaskia and Cahokia, and such recruits as he could muster in ten days, the whole amounting to only one hundred and seventy men. A large keel boat was fitted up as a galley, and mounted with two four-pounder cannon and four swivels, and furnished with a suitable supply of provisions, amunition, and military stores. This vessel was placed under the command of Captain John Rodgers, with a company of forty-six men, with orders to penetrate up the Wabash within a few miles of the mouth of White River, and there to take up his position and wait for further orders, permitting none to pass up or down the river.

On the 7th of February, Colonel Clark with the remainder of his force, amounting to one hundred and thirty men, set out upon a perilous march of one hundred and fifty miles through the wilderness, northeast, to Vincennes. The route was an Indian trace, which lay through deep forests and prairies; the weather was uncommonly wet; the water courses were out of their banks; and the larger streams had inundated their bottoms from bluff to bluff, often three or four miles in width; but the hardy backwoodsmen, under their intrepid and persevering leader, pressed forward in spite of every obstacle. On foot, with their rifles on their shoulders, and their knapsacks filled with parched corn and jerked beef, for six days they advanced along the trace, through forests, marshes, ponds, swollen streams, and inundated lowlands, for nearly one hundred miles, when they arrived at the crossings of the little Wabash, where the bottoms, to the width of three miles were inundated to the depth of three feet, never under two, and frequently over four. Through these lowlands the whole battalion were compelled to march, often feeling for the trace with their feet, and carrying their arms and ammunition over their heads to protect them from the water.

Five days more brought them to the Wabash, just below the mouth of the Embarras River, and nine miles below the post of Vincennes. Here great difficulty was encountered in crossing the river. No boats were within reach, and the galley had not arrived. Nearly two days were spent in unavailing efforts to cross the river; the men became discouraged, and starvation seemed to await them in their present situation. At length, on the evening of the 20th, a boat was captured, and preparations for crossing the low grounds and the river commenced. After great difficulty in crossing the river, they traversed low grounds by wading often up to their armpits, and reached the opposite highlands nearly exhausted by fatigue, fasting, and cold. Here they remained to recruit their exhausted bodies, and to prepare for their appearance before Fort Sackville. Such had been their hardships by day and at night, by hunger and exposure in the water, that the comparative mildness of the season alone prevented this gallant little band from perishing almost in sight of the object of their toils.[1]

The following extracts from Colonel Clark's journal, of the expedition against Vincennes, present a vivid picture of the sufferings of the party, and a correct account of their final success in the capture of the post, which put an end to British dominion in the Illinois country, and preserved the eastern States from further Indian depredations during the American revolution. The original manuscript of Colonel Clark's narrative, which is in the possession of Lyman C. Draper, Esq., of Madison, soon to be published by him is highly interesting.

"The most of the weather that we had on this march was moist and warm for the season. This was the coldest night we had, (February 21st.) The ice in the morning was from one-half to three-quarters of an inch

---

[1] Jefferson's Corresp. Randolph's ed., vol. 1., p. 451.

thick, near the shores and in still water. The morning (February 22d) was the finest we had on our march. A little after sunrise I lectured the whole. What I said to them I forget; but it may be easily imagined by a person that could possess my affections for them at that time. I concluded by informing them, that passing the plain that was then in full view, and reaching the opposite woods, would put an end to their fatigue; that in a few hours they would have a sight of their long wished for object; and immediately stepped into the water without waiting for any reply. A huzza took place. As we generally marched through the water in a line, before the third entered, I halted and calling to Major Bowman, ordered him to fall in the rear with twenty-five men, and put to death any man who refused to march, as we wished to have no such person among us. The whole gave a cry of approbation, and on we went. This was the most trying of all the difficulties we had experienced. I generally kept fifteen or twenty of the strongest men next myself, and judged from my own feelings what must be that of others. Getting about the middle of the plain, the water about mid-deep, I found myself sensibly failing; and as there were no trees nor bushes for the men to support themselves by, I feared that many of the most weak would be drowned. I ordered the canoes to make the land, discharge their loading, and ply backwards and forwards with all diligence and pick up the men; and to encourage the party, sent some of the strongest men forward with orders, when they got to a certain distance, to pass the word back that the water was getting shallow; and when getting near the woods to cry out "Land!" This stratagem had its desired effect. The men, encouraged by it, exerted themselves almost beyond their abilities—the weak holding by the stronger. * * * The water never got shallower, but continued deepening. Getting to the woods where the men expected land, the water was up to my shoulders; but gaining the woods was of great consequence; all the low men, and the weakly, hung to the trees, and floated on the old logs, until they were taken off by the canoes. The strong and tall got ashore and built fires. Many would reach the shore and fall with their bodies half in the water, not being able to support themselves without it.

"This was a delightful dry spot of ground of about ten acres. We soon found that the fires answered no purpose; but that two strong men taking a weaker one by the arms, was the only way to recover him,—and being a delightful day, it soon did. But fortunately, as if designed by Providence, a canoe of Indian squaws and children was coming up to town, and took through part of this plain as a nigh way. It was discovered by our canoes as they were out after the men. They gave chase and took the Indian canoe, on board of which was near half a quarter of a buffalo, some corn, tallow, kettles, &c. This was a grand prize and was invaluable. Broth was immediately made and served out to the most weakly, with great care: most of the whole got a little; but a great many gave their part to the weakly, jocosely saying something cheering to their comrades. This little refreshment and fine weather, by the afternoon gave new life to the whole. Crossing a narrow deep lake in the canoes, and marching some distance, we came to a copse of timber called the Warrior's Island. We were now in full view of the fort and town, not a shrub between us, at about two miles distance. Every man now feasted his eyes, and forgot that he had suffered any thing,—saying, that all that had passed was owing to good policy, and nothing but what a man could bear, and that a soldier had no right to think, &c. —passing from one extreme to another, which is common in such cases. It was now we had to display our abilities. The plain between us and the town was not a perfect level. The sunken grounds were covered with water, full of ducks. We observed several men out on horseback, shooting them, within half a mile of us; and sent out as many of our active young Frenchmen to decoy and take one of these men prisoner, in such a manner as not to alarm the others, which they did. The information we got from this person was similar to that which we got from those we took on the river; except that of the British having that evening completed the wall of the fort, and that there was a good many Indians in town.

"Our situation was now truly critical—no possibility of retreating in case of defeat—and in full view of a town that had at this time upwards of six hundred men in it, troops, inhabitants, and Indians. The crew of the galley, though not fifty men, would have been now a reinforcement of immense magnitude to our little army, (if I may so call it,) but we would not think of them. We were now in the situation that I had laboured to get ourselves in. The idea of being made prisoner was foreign to almost every man, as they expected nothing but torture from the savages if they fell into their hands. Our fate was now to be determined, probably in a few hours. We knew that nothing but the most daring conduct would insure success. I knew that a number of the inhabitants wished us well—that many were lukewarm to the interest of either—and I also learned that the grand chief, the Tobacco's son, had, but a few days before, openly declared in council with the British, that he was a brother and friend to the Big Knives. These were favourable circumstances; and as there was but little probability of our remaining until dark undiscovered, I determined to begin the career immediately, and wrote the following placard to the inhabitants:—

"'To the Inhabitants of Post Vincennes.

"Gentlemen—Being now within two miles of your village, with my army, determined to take your fort this night, and not being willing to surprise you, I take this method to request such of you as are true citizens and willing to enjoy the liberty I bring you, to remain still in your houses. And those, if any there be, that are friends to the king, will instantly repair to the fort and join the *hair-buyer* general, and fight like men. And if any such as do not go to the fort shall be discovered afterward, they may depend on severe punishment. On the contrary, those who are true friends to liberty may depend on being well treated; and I once more request them to keep out of the streets. For every one I find in arms on my arrival, I shall treat as an enemy.

"'(Signed,) G. R. CLARK.'

"A little before sunset we moved and displayed ourselves in full view of the town—crowds gazing at us. We were plunging ourselves into certain destruction or success. There was no midway thought of. We had but little to say to our men, except inculcating an idea of the necessity of obedience, &c. We knew they did not want encouraging, and that any thing might be attempted with them that was possible for such a number —perfectly cool, under proper subordination, pleased with the prospect before them, and much attached to their officers. They all declared that they were convinced that an implicit obedience to orders was the only thing that would ensure success—and hoped that no mercy would be shown the person that should violate them. Such language as this from soldiers, to persons in our station, must have been exceedingly agreeable. We moved on slowly in full view of the town; but as it was a point of some consequence to us to make ourselves appear as formidable, we, in leaving the covert that we were in, marched and counter-marched in such a manner that we appeared numerous. In raising volunteers in the Illinois, every person that set about the business had a set of colours given them, which they brought with them, to the amount of ten or twelve pair. These were displayed to the best advantage; and as the low plain we marched through was not a perfect level, but had frequent risings in it, seven or eight feet higher than the common level, (which was covered with water,) and as these risings generally run in an oblique direction to the town, we took the advantage of one of them, marching through the water under it, which completely prevented our being numbered; but our colours showed considerably above the heights, as they were fixed on long poles procured for the purpose, and at a distance made no despicable appearance; and as our young Frenchmen had, while we lay on the Warrior's Island, decoyed and taken several fowlers, with their horses, officers were mounted on these horses, and rode about, more completely to deceive the enemy. In this manner we moved, and directed our march in such a way as to suffer it to be dark before we had advanced more than halfway to the town. We then suddenly altered our direction, and crossed ponds where they could not have suspected us, and about eight o'clock gained the heights back of the town.

"The garrison was soon completely surrounded, and the firing continued without intermission, (except about fifteen minutes a little before day,) until about nine o'clock the following morning. It was kept up by the whole of the troops—joined by a few of the young men of the town, who got permission—except fifty men kept as a reserve. * * * I had made myself fully acquainted with the situation of the fort and town, and the parts relative to each. The cannon of the garrison was on the upper floors of strong block-houses at each angle of the fort, eleven feet above the surface; and the ports so badly cut that many of our troops lay under the fire of them within twenty or thirty yards of the walls. They did no damage except to the buildings of the town, some of which they much shattered; and their musketry, in the dark, employed against woodsmen, covered by houses, palings, ditches, the banks of the river, &c., was but of little avail, and did no injury to us, except wounding a man or two. As we could not afford to lose men, great care was taken to preserve them sufficiently covered, and to keep up a hot fire in order to intimidate the enemy as well as destroy them. The embrasures of their cannon were frequently shut, for our riflemen finding the true direction of them, would pour in such volleys when they were opened, that the men could not stand to the guns: seven or eight of them in a short time got cut down. Our troops would frequently abuse the enemy, in order to aggravate them to open their ports and fire their cannon, that they might have the pleasure of cutting them down with their rifles—fifty of which perhaps would be levelled the moment the port flew open; and I believe that if they had stood at their artillery, the greater part of them would have been destroyed in the course of the night, as the greater part of our men lay within thirty yards of the walls; and in a few hours were covered equal to those within the walls, and much more experienced in that mode of fighting.

* * * * * *

"Sometimes an irregular fire, as hot as possible, was kept up from different directions, for a few minutes, and then only a continual scattering fire at the ports as usual; and a great noise and laughter immediately commenced in different parts of the town, by the reserved parties, as if they had only fired on the fort a few minutes for amusement; and as if those continually firing at the fort were only regularly relieved. Conduct similar to this kept the garrison constantly alarmed.

"Thus the attack continued until about nine o'clock on the morning of the 24th. Learning that the two prisoners they had brought in the day before, had a considerable number of letters with them, I supposed it an express that we expected about this time, which I knew to be of the greatest moment to us, as we had not received one since our arrival in the country; and not being fully acquainted with the character of our enemy, we were doubtful that those papers might be destroyed; to prevent which, I sent a flag, with a letter, demanding the garrison."

(The following is a copy of the letter which was addressed by Colonel Clark to Lieutenant-governor Hamilton, on this occasion; it is extracted from Major Bowman's MS. Journal, as quoted in Perkins's Annals, p. 208.)

"Sir—In order to save yourself from the impending storm that now threatens you, I order you immediately to surrender yourself, with all your garrison, stores, &c. For if I am obliged to storm, you may depend on such treatment as is justly due to a murderer. Beware of destroying stores of any kind, or any papers or letters that are in your possession, or hurting one house in town—for by heavens! if you do, there shall be no mercy shown you.

(Signed,) G. R. Clark."

To this the governor replied that he could not think of being "awed into any action unworthy a British subject;" but perhaps his true feelings were exhibited, when he inquired of Captain Helm, (who was his prisoner,) if "Colonel Clark was a merciful man."

Finding the British unwilling to yield quietly, Colonel Clark renewed the firing with increased vigour; the soldiers of the fort did not dare to look out of the loop-holes, as several were shot by balls which came through these apertures: at length Hamilton sent out a flag with the following letter:—

"Lieutenant-governor Hamilton proposes to Colonel Clark a truce for three days; during which time he promises there shall be no defensive works carried on in the garrison, on condition that Colonel Clark shall observe on his part, a like cessation of any defensive work; that is, he wishes to confer with Colonel Clark as soon as can be; and promises that whatever may pass between them two, and another person mutually agreed upon to be present, shall remain secret till matters be finished, as he wishes, that whatever the result of the conference may be, it may tend to the honour and credit of each party. If Colonel Clark makes a difficulty of coming into the fort, Lieutenant-governor Hamilton will speak to him by the gate.

"(Signed,) HENRY HAMILTON.

"24th February, '79."

We now resume our extracts from Clark's MS. journal:—

"I was at a great loss to conceive what reason Lieutenant-governor Hamilton could have for wishing a truce of three days, on such terms as he proposed. Numbers said it was a scheme to get me into their possession. I had a different opinion, and no idea of his possessing such sentiments; as an act of that kind would infallibly ruin him. Although we had the greatest reason to expect a reinforcement in less than three days, that would at once put an end to the siege, I yet did not think it prudent to agree to the proposals, and sent the following answer:

"'Colonel Clark's compliments to Lieutenant-governor Hamilton, and begs leave to inform him, that he will not agree to any terms other than Mr. Hamilton's surrendering himself and garrison prisoners at discretion. If Mr. Hamilton is desirous of a conference with Colonel Clark, he will meet him at the church with Captain Helm.

"'(Signed,) G. R. C.

"'February 24th, '79.'

"We met at the church about eighty yards from the fort—Lieutenant-governor Hamilton, Major Hay, Superintendent of Indian Affairs, Captain Helm, their prisoner, Major Bowman, and myself. The conference began. Hamilton produced terms of capitulation, signed, that contained various articles, one of which was that the garrison should be surrendered, on their being permitted to go to Pensacola on parole. After deliberating on every article, I rejected the whole. He then wished that I would make some proposition. I told him that I had no other to make, than what I had already made—that of his surrendering as prisoners at discretion. I said that his troops had behaved with spirit; that they could not suppose that they would be worse treated in consequence of it; that if he chose to comply with the demand, though hard, perhaps the sooner the better; that it was in vain to make any proposition to me; that he, by this time, must be sensible that the garrison would fall; that both of us must regard all blood spilt for the future by the garrison as murder; that my troops were already impatient and called aloud for permission to tear down and storm the fort; if such a step was taken, many of course would be cut down, and the result of an enraged body of woodsmen breaking in, must be obvious to him; it would be out of the power of an American officer to save a single man. Various altercation took place for a considerable time. Captain Helm attempted to moderate our fixed determination. I told him he was a British prisoner, and it was doubtful whether or not he could with propriety speak on the subject. Hamilton then said that Captain Helm was from that, liberated, and might use his pleasure. I informed the captain that I would not receive him on such terms—that he must return to the garrison and await his fate. I then told Lieutenant-colonel Hamilton, that hostilities should not commence until five minutes after the drums gave the alarm. We took our leave and parted but a few steps, when Hamilton stopped and politely asked me if I would be so kind as to give him my reasons for refusing the garrison, on any terms than those I had offered. I told him I had no objections in giving him my real reasons, which were simply these: that I knew the greater part of the principal Indian partisans of Detroit were with him; that I wanted an excuse to put them to death, or otherwise treat them as I thought proper; that the cries of the widows and the fatherless on the frontiers, which they had occasioned, now required their blood from my hands, and that I did not choose to be so timorous as to disobey the absolute commands of their authority, which I looked upon to be next to divine; that I would rather lose fifty men, than not to empower myself to execute this piece of business with propriety; that if he chose to risk the massacre of his garrison for their sakes, it was his own pleasure; and that I might perhaps take it into my head to send for some of those widows to see it executed. Major Hay paying great attention, I had observed a kind of distrust in his countenance, which in a great measure influenced my conversation during this time. On my concluding, "Pray, sir," said he, "who is that you call Indian partisans?" "Sir," I replied, "I take Major Hay to be one of the principal." I never saw a man in the moment of execution so struck as he appeared to be—pale and trembling—scarcely able to stand. Hamilton blushed, and I observed was much affected at his behaviour. Major Bowman's countenance sufficiently explained his disdain for the one, and his sorrow for the other. * * * Some moments elapsed without a word passing on either side. From that moment my resolutions changed respecting Hamilton's situation. I told him that we would return to our respective posts; that I would reconsider the matter, and let him know the result; no offensive measures should be taken in the mean time. Agreed to, and we parted. What had passed, being made known to our officers, it was agreed that we should moderate our resolutions."

From Major Bowman's MS. journal, as quoted by Perkins, p. 212, the following is extracted:—

In the course of the afternoon of the 24th, the following articles were signed, and the garrison capitulated.

I. Lieutenant-governor Hamilton engages to deliver up to Colonel Clark, Fort Sackville, as it is at present, with all the stores, &c.

II. The garrison are to deliver themselves as prisoners of war; and march out with their arms, and accoutrements, &c.

III. The garrison to be delivered up at ten o'clock to-morrow.

IV. Three days' time to be allowed the garrison to settle their accounts with the inhabitants and traders of this place.

V. The officers of the garrison to be allowed their necessary baggage.

Signed at Post St. Vincent, (Vincennes,) 24th February, 1779.

Agreed for the following reasons: the remoteness from succour; the state and quantity of provisions, &c.; unanimity of officers and men in its expediency; the honorable terms allowed; and lastly the confidence in a generous enemy.

(Signed,) HENRY HAMILTON,
Lieutenant-governor and Superintendent.

The MS. of Colonel Clark further observes—

"The business being now nearly at an end, troops were posted in several strong houses around the garrison, and patroled during the night, to prevent any deception that might be attempted. The remainder on duty lay on their arms; and for the first time for many days past got some rest. * * * During the siege I got only one man wounded; not being able to lose many, I made them secure themselves well. Seven were badly wounded in the fort, through ports." * * *

The hardships endured by Colonel Clark's men, in this expedition, may best be shown by giving an extract from Major Joseph Bowman's journal, the MS. of which is quoted in Perkins, p. 202, as follows:—

"February 7th. Began our march early: made a good day's march for about nine leagues. The road very bad with mud and water. Pitched our camp in a square, baggage in the middle, every company to guard their own square.

8th. Marched early, through the waters which we now began to meet in those large and level plains, where from the flatness of the country, the water rests a considerable time before it drains off. Nothwithstanding, our men were in great spirits though much fatigued.

9th. Made another day's march. Rain part of the day.

10th. Crossed the river Petit Fort, upon trees which we felled for that purpose, the water being so high there was no fording it. Still raining and no tents. Encamped near the river. Stormy weather.

11th. Crossed the Saline River. Nothing extraordinary this day.

12th. Marched across Cat Plains. Saw and killed numbers of buffaloes. The road very bad from the immense quantity of rain that had fallen. The men much fatigued. Encamped on the edge of the wood. This plain being fifteen or more miles across, it was late in the night before the baggage and troops got together. Now 21 miles from St. Vincent's.

13th. Arrived early at the two Wabashes; although a league asunder, they are now but one. We set to making a canoe.

14th. Finished the canoe and put her into the river about four o'clock in the afternoon.

15th. Ferried across the two Wabashes, it being three miles in water to the opposite hills, where we encamped. Still raining. Ordered not to fire any guns in future, but in case of necessity.

16th. March all day through rain and water. Crossed the Fir River. Provisions begin to be short.

17th. Marched early. Crossed several runs very deep. Sent Mr. Kennedy, our commissary, with three men to cross the river Embarras, if possible, and proceed to a plantation opposite Post St. Vincent's, in order to steal boats or canoes to ferry us across the Wabash. About an hour by sun, we got near the river Embarras, and found the country all overflowed with water. We strove to find the Wabash. Travelled till three o'clock in mud and water, but could find no place to encamp on. Still keep marching on, but after some time, Mr. Kennedy and his party returned. Found it impossible to pass the Embarras River. We found the water falling, from a small spot of ground. Stayed there the remainder of the night. Drizzly and dark weather.

18th. At break of day, heard Governor Hamilton's morning guns. Set off and marched down the river. Saw some fine lands. About two o'clock came to the bank of the Wabash. Made rafts for four men to cross and go up to town and steal boats, but they spent the day and night in the water to no purpose, for there was not a foot of dry land to be found.

19th. Captain McCarty's company set to making a canoe. At three o'clock the four men returned, after spending the night on some old logs in the water. The canoe finished. Captain McCarty with three of his men embarked in the canoe, and made the next attempt to steal boats. But he soon returned, having discovered four large fires about a league distant from our camp, that seemed to him to be fires of whites and Indians. Immediately Colonel Clark sent two men in the canoe, down to meet the Batteau, with orders to come on day and night, that being our last hope from starving. Many of the men much cast down, particularly the volunteers. No provision of any sort for two days. Hard fortune.

20th. Camp very quiet, but hungry. Many of the Creoles, volunteers, talking of returning. Fell to making more canoes, when about 12 o'clock our sentry brought to, a boat with five Frenchmen from the post, who told us we were not as yet discovered; that the inhabitants were well pleased towards us, &c.

Captain Willing's brother, who was taken in the fort, had made his escape to us, and said that one Masonville, with a party of Indians, were then seven days in pursuit of him, with much news, more news in our favour, such as repairs done to the fort, &c. They informed us of two canoes they had seen adrift some distance above us. Ordered Captain Worthington, with a party of men, to go in search of them. Returned late with one only. One of our men killed a deer, which was distributed in the camp very acceptably.

21st. At break of day began to ferry our men over in our two canoes, to small hills called Mamelles, or breasts. Captain Williams with two men went to look for a passage; but were discovered by two men in a canoe, but could not bring them to. The whole army being over, we thought to get to town that night, so, plunged into the water, sometimes to the neck, for more than a league, when we stopped on the next hill of the same name, there being no dry land on any side for many leagues. Our pilot says we cannot get along—that it was impossible. The whole army being over, we encamped. Rain all this day. No provisions."

From the same journal, the following note is made by Perkins:—

"During the conference at the church, some Indian warriors who had been sent to the Falls of the Ohio, for scalps and prisoners, were discovered on their return, as they entered the plains near Post Vincennes. A party of the American troops commanded by Captain Williams went out to meet them. The Indians, who mistook this detachment for a party of their friends, continued to advance, with all the parade of successful warriors." "Our men," says Major Bowman, "killed two on the spot: wounded three; took six prisoners, and brought them into town. Two of them proved to be whites; we released them and brought the Indians to the main street before the fort-gate; there tomahawked them, and threw them into the river." (Major Bowman's MS. journal.)

---

## NOTE I. Page 170.

A search into the old journals of Congress on the subject of the cession by the States of the western lands, for the common benefit, and the future disposition of the territory by the United States, will produce some curious information. In April, 1784, a plan for the temporary government of the newly acquired territory was reported by Mr. Jefferson; it contained a provision prohibiting slavery northwest of the Ohio, after the year 1800; and this was the origin of the anti-slavery article embodied in the ordinance of 1787, and so often referred to in political writings and in congressional debate. Mr. Jefferson was in France as Minister in 1785–6–7, when the subject of the future government was often under discussion in Congress. It has been generally conceded, that to Nathan Dane, of Massachusetts, belongs the honour of having drawn up the ordinance of 1787, and of having been one of the most strenuous supporters of the anti-slavery proviso; but the original paternity of this important clause must in all juctice be ascribed to the apostle of liberty, Thomas Jefferson; later times, later events, and a later application of the principles of the renowned sixth article of the ordinance of 1787, have conspired to wrest the deserved honours from Jefferson and Dane, and to obscure its origin by giving it the name of the "Wilmot proviso."

On the 19th of April, 1784, Mr. Spaight, of North Carolina, moved to strike from Mr. Jefferson's plan, the clause prohibiting slavery after 1800, which motion prevailed. From that day until the 23d, the plan was debated and altered, and then passed unanimously, with the exception of South Carolina. By this proposition, the territory was to have been divided into States, by parallels of latitude, and meridian lines; this it was thought would have made ten States, which were to have been named as follows, beginning at the northwest corner and going southwardly:—Sylvania, Michigania, Chersonesus, Assenisipia, Metropotamia, Illinoia, Saratoga, Washington, Polypotamia, and Pelesipia. Surely, (says Sparks,) the hero of Mount Vernon must have shuddered to find himself in such company.

---

## Note K. Page 173.

The substance of the following note is taken from the remarks of Mr. Benton, of Missouri, made in the House of Congress on the 25th of April, 1854, on the subject of the provisions of the "Nebraska Bill;" the remarks exhibit in a lucid view the character and effect of the several compromises on the subject of slavery, which have their particular bearing on the north-western portion of the Union. Its importance may justify this note.

"There are three slavery compromises in our history, which connect themselves with the foundation and preservation of this Union. First, the territorial partition ordinance of 1787, with its clause for the recovery of fugitive slaves; secondly, the contemporaneous constitutional recognition of slavery, in the States which chose to have it, with the fugitive slave recovery clause in the same instrument; thirdly, the Missouri partition line of 1820, with the same clause annexed for the recovery of fugitive slaves.

"All three of these compromises are part and parcel of the same policy; and neither of them could have been formed without the other, nor either of them without the fugitive slave recovery clause incorporated in it. The anti slavery clause in the ordinance of 1787 could not have been adopted, (as was proved by its three years' rejection,) without the fugitive slave recovery clause added to it; the constitution could not have been formed without its recognition of slavery in the States which chose it, and the guarantee of the right to recover slaves fleeing into the free States; the Missouri controversy could not have been settled without a partition of Louisiana between free and slave soil; and that partition could not have been made without the addition of the same clause for the recovery of fugitive slaves. Thus all three compromises are settlements of existing questions, and intended to be perpetual. They are all three of equal moral validity; the constitutional compromise is guarded by a higher obligation, in consequence of its incorporation in that instrument; but it in no way differs from the other two, in the circumstances which induced it, the policy which guards it, or the consequences which would flow from its abrogation. A proposition to destroy the slavery compromises in the constitution, would be an open proposition to break up the Union; the attempt to abrogate the compromises of 1787 and 1820, would be virtual attempts to destroy the harmony of the Union, and prepare it for dissolution by destroying the confidence and affection in which it is founded.

"The Missouri compromise of 1820 is a continuation of the ordinance of 1787—its extension to the since-acquired territory west of the Mississippi; and no way differing from it, either in principle or in detail. The ordinance of 1787 divided the then territory of the United States about equally between the free and slave States; the Missouri compromise line did the same by the additional territory of the United States as it stood in 1820: and in both cases it was done by act of Congress, and was the settlement of a difficulty which was to last for ever. They are both, with their fugitive slave recovery clauses, and the similar clause in the constitution, part and parcel of the same transaction—different articles in the same general settlement. Thus the three measures are one, and the ordinance of 1787 father of the other two. It led to the adoption of the fugitive slave clause in the constitution, and we may say, to the formation of the constitution itself, which could not have been adopted without that clause, and the recognition of slave property in which it was founded. This vital fact results of itself from the history of the case. In March, of the year 1784, the Virginia delegation in the then Congress of the confederation, headed by Mr. Jefferson and Mr. Monroe, conveyed the north-western territory to the thirteen United States. In the month of April ensuing, the organizing mind of Mr. Jefferson, always bent upon systems and administration, brought in an ordinance for the government of the territory so conveyed, with the anti-slavery clause as a part of it, to take effect in the year 1800; but without a clause for the recovery of fugitive slaves. For the want of this provision, the anti-slavery clause was opposed by the slave-holding States, and rejected; and the ordinance passed without it. In July, of the year 1787, the ordinance was remodelled; the anti-slave clause, with the fugitive slave recovery clause, as they now stand, were inserted in it; and, in that shape, the ordinance had the unanimous vote of every State present—eight in the whole—and an equal number of slave and free States present. Thus it is clear that the anti-slavery clause in the ordinance of 1787, could not have passed without the fugitive slave recovery clause annexed. They were inseparable in their birth, and must be so in their life; and those who love one, must accept the other.

"This was done in the month of July, in the city of New York, where the Congress of the confederation then sat. The National Convention was sitting at the same time, in the city of Philadelphia, at work upon the Federal Constitution. The two bodies were in constant communication with each other, and some leading members (as Mr. Madison and General Hamilton) were members of each, and attending by turns in each. The constitution was finished in September, and received the fugitive slave recovery clause immediately after its insertion in the ordinance. It was the work of the same hands, and at the same time, in both instruments; and it is well known that the constitution could not have been formed without that clause. Thus the compromise clause in the ordinance is father to the compromise clause in the constitution, and the Missouri compromise results from both. All three are founded in the same circumstances, induced by the same considerations, and directed by the same policy—that of the peace, harmony, and perpetuity of this Union."

In the memorable debate in the Senate of the United States, in January, 1830, Mr. Webster, in reply to Mr. Hayne, took occasion to advert to the ordinance of 1787, giving full credit to both Mr. Jefferson and to Nathan Dane, for their framing, modifying, and supporting that instrument, and the very important principles contained in it. In the course of his remarks, speaking of the provision introduced by Mr. Jefferson in 1784, viz., "that, after the year 1800, there shall be neither slavery, nor involuntary servitude in any of the said States, otherwise than in punishment of crimes, of which the party shall have been duly convicted," he observes that Mr. Spaight moved to strike out this paragraph; on the question, "Shall these words stand as part of the plan?" &c., seven States, New Hampshire, Massachusetts, Rhode Island, Connecticut, New York, New Jersey, and Pennsylvania, voted in the affirmative; three States, Maryland, Virginia, and South Carolina, voted in the negative; and North Carolina was divided. As the consent of nine States was necessary, the words could not stand, and were struck out accordingly. Mr. Jefferson voted for the clause, but was overruled by his colleagues.

In March, 1785, Mr. King, of Massachusetts, seconded by Mr. Ellery, of Rhode Island, proposed the formerly rejected article, with this addition, "and that this regulation shall be an article of compact, and remain a fundamental principle of the constitution between the thirteen original States, and each of the States, as described in the Resolve," &c. On this clause, which provided the adequate and thorough security, the eight northern States at that time voted affirmatively, and the four southern States negatively. The votes of nine States were not yet obtained, and thus the provision was again rejected by the southern States. The perseverance of the north held out, and two years afterward the object was attained.

The ordinance of 1787 expresses just sentiments on the great subject of civil and religious liberty; such sentiments were common, and abound in the state papers of that day. But this ordinance did that which was not so common, and which is not, even now, universal. It set forth and declared *as a high and binding duty of government itself*, to encourage schools and advance the means of education; on the plain reason, that religion, morality, and knowledge are necessary to good government, and to the happiness of mankind. One observation further: the important provision incorporated into the constitution of the United States, and several of those of the States, restraining legislative power, in questions of private right, and from impairing the obligation of contracts, is first introduced and established, (as far as I am informed,) as matter of expressed, written, constitutional law, in this ordinance of 1787.

# NOTES TO CHAPTER IV.

## Note A. Page 178.

### WAYNE'S VICTORY.

These two posts were not the only ones which the British occupied in derogation of the treaty; others also were withheld, and new places of defence erected.

The following correspondence between the British commander of a fort on the Maumee, and General Anthony Wayne, the day after the victory of the latter over the confederated Indians, on the Maumee, will be interesting, as showing the feelings of the American commander at the unwarrantable retention and occupation of the frontier posts by the British; and the slight thread upon which hung, at that time, the event of a renewal of hostilities between the United States and Great Britain. Very little was wanting of provocation on the part of Major Campbell, to have induced Wayne to attack the fort, and add its destruction to that of the property of the Indians in the vicinity, and even within pistol-shot of the fort. General Wayne, in his report says, "the garrison were compelled to remain tacit spectators to this general devastation and conflagration, among which were the houses, stores, and property of Colonel McKee, the British Indian Agent, and principal stimulator of the war now existing between the United States and the savages." Marshall, in his Life of Washington, remarks that "hostilities were only avoided by the prudent acquiescence of the British commander, in this devastation of property, within the range of his guns."

*Correspondence reported by General Wayne.*

No. I.

Miami, Maumee River, August 21st, 1794.

Sir—An army of the United States of America, said to be under your command, having taken post on the banks of the Miami, (Maumee,) for upwards of the last twenty-four hours, almost within the reach of the guns of this fort, being a post belonging to his majesty the King of Great Britain, occupied by his majesty's troops, and which I have the honour to command, it becomes my duty to inform myself, as speedily as possible, in what light I am to view your making such near approaches to this garrison. I have no hesitation, on my part, to say, that I know of no war existing between Great Britain and America.

I have the honour to be, sir, with great respect, your most obedient and very humble servant,

William Campbell,
Major 24th Regiment, commanding a British post on the banks of the Miami.

To Major-General Wayne, &c.

No. II.

Camp on the Bank of the Miami, (Maumee,)
August 21st, 1794.

Sir—I have received your letter of this date, requiring from me the motives which have moved the army under my command to the position they at present occupy, far within the acknowledged jurisdiction of the United States of America. Without questioning the authority or the propriety, sir, of your interrogatory, I think I may, without breach of decorum, observe to you, that were you entitled to an answer, the most full and satisfactory one was announced to you from the muzzles of my small arms, yesterday morning, in the action against the horde of savages in the vicinity of your post, which terminated gloriously to the American arms; but had it continued until the Indians, &c. were driven under the influence of the post and guns you mention, they would not have much impeded the progress of the victorious army under my command, as no such post was established at the commencement of the present war between the Indians and the United States.

I have the honour to be, sir, with great respect, your most obedient and very humble servant,

Anthony Wayne,
Major-general and Commander-in-chief of the Federal Army.

To Major Campbell, &c.

No. III.

Fort Miami, August 22d, 1794.

Sir—Although your letter of yesterday's date fully authorizes me to any act of hostility against the army of the United States in this neighbourhood under your command, yet, still anxious to prevent that dreadful decision which, perhaps, is not intended to be appealed to by either of our countries, I have forborne, for these two days past, to resent those insults you have offered to the British flag flying at this fort, by approaching it within pistol-shot of my works, not singly, but in numbers, with arms in their hands. Neither is it my wish to wage war with individuals; but, should you, after this, continue to approach my post in the threatening manner you are at this moment doing, my indispensable duty to my king and country, and the honour of my profession, will oblige me to have recourse to those measures, which thousands of either nation may hereafter have cause to regret, and which, I solemnly appeal to God, I have used my utmost endeavours to arrest.

I have the honour to be, sir, with much respect, your most obedient and very humble servant,

William Campbell,
Major 24th Regiment, commanding at Fort Miami.

Major-General Wayne, &c.

No. IV.

Camp, Banks of the Miami, 22d August, 1794.

Sir—In your letter of the 21st instant, you declare, "I have no hesitation on my part to say, that I know of no war existing between Great Britain and America." I, on my part, declare the same, and that the only cause I have to entertain a contrary idea at present, is the hostile act you are now in commission of, *i. e.* by recently taking post far within the well-known, and acknowledged limits of the United States, and erecting a fortification in the heart of the settlements of the Indian tribes now at war with the United States. This, sir, appears to be an act of the highest aggression, and destructive to the peace and interest of the Union. Hence it becomes my duty to desire, and I do hereby desire and demand, in the name of the President of the United States, that you immediately desist from any further act of hostility or aggression, by forbearing to fortify, and by withdrawing the troops, artillery, and stores under your orders and direction, forthwith, and removing to the nearest post occupied by his Britanic majesty's troops at the peace of 1783, and which you will be permitted to do, unmolested by the troops under my command.

I am, with very great respect, sir, your most obedient and very humble servant,

Anthony Wayne.

Major William Campbell, &c.

No. V.

Fort Miami, 22d August, 1794.

Sir—I have this moment to acknowledge the receipt of your letter of this date; in answer to which I have only to say, that, being placed here in command of a British post, and acting in a military capacity only, I cannot enter into any discussion either on the right or impropriety of my occupying my present position. Those are matters that I conceive will be best left to the ambassadors of our different nations.

Having said this much, permit me to inform you that I certainly will not abandon this post, at the summons of any power whatever, until I receive orders for that purpose from those I have the honour to serve under, or the fortune of war should oblige me. I must still adhere, sir, to the purport of my letter this morning, to desire that your army, or individuals belonging to it, will not approach within reach of my cannon, without expecting the consequences attending it.

Although I have said in the former part of my letter, that my situation here is totally military, yet, let me add, sir, that I am much deceived, if his majesty the King of Great Britain had not a post on this river, at and prior to the period you mention.

I have the honour to be, sir, with the greatest respect, your most obedient and very humble servant,

William Campbell,
Major 24th Regiment, commanding at Fort Miami.

To Major-General Wayne, &c.

The only notice taken of this letter was by immediately setting fire to and destroying every thing within view of the fort, and even under the muzzles of the guns. Had Mr. Campbell carried his threats into execution, it is more than probable he would have experienced a storm. (Remark in Dunlap & Claypole's Am. Daily Adver., October 3d, 1794.)

---

## Note B. Page 186.

In the testimony given by Major Ferguson, in the investigation of the causes of Harmar's defeat, is found the following account of the militia drafted from Kentucky. (See American State Papers, vol. xii. 20.)

"They were very ill equipped, being almost destitute of camp kettles and axes, nor could a supply of these essential articles be procured. Their arms were generally very bad and unfit for service. * * * They came under my inspection in making repairs; as a specimen, one rifle was brought to be repaired without a lock, and another without a stock. * * * They were told in Kentucky that all repairs would be made at Fort Washington. * * The general had many difficulties to encounter in organizing the Kentucky militia on their arrival. Colonel Trotter aspired to the command, although Colonel Hardin was the eldest officer, and in this he was encouraged both by men and officers, who openly declared, unless Colonel Trotter commanded them they would return home. After two or three days, the business was settled, and the Kentucky men were formed into three battalions under the command of Colonel Trotter, and Colonel Hardin had the command of all the militia, both Pennsylvania and Virginia. * * * The last of the Pennsylvania militia arrived on the 25th of September; they were equipped nearly as the Kentucky, but were worse armed, several were without any. * * * The general ordered all the arms in store to be delivered to those who had none, and those whose guns could not be repaired. Among the militia were a great many hardly able to bear arms, such as old, infirm men, and young boys; they were not such as might be expected from a frontier country, smart, active woodsmen, well accustomed to arms, eager and alert to revenge the injuries done them and their connections; no, there were a great many of them substitutes, who probably had never fired a gun. Major Paul, of Pennsylvania, told me that many of his men were so awkward, that they could not take their gun-locks off to oil them and put them on again, nor could they put in their flints so as to be useful; and even of such materials, the numbers came far short of what was ordered, as may be seen by the returns.

---

## Note C. Page 187.

The troops were organized and moved forward as follows:—

The Kentuckians composed three battalions, under the Majors Hall, McMullen, and Ray, with Lieutentant-colonel Commandant Trotter, at their head. The Pennsylvanians were formed into one battalion under Lieutenant-colonel Trubley, and Major Paul, the whole to be commanded by Colonel John Hardin, subject to the orders of General Harmar. The 30th, the general having got forward all the supplies that he expected, he moved out with the Federal troops, formed into two small battalions under the immediate command of Major Wyllys and Major Doughty, together with Captain Ferguson's company of artillery, and three pieces of ordnance. On the 3d of October, General Harmar joined the advanced troops early in the morning; the remaining part of the day was spent in forming the line of march, the order of encampment, and battle, and explaining the same to the militia field-officers. On the 4th, the army took up the order of march; and on the 5th a reinforcement of horsemen and mounted infantry, joined, from Kentucky. The dragoons were formed into two troops; the mounted riflemen made a company, and this small battalion of light troops were put under the command of Major Fontaine.

The whole of General Harmar's command, then, may be stated thus:—

| | | |
|---|---|---|
| Three battalions of Kentucky militia, <br> One " of Pennsylvania militia, <br> One " of light troops mounted, militia, | Total, | 1133 |
| Two battalions of Federal troops, | | 320 |
| | Grand total, | 1453[1] |

## NOTE D. Page 188.

The utter want of discipline in the army, may be conceived from the perusal of the following extracts from the evidence of Captain Armstrong, (then lieutenant,) which was given before the court of inquiry. Lieutenant Armstrong was with Colonel Trotter during the 18th of October, and also with Colonel Hardin on the 19th, when the encounter with the Indians occurred. (See American State Papers, xii. 26.)

On the 18th of October, says Armstrong, after we had proceeded about a mile, the cavalry gave chase to an Indian, who was mounted; him they overtook and killed. Before they returned to the column, a second appeared, on which the four field officers left their commands and pursued, leaving the troops near half an hour without any directions whatever. The cavalry came across the second Indian, and, after he had wounded one of their party, killed him also. When the infantry came up to this place they immediately fell into confusion, upon which I gained permission to leave them some distance on the road, where I formed an ambuscade. After I had been some time at my station, a fellow on horseback came to me, who had lost the party in pursuit of the first Indian; he was much frightened, and said he had been pursued by fifty mounted Indians. On my telling this story to Colonel Trotter, notwithstanding my observations to him, he changed his route, and marched in various directions until night, when he returned to camp.

On our arrival in camp, General Harmar sent for me, and after asking me many questions, ordered one subaltern and twenty militia to join my command. With these I reached the river St. Joseph about ten at night, and with a guide proceeded to an Indian town, about two miles distant, where I continued with my party until the morning of the 19th. About nine o'clock I joined the remainder of the detachment under Colonel Hardin. We marched on the route Colonel Trotter had pursued the day before, and after passing a morass about five miles distant, we

[1] American State Papers, xii. 24.

came to where the enemy had encamped the day before. Here we made a short halt, and the commanding officer disposed of the parties at a distance from each other; after a halt of half an hour, we were ordered to move on, and Captain Faulkner's company was left on the ground; the colonel having neglected giving him orders to move on.

After we had proceeded about three miles we fell in with two Indians on foot, who threw off their packs, and the brush being thick, made their escape. I then asked Colonel Hardin where Captain Faulkner was? He said he was lost, and then sent Major Fontaine with part of the cavalry in search of him, and moved on with the remainder of the troops. Some time after I informed Colonel Hardin that a gun had fired in our front, which might be considered as as alarm gun, and that I saw where a horse had come down the road and returned again; but the colonel still moved on, giving no orders, nor making any arrangements for an attack. Some time after, I discovered the enemy's fires at a distance, and informed the colonel, who replied, that they would not fight, and rode in front of the advance, until fired on from behind the fires; when he, the colonel retreated, and with him all the militia except nine, who continued with me, and were instantly killed, with twenty-four of the Federal troops; seeing my last man fall, and being surrounded by the savages, I threw myself into a thicket, and remained there three hours in daylight; during that time I had the opportunity of seeing the enemy pass and repass, and conceived their numbers did not amount to one hundred men; some were mounted, others armed with rifles, and the advance with tomahawks only. I am of opinion that had Colonel Trotter proceeded, on the 18th, agreeably to his orders, having killed the enemy's sentinels, he would have surprised their camp, and with ease defeated them; or had Colonel Hardin arranged his troops or made any military disposition, on the 19th, that he would have gained a victory. Our defeat I therefore ascribed to two causes; the unofficer-like conduct of Colonel Hardin, (who I believe was a brave man,) and the cowardly behaviour of the militia; many of them threw down their arms loaded, and I believe that none, except the party under my command, fired a gun.

Note.—It is proper to add, that accounts in addition to this statement of Lieutenant Armstrong, say that he was in a swamp or pond up to his neck. (Butler, 192, Cist's Cincinnati Miscellany, i. 183.) Other accounts say he was merely concealed in the swamp, or up to his waist in water. (Cin. Miscel. i. 39. McClung's Sketches, 241.)

## NOTE E. Page 189.

Captain Asheton, in his examination before the court of inquiry, makes the following statement of the occurrences on the 22d of October; it is given in the *third* person, but here changed to the *first*, as Perkins has it in his Annals, p. 342. See also American State Papers, xii. 28, 34. Cist's Cincinnati Miscellany, i. 183. McClung's Sketches, 241.

The detachment marched in three columns, the Federal troops in the centre, at the head of which I was posted, with Major Wyllys and Colonel Hardin in my front; the militia formed the columns to the right and left. From delays occasioned by the militia's halting, we did not reach the banks of the Omee (Maumee) till some time after sunrise. The spies then discovered the enemy, and reported to Major Wyllys, who halted the Federal troops, and moved the militia on, some distance in front, when he gave his orders and plan of attack to the several commanding officers of corps. Those orders were not communicated to me. Major Wyllys reserved the command of the Federal troops to himself. Major Hall, with his battalion, was directed to take a circuitous route round the bend of the Omee river, cross the Pickaway fork, (or St. Mary's,) which brought him directly in the rear of the enemy, and there wait until the attack should commence with Major McMullen's battalion, Major Fontaine's cavalry, and Major Wyllys with the Federal troops, who all crossed the Omee at, and near, the common fording place. After the attack commenced, the troops were by no means to separate, but were to embody, or the battalions to support each other, as circumstances required. From this disposition it appears evident, that it was the intention of Major Wyllys to surround the enemy, and that if Colonel Hall, who had gained his ground undiscovered, had not wantonly disobeyed his orders, by firing on a single Indian, the surprise must have been complete. The Indians then fled with precipitation, the battalions pursuing in different directions. Major Fontaine made a charge upon a small party of savages—he fell, the first fire, and his troops dispersed. The Federal troops, who were then left unsupported, became an easy sacrifice to much the largest party of Indians that had been seen that day. It is my opinion that the misfortunes of that day were owing to the separation of troops, and disobedience of orders. After the Federal troops were defeated, and the firing in all quarters nearly ceased, Colonel Hall and Major McMullen, with their battalions, met in the town, and after discharging, cleaning, and fresh loading their arms, which took up about half an hour, proceeded to join the army unmolested. I am convinced that the detachment, if it had kept embodied, was sufficient to have answered the fullest expectations of the general, and needed no support; but I was informed a battalion under Major Ray was ordered out for that purpose.

"In Hardin's first day's encounter, twenty-three out of thirty of the regulars in Lieutenant Armstrong's company were killed; the remaining seven made their way back to camp. In the second fight, Major Wyllys, with Lieutenant Farthingham, and fifty of the regulars, were left dead on the field, together with one hundred of the militia."

NOTE.—These battles were fought on ground near the junction of the St. Mary's and St. Joseph's Rivers, the site of Fort Wayne; of this fact there is no doubt, but some authorities might lead the reader into error in this matter, without examination. Marshall, in his Life of Washington, says, "the attack was made on Hardin, about ten miles west of *Chillicothe*, where the main body of the army lay." Other writers have stated the same matter in the same language. But it must be understood that the Shawanese had several locations of villages, at different periods, each of which was called "Chillicothe;" this being with them a favourite name. It is sufficient now, to know that the battles were not fought near Chillicothe on the Scioto, this being the only "Chillicothe" known at this day. W. R. S.

---

## NOTE F. Page 193.

We extract the following remarks on these several movements at this period, as presenting a correct summary of events and results; they are found in Perkins's Annals, 353. Colonel Wilkinson, in his report, after destroying the Eel Biver town and cornfields, says, "I commenced my march for the Kickapoo town in the prairie." Perkins remarks—

"The Kickapoo prairie metropolis was not reached; the horses were too sore, and the bogs too deep; but various cornfields were destroyed, (Wilkinson says four hundred and thirty acres of corn,) and a respectable Kickapoo town given to the flames; for which the general was duly thanked by his country. Meanwhile, Proctor was attempting to hurry the slow-moving Iroquois, who told him it took them a great while to think, (this was said by Red Jacket;) and Wilkinson was floundering up to his armpits in mud and water among the morasses of the Wabash; (his own words in his official report;) the needful preparations were constantly going forward for the great expedition of St. Clair, which, by founding posts throughout the Western country from the Ohio to Lake Erie, and especially at the head of the Maumee, was to give the United States a sure means of control over the savages. At a very early period, (1785,) the admirable position of the Miami village at the junction of the St. Mary and St. Joseph, had struck Washington's sagacious mind, as we know from his correspondence; and when Harmar's expedition was undertaken, one purpose of it would doubtless have been the founding of a military post at the Miami town, had it been compatible with the public finances. But Harmar's defeat having proved the necessity of some strong check upon the northern savages, it became the main purpose of the effort of 1791 to build a fort at the point designated, which was to be connected by other intermediate stations, with Fort Washington and the Ohio. Of this we have proof in the language of government after St. Clair's defeat: 'The great object of the campaign,' says General Knox, in his official report dated December 26th, 1791, 'was to establish a strong military post at the Miami village;' this language was used more than once, and this object, too, was to be attained if possible, even at the expense of a contest which might be otherwise avoided."

---

## NOTE G. Page 195.

We make the following extracts from the official report of General St. Clair to the secretary of war, of this melancholy affair. (Am. State Papers, v. 137.)

"The right wing, composed of Butler's, Clarke's, and Patterson's battalions, commanded by Major-general Butler, formed the first line; and the left wing, consisting of Bedinger and Gaither's battalions and the second regiment, commanded by Liutenant-colonel Darke, formed the second line, with an interval between them of about seventy yards, which was all the ground would allow. The right flank was pretty well secured by the creek; a steep bank and Faulkner's corps, some of the cavalry and their pickets, covered the left flank. The militia were thrown over the creek, and advanced about one-quarter of a mile, and encamped in the same order. There were a few Indians who appeared on the opposite side of the creek, but fled with the utmost precipitation on the advance of the militia. At this place, which I judged to be about fifteen miles from the Miami village, I determined to throw up a slight work, the plan of which was concerted that evening with Major Ferguson, wherein to have deposited the men's knapsacks, and every thing else that was not of absolute necessity, and to have moved on to attack the enemy as soon as the first regiment was come up. But they did not permit me to execute either; for on the 4th, about half an hour before sunrise, and when the men had just been dismissed from parade, (for it was constant practice to have them all under arms a considerable time before daylight,) an attack was made upon the militia. Those gave way in a very little time, and rushed into camp through Major Butler's battalion, (which, together with a part of Clarke's, they threw into considerable disorder, and which, notwithstanding the exertions of both those officers, was never altogether remedied,) the Indians following close at their heels. The fire, however, of the front line, checked them; but almost instantly, a very heavy attack began upon that line; and in a few minutes it was extended to the second likewise. The great weight of it was directed against the centre of each, where the artillery was placed, and from which the men were repeatedly driven with great slaughter. Finding no great effect from our fire, and confusion beginning to spread, from the great number of men who were falling in all quarters, it became necessary to try what could be done by the bayonet. Lieutenant-colonel Darke was accordingly ordered to make a charge with part of the second line, and to turn the left flank of the enemy. This was executed with great spirit. The Indians instantly gave way, and were driven back three or four hundred yards; but for want of a sufficient number of riflemen to pursue this advantage, they soon returned, and the troops were obliged to give back in their turn. At this moment they had entered our camp by the left flank, having pushed back the troops that were posted there. Another charge was made here by the second regiment, Butler's and Clarke's battalions, with equal effect, and it was repeated several times, and always with success; but in all of them many men were lost, and particularly the officers, which with so raw troops was a loss altogether irremediable. In that I just spoke of, made by the second regiment and Butler's battalion, Major Butler was dangerously wounded, and every officer of the second regiment fell except three, one of whom, Mr. Greaton, was shot through the body.

"Our artillery being now silenced, and all the officers killed except Captain Ford, who was very badly wounded, and more than half of the army fallen, being cut off from the road, it became necessary to attempt the regaining it and to make a retreat if possible. To this purpose, the remains of the army was formed as well as circumstances would admit, toward the right of the encampment, from which, by the way of the second line, another charge was made upon the enemy, as if with the design to turn their right flank, but in fact to gain the road. This was effected, and as soon as it was open, the militia took along it, followed by the troops; Major Clarke with his battalion covering the rear.

"The retreat, in those circumstances, was, you may be sure, a very precipitate one. It was, in fact, a flight. The camp and the artillery were abandoned; but that was unavoidable, for not a horse was left alive to have drawn it off, had it otherwise been practicable. But the most disgraceful part of the business is, that the greatest part of the men threw away their arms and accoutrements, even after the pursuit, which continued four miles, had ceased. I found the road strewed with them for many miles, but was not able to remedy it; for having had all my horses killed, and being mounted upon one that could not be pricked out of a walk, I could not get forward myself; and the orders I sent forward either to halt the front, or to prevent the men from parting with their arms, were unattended to. The rout continued quite to Fort Jefferson, twenty-nine miles, which was reached a little after sun-setting. The action began about half an hour before sunrise, and the retreat was attempted at half an hour after nine o'clock. I have not yet been able to get returns of the killed and wounded; but Major-general Butler, Lieutenant-colonel Oldham, of the militia, Major Ferguson, Major Hart, and Major Clarke, are among the former; Colonel Sargent, my adjutant-general, Lieutenant-colonel Darke, Lieutenant-colonel Gibson, Major Butler, and the Viscount Malartie, who served me as an aid-de-camp, are among the latter; and a great number of captains and subalterns in both.

---

## Note H. Page 197.

At the great council held at Sandusky, Simon Girty acted as interpreter; at the first meeting, many chiefs wished to know distinctly, and *merely*, if the United States would or would not make the Ohio the boundary. To this inquiry the commissioners replied in writing, setting forth the American claims, the grounds of them, and the impossibility of making the Ohio the line of settlement. The *ultimata* of the Indians is contained in the following speech which was delivered orally, and is both able and characteristic. We give it entire from American State Papers, v. 349.

"Brothers—We are all brothers you see here now. Brothers: It is now three years since you desired to speak with us. We heard you yesterday, and understood you well—perfectly well. We have a few words to say to you. Brothers: You mentioned the treaties of Fort Stanwix, Beaver Creek, (Fort McIntosh,) and other places. Those treaties were not complete. There were but a few chiefs who treated with you. You have not bought our lands. They belong to us. You tried to draw off some of us. Brothers: Many years ago, we all know that the Ohio was made the boundary. It was settled by Sir William Johnston. This side is ours. We look upon it as our property. Brothers: You mentioned General Washington. He and you know you have your houses and your people on our land. You say you cannot move them off; and we cannot give up our land. Brothers: We are sorry we cannot come to an agreement. The line has been fixed long ago. Brothers: We don't say much. There has been much mischief on both sides. We came here upon peace, and thought you did the same. We shall talk to our head warriors. You may return whence you came and tell Washington."

The council here breaking up, Captain Elliott went to the Shawanee chief, Ka-kia-pilathy, and told him that the last part of the speech was wrong. That chief came back, and said it was wrong. Girty said that he had interpreted truly what the Wyandot chief spoke. An explanation took place; and Girty added as follows: "Brothers: Instead of going home, we wish you to remain here for an answer from us. We have your speech in our breasts, and shall consult our head warriors."

The head warriors having been consulted, the final answer came, fully detailing all their views of the question of boundary, and insisting on the Ohio as such limit between the white and red men.

---

## Note I. Page 199.

We are indebted to Perkins's Annals for the following note:—

"The authenticity of this speech has been questioned; it was doubted at the time even. George Clinton, of New York, sent the proof of its genuineness to Washington, March 20, 1794, and both he and the President thought it authentic. Judge Marshall, (Life of Washington, v. 535,) states it is not authentic, and Sparks, (Washington Papers, x. 394, note,) seems to agree with him; but Mr. Stone found among Brant's papers, a certified MS. copy from which the above extracts are taken, (Stone's Brant, ii. 368, note); and Mr. Hammond, the British minister, in May, 1794, acknowledged it to be genuine. (American State Papers, i. 462. See also v. 480.)

---

## Note K. Page 204.

The following extracts are from the official report of General Wayne, of the battle of the 20th of August, 1794. The full report is found in American State Papers, v. 492.

"The forces moved down the north bank of the Maumee, the legion on the right, its flank covered by the Maumee; one brigade of mounted volunteers on the left, under Brigadier-general Todd, and the other in the rear under Brigadier-general Barbee. A select battalion of mounted volunteers moved in front of the legion, commanded by Major Price, who was directed to keep sufficiently advanced, so as to give timely notice for the troops to form in case of action, it being yet undetermined whether the Indians would decide for peace or war.

"After advancing about five miles, Major Price's corps received so severe a fire from the enemy, who were secreted in the woods and high grass, as to compel them to retreat. The legion was immediately formed in two lines, principally in a close thick wood, which extended for miles on our left, and for a very considerable distance in front; the ground being covered with old fallen timber, probably occasioned by a tornado, which rendered it impracticable for the cavalry to act with effect, and afforded the enemy the most favourable covert for their mode of warfare. The savages were formed in three lines, within supporting distance of each other, and extending for near two miles at right angles with the river. I soon discovered, from the weight of the fire and extent of their lines, that the enemy were in full force in front, in possession of their favourite ground, and endeavouring to turn our left flank. I therefore gave orders for the second line to advance and support the first; and directed Major-general Scott to gain, and turn the right flank of the savages, with the whole of the mounted volunteers, by a circuitous route; at the same time I ordered the front line to advance, and charge with trailed arms, and rouse the Indians from their covert at the point of the bayonet, and when up, to deliver a close and well-directed fire on their backs, followed by a brisk charge, so as not to give them time to load again.

"I also ordered Captain Mis Campbell, who commanded the legionary cavalry, to turn the left flank of the enemy next the river, and which afforded a favourable field for that corps to act in. All these orders were obeyed with spirit and promptitude; but such was the impetuosity of the charge by the first line of infantry, that the Indian and *Canadian militia and volunteers* were drove from all their coverts in so short a time, that although every possible exertion was used by the officers of the second line of the legion, and by Generals Scott, Todd, and Barbee, of the mounted volunteers, to gain their proper positions, but part of each could get up in season to participate in the action; the enemy being drove in the course of one hour, more than two miles, through the thick woods already mentioned, by less than one half of their numbers. From every account the enemy amounted to two thousand combatants. The troops actually engaged against them, were short of nine hundred. This horde of savages, with their allies, abandoned themselves to flight, and dispersed with terror and dismay, leaving our victorious army in full and quiet possession of the field of battle, which terminated under the influence of the guns of the British garrison, as you will observe by the enclosed correspondence between Major Campbell, the commandant, and myself, upon the occasion." (Vide supra, note A.)

---

## Note L. Page 207.

On the exchange of prisoners, a scene occurred, which may not be considered as out of place to be here noted. The account is taken from the narrative of John Brickell, or Bickell, who had been a captive for four years among the Delawares, and adopted into the family of Whingwy Pooshies, or Big Cat, a noted warrior of that tribe. Brickell's narrative is given at length in the American Pioneer, i. 53. He says—

"On the breaking up of spring we all went up to Fort Defiance, and on arriving on the shore opposite, we saluted the fort with a round of rifles, and they shot a cannon thirteen times. We then encamped on the spot. On the same day Whingwy Pooshies told me I must go over to the fort. The children hung round me crying, and asked me if I was going to leave them? I told them I did not know. When we got over to the fort, and were seated with the officers, Whingwy Pooshies told me to stand up, which I did; he then rose and addressed me in about these words:—'My son, there are men the same colour with yourself. There may be some of your kin there, or your kin may be a great way off from you. You have lived a long time with us. I call on you to say if I have not been a father to you? If I have not used you as a father would use a son?' I said, 'You have used me as well as a father could use a son.' He said, 'I am glad you say so. You have lived long with me; you have hunted for me; but our treaty says you must be free. If you choose to go with the people of your own colour, I have no right to say a word, but if you choose to stay with me, your people have no right to speak. Now reflect on it, and take your choice, and tell us as soon as you make up your mind.'

"I was silent a few minutes, in which time it seemed as if I thought of almost every thing. I thought of the children I had just left crying; I thought of the Indians I was attached to, and I thought of my people which I remembered; and this latter thought predominated, and I said, 'I will go with my kin.' The old man then said, 'I have raised you,—I have learned you to hunt. You are a good hunter,—you have been better to me than my own sons. I am now getting old, and I cannot hunt. I thought you would be a support to my age. I leaned on you as on a staff. Now it is broken—you are going to leave me, and I have no right to say a word, but I am ruined.' He then sank back, in tears, to his seat. I heartily joined him in his tears—parted with him, and have never seen nor heard of him since."

---

## NOTE M. Page 208.

Mr. Jay reached England June 15th, 1794. His treaty was concluded November 19th. It was received by the President March 7th, 1795. It was submitted to the Senate June 8th; was agreed to by them on the 24th of the same month; and was ratified by the President on the 14th of August, 1795.

---

## NOTE N. Page 216.

At this time, (1797,) there was a strong military force in Canada, and there were persons in the United States who would gladly have joined even a British invasion of Louisiana; and although the British cabinet disavowed any such intentions, the provincial authorities of Canada no doubt seriously contemplated such an event, as did men of influence in the United States. At the very time that Gayoso was deferring the fulfilment of the treaty, his allusion to a British invasion was not without foundation. As was subsequently ascertained, Senator William Blount, from Tennessee, who had enjoyed the confidence of the Federal government, as "Governor of the Southwestern Territory, and Indian Agent," and was intimately acquainted with the southern country, people, and Indian tribes, where he had great influence, conceived the design of a conspiracy to aid the British forces of Canada, by way of Lake Michigan, Chicago, and the Illinois River, to invade Louisiana, and capture New Orleans. The troops of Great Britain in Canada had actually embarked from Quebec for the lakes. Blount's plan of operations contemplated a strong reinforcement from the Ohio, the Tennessee, and Cumberland rivers, with supplies of military stores and provisions, to meet the invading forces at the mouth of the Ohio. Blount having disclosed his plans to Mr. Liston, the British minister, was referred by him directly to the British cabinet. The cautious mystery of the American senator led to his detection, and having been found guilty of entertaining the treasonable plot, he was unanimously expelled from the United States Senate. (See American State Papers, iii. 335, Boston edition. Martin's Louisiana, ii. 139. Marbois's Louisiana, 163. Journals of Congress—Senate.)

## NOTE O. Page 217.

We are indebted to Monette for the following pertinent remarks:—"The temerity of this last intrigue put in operation by the Governor of Louisiana, astonishes every reflecting mind. But General Wilkinson was a talented and ambitious man; he had received many favours from the Spanish governors nearly ten years before; he had received exclusive privileges in the commerce with Louisiana; a long and confidential intercourse had existed between him and Governor Miro; he was known to have indulged a predilection for the Spanish authority, and was ambitious of power and distinction; he was now at the head of the Western armies, and with the power and influence of his station he might effectually bring about a separation of the West, the formation of a new republic, of which he himself might be the supreme ruler, and conduct the alliance with Spain. Such may have been the reasoning of Baron de Carondelet at this period." (Monette, i. 536.)

# NOTES TO CHAPTER V.

## Note A. Page 226.

In January, 1802, Governor Harrison communicated to the President a letter detailing some very singular and curious land speculations. We take it from American State Papers, xvi. 123.

"The court established at this place under the authority of the State of Virginia, in the year 1780, assumed to themselves the right of granting lands to every applicant. Having exercised this power for some time without opposition, they began to conclude that their right over the land was supreme, and that they could with as much propriety grant to themselves as to others. Accordingly an arrangement was made by which the whole country to which the Indian title was supposed to be extinguished, was divided between the members of the court; and orders to that effect entered on their journal, each member absenting himself from the court on the day that the order was to be made in his favour, so that it might appear to be the act of his fellows only. The tract thus disposed of, extends on the Wabash twenty-four leagues from La Pointe Coupèe, to the mouth of White River, and forty leagues into the country west, and thirty east, from the Wabash, excluding only the land immediately surrounding this town, (Vincennes,) which had before been granted to the amount of twenty or thirty thousand acres.

"The authors of this ridiculous transaction soon found that no advantage could be derived from it, as they could find no purchasers, and I believe that the idea of holding any part of the land was by the greater part of them abandoned a few years ago; however, the claim was discovered, and a part of it purchased, by some of those speculators who infest our country, and through these people, a number of others in different parts of the United States have become concerned, some of whom are actually preparing to make settlements on the land the ensuing spring. Indeed, I should not be surprised to see five hundred families settling under these titles in the course of a year. The price at which the land is sold enables anybody to become a purchaser; one thousand acres being frequently given for an indifferent horse or a rifle gun. And as a formal deed is made reciting the grant of the court, (made as it is pretended under the authority of the State of Virginia,) many ignorant persons have been induced to part with their little all, to obtain this ideal property, and they will no doubt endeavour to strengthen their claim, as soon as they have discovered the deception, by an actual settlement. I am now informed that a number of persons are in the habit of repairing to this place, where they purchase two or three hundred thousand acres of this claim, for which they get a deed properly authenticated and recorded, and then disperse themselves over the United States, to cheat the ignorant and credulous. In some measure to check this practice, I have forbidden the recorder and prothonotary of this county from recording or authenticating any of these papers; being determined that the official seals of the territory should not be prostituted to a purpose so base as that of assisting an infamous fraud.

"WM. H. HARRISON.

"To JAMES MADISON, Secretary of State."

---

## NOTE B. Page 227.

Rock Island is certainly a beautiful and fertile spot of land, reposing in a noble field of crystal waters; the scenery around it is not surpassed in beauty by any other on the Upper Mississippi. The Rock, and remarkable cave at its base, which is washed by the Mississippi, are prominent and romantic features in the imposing landscape which presents itself to the view on ascending the river. At this day, the high state of cultivation which distinguishes both the Illinois and the Iowa banks of the river, and the large and flourishing cities of Rock Island and Davenport, gracefully and beautifully adorning each side of the Mississippi, which majestically flows between them, present a picture that the wild Indian could never have imagined, nor the early explorers of the country ever have anticipated. Old Fort Armstrong, built on the summit of the Rock, was formerly not the least of the handsome objects in the panorama.

Black Hawk has thus described this favourite dwelling-place of the Sacs, and gives the Indian tradition of the tutelary spirit of the island: "Here we found that troops had arrived to build a fort at Rock Island. We did not object to their building the fort, but were very sorry, as this was the best island on the Mississippi, and had long been the resort of our young people during the summer. It was our garden, (like the white people have near to their big villages,) which supplied us with strawberries, blackberries, gooseberries, plums, apples, and nuts of different kinds; and its waters supplied us with fine fish, being situated in the rapids of the river. In my early life I spent many happy days on this island. A good spirit had care of it, who lived in a cave in the rocks immediately under the place where the fort now stands, and has often been seen by our people. He was white, with large wings like a swan's, but ten times larger. We were particular not to make much noise in that part of the island which he inhabited, for fear of disturbing him. But the noise of the fort has since driven him away, and no doubt, a *bad spirit* has taken his place." (See Black Hawk's Life, by himself.)

---

## NOTE C. Page 228.

This treaty, generally called the Treaty of St. Louis, was made November 3d, 1804, by Governor William Henry Harrison, sole commissioner on part of the United States, and the chiefs and head men of the United Sac and Fox tribes. It is signed on the part of the Indians by "Layouvois, or Laiyuwa, Pashepapo, or the Giger, Quashquame, or Jumping Fish; Outchequaha or Sunfish, and Hah-she-quax-hi-qua, or the Bear. It must be allowed that these are very few representatives of the different bands of the Sacs and Foxes; and considering the immense extent of country ceded by the signers of the treaty, which embraced nearly all of the present State of Wisconsin south of the Wisconsin River, together with a considerable portion of the States of Illinois and Missouri; also taking into view the absolutely trifling consideration named for the grant, which was "goods in hand to the amount of two thousand two hundred and thirty-four dollars and fifty cents; and a yearly annuity of one thousand dollars, of which six hundred dollars was for the Sacs and four hundred dollars for the Foxes, to be paid in goods valued at first cost," this treaty may be considered as a most extraordinary one. In all subsequent treaties made with the Indians of the Upper Mississippi this treaty of November 3d, 1804, is referred to, and its validity acknowledged, when necessary. Black Hawk always denied the validity of this treaty, as having been made and signed by persons of no authority, or possessing no authority to sell the lands of the Sacs and Foxes. In a subsequent treaty, made 13th of May, 1816, this treaty of 1804 is acknowledged and confirmed. The treaty of 1816 is made with the Sacs of Rock River, and is signed by twenty-two chiefs, among whom is found Muck-etama-che-ka-ka, or Black Sparrow Hawk; but he afterward asserted that he was deceived and was ignorant of what he was then doing. Another signer to this latter treaty is Matchequawa, or the *Bad Axe*, a name most ominous to Black Hawk, as subsequent events gave evidence.

## NOTE D. Page 239.

Governor John Reynolds, in his "Pioneer History of Illinois," gives this account of Keokuk:—

"Keokuk was made a war chief by his merit, and not by birth. In the late war with England, the Sauk and Fox Indians were about to be destroyed, as they supposed, by the army under General Howard in 1813. The whole nation at Rock Island, except a very few, commenced lamentations and shedding tears of distress, thinking the Long Knives were about to kill them all. Keokuk was then a mere youth, but his great native mind and his true patriotism made him stand out the champion of the nation, to defend them and the country against General Howard and his army. A few other choice spirits of the young warriors joined him and marched out to meet the American army, preferring death to the surrender of their country. It so happened that the Americans were not near them, and the panic arose without foundation. I was with the army under General Howard, and we were almost as much alarmed at the Indians as the Indians were at us. They had three or four-fold over our numbers.

"This movement made Keokuk a war-chief of the nation; and General Scott and myself, as commissioners at the treaty of Rock Island, in 1832, with the Sauk and Fox Indians, confirmed him in this office. Keokuk had sound good sense; he took the newspapers, and got them explained to him."

Black Hawk gives an account to the same effect: he says, "that on his return, he learned that the nation had been reduced to so small a party of fighting men by the absence of the braves with him, that they felt unable to defend themselves if the Americans should attack them; that all the women and children, and old men belonging to the warriors who had joined the British, were left with them to provide for. That a council had been held, and it was determined that several chiefs, and such men, women, and children as chose to accompany them, should descend the river and place themselves under the protection of the American chief at St. Louis. Accordingly the 'peace party' went to St. Louis, and were received as the friendly band of Sacs and Foxes, while their friends were assisting the British. That some time afterward the spies reported that a large American force had been seen going toward Peoria; that fears were entertained of an attack on their village; that a council was held, to which Keokuk was admitted by *special permission*, as he never had killed an enemy, and therefore was no chief; that there was a serious question on deserting their village, and the graves of their fathers; that Keokuk resisted such action, and offered to defend the village; that he was thereupon constituted a war chief by the council, and marched with his braves on the trail leading to Peoria, but returned without seeing an enemy. The Americans did not disturb the village, and all were satisfied with the appointment of Keokuk."[1]

---

## Note E. Page 241.

(From the Montreal Herald of August 8th.)

Mackinac, July 17th, 1811.

Capitulation

Agreed upon between Captain Charles Roberts, commanding his Britanic Majesty's forces, on the one part, and Lieutenant Hanks, commanding the forces of the United States, on the other.

Articles.

I. The fort of Mackina shall immediately be surrendered to the British forces. Granted.

II. The garrison shall march out with the honours of war, lay down their arms, and become prisoners of war, and shall be sent to the United States of America by his Britannic Majesty. Not to serve in this war until regularly exchanged; and for the due performance of this article the officers pledge their word of honour. Granted.

III. All the merchant vessels in the harbour, with their cargoes, shall be in the possession of their respective owners. Granted.

IV. Private property shall be held sacred. Granted.

V. All citizens of the United States of America who shall not take the oath of allegiance to his Britannic Majesty, shall depart with their property from the island in one month from the date hereof. Granted.

Signed, Charles Roberts,
Commanding H. B. Majesty's Forces,
P. Hanks,
Commanding the Forces of the United States of America.

Remarks.—His Britannic Majesty's force consisted of forty regulars of the royal veteran battalion.

Two hundred and sixty Canadians, with their bourgeois or employèes.

Four hundred Indians—Sioux, Folle Avoines, Puans, Chippewas of St. Joseph's, St. Mary's, &c.

---

[1] Doc. History. Black Hawk War.

Artillery—Two six-pounders, which embarked at St. Joseph's, on board the Caledonia, N. W. Co.'s ship; ten batteaux, and seventy canoes.

The American garrison consisted of sixty-three regulars, and nine vessels in the habour, having on board forty-seven men; in all, one hundred and ten.

After the capitulation, two American vessels arrived, laden with seven hundred packs of furs, which became prize to his Majesty's forces.

In the Montreal Herald of August 4, is found a letter from John Askin, Jun., dated July 18th, giving an account of the capitulation of Mackinac; in which the writer exhibits a true specimen of British magnanimity in the following language:—"It was a fortunate circumstance the fort capitulated without firing a single gun, for had they done so, *I firmly believe not a soul of them would have been saved!* My son, Charles Langlade, Augustin Nolin, and Michael Badotte, Jun., have rendered me great service in *keeping the Indians in order*, and in executing from time to time, such commands as were delivered to me by the commanding officer. I never saw *so determined a set of people* as the Chippewas and Ottawas were."

Lieutenant Hanks, in his official report of the surrender of the fort, made to General Hull, and dated at Detroit, August 4th, says, "That the summons to surrender the fort and island to his Britannic Majesty's forces, was the first intimation he had received of the declaration of war." He also states that the British force, of regulars, Canadians, and Indians, amounted to 1021; and, two days after the capitulation, one hundred and fifty Chippewas and Ottawas joined the British.

A gentleman in the Indian department, who had been made prisoner and taken to the British and Indian camp, writes from Detroit, August 6th, to the secretary of war, and says, "The persons who commanded the Indians are, Robert Dickson, Indian trader, and John Askin, Jun., Indian agent, and son. The latter two were painted, dressed, and armed after the manner of the Indians. Those who commanded the Canadians are, John Johnson, Crawford, Pothier, Armitingen, La Croix, Rolette, Franks, Livingston, and others, all Indian traders; some of whom were lately concerned in smuggling British goods into the Indian country, and who, in conjunction with others, have been using their utmost efforts several months before the declaration of war, to excite the Indians to take up arms against the United States." The same writer also says, "The least resistance from the fort would have been attended with the destruction of all the persons who fell into the hands of the British, as I have been assured by some of the British traders; and the same fate, as I have been assured, would have attended the officers and soldiers, had a single Indian been killed. Nothing else, it is said, would have satisfied the Indians, and it was not without great difficulty they were prevented from taking the lives of several Americans after the fort had capitulated."

---

## Note F. Page 242.

The following data are extracted from Captain Heald's account of the evacuation of Fort Dearborn, and the subsequent massacre of the garrison and inhabitants; Captain Heald's letter is found in Niles's Register, vol. iii. 155, iv. 160.

On the 9th of August, orders to evacuate the post were received from General Hull; Captain Heald was at liberty to dispose of the public property at his discretion.

On the 14th of August, the captain delivered to the Indians all the goods in the factory store, and a considerable quantity of provisions which he could not take with him. He destroyed the surplus arms and ammunition.

On the 15th, the garrison marched, and were attacked about a mile and a half from the fort; the captain, after a short but fruitless resistance, surrendered to the chief "Black Bird," and the remains of his command and party were taken back to the fort as prisoners and distributed among the several tribes of Indians.

The number of the Indians was between four and five hundred, mostly Pottawatamies; their loss in the battle was about fifteen.

Captain Heald's command was fifty-four regulars, and twelve militia-men; out of which twenty-six regulars, and all the militia were killed; also two women and twelve children.

On the 16th, the Indians set fire to the fort and left the place, taking their prisoners with them.

Lieutenant Lina T. Helm, with twenty-five non-commissioned officers and privates, and eleven women and children, were left as prisoners when Captain Heald was separated from them. Mrs. Heald and the captain, (both being badly wounded,) were taken to the house of Mr. Burnett, an Indian trader, at the mouth of St. Joseph River, where they were left, and from which place they afterward reached Detroit.

The following synopsis is taken from Lanman's History of Michigan:—

"General Hull had sent word to the commander at Fort Dearborn, (Chicago,) Captain Heald, of the loss of Mackinac, and directed him to distribute his stores among the Indians and retire to Fort Wayne. The garrison had at that time the amplest means of defence, but the order was received on the 9th of August and left nothing to the discretion of the commandant. The fidelity of the Pottawatamies was doubted on substantial grounds, and the advice of Captain Wells, to evacuate the fort immediately, before the Indians should have time to concentrate around it, was unfortunately disregarded. Before Captain Heald had completed his arrangements to leave the fort, about four hundred Indians had collected in the neighbourhood. A promise was made that all the surplus stores of the fort should be at their disposal, if they would forbear harassing the garrison on their march. It was conceived that a large quantity of powder and whiskey, which had been collected in the fort, would be an impolitic gift to the Indians; and Captain Heald therefore ordered the powder to be thrown into the well, and the whiskey wasted; which was accordingly done. During the night, by some means which are not known, the Indians received information of this fact, and regarded the waste as an infringement of their vested rights. The act naturally tended to exasperate them greatly, and they therefore assembled in considerable numbers around the fort. It was then suggested by Captain Wells, and Mr. Kenzie, an Indian agent, that a retreat would be unsafe at that time; but without effect. The whiskey having been destroyed and the ammunition lost, the means of defending the fort were gone; and the garrison, comprising several families, twelve militia-men, and also fifty-four regular troops, took their line of march from the fort. When about a mile from the fort, the Indians were perceived making preparations for an attack, and the garrison also prepared for a defence. After a short conflict, Captain Heald surrendered, when several women, children, and about half his garrison had been killed. The prisoners were distributed among the tribes, and on the following morning the fort was burned to the ground.

" Lieutenant Helm, one of the prisoners, was taken to Au Sable, on the Illinois River; he was afterward ransomed from the Indians, by the trader Thomas Forsyth.

" Captain Wells was an early victim to this disastrous conflict. Disappointed at the blind wilfulness of Captain Heald, in accordance with the habits of the savages in fits of disappointment, he had blackened his face, and was thus found among the slain. Captain Wells was a remarkable man. He had been captured when a mere child, by the Indians, and was adopted by Mackinac, the Little Turtle, one of the fiercest warriors who has figured in Indian history. During the sanguinary defeats of Harmar and St. Clair, Captain Wells had commanded an Indian force of about three hundred young warriors. These were posted immediately in front of the artillery, and covering themselves behind logs and posts, under knolls on which the guns were placed, they literally heaped up around the guns the bodies of the artillerists. After those contests, Wells, foreseeing the advancing power of the whites, resolved to abandon the savages. His mode of expressing his determination was peculiar to the savage custom. Being alone in the wilderness with his adopted father, he remarked, 'When the sun reaches the meridian, I leave you for the whites; and whenever you meet me in battle, you must kill me, as I shall endeavour to do the same to you.' Captain Wells shortly after joined the army of General Wayne, and by his knowledge of Indian customs was of essential service to the American forces, and fought with signal success. When, however, the war was concluded, and peace was restored between the Indians and the United States, he returned to his foster-father, the Little Turtle, and continued in unbroken friendship with him, until the latter died in 1812. It is alleged that when the body of Captain Wells was found at Chicago, by the Indians, they drank his blood, as they had imbibed a superstition that they should thus inherit his extraordinary military endowments."

By the stipulations of the treaty made at Prairie du Chien, July 29th, 1829, the Chippewa, Ottawa, and Pottawatamie Indians, of the waters of the Illinois, Milwaukee, and Manitoouck rivers, agree that the sum of eleven thousand six hundred and one dollars shall be paid to certain persons named in the schedule, in full satisfaction of claims brought against the said Indians, and which they acknowledge to be justly due. Among these claims we find the following:—To Antoine Ouilmette, for depredations committed on him by the Indians at the time of the massacre at Chicago, and during the war, $800. To the heirs of John Kenzie, late of Chicago, for depredations committed on him at the time of the massacre at Chicago and at St. Joseph, during the winter of 1812, $3500. To Margaret Helm, for losses sustained at the time of the capture of Fort Dearborn, in 1812, by the Indians, $800.

---

## Note G. Page 245.

By the 7th section of the act of Congress, approved April 18th, 1818, entitled "An Act to enable the people of Illinois Territory to form a constitution and state government, and for the admission of such State into the Union on an equal footing with the original States," it was enacted, "That all that part of the territory of the United States lying north of the State of Indiana, and which was included in the former Indiana Territory, together with that part of the Illinois Territory which is situated north of, and not included within the boundaries prescribed by this act, to the state thereby authorized to be formed, shall be and hereby is attached to, and made a part of the Michigan Territory, from and after the formation of the said state, subject, nevertheless, to be hereafter disposed of by Congress according to the right reserved in the fifth article of the ordinance aforesaid, (of 1787,) and the inhabitants therein shall be entitled to the same privileges and immunities, and subject to the same rules and regulations in all respects with the other citizens of the Michigan Territory." (Laws of Congress, 1818.)

---

## Note H. Page 255.

General Gaines, in a letter dated at Rock Island, June 20th, 1831, gives the following account of his expedition, and his views of the future action of Black Hawk's band:—

"I have visited the Rock River villages with a view to ascertain the localities, and, as far as possible, the dispositions of the Indians. They confirm me in the opinion that I had previously formed, that whatever may be their feelings of hostility, they are resolved to abstain from the use of their tomahawks and fire-arms, except in self-defence. But few of their warriors were to be seen—their women and children, and their old men appeared anxious, and at first somewhat confused, but none attempted to run off. Having previously notified their chiefs that I would have nothing more to say to them, unless they should desire to inform me of their intention to *move forthwith*, as I had directed them, I did not speak to them, though within fifty yards of many of them. I had with me on board the steamboat, some artillery, and two companies of infantry. Their village is immediately on Rock River, and so situated that I could from the steamboat destroy all their bark houses (the only kind of houses they have) in a few minutes, with the force now with me, probably without the loss of a man. But I am resolved to abstain from firing a shot without some bloodshed, or some manifest attempt to shed blood, on the part of the Indians. I have already induced the one-third of them to cross the Mississippi to their own land. The residue, however, say, as the friendly chiefs report, that they *never will move;* and what is very uncommon, their women urge their hostile husbands to fight, rather than to move, and thus to abandon their homes.

# NOTES TO CHAPTER VI.

## NOTE A. Page 264.

### AN INDIAN TALK,

Delivered at the head of the Four Lakes, May 25th, 1832, to the Winnebagoes, by Henry Gratiot, sub-Indian-agent, and General Henry Dodge, in the presence of fifty mounted volunteers, commanded by Captains James H. Gentry, and John H. Rountree.

General Dodge said—

"My friends: Mr. Gratiot, your father, and myself have met to have a talk with you; having identified us both, as your friends, in making a sale of your country to the United States, you will not suspect us for deceiving you.

"The Sacs have shed the blood of our people; the Winnebago Prophet, and as we are told one hundred of your people have united with Black Hawk and his party; our people are anxious to know in what relation you stand to us, whether as friends or enemies.

"Your residence being near our settlements, it is necessary and proper that we should explicitly understand from you, the chiefs and warriors, whether or not you intend to aid, harbour, or counsel the Sacs in your country; to do so will be considered as a declaration of war on your part.

"Your great American father is the friend of the Red Skins; he wishes to make you happy. Your chiefs who have visited Washington, know him well; he is mild in peace, but terrible in war; he will ask of no people what is not right, and he will submit to nothing wrong; his power is great, he commands all the warriors of the American people; if you strike us, you strike him, and to make war on us, you will have your country taken from you, your annuity money will be forfeited, and the lives of your people must be lost. We speak the words of truth; we hope they will sink deep in your hearts.

"The Sacs have killed eleven of our people, and wounded three; our people have killed eleven of the Sacs; it was but a small detachment of our army who were engaged with the Sacs; when the main body of our army appeared, the Sacs run.

"The Sacs have given you bad counsel, they tell you lies and no truth;

stop your ears to their words; they know death and destruction follows them; they want you to unite with them, wishing to place you in the same situation with themselves.

"We have told you the consequences of uniting with our enemies; we hope, however, that the bright chain of friendship will still continue; that we may travel the same road in friendship, under a clear sky.

"We have always been your friends; we have said that you would be honest, and true to your treaties; do not let your actions deceive us. So long as you are true and faithful we will extend the hand of friendship to you and your children; if unfaithful to your treaties, you must expect to share the fate of the Sacs."

---

## NOTE B. Page 265.

MINERAL POINT, May 8th, 1832.

His Excellency JOHN REYNOLDS:

Dear Sir—The exposed situation of the settlements of the mining district to the attack of the Indian enemy, makes it a matter of deep and vital interest to us, that we should be apprized of the movements of the mounted men under your excellency's immediate command. Black Hawk and his band, it is stated by the last advices we have had on this subject, was to locate himself about twenty miles above Dixon's Ferry, on Rock River. Should the mounted men under your command make an attack on that party, we would be in great danger here; for should you defeat Black Hawk, the retreat would be on our settlements. There are now collected within twenty miles above our settlements, about two hundred Winnebagoes, and should the Sauks be forced into the Winnebago country, many of the wavering of that nation would unite with the hostile Sauks. I have no doubt it is part of the policy of this banditti to unite themselves as well with the Pottawatamies, as Winnebagoes. It is absolutely important to the safety of this country, that the people here should be apprized of the intended movements of your army. Could you detach a part of your command across the Rock River, you would afford our settlements immediate protection, and we would promptly unite with you, with such a mounted force as we could bring into the field. Judge Gentry, Colonel Moore, and James P. Cox, Esq., will wait on your excellency and receive your answer.

I am, sir, with respect and esteem, your obedient servant,

HENRY DODGE,
Commanding Michigan Militia.

## Note C. Page 267.

Narrative of the killing of Felix St. Vrain, Indian agent of the Sauks and Foxes, Aaron Hawley, and others, during the Black Hawk War. Compiled from the personal narrative of Mr. Asahel Higginbotham, and Mrs. Phebe Baldwin, the widow of Mr. Hawley:

"Aaron Hawley, William Hale, John Fowler, and another person, left Dixon's Ferry, on Rock River, on the 22d of May, 1832, for the purpose of examining the country, in order to make settlements. They travelled as far as Buffalo Grove, and there found a white man lying dead in their path; he was known to them, his name was Dearley or Durley. The party then immediately returned to Dixon's, and stayed until the next day. On the following morning they were joined by Mr. St. Vrain, the Indian agent, Alexander Higginbotham, Aquilla Floyd, and one Kinney. This party then came to Buffalo Grove, and buried the body of Durley. They then started for Hamilton's settlement, (Wiota,) and having travelled about ten miles in that direction, camped for the night.

"At daylight the next morning they again started, proceeded about three miles, and then stopped to cook breakfast. While this was being prepared, Higginbotham discovered some tracks of ponies or Indian horses, and informed his companions. They immediately pursued their journey some three-fourths of a mile, when they discovered an Indian on their right, and instantly afterward saw one band of Indians collected on their right, then, another band in their front, and next, a third band in their rear. The whole number of these Indians, as it was afterward learned, was thirty-nine. The whole party of the whites fled, and were followed by the Indians. John Fowler was killed in about a quarter of a mile from the place where the Indians were first seen, St. Vrain in half a mile, and Hale in a mile; the party lost sight of the Indians after running about eight or ten miles.

"They then travelled five or six miles, and directed their course toward Galena; they pursued this direction for some three or four miles, and then fell in again with the same band of Indians, who gave them chase for five or six miles, and they then lost sight of that band altogether. The party then crossed Brush Creek, and fell in with another band; they immediately turned back and recrossed the creek. After crossing back, they travelled some six or eight miles to the waters of Plum River, and laid by until it was dark, and then started for Galena. They travelled all night, and laid by all the next day; travelled all the second night, and on the morning of the third day arrived at Galena.

"Aaron Hawley's horse being the fastest, he left the company when the Indians were first seen, and was, as supposed, cut off by them. The last that was seen of him, he was making his course toward the Pecatonica; the body of Mr. Hawley was never found. It is conjectured that his horse was mired in the low grounds, and he was thus killed. The bodies of the other persons who were killed, were found and buried about a week after they were killed.

"The above account has been procured from a son of Mr. Hawley, who resides at Argyle, Lafayette county, about two miles from the scene of the battle of the Pecatonica."

After the Black Hawk War was over, treaties were made at Rock Island with the Sacs and Foxes, and with the Winnebagoes, in which was a stipulation for the delivering up to the Americans, for punishment, the murderers of St. Vrain, the Indian agent. In connection with this subject, the following talk, delivered by General Dodge to the Winnebago chiefs, sufficiently explains itself:—

An Indian Talk, delivered to the Chiefs of the Winnebago nation, after the Treaty at Rock Island, on the subject of the murderers of St. Vrain and others.

General Dodge said—"Chiefs of the Winnebagoes: When I last met you at the Four Lakes, I told you that a cloud of darkness would rest on your nation until you delivered up the eight murderers taken by you last fall, under a stipulation of the treaty made at Rock Island. You acted in that respect in good faith: the murderers have made their escape, and have received your aid and protection during the winter on Rock River. Your agent, Mr. Gratiot, stated to me that he had seen four of them: he identified the Indian who killed the agent of the Sacs and Foxes, Mr St. Vrain.

"It becomes my duty to demand of you, the chiefs, that these murderers be delivered to me, to be dealt with as the law directs; their escape from justice is no acquittal of them. Is it right, is it just, that men who professed to be our friends, and when the government of the United States was in a state of peace with them, that a part of your nation should unite with the Sacs and Fox Indians to kill our weak and defenceless citizens on this frontier, and charge their crimes on the Sacs? The men who participated in killing the United States Indian agent, and his murderer, whom, as Mr. Gratiot, your agent, states, Mr. St. Vrain had fed and treated with hospitality and friendship, at his house on Rock Island, but two weeks before he was killed!—the Indian who barbarously cut off his hands and feet before his death!—have been permitted by you to go at large, covered with the blood of an innocent man!—without any attempt, since the escape of these murderers, on your part, to bring them to justice! This state of things is in direct violation of every principle of justice, and contrary to all usage among friendly nations, for you to harbour and conceal the murderers of our people.

"I now distinctly give you to understand, that if you fail to adopt measures for the apprehension of these fugitives from justice, that it will lead to a stoppage of your annuities by the government; and that your chiefs are liable to be arrested and detained until the delivery of the murderers.

"Your great father, the President of the United States, deals justly with all nations; whether they are strong or weak people, he will ask nothing of them that is not right; and he will submit to nothing that is wrong. He will do justice to all the red skins. Had our citizens killed any of the Winnebagoes, when in a state of peace, they would have been punished according to the laws of the country where the injury was committed. If your people kill ours, they must be punished in the same manner. The laws are made for the protection of all, as well as for the punishment of all who violate them.

"If you deliver the murderers, to be dealt with according to law, you will give us a proof of your friendly disposition, and that you are disposed to conform to those friendly relations that should exist among different nations of people; then the bright chain of friendship will remain entire and unbroken between us.

"Should you, however, fail to deliver the murderers, your road will be filled with thorns; and the sun will be covered with a dark cloud, which will rest on your nation until the blood of the innocent is avenged!"

---

## NOTE D. Page 273.

Address delivered by Colonel Henry Dodge, to the volunteers at Kirker's place, (on the head of Apple River,) on their march to Rock River, June, 1832:—

Volunteers: We have met to take the field; the tomahawk and scalping-knife are drawn over the heads of the weak and defenceless inhabitants of our country. Although the most exposed people in the United States and territories, living as we do, surrounded by savages, not a drop of the blood of the people of this part of the Territory of Michigan has been shed. Let us unite, my brethren in arms; let harmony, union, and concert exist; be vigilant, silent, and cool. Discipline and obedience to orders will make small bodies of men formidable and invincible; without order and subordination, the largest bodies of armed men are no better than armed mobs. We have every thing dear to freemen at stake, the protection of our frontiers, and the lives of our people. Although we have entire confidence in the government of our choice, knowing as we all do that ours is a government of the people, where the equal rights of all are protected, and that the power of our countrymen can crush this savage foe, yet it will take time for the government to direct a force sufficient to give security and peace to the frontier people. I have, gentlemen, as well as yourselves, entire confidence, both in the President of the United States, and the present distinguished individual at the head of the war department, that our Indian relations are better understood by those distinguished individuals, than by any two citizens who could be selected to fill their stations. They have often met our savage enemies on the field of battle, where they have conquered them, as well as in council. They understand well all the artifice, cunning, and stratagem for which our enemies are distinguished; they well know our wants, and will apply the remedy. In General Atkinson, in whose protection this frontier is placed, I have the most entire confidence; he is well advised of our situation. You will recollect the responsibility he assumed for the people of this country in 1827, by ascending Wisconsin with six hundred infantry, and one hundred and fifty mounted men, to demand the murderers of our people; many of us had the honour of serving under him on that occasion. He has my most entire confidence, both as a man of talents in his profession, a soldier, and a gentleman. If our government will let him retain the command, he will give us a lasting peace, that will insure us tranquillity for years. He knows the resources as well as the character of the Indians we have to contend with; let the government furnish him the means, and our troubles will be of short duration.

What, my fellow soldiers, is the character of the foe we have to contend with? They are a faithless banditti of savages, who have violated all treaties; they have left the country, and the nation, of which they form a part; the policy of these marauders and robbers of our people appears to be, to enlist the disaffected and restless of other nations, which will give them strength, and resources to murder our people and burn their property. They are the enemies of all people, both the whites and Indians; their thirst of blood is not to be satisfied; they are willing to bring ruin and destruction on other Indians, in order to glut their vengeance on us. The humane policy of the government will not apply to these deluded people: like the pirates of the sea, their hand is against every man, and the hand of every man should be against them. Faithless to the government in every thing, it will surely be the policy of the government to let them receive that kind of chastisement which will quiet them effectually, and make a lasting example for others. The future growth and prosperity of our country is to be decided for years by the policy that is now to be pursued by the government in relation to the Indians. Our existence as a people is at stake, and great, gentlemen, as the resources of our government are, the security of the lives of our people depends on our vigilance, caution, and bravery. The assistance of our government may be too late for us; let us not await the arrival of our enemies at our doors, but advance upon them, fight them; watch them, and hold them in check. Let us avoid surprise and ambuscades; let every volunteer lie with his arms in his hands, ready prepared for action, so that when each volunteer rises to his feet, the line of battle will be formed. If attacked in the night, we will charge the enemy at a quick pace and even front. The eyes of the people of our country are upon us; let us endeavour by our actions to retain the confidence and support of our countrymen.

H. Dodge,
Col. commanding Mounted Militia.

*Gratiot's*, June, 1832.

---

## Note E. Page 273.

Letter of General Dodge to John Achison, Esq., on the subject of supplying provisions to the citizens of the mining country:—

Gratiot's Grove, June 14th, 1832.

Dear Sir—I was at the head-quarters of General Atkinson, at the mouth of the Fox River of the Illinois, on the 11th of this instant; he is actively engaged in making preparations to march against the hostile Indians. He will bring into the field about 3000 men. I will copy for your information that part of my order as it respects the supplies of provisions for the use of the troops under my command:—"Your detached situation renders it impossible for me to furnish subsistence for your troops; you will therefore procure supplies upon the best terms practicable, and in the issue, not exceed the United States allowance, and at the same time be careful to have the accounts kept accurately."

I have copied that part of General Atkinson's order in which you are interested; although it would seem from his order, that the rations furnished those not under arms, would not be paid for, the government of the United States will certainly pay for rations furnished the inhabitants, the protection of whose lives makes it necessary for them to *fort* themselves to avoid the tomahawk and scalping-knife. The people of the country have been invited here by the agents of the government to settle in this country, to work the lead-mines; they are neither intruders nor squatters on the public lands of the United States. The government has, by the industry and enterprise of the people of the mining country, derived all the advantages which they could have anticipated in the working and exploration of their mines; the government has no regular troops here to afford protection to our exposed settlements, and I have no hesitation in saying that the rations furnished women and children will be paid for by a special appropriation to be made by Congress.

The only difference with you, as I confidently believe, will be, that the amount due you for furnishing the troops under my immediate command will be paid for promptly by the war department of the government, and for the residue, a special law will have to be passed. This is a subject of great importance to the inhabitants who have been driven from their homes by the savages. Unless they can be furnished on the credit of the government, starvation must ensue, as many of them are unable to leave this country, and they are also unable to furnish themselves. I will thank you to write me on this subject, as early as possible.

I am, with much respect, your obedient servant,

H. Dodge,

Col. commanding the Militia of Iowa County, W. T.

Mr. John Atchison, Galena.

---

## Note F. Page 276.

### BATTLE OF THE PECATONICA.

John Messersmith, Esq., of Iowa county, relates as follows:—"Captain John Sherman commanded a company of volunteers at the Blue Mounds.

"Aubrey and his family kept house for Ebenezer Brigham at the Mounds.

"On the 6th of June, 1832, on the day that Aubrey was killed by the Indians, John Messersmith and his family left Mound Fort, and on the same evening came to his own residence at Messer Grove, about fifteen miles west of the mounds. About midnight, an express arrived from Dodge's Fort, and informed him of the killing of Aubrey; and Mrs. Dodge having sent a horse for Mrs. Messersmith, the family left home again, and arrived at Dodge's Fort at the dawn of day. Here they remained, and some days after, General Dodge came home, together with Thomas Jenkins and John Messersmith, Jun., from an excursion down in Illinois. On the same night, an express arrived from Colonel William S. Hamilton, informing General Dodge of the killing of the men at Spafford's Creek, and requesting his immediate presence at Hamilton's Fort. General Dodge immediately sent off the same express to Captain James H. Gentry at Platte Mounds, with orders to collect as many men as he could, and to proceed instantly to Wiota, Hamilton's Settlement. On the next morning, General Dodge, Thomas Jenkins, and John Messersmith, Jun., proceeded to the Blue Mounds."

The remainder of this narrative is the substance of the relation of John Messersmith, Jun., to his father.

"From the Blue Mounds, we three proceeded toward Hamilton's Settlement, and slept that night at Fretwell's diggings. The next morning, we pursued our course toward Hamilton's. There was a field about three-fourths of a mile from the fort; one path passed around the field, and another nigher path avoided the field, and intersected the road between the field and the fort. Near this intersection the Indians were lying in ambush. General Dodge and his two companions took the nigh path, and struck the road nearer to the fort than where the Indians were lying, perhaps about sixty yards from them. Here they met a German named Apple, on horseback, who said he was going up to his cabin, near the field, for his blanket, and would join them immediately. Captain Gentry's men in the mean while had arrived at the fort the preceding day, and their horses were already saddled, and all prepared for service. In a few minutes General Dodge and his companions arrived at the fort, and before they dismounted they heard the report of guns, and immediately Apple's horse came galloping back, bloody and without a rider. All immediately mounted and rode with speed up the road; they soon found the mutilated body of Apple, and riding into the hazel thickets skirting the road, discovered the ground where the Indians had been in ambush. They followed in pursuit, and soon came in sight of the flying savages, fourteen in number, who gave their war-cries tauntingly and beckoned for our men to follow. They were pursued for about five miles, when our men came to the east branch of the Pecatonica. Here General Dodge, having twenty-eight men, detailed eight, some to hold the horses and others to keep a look-out, and with the remainder, dismounted and waded the river; the opposite bank was covered with scattered timber and undergrowth, and the ground was much cut up and indented with the floods of the river, causing deep cavities and miry sloughs. The men were ordered to trail arms and keep a good look-out for Indians.

In less than five minutes, the Indians, who were lying concealed in the cavities caused as above stated, delivered their fire, by which three of our men fell. The battle was fought hand to hand, and it was over directly." The descriptive language of Mr. Messersmith, as to time, is thus :—"I fired my yager, let it drop—drew out my left pistol, fired at an Indian, let the pistol fall—drew out my right pistol, fired at another Indian, and was pouring powder in my hand to reload, when one of our company said, 'They are all dead!' The fact was so, or nigh to it, as the whole number of Indians except one were killed."

William S. Hamilton had gone up the Mississippi to get the Sioux and Menominees to assist us. He arrived with them, (about two hundred,) the same day of the battle. They went out and held a powwow over the bodies of the dead Indians, and literally cut them to pieces. They did not remain with us, but on the next day returned to their homes.

---

## NOTE G. Page 281.

The following letter appeared in the Missouri Republican Extra, of the 1st August, 1832, and was viewed as an official report of the battle of Wisconsin Heights:—

"CAMP WISCONSIN, July 22, 1832.

"We met the enemy yesterday, near the Wisconsin River, and opposite the old Sac village, after a close pursuit for near 100 miles. Our loss was one man killed and eight wounded; from the scalps taken by the Winnebagoes, as well as those taken by the whites, and the Indians carried from the field of battle, we must have killed 40 of them. The number of wounded is not known; we can only judge from the number killed, that many were wounded. From their crippled situation I think we must overtake them, unless they descend the Wisconsin by water. If you could place a field-piece immediately on the Wisconsin that would command the river, you might prevent their escape by water. General Atkinson will arrive at the Blue Mounds on the 24th with the regulars, and a brigade of mounted men. I will cross the Wisconsin to-morrow, and should the enemy retreat by land, he will probably attempt crossing some twenty miles above Prairie du Chien; in that event the mounted men would want some boats for the transportation of their arms, ammunition and provisions. If you could procure for us some Mackinaw boats, in that event, as well as some provision supplies, it would greatly facilitate our views. Excuse great haste.

"I am, with great respect your obedient servant,

(Signed,) H. DODGE,

"Col. commanding Michigan Mounted Volunteers."

The above letter is extracted from Niles's Register of August 18th, 1832, and it does not appear to whom it is addressed; but it is highly probable that it is the letter which was sent to the commandant of Fort Crawford, at Prairie du Chien, which Captain Estes carried as express.

The singularity of the language of the letter will be evident, when it is considered that General Henry had the chief command at the battle of Wisconsin Heights, and not Colonel Dodge.

---

## NOTE H. Page 283.

### GENERAL ORDERS AFTER THE BATTLE OF BAD AXE.

HEAD QUARTERS, FIRST ARMY CORPS OF THE NORTHWESTERN ARMY,
*Banks of the Mississippi River, near Bad Axe River,*
Aug. 3d, 1832.

Order No. 65.

The victory achieved by the volunteers and regular troops over the enemy yesterday on this ground, affords the commanding general an opportunity of expressing his approbation of their brave conduct. The whole of the troops participated in the honour of the combat; some of the corps were however more fortunate than others, in being thrown from their position in order of battle, more immediately in conflict with the enemy. These were Henry's brigade, Dodge's battalion, the regular troops, Leach's regiment of Posey's brigade, and the Spy battalion of Alexander's brigade.

In order that individual merit, and the conduct of the corps may be properly represented to the department of war, and the general commanding the Northwestern Army, the commanding general of this division directs that commanding officers of brigades and independent corps, make to him written reports of the conduct and operation of their respective commands in the action.

By order of Brigadier-general ATKINSON.

ALB. S. JOHNSTON,
A. D. C. and A. Adjutant-general.

## NOTE I. Page 284.

The following letter from General Scott to Governor Reynolds, is taken from the Louisville Advertiser of July 27th, 1832:—

HEAD QUARTERS N. W. ARMY,
Chicago, July 15th, 1832.

Sir,

To prevent, or to correct the exaggerated rumours in respect to the existence of cholera at this place, I address myself to your excellency. Four steamers were engaged at Buffalo, to transport United States troops and supplies to Chicago. In the headmost of these boats, the Sheldon Thompson, I, with my staff, and four companies, a part of Colonel Eustis's command, arrived here on the night of the 10th instant. On the 8th, all on board were in high health and spirits; but the next morning, six cases of undoubted cholera presented themselves. The disease rapidly spread itself for the next three days. About one hundred and twenty persons have been affected.

Under a late act of Congress, six companies of rangers are to be raised and marched to this place. General Dodge, of Michigan, is appointed major of the battalion, and I have seen the names of the captains, but I do not know where to address them. I am afraid that the report from this place, in respect to cholera, may seriously retard the raising of this force. I wish, therefore, that your excellency would give publicity to the measures I have adopted to prevent the spread of this disease, and of my determination not to allow any junction or communication between uninfected and infected troops. The war is not at an end, and may not be brought to a close for some time. The rangers may reach the theatre of operations in time to give the final blow. As they approach this place, I shall take care of their health and general wants.

I have the honour to be, &c., &c.,

WINFIELD SCOTT.

His Excellency GOVERNOR REYNOLDS.

The ravages made by this dreaded disease, in General Scott's army, has been thus estimated:—Of the two hundred and eight recruits attached to the command of Colonel Twiggs, thirty died of the cholera, and one hundred and fifty-five deserted for fear of it. Of the three companies of artillery under Colonel Twiggs, consisting of one hundred and fifty-two men, twenty-six died, and twenty deserted. Of Colonel Cumming's detachment, eighty men, twenty-one died, and four deserted. Of Colonel Crane's artillery, two hundred and twenty men, fifty-five died. Of the eight hundred and fifty men who left Buffalo, not more than two hundred were left, fitted to take the field, at the latest accounts from the army under Major-general Scott. (Niles's Register, vol. xlii. 423.)

Of the men who deserted, the following extract of a letter from John Norvell, of Detroit, dated July 12th, 1832, gives a most deplorable and melancholy account:—

"Of the deserters scattered all over the country, some have died in the woods, and their bodies been devoured by wolves; (I use the language of a gallant young officer;) others have taken their flight to the world of spirits without a companion to close their eyes, or console the last moments of their existence. Their straggling survivors are occasionally seen marching, some of them know not whither, with their knapsacks on their backs, shunned by the terrified inhabitants as the source of a mortal pestilence." (Pennsylvania Inquirer, 1832.)

---

## Note K. Page 295.

The following note, condensed from the report of Judge A. B. Woodward, on the land titles in the Michigan Territory, made on the 12th of March, 1806, to the House of Representatives, exhibits a curious picture of *tenure* in the French colonist, and may be viewed as a powerfully operating check to the early settlement of the French possessions by agriculturists. The policy of the United States, in the encouragement of occupation of the country by agricultural settlement, affords a vivid contrast to that which was pursued both by the French and English, while the western region was under their control.

Judge Woodward observes, "that the French conceived the bold project of connecting their settlements by a chain of fortifications from the St. Lawrence to that of the Mississippi; and, by tightening it on the back of the British possessions, to reduce them to the smallest possible limits. The western parts of New York and Pennsylvania, the State of Ohio, and the Territory of Michigan, still exhibit the monuments of their labours. But what can the best conceived designs avail against a defect of physical force? Agriculture is the only sure basis on which to support a distant settlement, and the English soon discovered the necessity of application to it. The French, relying on the military ardour of their nation, and neglecting those minute causes from which the sources of all permanent pre-eminence must be derived, gave scarcely the least encouragement to agriculture.

"Among the earlier claims is the grant of De la Mothe Cadillac to an inhabitant of Detroit, Francois Fafard de Lorme, in the year 1707, the conditions of which are nearly similar to that of the Marquis de Beauharnois, governor and lieutenant-general of New France and Louisiana, to St. Aubin, which is another of the said claims. That of De la Mothe conveys two arpens of front, by twenty of depth, (about thirty-two American acres,) for a colonist and his family in an American wilderness. But what are the conditions of these grants, contrasted with an American estate in fee-simple?

"They are no less than these:—

"I. To pay a reserved rent of fifteen livres a year to the crown, for ever.

"II. To begin to clear and improve the concession within three months from the date of the grant.

"III. All of the timber is reserved to the crown, whenever it may be wanted for the fortifications, or for the construction of boats, or other vessels; (that is to say, when reduced to plain language, it may be taken at the pleasure of any military officer who may happen to have the command of the country.)

"IV. The property of all mines and minerals, if any be found, does not pass by the grant.

"V. The privilege of hunting hares, rabbits, partridges and pheasants does not pass.

"VI. The grantee is to come and carry, plant or help to plant, a long maypole before the door of the principal manor-house, on the first day of May in every year.

"VII. All the grains of the grantee are to be carried to the *moulin bannal*, or mill of the manor, to be ground, paying the tolls sanctioned by the *coutûme de Paris*.

"VIII. On every sale of the land a species of duty is to be paid, termed the *lôds et vente;* which in the English law might bear the name of *a fine of alienation*, but is more intelligible to an American ear under the appellation of *a tax on the sale of the land.* This tax, by the *coutûme de Paris*, forms no inconsiderable proportion of the value of the whole.

"IX. Previous to a sale, the grantee is to give information to the government, and if the government is willing to take it at the price offered to him, it is to have it.

"X. The grantees cannot mortgage it without the consent of the government previously obtained.

"XI. For ten years the grantee is not permitted to work, or cause any person to work, directly or indirectly, at the profession and trade of a blacksmith, locksmith, armorer, or brewer.

"XII. All effects and articles of merchandise sent to or brought from Montreal, must be sold by the grantee himself, or other person, who, with his family, is a French resident, and not by *engagées*, or clerks, or foreigners, or strangers.

"XIII. The grantee is not to sell to a foreigner, without special permission.

"XIV. If he sells to a foreigner with permission, the rent reserved is greatly increased; and the duties of the *coutûme*, in such cases, are to be paid.

"XV. He is not to sell or trade brandy to the Indians, on pain of confiscation.

"XVI. The public charges and servitudes, and royal and seigneurial rights of the *coutûme de Paris*, are reserved generally.

"XVII. The grantee is to suffer on his lands that, which may be thought necessary for the public utility.

"XVIII. The grantee is to make his fences as it shall be regulated.

"XIX. He is to assist in making his neighbour's fences when called upon.

"XX. He is to cause his land to be *alienated*, that is, surveyed, *set apart*, at his expense.

"XXI. He is to obtain a brevet of confirmation, from Europe, within two years.

"With a system of policy so narrow and illiberal, it was impossible for France to raise in her settlements a strong agricultural interest, alike the support of colonies in peace, and their defence in war.

"In the Territory of Michigan, the policy of Great Britain was not better than that of France. During the twenty years this territory belonged to her, she withheld all grants of land."

---

## NOTE L. Page 297.

Letter of General Henry Dodge, to the Hon. Austin E. Wing, delegate in Congress from Michigan, on a division of the Territory:—

DODGEVILLE, February 10th, 1829.

Dear Sir,

In my last communication, I promised you, as early as possible, to present my views as to the claims the people have on the national legislature for a division of the territory. To you the subject is not a new one; you know well the many inconveniences and hardships the people have to encounter in this remote part of the Territory of Michigan. Our relations are entirely with the General Government, and not with the peninsula of Michigan; our trade is immediately with the States of Illinois and Missouri; taxation and representation should go together, and it will readily appear, on examination of the returns made by the superintendent of the United States' lead-mines, that the people of this mining country have paid a greater amount of taxes than any equal number of citizens in the United States, or Territories; and *that*, a direct tax upon the labour of the whole community. It cannot be expected, that a delegate, elected from the peninsula of Michigan, can understand the wants of a people so detached and remote from him, however talented and zealous he may be to represent truly the interests of this detached territory of the United States. There is no branch of the government in which the people are more interested, than the just and impartial administration of the laws of the country, and those laws should be made to suit the condition of the people over whom they are to operate: hence the necessity of a local legislation, following a division of the territory. At present, we have but two representatives for five counties; there are thirteen in the territory, and the seat of our territorial legislature is from 800 to 1000 miles from us. It is not to be expected that so small a representation can effect any important measure for this remote section of the territory, when the legislature is permitted to sit but sixty days; it is, in fact, but a nominal representation. The great interests of a growing and interesting territory, which bids fair soon to become a member of the great confederation of States, must show the propriety of granting the division of the territory; for it cannot be expected that the General Government will permit the people of this country to be attached to the State of Michigan. The legislative council have twice memorialized Congress on this subject, as well as the legislature of the State of Missouri. Michigan never can become a State, with us attached to them. Another strong reason why we should be separated from the Territory of Michigan, is, we are surrounded by Indians; some friendly, others, who are still hostile to the extension of the American empire, and to the people of this country. A local legislature, and a separate government here, would place the people of this country in a situation to defend themselves, and have the aid of the constituted authorities near them; it would be almost impossible to receive aid from the peninsula of Michigan. Mounted companies of riflemen would be the best arm of defence to afford this country protection; the couutry is well adapted for mounted men to act effectually and promptly. Recent events at Rock Island prove the secret influence that exists over the minds of the Indians; and I have no hesitation in saying, that so long as that influence exists, we will have occasional difficulties with the Indians on our borders.

I fear I have trespassed on your time and patience; the importance of the subjects, connected with the best interests of this country, must plead my apology.

I am, dear sir, with great respect and esteem,

Your obedient servant,

H. Dodge.

**END OF VOLUME I.**

STEREOTYPED BY L. JOHNSON AND CO.
PHILADELPHIA.

www.ingramcontent.com/pod-product-compliance
Lightning Source LLC
LaVergne TN
LVHW021146110826
845150LV00005B/1137

* 9 7 8 1 4 2 5 5 4 6 8 7 8 *